MW01258705

THE MASTER MUSICIANS

MACDOWELL

SERIES EDITED BY R. LARRY TODD
FORMER SERIES EDITOR, THE LATE STANLEY SADIE

THE MASTER MUSICIANS

Titles Available in Paperback

Bach • *Malcolm Boyd*   Monteverdi • *Denis Arnold*

Beethoven • *Barry Cooper*   Mozart • *Julian Rushton*

Berlioz • *Hugh Macdonald*   Mussorgsky • *David Brown*

Handel • *Donald Burrows*   Puccini • *Julian Budden*

Liszt • *Derek Watson*   Schumann • *Eric Frederick Jensen*

Mahler • *Michael Kennedy*   Vivaldi • *Michael Talbot*

Titles Available in Hardcover

Byrd • *Kerry McCarthy*   Schoenberg • *Malcolm MacDonald*

Rossini • *Richard Osborne*   Tchaikovsky • *Roland John Wiley*

Verdi • *Julian Budden*

MACDOWELL

E. DOUGLAS BOMBERGER

OXFORD
UNIVERSITY PRESS

OXFORD
UNIVERSITY PRESS

Oxford University Press is a department of the University of Oxford.
It furthers the University's objective of excellence in research, scholarship,
and education by publishing worldwide.

Oxford   New York
Auckland   Cape Town   Dar es Salaam   Hong Kong   Karachi
Kuala Lumpur   Madrid   Melbourne   Mexico City   Nairobi
New Delhi   Shanghai   Taipei   Toronto

With offices in
Argentina   Austria   Brazil   Chile   Czech Republic   France   Greece
Guatemala   Hungary   Italy   Japan   Poland   Portugal   Singapore
South Korea   Switzerland   Thailand   Turkey   Ukraine   Vietnam

Oxford is a registered trademark of Oxford University Press
in the UK and certain other countries.

Published in the United States of America by
Oxford University Press
198 Madison Avenue, New York, NY 10016

Library of Congress Cataloging-in-Publication Data
Bomberger, E. Douglas, 1958–
MacDowell / E. Douglas Bomberger.
pages cm. – (The master musicians)
ISBN 978–0–19–989929–6 (hardback : alk. paper)
1. MacDowell, Edward, 1860-1908.   2. Composers–United States–Biography.   I. Title.
ML410.M12B66 2013
780.92–dc23
[B]
2013013463

Publication of this book was supported in part by the John Daverio Fund of the
American Musicological Society

1 3 5 7 9 8 6 4 2
Printed in the United States of America
on acid-free paper

To Margery Morgan Lowens

Contents

Preface   ix
List of Musical Examples   xiii
List of Bibliographic Abbreviations   xv

Book One: The Education of Edward MacDowell

1 Quaker Roots 3

2 The Latin American Connection 14

3 The Paris Conservatory 24

4 A Fourth-Rate Conservatory and a First-Rate Mentor 40

5 The Big Break .54

6 Establishing a Career in Germany 71

7 Married Life. 91

8 Templeton Strong, Loyal Friend 106

Book Two: Edward MacDowell in Boston

9 The Prodigal Returns 125

10 The Politics of Musical Boston 147

11 MacDowell the Pianist. 156

12 The Darkest Winter 169

13 International Tastes vs. American Opportunities 180

14 A Cabin in the Woods 198

Book Three: Edward MacDowell in New York

15 Columbia University, 1896–1901 211

16 Outside the University 224

17 The Price of Fame 233

18 Columbia University, 1901–1904 242

19 A Living Death 267

20 MacDowell's Legacy 284

Appendices

A. Calendar 293

B. List of Works 305

C. Personalia 312

Bibliography 325

Index 339

Preface

The really important things in any biography are what someone thinks and feels and not what he has done.

—Glenn Gould

E DWARD MACDOWELL IS AT ONCE THE MOST ICONIC AND ENIGMATIC of nine-teenth-century American composers. He was the first composer of art music to achieve a genuine international reputation. He created works of extreme complexity, but he also wrote enduring pieces of charming simplicity. He composed several works that are quintessentially American, but he objected to "Americanism" on principle, fighting against American concerts and stylistic Americanism at every opportunity. He was a loner, not a joiner, who managed to alienate many of his professional colleagues while winning an unprecedented audience for his works. His birthdate, his cause of death, and many other biographical details are shrouded in mystery. This book aims to peel back the legends and biases to understand the man and his music.

MacDowell's life divides naturally into four periods: his childhood in New York (1860–1876), his years in Europe (1876–1888), his years of growing fame in Boston (1888–1896), and his years of international renown in New York (1896–1908). Of these four, the first two are the least known, in part because so little evidence has survived and in part because the foreign-language sources are so difficult to decipher. But these early years shaped his personality, planting the seeds that would later bear fruit in his mature work as artist, performer, and teacher. The experiences and attitudes of the early years have a direct bearing on his adult personality, giving new perspectives on why his career developed—and ended—as it did. For this reason, I have chosen to reverse the emphasis of previous biographers by devoting more space to his early years and less to his years of fame.

Musical biography is a genre that overlaps others, most notably music history and musical analysis. It is my intention to focus primarily on telling the story of one unique individual and his life rather than to provide a comprehensive historical survey or an extensive review of his compositions. This book will therefore discuss historical events only as they pertain to MacDowell's life. Musical discussions will be accessible rather than exhaustive, and they will be incorporated into the story to elucidate the development of his personality and career rather than segregated in a separate section as has been traditional in musical biographies.

The telling of this story is made possible by the thousands of letters preserved by MacDowell and his admirers. Among the most valuable are the letters he exchanged with his friend Templeton Strong after moving to Boston in 1888. The two men promised to be completely frank in their comments and to burn their letters after reading them. Fortunately, they both reneged on the second half of the agreement. When Strong donated a cache of more than one hundred letters to the Library of Congress in 1931, MacDowell's widow, Marian, feared their inflammatory content and had them sealed for fifty years. It is my belief that contemporary letters allow us to hear the composer's voice better than any other medium, and therefore I have quoted liberally from them. To retain their spirit, I have kept MacDowell's expressive system of underlining and double underlining rather than replacing them with italics. His unconventional contractions have been silently corrected to current usage.

As I have lived with the MacDowell documents and delved ever deeper into his life and personality, I have become convinced that his example continues to resonate beyond his time and place. Although his career was a product of the Victorian era, it raises questions that are relevant today. How does a person born in a restrictive religious and cultural environment transcend his upbringing to achieve his personal goals? What are the advantages and limits of an intensely ambitious parent who continues to guide her son's career after he has left home? How can a creative and original artist maintain his independence while also earning a living? What is a fair division of profit between the artist and those who make his work available to the world? Edward MacDowell's life story forces consideration of all these questions, and his solutions to the problems he faced are not so different from those of artists in the YouTube era.

The scope of this project required the help of many librarians and archivists on both sides of the Atlantic. I am particularly indebted to Robin Rausch of the Library of Congress, Jonathan Hiam of the New York Public Library, Maryalice Perrin-Mohr of the New England Conservatory Library, Diane Ota of the Boston Public Library, Christopher Densmore of the Friends Historical Library at Swarthmore College, Kathy Kienholz of the American Academy of Arts and Letters, Thekla Kluttig of the Sächsisches Staatsarchiv Leipzig, and the staff members of the Library and Archives of Canada, the Archives Nationales in Paris, the Universitätsbibliothek Frankfurt, and the Special Collections department of the Butler Rare Book and Manuscript Library at Columbia University.

Elizabethtown College in Elizabethtown, Pennsylvania, provided outstanding support for this research by granting me a sabbatical leave in fall 2009 and providing a generous CISP (Collaborative Interdisciplinary Scholarship Program) grant in support of a MacDowell Festival and Symposium on the occasion of the composer's 150th birthday. Anna Pilston, Sylvia Morra, and Louise Hyder-Darlington of the college's High Library were gracious and diligent in obtaining materials through interlibrary loan and purchasing materials for the collection. Amy Reynolds, Department Assistant in Fine and Performing Arts, was helpful throughout.

I am grateful for the advice and encouragement of scholarly colleagues who share my interest in MacDowell, especially Richard Crawford, N. Lee Orr, Michael Pisani, and Judith Tick. The presenters at the MacDowell Festival and Symposium at Elizabethtown College in December 2010 were an inspiration as well: Javier Albo, Paul Bertagnolli, Marianne Betz, Marvin Blickenstaff, Francis Brancaleone, Charles Freeman, John Graziano, Michael Joiner, Margery Morgan Lowens, Brian Mann, Laura Pita, Mark Radice, and Robin Rausch.

Suzanne Ryan and her colleagues at Oxford University Press have been helpful and supportive. I am grateful to her for believing in the project and to R. Larry Todd and the external readers for insightful suggestions. The publication was also supported by a subvention from the Daverio Endowment of the American Musicological Society.

My family has been extremely supportive of the project. My son Joe worked as a research assistant in the summer of 2009; my son Matt helped with the Personalia entries; my parents, James and Doris, offered important perspectives and enthusiastic support; my sister, Cathy, contributed expert medical advice; and my wife, Teresa, read multiple drafts of the manuscript.

Anyone studying the life and works of Edward MacDowell is indebted to Margery Morgan Lowens, whose 1971 dissertation established the groundwork for future research. She shared her knowledge unstintingly and provided me with full access to her collection of MacDowelliana gathered since the 1960s. This book is dedicated to her with gratitude.

Musical Examples

5.1 First Piano Concerto, op. 15: I, mm. 1–6   79

5.2 First Piano Concerto, op. 15: I, principal theme, mm. 13–14

    80

5.3 First Piano Concerto, op. 15: I, second theme, rehearsal D   80

11.1 "Shadow Dance," op. 39, no. 8, mm. 25–32   189

11.2 "Scherzino," op. 39, no. 11, mm. 1–4   190

11.3 J. S. Bach "Minuet in G," arranged by MacDowell, mm. 1–16   192

11.4 *Sonata Tragica*, op. 45, mm. 1–4   194

11.5 *Sonata Tragica*, op. 45, mm. 18–25   195

11.6 *Sonata Eroica*, op. 50, mm. 1–9   199

11.7 *Sonata Eroica*, op. 50, mm. 55–60   199

12.1 "Dance of Gnomes," op. 41, no. 2, mm. 1–6   210

13.1 "Waldgeister" from *Suite for grosses Orchester*, op. 42, rehearsal C   223

13.2 "Waldgeister" from *Suite for grosses Orchester*, op. 42, 8 measures before rehearsal O   223

14.1 "From Uncle Remus" from *Woodland Sketches*, op. 51, no. 7, final 10 measures   239

14.2 "To a Wild Rose" from *Woodland Sketches*, op. 51, no. 1, mm. 1–8   240

14.3 "To a Wild Rose" from *Woodland Sketches*, op. 51,
     no. 1, mm. 21–28   240

14.4 "Will o' the Wisp" from *Woodland Sketches*, op. 51,
     no. 2, mm. 5–12   241

14.5 "To a Water-Lily" from *Woodland Sketches*, op. 51,
     no. 6, mm. 1–8   242

14.6 "To the Sea" from *Sea Pieces*, op. 55, no. 1,
     mm. 27–32   244

14.7 "Long Ago," op. 56, no. 1, mm. 1–4   246

18.1 "Mid-Winter" from *New England Idyls*, op. 62, no. 3,
     mm. 1–8   295

18.2 "From Puritan Days" from *New England Idyls*,
     op. 62, no. 8, mm. 1–4   296

Bibliographic Abbreviations

APS	Arthur P. Schmidt
B&H	Breitkopf & Härtel
EAM	Edward A. MacDowell
EMMC	Edward and Marian MacDowell Collection, Library of Congress Music Division
MC	*Musical Courier*
MM	Marian MacDowell
MQ	*Musical Quarterly*
NYPL	New York Public Library Music Division
NYT	*New York Times*
TS	Templeton Strong

BOOK ONE

The Education of Edward MacDowell

CHAPTER ONE

Quaker Roots

I N A LAND RICH WITH RELIGIOUS AND CULTURAL DIVERSITY, IT IS HARD TO imagine a less promising wellspring for a future composer than the Religious Society of Friends in nineteenth-century America. The Quakers, as they were familiarly known, did not allow music in their meetings or their homes, and the Quaker *Discipline* forbade attendance at concerts and other musical events. That Edward Alexander MacDowell, America's most renowned composer of art music before World War I, was raised in a Quaker home reflects the depth of his musical gifts and his determination to follow his chosen career. But his unique artistic personality was also formed by this environment and not merely in spite of it. To understand his complex personality and reconstruct the stirrings of his remarkable creative achievement, we must begin by understanding the close-knit group from which he emerged.

Edward's paternal great-grandfather, Dr. Alexander McDowell (the family used this spelling until Edward changed it around 1877) had moved from his native Scotland to Belfast, Ireland, in the late eighteenth century to escape religious persecution for his Quaker beliefs. He married an Irish woman named Ann McMurran, with whom he had seven children, including Edward's grandfather Alexander McDowell (1800–1877). After her husband's death, Ann married Thomas Fair, and the family immigrated to America in 1812. Alexander married Sarah Thompson (1798–1883) of Canterbury, New York, in 1822. The fourth of their eight children, Edward's father, Thomas Fair McDowell (1829–1910), was named after his step-grandfather.

This family lineage was important in the Society of Friends, which made a distinction between members and non-members. Being born of Quaker parents allowed one to participate fully as a birthright member of this group, which kept remarkably detailed records for the purpose of distinguishing those on the inside from those on the outside. The McDowell family had an enviable pedigree of Quaker ancestry stretching back to the British Isles, and they participated actively in the Quaker meetings in Cornwall, New York, where Thomas was born, and later in lower Manhattan, where they moved when Thomas was six years old. Alexander's family and later Thomas's family were part of the Fifteenth Street Meeting House of the Hicksite branch of the Society of Friends. The beliefs and practices of this group were crucial to Edward's formative years.

At the heart of Quaker belief and practice lies the principle of the "Inward Light." The Society's founder, George Fox (1624–1691), stressed the idea that the truth of God was ongoing, and that Christian doctrine was not fixed in orthodox dogma but was instead responsive to new insights and truths that God continues to give to believers who are open to the movement of this "Light Within." This profoundly affected their style of worship, as they were suspicious of professional clergy who knew doctrine and Scripture but might not be open to the Inward Light. They believed that hymns and sacred songs were detrimental to worship, since these did not reflect the direct experiences of the believer but rather those of another believer at a different place and time.

The worship experience of the Society of Friends consists of a silent meeting. There are no clergy, no musicians, no liturgy, and no predetermined order of service. Instead, the members gather in silence and listen to the Inward Light. When they receive an inspiration that they believe is meant for the group as a whole, they share it verbally. If no one receives an inspiration, the entire meeting may be passed in silence and individual contemplation. These experiences of silent contemplation must have been among Edward McDowell's earliest childhood memories.

Because of the fundamental human dignity of this principle of direct communication with the Divinity, Quakers emphasized equality from the very beginning. Women and men were considered equal, with family life and the conduct of meetings reflecting this principle. Quakers refused to doff their hats to nobility or government officials, and Quaker merchants refused to bargain in commercial transactions, preferring instead to establish fair prices and stick with them. In the nineteenth century, Quakers were leaders in the abolition movement, believing that no man should enslave another. Perhaps the most basic expression of the principle of equality is the doctrine of peace, which is a literal adherence to the scriptural commandment against killing. Quakers do not believe in military service, and their members were conscientious objectors to the Revolutionary War and all subsequent wars.

It is easy to imagine that a society giving primacy to individual inspiration could be subject to disagreements and even anarchy. Counterbalancing the principle of the Inward Light is the Discipline, a set of rules that members of the Society agree to follow. Initially established by George Fox in the seventeenth century, these rules have been modified through the centuries as conditions changed and new revelations were given to the members. The Discipline was taken seriously, and the ultimate punishment for continued disregard of any of its principles was disownment, or exclusion from the Society. Changes to the Discipline and other business matters are attended to at the Monthly Meetings, whose proceedings have been carefully recorded and preserved for centuries. It is thus possible to determine how the Discipline evolved over the years, and when certain rules were no longer enforced.[1] The nineteenth century was a time of significant changes in the Discipline, especially in the decades around the Civil War, when both branches of the Society of Friends went through a period of liberalization.[2] Disownments, which had been a common means of control within the Society in the eighteenth century, became rare after the Civil War.

Traditional Quakers set themselves apart from the world not only through the rules of the Discipline but also through clothing and speech. Quaker garb consisted of plain, archaic clothing in somber shades of gray or black, while in speech they used the archaic pronouns thee, thou, and thy. In New York City, the members of the Society of Friends were perhaps more fully assimilated into society than their rural brethren, but even in the heart of Manhattan, they thought of themselves as a group apart from their surroundings. This was the world in which Thomas Fair McDowell was born and in which he no doubt expected to marry and raise his family. But Thomas McDowell did not marry within the Quaker community. Instead, he fell in love with a woman from outside who brought radically different values and practices into his home that would profoundly affect his family.

Frances Mary Knapp was born in Fredonia, New York, on 30 December 1837 into a very different family from the stable, traditional Quaker family in which Thomas was raised. Her father, Darius Knapp (1789–1879), was a widower with five children when he married Mary Morey Shults (1804–1885), a widow who had five children of her own, in 1834. Frances (or Fanny, as she preferred to be called) was the second of four daughters born to this prolific couple. She left home as a teenager, reportedly to teach school in New York City. There she came to know the McDowell family and so captivated Thomas that he "married out" to her on 8 September 1856.[3] For a member of the Religious Society of Friends, this was an action with serious consequences.

---

1. Changes in the Discipline of the New York Yearly Meeting are tracked in *The Old Discipline: Nineteenth-Century Friends' Disciplines in America* (Glenside, PA: Quaker Heritage Press, 1999).

2. The Society split in 1828, from which time the traditional group called itself Orthodox Friends, and the liberal group called itself Hicksite Friends. The McDowells were members of the Hicksite group.

3. Their wedding certificate is in the MacDowell Collection, NYPL.

If their marriage had been a generation earlier, Thomas—and his parents, if they supported the marriage—would have been disowned. By the late 1850s, the Discipline had been relaxed enough that Thomas was not disowned by the Society of Friends. But neither was Fanny welcomed. Instead, she was officially ignored. It is the job of the recorder of the Monthly Meeting to note in the minutes all marriages, births, relocations from one meeting to another, and other changes in the status of members. When Thomas's older brother Joseph had married a Quaker woman, Isabella Stratton, the two presented their application to the Monthly Meeting on 7 April 1852, and a committee of Quaker leadership reported that they were free of obstructions on 5 May 1852. The following day, 6 May 1852, the two declared publicly that they were married, without the help of a minister or public official, and this declaration was entered in the records of the New York Monthly Meeting and signed by thirty witnesses. At the next monthly meeting on 2 June 1852, the committee to attend the marriage reported that everything had been done according to Quaker practice. The same procedure was followed when Thomas's older sister, Elizabeth Ann, married Mordecai Buzby of Philadelphia on 9 June 1853 before sixty witnesses. The births of the children of these two unions were noted in the minutes, as were their deaths many years later. By contrast, the records make no mention of Thomas's betrothal or marriage to Fanny.

The wedding took place at the house of Thomas C. Thompson on the corner of Eighth Avenue and Twenty-fifth Street. The ceremony was conducted by Isaac O. Barker, an alderman of the fifteenth ward and president of the board of aldermen, and officially witnessed by Thompson and Mordecai Buzby. Since it was not performed by a clergyman, the wedding ceremony itself was acceptable to the Religious Society of Friends, but Thomas's marriage did not receive the same recognition as those of his siblings, because he had "married out."

The issue became especially important when their children were born. The Society of Friends was essentially a closed society, in that a "birthright" member was one who had been born of two Quaker parents. A child who was born to a mixed marriage was not recognized as Quaker and could join only by request. On 27 July 1857, Fanny gave birth to twin boys, Walter and Frank. This happy event was not mentioned in the records of the New York Monthly Meeting, although the birth of Joseph's son Charles on 30 September 1857 was noted. The young couple must have had a challenging time with the twins, since Thomas's parents, Sarah and Alexander, with their two remaining children had moved back to Cornwall on 2 June 1857 (an event that *was* recorded in the minutes). Thirteen months later, Frank died, leaving Fanny deeply sorrowful.[4] Again this death was not recorded in the records, although the death of

---

4. On Walter's nineteenth birthday, Fanny wrote to him, "Your mother prays for you always, and if you lead such a life that when you die you can meet that little brother who for nearly 18 years

Joseph's son Henry on 9 August 1859 was noted. On 1 December 1860, the birth of Theodore McDowell to Joseph and Isabella was recorded in the minutes. The birth of his cousin Edward Alexander McDowell, youngest son of Thomas and Fanny, on 18 December 1860, was not recorded. Edward's name never appeared in the minutes of the New York Monthly Meeting. Although he attended Quaker meetings as a child, officially he and his brother and their mother did not exist for the Society.

Thomas and Fanny McDowell were proof of the old adage that opposites attract. In the words of Edward's friend Templeton Strong:

> Mr. Thomas MacDowell was a gentleman of medium height, slight in figure, quiet and reserved in manner, and gentle of speech...Although his reserve prevented him from being a conversationalist, yet his observations, whenever he vouchsafed to make any, were always pungent and to the point. He was a good, kindly, and charming man. Edward more resembled his mother, both in physique, mental activity, and general energy, as also in charm of manner, and I should imagine that she it was, perhaps more than his father, who fostered the development of his talent. His poetic instinct may have been transmitted to him by his father, and his energy, which was great indeed, by his mother.[5]

Already by the time of the first extant family letters in the late 1860s, a clear family pattern had been established: Thomas was silent and circumspect, while Fanny was a garrulous risk-taker. There are very few surviving letters from Thomas, all of which are short and businesslike. Fanny, by contrast, left dozens of extant letters, which are long, detailed explications of the minutiae of her life. Characteristically, she filled both sides of every sheet with no margins; if she filled her allotted sheets completely but still had more to say, she went back to page one and wrote over the beginning of the letter in perpendicular lines. Her sentences are long and complex, and her letters are filled with perceptive observations on people, as in this passage from a letter to her son Walter:

> The Magazines sent to Burnton's to be bound, will be done by the time you receive this, the Harpers, Atlantic and Scribner were to be $1.40 a volume. The Young Folks and Galaxy and St. Nicholas were to be $1.15, I think. Keep these well pressed together for a month or so after they come home, for they will be so freshly bound that the backs will

has been an Angel in Heaven then will Mamma's prayers have been answered." Letter, Fanny McDowell to Walter McDowell, 12 July 1876, NYPL.

5. Templeton Strong, "Edward MacDowell as I Knew Him, seventh paper," *Music Student* 8/6 (February 1916): 151. Strong's article states that this visit took place during the summer of 1887, but I have not found independent confirmation of the date. The MacDowell parents did visit Europe during the summer of 1889, and this may have been the occasion Strong remembers. Their names are found on the passenger list of the SS *Gallia*, which arrived in New York harbor on 6 September 1889 [www.ancestry.com, accessed 14 December 2009].

spring open unless they are pressed together so, pack them in the bookcase as tightly as you can and leave them there for some time. <u>Don't</u> lend any of my books to <u>any one</u>. I don't care who asks you for them. Just say you would be very glad to do so but Mamma made you promise not to lend them to any one. Not even to your Great Grandmother. Keep the bookcase <u>locked</u>, not <u>to be able</u> to find the key is a most excellent excuse for not lending books, and by lending them I should be sure to lose some, and books are too valuable to me for that. So remember you are not to lend a book to any body.[6]

In an 1892 letter to his wife, Edward joked that "if she [Fanny] had been one of the disciples, Jesus Christ would have never got a word in and the Christian Religion would have been wrecked."[7]

Fanny brought to her marriage with Thomas a very different attitude toward childrearing than the one he had known as a son of Quaker parents. According to the Discipline, overindulgence of children was an offense punishable by disownment. Quaker parents were specifically forbidden to allow their children to read plays and romances or to attend public pastimes and diversions. Ignoring this directive, Fanny lavished her boys with fairy tales and books on knights and chivalry, which became Edward's favorites. The earliest descriptions of the boy recall his lying on the floor reading books, and he continued to stimulate his imagination in this way throughout his adult life. When they reached school age, he and Walter were enrolled in public schools rather than in one of the Quaker parochial schools.[8]

We do not know much about Thomas's friendships, but he seems to have been content with the family relationships and those with his business associates. Fanny, on the other hand, was a very social person who delighted in making new acquaintances and who knew how to use influential friendships to advance her family interests. This is not to say that persons saw her as conniving; on the contrary she had many genuinely loyal and affectionate friends. It was reported that when the Polish pianist Ignace Paderewski met Fanny for the first time, he said, "Now I understand where Edward MacDowell got his genius."[9] As she told Walter, she believed in the importance of social connections:

Your letter came today telling me of all your new Years fun, and we were all very much amused over it. I hope that William Poole is a young man who is in every way nice, if

6. Letter, Fanny McDowell to Walter McDowell, 6 May 1876, NYPL.

7. Letter, EAM to MM, 4 November 1892, EMMC box 31/54.

8. The Certificate of Merit that Edward received for his work in second grade on 31 January 1869 is preserved in his scrapbook titled "SKETCHES, Presented By Mamma. March 7th 1874," EMMC box 28.

9. Ruth Payne Burgess, "Teresa Carreño as a Teacher: Memories of a Remarkable Woman and Musician," Etude 48/11 (November 1930): 779.

he is not, I would not like you to associate with him, because you see the friends you make now are most important—as giving you a place in the social circle. Talk it well over with papa and unless you <u>both</u> conclude that Poole is one of whom your Mamma would quite approve, please drop his acquaintance. Papa will always advise you for the best.[10]

When Edward (known as Eddie) was in early elementary school, the family moved from their Clinton Street house in lower Manhattan to an apartment on Eighteenth Street. The parents moved several times subsequently but always remained close to the fashionable Gramercy Park area.

The differences between Thomas and Fanny went deeper than these personality traits. A fundamental hallmark of the Religious Society of Friends was opposition to war. But a source of pride for Fanny was the fact that her father Darius Knapp had fought in the War of 1812, and her grandfather Benjamin Knapp had fought for three years in the Revolutionary War.[11] Thomas was too old to be conscripted in the Civil War, and his sons were too young, but their Quaker friends and relatives struggled to reconcile their opposition to slavery with their opposition to war. The family supported the party of Lincoln in later years, but they were not directly confronted with the choice of whether to enlist.

The parents' disagreements over war may have been responsible for one of Eddie's earliest experiences with music. The story came from his cousin Charles, who was visiting their grandparents' farm in Cornwall during the Civil War. Fanny taught the boys (Eddie must have been no more than four, Walter and Charles three years older) the song "Tramp! Tramp! Tramp! or The Prisoner's Hope," composed in 1864 by George F. Root. This song was one of the most popular and enduring to come out of the Civil War. Charles said that Fanny had them march around the room, keeping time to the music and imagining the plight of Union soldiers held in Confederate prisons. Eddie, the youngest of the cousins, caught on quickest to the rhythm and melody.[12]

That Fanny could exercise her individuality in raising her children and even flaunt the Quaker Discipline is a reflection of the principle of equality in the Society of Friends. Quakers believed that men and women were equal, and thus Thomas did not exert the control over his wife that many American men might have done. The strong-willed Fanny had married into a group that supported her right to exercise her will, creating a home that was unconventional by Quaker

10. Letter, Fanny McDowell to Walter McDowell, 18 January 1876 [recte 1877], NYPL.

11. These facts were entered by Fanny McDowell in a family Bible.

12. Abbie Farwell Brown, *The Boyhood of Edward MacDowell* (New York: Frederick A. Stokes, 1924), 31–33.

standards. For the future composer and pianist, the most important arena where she exercised her freedom to flaunt Quaker Discipline was music.

The language of George Fox's original Discipline was still in effect during Edward's childhood:

> Friends are not to attend stage plays, horse races, places of music or dancing, or other places of diversion; nor lay wagers, nor be concerned in lotteries, nor practice any other kind of gaming: but should any be concerned in, or give way to either of these practices, and they cannot, after tender labour in the spirit of restoring love, be brought to a due sense of their misconduct, monthly meetings should manifest their disunion with them by separating them from the Society.[13]

Long before the restrictions on music were officially modified in the Discipline, there was a debate that showed how divided the Society was on this topic. This debate took place in 1868, about the time Eddie McDowell began piano lessons.

When the first Discipline had been crafted in England, musical conditions were very different than in the nineteenth century. In seventeenth-century England, public music houses were associated with a variety of vices, and musical instruments like harpsichords were so expensive that only the wealthy could afford them. The Quaker Disciplines continued to lump music with stage plays, gambling, and horseracing well into the nineteenth century after the culture had changed significantly. The industrial revolution altered the music industry, as mass-produced pianos came within the price range of middle-class families by midcentury, and the lithographic process made the price of printed music easily affordable. In many American homes, music lessons became an important part of a young person's education. Any stigma that society in general had held against music in the seventeenth century disappeared by the mid-nineteenth century, but Quakers continued to enforce the old discipline. The reasons for continued opposition to music were articulated in a lengthy essay delivered to the Philadelphia Yearly Meeting in 1852:

> Friends early bore a testimony against singing, music, and all other idle pastimes; and many faithful laborers among them were concerned from time to time to warn the people against their pernicious consequences....We do not, however, mean to be understood as objecting to melodious sounds, raised in thankfulness to the Author of our being, or to the innocent song of childhood. It is the scientific cultivation of the art—the vain and idle indulgence connected with it, either vocally or instrumentally—that we testify against....Friends believe music a sensual gratification, and that it takes the place in the affections of intellectual enjoyments: they believe it to be the handmaid of folly and voluptuousness, and that it leads into fashion, balls, theatres, and other places of vain amusements....They also urge the waste of time and expense incurred

13. *The Old Discipline*, 374.

in obtaining a scientific knowledge of it; besides which, it seduces the youthful mind away from the pursuit of more substantial and intellectual acquirements, that fit it for the practical duties of life.[14]

Over a period of several months in spring 1868, a series of letters to the editor of the *Friends' Intelligencer*, the weekly journal of the Hicksite Friends, demonstrated just how divergent the members' practices had become.

On one side were a series of correspondents who felt that any relaxation of the discipline would undermine traditional Quaker beliefs. As recently as 1854, the New York Monthly Meeting had issued a statement against pianofortes in Quaker homes along with an admonition against piano instruction for children.[15] The reasons for this prohibition were summed up by a correspondent identified only as "W": "I have noticed, rather with regret, the discussion…upon the subject of Music. I do not believe any advantage will result from it. The youth of our Society are certainly not suffering from over-restraint in this direction. Music in its most enchanting and exquisite form is so wrought up with that which tends to lead the mind of its votary from beneath the restraining power of Divine grace, that safety consists rather in abstinence than indulgence."[16]

The advocates of change argued that music was not inherently wrong, since the Bible lists many instances of vocal and instrumental music. Another correspondent, "J. D. H.," invoked the principle of the Inward Light, pointing out the Society's tradition of allowing new revelations to supersede older rules. The writer noted that times had changed, and music in the nineteenth century no longer had the immoral associations of George Fox's day: "Let us then see that we call only that evil which upon examination we find to be so, remembering always that the manna gathered yesterday will not suffice for to-day—that though principles are unchangeable, testimonies may change."[17]

A contributor identified only as "S." summarized the discussion and tried to mediate the differences by pointing out that the lively discussion indicated the matter had not been resolved. Sincere and thoughtful persons on both sides of the debate arrived at different conclusions on this issue, and thus it would be best to leave it open:

> In regard to music, the question now under discussion is not whether it shall be introduced into Friends' families, but, whether, being already in many of them, it shall be

---

14. "Essay on the Subject of Music," *Friends' Intelligencer* 25/1 (7 March 1868): 3–5; 25/2 (14 March 1868): 18–20.

15. A Friend, "Music," *Friends' Intelligencer* 25/3 (21 March 1868): 38–39.

16. W., "For Friends' Intelligencer," *Friends' Intelligencer* 25/9 (2 May 1868): 136.

17. J. D. H., "Music," *Friends' Intelligencer* 25/6 (11 April 1868): 86–88.

tolerated. Singing, and the use of the simpler musical instruments, have been indulged in, and the indulgence at least winked at, in our Society, as far back, it is believed, as the earliest recollection of the mothers and grandmothers of the oldest among us, and it was not until the introduction of the piano into Friends' parlors that attention was called to the subject. It would appear, then, that we have permitted music in its simpler forms, as one of the things in which the young might be indulged, but that we now wish to set a limit beyond which they must not pass....These things must of necessity be left to individual conscience and good sense.[18]

This solution was the one that prevailed. The Discipline was not changed, but after the debate subsided in the summer of 1868, the Society seems to have adopted a "don't ask, don't tell" policy. This was fortunate for the McDowell family, since tax records indicate that they had acquired a piano by April 1866.[19]

In summary, Edward McDowell's Quaker upbringing helps to explain some aspects of his personality. As might be expected from someone who was accustomed to the Quaker meeting, he was extremely sensitive to aural stimuli. He did not enjoy attending church services in other denominations as an adult because he found the sounds too overwhelming. He did not attend many concerts, either, because the stimulation overexcited his nerves. It was reported that he would leave in the middle of concerts and come back at the end in order to spare his nerves.[20]

Without a childhood background in church music, he missed out on a repertoire that many musicians take for granted. McDowell's Quaker background meant that his musical mind was virtually a blank slate. He did not have the background in Roman Catholic liturgy that his classmates at the Paris Conservatory would have; he did not share a repertoire of Lutheran chorales with his German colleagues; and he did not know the Protestant hymns that were second nature to his Boston colleagues in later years. What he did know was the music of his own soul, and it is not hard to see a parallel to the Inward Light. A composer's greatest asset is originality, and McDowell had the uncanny ability to look inside and come up with sounds that were like no other composer's. Critics agreed that McDowell sounded like no one but himself.

The principle of the Inward Light also helps to explain MacDowell's pattern of revisions. Like Chopin, MacDowell never considered his compositions finished, even after they were published. His restless intellect was always open to a better

18. S., "Music," *Friends' Intelligencer* 25/11 (16 May 1868): 163.

19. IRS Tax Records, Special Excise Tax, April 1866, www.ancestry.com, accessed 6 December 2009. There was no piano listed in 1864, and I have not been able to locate the records for 1865.

20. T. P. Currier, "Edward MacDowell as I Knew Him," *MQ* 1/1 (January 1915): 42.

solution to a compositional problem, and he did not hesitate to correct his youthful errors. As a consequence, many of his works were later published in revised editions. Clearly he subscribed to J.D.H.'s view: "the manna gathered yesterday will not suffice for to-day."

Edward began his piano lessons at a time when music was officially forbidden and considered dangerous and subversive by many Friends. But since their earliest days, Quakers had been known for defying authority, and the desire to follow principle and do what they felt was right superseded the rules, even those established by the Society. As an adult, Edward was drawn to musical styles that were progressive, avant-garde, and risky. He admired Liszt and Wagner, detested Brahms, and had little patience for composers of conservative music. These predilections may be traced to the rebellious connotations of music in his childhood.

Eddie grew up in a home with deep unresolved conflicts between the parents, which may help to explain his extreme shyness. He found it difficult to form new friendships, but when he found a true friend, he was intensely loyal. McDowell was torn throughout his life between the example of his quiet, reserved father and his gregarious, talkative mother. This contrast is nowhere more evident than in his life-long vacillation between the vocations of composer and performer, which demand very different skills and personality traits. From both parents, though, he learned the value of a strong work ethic.

But most important to Edward's personality was the feeling of being an outsider. Because of his father's marriage to a non-member, and additionally because of family activities that could have conflicted with Quaker beliefs, the family was tangential to the Friends meeting. Even as an adult, Edward would never be able to shake the feeling of being an outsider. He was not a person to cultivate popularity, and his best friends were mavericks like him. Characteristic of someone accustomed to living on the fringes of his group, McDowell was not a "joiner." He was loath to commit himself to clubs and other organizations, which was interpreted as aloofness or even disdain after he became famous. Like the stern Quakers he had known as a child, McDowell grew into a man of principle. He could be stubborn, even when it was not to his political advantage, but he knew what he believed and was willing to stand on principle rather than bow to expediency. This trait would serve him well in his creative life, where inspiration and commitment to a personal vision are vital. It would be less useful in professional situations where diplomacy and tact are needed in order to advance. And in the one situation where the best course of action would have been to admit defeat and accept compromise graciously, this trait would prove to be his undoing, with devastating consequences.

CHAPTER TWO

The Latin American Connection

THE MCDOWELLS WERE A LETTER-WRITING FAMILY. DURING THEIR YEARS APART,
they typically wrote at least one long letter per week to each other, along
with numerous letters to other friends and business associates. In light of this pattern, it is interesting to read the very first letter that the family preserved:

Sunday May 16, 1869

Dear Grandma,

Please excuse me for not writing sooner because I did not have much time Saturday
before last the semflers and Mamma Eddie and I went to the park Except George and
Alfred Fair he is Georges cousin who is staying with him. First we went to the Lake there
we met Cora Minnie and Mr Buitrag [sic] who is a friend of ours. Then we went in a
nice little summer house there were no body in it we ate our dinner on a big rock. The
violets are coming out the bank was completely covered with them They looked very
nice to a boy who has not been out of the city in a long time there are many birds in the
park and they are so tame that they came quite near us. There are some peacoks [sic] in
the park. One came in the summer house. There are many vellocipedes [sic] in the park
on Saturday. We had a sail on the lake but mamma did not want to go. Ned went to sleap
[sic] on my sholder [sic] when we were on the lake and then wecome [sic] home. Good
by Give my love to grandpa and the rest of the folks and your self. From your loving
Grandson

Walter Thomas McDowell

232 E. 18 St

my city

PS write soon.[1]

1. Letter, Walter MacDowell to "Grandma," 16 May 1869, NYPL.

Twelve-year-old Walter was still learning the finer points of spelling and punctuation, but this letter to his grandmother tells us a lot about the family dynamic. His apology for not writing sooner indicates that letter writing was already a routine for him, and in this case he had exciting news to share. A visit to Central Park—three miles from the upscale home on Eighteenth Street where they had relocated from Eddie's humble birthplace on Clinton Street—was a treat that the boys anticipated with pleasure. There they could see a bit of nature and have a break from the routine of school and home life. Peacocks and velocipedes were exotic sights, and a boat ride on a spring afternoon was so relaxing that Ned (the name was used interchangeably with Eddie) fell asleep on his big brother's shoulder. "Mamma" was not in the habit of doing things she did not want to do, but in all likelihood she did not stay in the summerhouse alone. Their gallant South American friend Mr. Buitrago probably stayed on shore to keep her company.

How did this Quaker family become acquainted with a musician from Colombia? One can easily imagine Fanny's desire for more color in her life, but the odds of such an encounter were very small. According to the census records of 1870, the state of New York was home to 1,824 persons born in Cuba, 442 persons born in South America, and 49 persons born in Central America.[2] These persons constituted just over .05 percent of the total population of 4,387,464, or 1 in 1,895. Like Quakers, Latin Americans were an extremely small minority at this time, creating a bond between the McDowells and their Latin American friends. The family not only belonged to a minority group themselves, but because of Thomas's "marrying out," they were marginalized by that minority group. Even though their Spanish-speaking friends were very different, they shared an understanding of what it means to live on the fringes of society. It was through these family friends that Eddie received his earliest training in music.

There is no record of the family's first meeting with Juan Buitrago, but he was already an important part of their family life by the late 1860s. He would eventually introduce them to numerous other Latin Americans and shape their family's life profoundly. Buitrago was a violinist born in Bogotá, Colombia, in 1834, making him younger than Thomas and older than Fanny.[3] He spent most of his life in the United States, from the early 1860s until shortly before his death on 7 June 1914 in Florence,

---

2. Francis A. Walker, *The Statistics of the Population of the United States* (Washington: Government Printing Office, 1872), 338, 342.

3. When he returned to New York on 4 February 1879, the ship's manifest listed his age as forty-three, placing his birth in 1835 or 1836. The 1870 U.S. Census, conducted on 8 June 1880, gives his age as 48, placing his birth in 1831 or 1832. When he returned to New York on 18 July 1908, the ship's manifest listed his age as seventy-four, placing his birth date in 1833 or 1834. These three documents were found at www.ancestry.com, accessed 29 November 2009.

Italy.[4] Despite spending such a long time in the United States, he never learned to speak or write English well, retaining a thick accent even as an old man. The violinist Albert Spalding, who studied with him around 1900, recalled:

> He had the courtly manners of a Spanish grandee, but the gentle morals of Ferdinand the Bull. I never heard a harsh word from his lips nor an unkind sentiment about anyone. Aunt Sally took to him at once in spite of his broken English heavily laden with Spanish phrases. She never succeeded in teaching him bezique, her favorite game, but daily she enlisted his services in reading to her, from the newspaper, the death and obituary notices and an occasional account of a local murder, and then one of the Psalms. These Mr. Buitrago would intone majestically and emotionally although the matter was entirely incomprehensible. Nothing daunted, however, Aunt Sally would lean forward with absorbed interest and never fail to exclaim: "How beautifully you do read, Mr. Buitrago."[5]

"Ferdinand the Bull" refers to the 1936 children's book by Munro Leaf titled *The Story of Ferdinand*, about a bull who would rather smell flowers than fight the matador. Fanny confirmed this aspect of Buitrago's personality as well as his difficulty with writing when she wrote to Walter in 1878, "You know Mr. Buitrago is not mighty with the <u>pen</u>, any more than he would be with the <u>sword</u>."[6]

At some point in the late 1860s, Buitrago began to teach Eddie and Walter to play the piano. We do not know for certain when Eddie began his studies, but it was undoubtedly much later than age four or five, when the greatest virtuosos typically start to play. Though he was a good player who soon began to attract attention, he did not possess the ease and facility that characterize the prodigy. He also found himself distracted by other interests, particularly reading and drawing, which kept him from focusing on piano. One story that was passed down through the family had Edward pay Walter two cents an hour to practice in his place so that he could read a book.[7] Nonetheless, Buitrago seems to have been an ideal teacher to begin his instruction. He was not a pianist himself, but he could teach his pupil general musical principles and basic piano technique without discouraging him. Spalding noted that as a teacher, Buitrago was "an excellent drill master with a kind of

---

4. "Juan Buitrago" [obituary], *NYT* (9 June 1914).

5. Albert Spalding, "Boy with Violin: Beginning a Musical Autobiography," *Harper's Magazine* 184/1102 (March 1942): 358. Copyright 1942 by Harper's Magazine. All rights reserved. Reproduced from the March issue by special permission.

6. Letter, Fanny McDowell to Walter McDowell, 2 August 1878, NYPL.

7. Abbie Farwell Brown, *The Boyhood of Edward MacDowell* (New York: Frederick A. Stokes, 1924), 45–46.

persistent perseverance that was as obstinate as his nature was mild."[8] After several years, he realized that Eddie needed more expertise than he could offer, and he found another teacher who was a professional pianist and could take the student to the next level.

Pablo Desvernine (1823–1910) was a Cuban pianist who had studied at the Paris Conservatory in the 1840s. He immigrated to New York in 1869 with his large family and taught music there.[9] With Desvernine in charge, Eddie's piano lessons took on a new seriousness, and he began to make real progress. It seems to have been Desvernine who first encouraged the McDowell family to send their son to Paris for advanced training. In a letter written to Edward in 1892, Desvernine recalled their time together in this way: "I only claim the honor of having guided your first steps in the Art, and the satisfaction of having recognized in you, before anyone, a true artist, as I predicted and assured Mrs. McDowell when she consulted me on this subject."[10]

The third Latin American musician whom the McDowells invited into their home was not his formal piano teacher but would later become the most important professional contact for advancing his career. Teresa Carreño (1853–1917) at the age of eight emigrated with her family from Caracas, Venezuela, in the face of political instability. Their property was seized, forcing her parents to rely on Teresa's skills as a child prodigy to support the family. The child astounded the audience at her debut recital in Irving Hall, New York, on 25 November 1862, and she went on to a brilliant career as a piano virtuosa in Europe and the United States. An extremely emotional player, she epitomized to many the Latina temperament.[11]

The origins of Carreño's friendship with the family are uncertain, but by the early 1870s she made the acquaintance of Fanny McDowell, and the two became fast friends.[12] There was a special bond between them that lasted until Fanny's death in 1909. Both temperamental women, they had their share of disagreements and

---

8. Spalding, "Boy with Violin," 358.

9. The 1870 census, which does not specify family relationships, lists sixteen persons named Desvernine living together on 33rd Street. The 1880 census lists ten in the household [www.ancestry.com, accessed 29 November 2009].

10. Letter, Paul [Pablo] Desvernine to Eddie MacDowell, 28 October 1892, EMMC box 30.

11. The best introduction to Carreño's life is Marta Milinowski, *Teresa Carreño "by the grace of God"* (New Haven: Yale University Press, 1940; repr. New York: Da Capo, 1977).

12. Hazel Gertrude Kinscella, who interviewed the pianist in 1916, wrote, "From the time of Carreño's return to America from Paris at the age of eighteen her father and mother and the McDowells were intimate friends. 'We were as one family,' said Mme Carreño." Hazel Gertrude Kinscella, "A Half Century of Piano Playing as Viewed Through Teresa Carreño's Eyes," *Musical America* 25/9 (30 December 1916): 5.

temporary estrangements over the years, but the friendship was perhaps the closest that either of them had outside their marriages. Carreño was married four times: to the French violinist Émile Sauret from 1872 to 1877, to the Italian baritone Giovanni Tagliapietra from 1877 to 1889, to the German pianist Eugen d'Albert from 1892 to 1895, and to Giovanni's brother Arturo Tagliapietra from 1902. Her turbulent personal life made for salacious coverage in the press, and Fanny played the faithful friend through all this turmoil.

Teresa was instrumental in Eddie's early development. She later recalled that already in 1872, he was "so sensitive and shy that it was painful to watch him."[13] When she first came to know the family, he was bored with piano lessons and did not apply himself to practicing in the way she felt he could. She devised a method of sitting with him and practicing, not as a teacher but as a friend or a sister. This rejuvenated his interest and made him more receptive to Desvernine's teaching.[14] When he was a bit older, she became exasperated with his lackluster practice on the Chopin B-flat minor Scherzo. She made a bet with him that she could learn it herself in an afternoon—if she failed to play it perfectly, she would give him a present; if she succeeded, he would give her a kiss. That evening she returned to play the piece flawlessly by memory, but when she looked for Eddie after the final cadence, he was nowhere to be seen. She had to chase him through the house until she cornered him in the cellar, extracting the promised kiss.[15] Carreño's most important contribution to his career, however, was her adoption of his piano works into her own repertoire starting in the 1880s. At the crucial point when he most needed help to spread his reputation, she generously introduced his solo works and concertos into her concerts, helping to establish his reputation in America while he still lived in Europe.

Although Buitrago was no longer Eddie's piano teacher after Desvernine took over, he was by no means absent. For almost forty years, he would be integral to the McDowell family: as a boarder in their New York home, as a traveling companion for Eddie and Fanny from 1876 to 1878 (and for Fanny alone when she returned to the United States in 1879), and as someone who was constantly near at hand. Fanny's letters from Paris nearly all begin with a report on "Mr. Buitrago's" activities before proceeding to what she and Eddie were doing. The 1880 census lists Buitrago as a boarder in the McDowell home, and he continued to be close to the family in the 1890s, when Edward lived in Boston.

13. Ibid., 5.

14. Emilie Frances Bauer, "Teresa Carreño Tells of MacDowell's Youth," *New York Evening Mail*, 31 March 1908, 7.

15. Milinowski, *Teresa Carreño*, 122–23.

The McDowell family's interest in foreign languages and cultures did not end with their Latin American friends. They were also attracted to French culture at the time when it was least fashionable to do so. Tensions between France and the German states had grown throughout the 1860s, and in 1870 they finally broke out in the Franco-Prussian War. In the United States, public opinion was solidly on the side of the Germans in this conflict, in part because of the large percentage of German-Americans. In New York State, the 1870 census listed 151,216 persons who had been born in Germany and only 8,265 who had been born in France. Not surprisingly, New Yorkers had little sympathy for the French during the Franco-Prussian War. But given what we know of the McDowells, it is also not surprising that they felt differently. It was about this time that Edward was taken out of Public School No. 40, where he had begun his schooling, and enrolled in the Charlier Institute, a bastion of French culture in Manhattan.

Elie Charlier (1826–1896), from Lyon, France, established a private preparatory school in Manhattan in the early 1850s. He promoted it as a place for sons of wealthy families to prepare for careers in government and diplomatic service. The school became one of New York's most fashionable, educating future leaders in business, government, and the arts. Among those who attended the Charlier Institute at the same time as Edward McDowell were Lucius Littauer (1859–1944), a Republican congressman from 1897–1907; Joseph Johnson Hart (1859–1926), a newspaper owner, a Democratic congressman from 1894–96, and the deputy tax commissioner of the city of New York from 1907–1926; and Alfred Stieglitz (1864–1946) the renowned American photographer and husband of painter Georgia O'Keefe.[16] Fanny may have hoped that this school could further her son's social climbing, but there is no evidence that the painfully shy Edward ever used any of these childhood connections in adulthood.

In the summer of 1873 (not 1874 as has been asserted previously), the twelve-year-old Eddie and his mother saw France firsthand during a package tour of Europe with the Cook agency. The two arrived in June and returned aboard the RMS *Russia* on 28 August.[17] During nearly three months they had the opportunity to visit Ireland, Scotland, England, Belgium, Germany, Switzerland, and France. The

16. Charlier's great-grandson was the folksinger Pete Seeger, who discusses the school in Alec Wilkinson, *The Protest Singer: An Intimate Portrait of Pete Seeger* (New York: Knopf, 2009), 30–32.

17. Fanny's passport was issued on 16 May 1873 in New York. The names of "Fanny McDowell" and "Master McDowell" are found on the passenger list filed by the master of the SS *Russia* on reaching New York, 28 August 1873. The person compiling the list may have been estimating their ages, which are given as forty and seventeen, rather than thirty-five and twelve. Passenger list and passport application found on www.ancestry.com, accessed 1 December 2009.

trip allowed Eddie to form visual images of the places he had read about and also to practice the French he was learning at the Charlier Institute.

The age of twelve is poised between childhood and adolescence. This is an age when tears come easily, when the rapidly changing body is clumsy and awkward, when the mind has remarkable flashes of insight followed by inexplicable lapses into stupidity. This is an age that tries the patience of both parent and child, but it is also when the remnants of juvenile openness combine with the awakenings of adult awareness to provide a window of remarkable receptivity to new experiences. For McDowell, the tour could not have come at a better time.

Eddie recorded his impressions of Europe through drawings and paintings, which were eventually pasted into a scrapbook along with a few receipts, advertisements, and other mementos of the trip. The artwork, in particular, shows remarkable maturity for a boy of twelve. We know nothing about his instruction in art, but the young McDowell had already learned a wide range of techniques in shading and value that allowed him to portray contours convincingly. Some of the drawings are studies of hands, feet, eyes, lips, and even a nose, but many of the works are finished scenes or portraits. He had a confidence in portraying both landscapes and portraiture that belied his youth. Most importantly, his paintings and drawings are emotionally evocative, as a convincing portrait in pen and ink, pencil, and pastel titled *The Hen with the Golden Eggs* reveals. The portrait shows a woman with a troubled expression sitting on a curb holding a dead chicken. On the ground beside her are a bloody knife and three eggs. The portrait has an emotional immediacy that effectively communicates the meaning of the old story.

Eddie chronicled his trip through Europe with his drawings. The excursion began in the British Isles with visits to London, Ireland, and Scotland. In London, which must have reminded Eddie of New York at this time, he sketched Trafalgar Square and the view from their room in the Charing Cross Hotel looking toward St. Paul's Cathedral. In Scotland, he sketched Edinburgh Castle and Stirling Castle, but he was equally drawn to a man wearing a kilt and full Scottish garb. In Ireland they purchased photographs of the Lake of Killearney and other sites that the young artist embellished with paint. After visiting Brussels, they boarded a Rhine steamer and traveled to Switzerland. Along the way, Eddie was captivated by the castles, painting one after another as they passed by on either side of the river. He created a memorable view of Cologne with its famous cathedral, and also the fort of Coblenz. In Switzerland he had his first view of Lake Geneva, which would be the site of enjoyable summers as an adult. He sketched the lake and several Alpine scenes, and he saved an advertisement for a hotel in Lucerne. In Paris, he sketched the Notre Dame Cathedral.

Paging through this sketchbook, one is struck by the portraits. As might be expected from a child with a sense of humor, there are a few caricatures, for instance the drawing of an elegantly dressed woman leading a hippopotamus on a leash with the words "Come along Fido!!" Most of them, however, show a poignant interest in their subjects, which cover a range of humanity, from beautiful girls to old men. There are persons with unusual clothing and hairstyles, as well as various racial and ethnic types such as Chinese and Mongolian. There are stylized pictures of famous musicians like Schubert, Mozart, and Wagner, while there are some portraits that seem to have been copied from other artists. Most of the portraits in this sketchbook and another from a year later have a realism that reflects not only excellent technique but also an artist's eye for observation.

In later years he told a few choice stories from this summer's trip, and it is instructive to note which ones he considered worth retelling. The traveling companions on this trip were all strangers, and most were women. In Paris, they discovered that he had enough French to help them with their shopping, and he was enlisted as a translator. On one occasion he managed to get alone long enough to do a little shopping for himself. Preadolescent boys are constantly hungry, so his goal was to find a candy shop. Thinking he had found what he wanted, he entered a shop with the sign Confections over the door. It turned out that there was no candy to be found, only lingerie. The shopgirls made merry of his request for "confection" by pulling out boxes of intimate apparel and giggling over his discomfort.[18]

Another incident was perhaps more significant in shaping his perspectives on himself and his countrymen. He was traveling by train with a group of fellow American tourists who made disparaging comments about the appearance of the French persons in the same compartment, assuming they could not be understood. After some time, one of the French women rebuked the Americans in English, causing them well-deserved embarrassment.[19] This childhood experience with "ugly Americans" must have made a strong impression, for as an adult, McDowell did his best to become acculturated, first to France and later to Germany. Because he was shy and introverted, he yearned to blend in with the surrounding culture rather than stand out as different. It is no accident that his best friend in Europe, Templeton Strong, would also be an American expatriate who was committed to adopting European ways.

Upon his return to New York, he continued his schooling at the Charlier Institute and his piano studies with Desvernine. As his piano repertoire became more advanced, he had the opportunity to perform in recitals presented by Desvernine's students. On 7 March 1874, he played Beethoven's "Moonlight" Sonata, op. 27, no. 2, and by 17 April 1875, he was one of the most advanced

18. Brown, *Boyhood of Edward MacDowell,* 92–96.
19. Ibid., 86–87.

students in the recital, performing the Mendelssohn G-minor Concerto and also the Grand duet for two pianos "sur Puritani" by Liszt, Thalberg, and Herz. The second selection was played with another piano student by the name of Michael Castellanos, nicknamed "Chichi." Like Desvernine, Michael's father, Miguel Castellanos, had been born in Cuba. Michael was born on 11 July 1862, after the family moved to New York. Eddie and Chichi played the most advanced repertoire on both recitals, and one can imagine that there was a friendly rivalry between the two aspiring pianists. Eddie continued his excellent work at school, receiving two certificates, or "Billets de Satisfaction," from the Charlier Institute in December 1874. One of these recognized him for being first in the third English class, while the other recognized him as second in the fourth French class.[20]

In December 1874, Teresa Carreño visited the McDowell family and took the opportunity to give Eddie a photograph and write a musical autograph card that encapsulates a scene from the life of this unusual family (Plate 3). In the center of the card are scales representing vocal exercises on the words "Fi Fi Fi" (Carreño was studying singing with Herminia Rudersdorff at the time in preparation for her operatic debut as Zerlina in Mozart's *Don Giovanni*). The tempo marking is *Allegro furioso*, while the words "con molto espress." are found below the staff. This little excerpt is signed "Teresita Carreño Sauret, Dec. 26th 1874." In the corners of this card are written in tiny letters that can only be deciphered with effort, "Fanny Oh! Fanny! If it is thy wish that I should dye your dresses etc. etc. etc. Don't be sorrowful darling Don't be sorrowful pray for take the year together you'll always find the money."[21] This dramatic scene is missing some crucial details, but we can fill in the blanks with a little speculation. The person who is placating Fanny is most likely Thomas, because of the Quaker "thy." The comment about dying her dresses may be a reference to some demands that are now obscure. But the final sentence granting permission to "take the year together" despite the cost almost certainly refers to spending a year in Europe with Eddie.

The unanswered question in this little scene is where the idea of the European trip originated. Was it Eddie's wish to study in Europe? Had Fanny enjoyed their summer trip so much that she wanted to live there longer? Or was there another reason for wanting to travel? We cannot know for sure, but we do know that within a few weeks of this autograph, Eddie withdrew from the Charlier Institute in order to devote himself full time to his piano studies, and that in a little over a year he

20. Both certificates were pasted into the scrapbook "SKETCHES, Presented By Mamma. March 7th 1874," EMMC box 28.

21. "SKETCHES, Presented By Mamma. March 7th 1874," EMMC box 28.

moved to Paris to study not for one year but for several years. His teacher at the Charlier Institute, J. McManus, wrote: "Master McDowell—a <u>good</u> pupil: leaves behind him, in my experience, an excellent character in conduct and lessons, and much regret for his withdrawal."[22] From this point on, Eddie's formal studies would all be in music, while his general education would proceed through his own reading. Although he was an avid reader throughout his adult life, his teachers at the Charlier Institute must have felt that he was missing out on a well-rounded education. Given the timing of his withdrawal, it seems likely that his energies were being directed toward gaining admission to the Paris Conservatory, where Desvernine had studied years before.

In spring 1875, Eddie had another reason to aim for Paris. His duet partner, Chichi Castellanos, sailed with his father to France, where he enrolled in the Paris Conservatory. He gained admission through a competitive audition on 25 October 1875, joining the piano class of Antoine-François Marmontel on 3 November. His example must have added weight to Desvernine's arguments, for in April 1876, Eddie, Fanny, and Buitrago set sail for Paris, where he intended to audition for the Paris Conservatory as his friend had done the year before.

It is not a cliché to say that his European study was a life-changing experience. During the next twelve years, he would become thoroughly immersed in European ways of life, and the musical attitudes imparted by his European teachers would form the basis of his aesthetic views throughout his life. The decision to study in France would be crucial for his own professional future and, because of the stature he eventually attained, for the future of music in America. But for the fifteen-year-old Quaker boy and his mother, the example of their Latin American friends Buitrago, Carreño, Desvernine, and Castellanos was crucial in bringing them to this decision.

22. This evaluation, dated 27 January 1875, was sent to the McDowells by Elie Charlier on 30 March 1875. The note is pasted over a drawing—presumably by Eddie—of a man in profile identified as "Napoleon Trois." Archives of the American Academy of Arts and Letters, New York.

CHAPTER THREE

The Paris Conservatory

HE MACDOWELL LEGEND, AS TOLD IN LATER YEARS, BEGINS IN PARIS. HERE tradition tells us that MacDowell worked diligently for two years, earning one of only two scholarships for free admission to the prestigious conservatory. After his second year, however, he heard the Russian pianist Nicolai Rubinstein play at the Exposition Universelle and turned to his mother with the words, "Mother, I want to play like that man, and I will never do it if I remain in Paris." She promptly made arrangements to move to Germany, where he flourished and established his career. This version of the story first appeared in an anonymous—and francophobic—interview in the *Musical Times* in 1904 and has been repeated by biographers and record jacket annotators ever since.[1] In fact, the only verifiable part of the legend is that he worked diligently for two years in Paris. The real story, as told in recently discovered documents from the conservatory, is not so heroic (or nationalistic), but it shows MacDowell as a much more believable human being, one whose insecurities, personal loyalty, and passionate adherence to principle forced him to make perhaps the most crucial decision of his youth.

In late April 1876, Fanny and Eddie set sail for France, and on 6 May, after eleven days at sea, they spotted land at Plymouth harbor in southern England. Both travel-

---

1. "Edward MacDowell: A Biographical Sketch," *Musical Times* 44 (1 April 1904): 221. The story was repeated in Lawrence Gilman, *Edward MacDowell: A Study* (New York: John Lane, 1908), 6–7, and in Emilie Frances Bauer, "Teresa Carreño tells of MacDowell's Youth," *New York Evening Mail,* 31 March 1908, 7.

ers wrote to Walter on that day, and their respective letters show their excitement and anticipation. Fanny's letter reflects on the important step in their family life:

> Well, our long journey which each day has carried us farther and farther away from my two darlings (yourself and your dear Papa) is rapidly approaching its end, and soon our ship's company, an exceptionally pleasant one will be quite separated each going in their own direction and we will be surrounded only by frog-eating French people. It makes me homesick to think of, but we must all keep up a brave spirit, and anxiously look forward to the time when we shall be reunited once more. I hardly dare hope that we shall ever be as we once were, for Eddie naturally in his profession, will lay little claim, when he has once fairly started on his career, to the family roof tree from his abiding place, and so it is with a sad heart that I think of the probable and possible changes which may come to us all to decide our future; but I won't allow myself to get homesick today over it. We will look on the bright side and trust in that Providence which alone can protect us.[2]

This letter is a mixture of regret, anxiety, and—in the other seven pages of this long epistle—instructions on how to behave and how to take care of her things.

And what about the fifteen-year-old Eddie from whom so much was expected? He began his letter, "Dear Walter, I wrote you a letter yesterday but Mamma said that it wouldn't do so I begin this." The letter shows a young man who is very observant of the foibles of his fellow passengers. He begins by exposing the pretensions of an aspiring female piano student and goes on to relate how he and his mother laughed at a maudlin speech by the American consul to Havre. The majority of the letter, though, is reserved for an anecdote designed to appeal to his brother and childhood playmate:

> There is a little boy on board who is only eleven years old who is one of the smartest little fellows I ever saw. He is going to a College in Paris and is travelling all alone and is always in mischief. There was a Mr. Cook (He left at Plymouth) on board + they were always "fighting". The other day Mr. Cook was playing at "Shuffleboard" with a Mr. Greene (both "spoony" on Miss Quesada) when this little "Chuck" as they call him took his bunch of keys and tied them to a string (He was standing on the upper deck while Cook was on the lower) and let them down on Cook + then pulled them back which made Cook awfully mad who watching his opportunity caught the keys and threw them overboard. Chuck immediately walks down stairs and as Cook's coat was hanging up he took his handkerchief out of one of the pockets. Then he marched up stairs again and attached the handkerchief to the string and let it down on Cook who with an air of determination threw it overboard also. Of course all the passengers laughed at him. The day before we got to Plymouth Chuck thinking to do something smart to pay for his keys

2. Letter, Fanny McDowell to Walter McDowell, 6 May 1876, NYPL.

went to Cook's cabin and took 1 vest, a Clothes brush 3 Hats a trunk strap and threw them overboard and went down stairs for a pair of Pantaloons when Cook's son came and "bounced" him. Cook thought that some steerage passengers had stolen his things.[3]

Eddie was still a boy at heart and no doubt envious of the mischievous fellow traveling alone without a mother to keep him in line.

Upon arrival in Paris, the McDowells took rooms in a house with a Cuban family. This did not work out well, as Eddie reported in a letter to Madame Aubert, one of his former teachers at the Charlier Institute: "At first Mamma was horribly homesick but that was partly owing to our boarding with a Cuban family who were not congenial and whose manner of living differed entirely from that which Mamma had been accustomed to."[4] By mid-June, however, they were ensconced in a comfortable fourth-floor apartment at 30 Rue de Dunkerque, where they would remain for their entire stay in Paris. This building was one block from the Gare du Nord, the railway station serving northern Paris that had been completed just twelve years before their arrival. Eddie's multicolored drawing of the layout shows that he and Mr. Buitrago shared a room in the northeast corner, which was connected by a hall to Fanny's room in the northwest corner. Next to her room on the west side were a dining room and a parlor with a grand piano. The entire southern half of the floor, occupying as much space as these four rooms combined, is labeled "Mrs. Thurber's apartment."[5]

Jeannette Meyer Thurber (1850–1946) would play a crucial role in the McDowells' lives and also in the development of American music in the 1880s and 1890s. The daughter of a Danish immigrant violinist, she had studied at the Conservatoire National in Paris as a teenager and married the wealthy American businessman Francis Beattie Thurber in 1869. Beginning in the 1870s, she initiated a long series of projects allowing her to use her wealth to enhance musical life in the United States.[6] Her love for Paris caused her to return there often, including an extended stay in 1876/77 during which she shared lodgings with the McDowells. It is not clear how or when they met, but Fanny had a knack for making and keeping influential friends. In a letter of 5 October 1876, she told Walter that she and Mrs. Thurber had visited the Louvre three days in a row, followed by a day at the zoo.

3. Letter, Eddie McDowell to Walter McDowell, 6 May 1876, EMMC box 29/1.

4. Letter, Eddie McDowell to Madame Aubert, 18 June 1876, NYPL.

5. Drawing by Juan Buitrago and Eddie McDowell labeled "Daniel in the Lion's Den," EMMC.

6. Thurber's life work has been documented extensively by Emanuel Rubin. See especially "Jeannette Meyers Thurber and the National Conservatory of Music," *American Music* 8/3 (Fall 1990): 294–325; "Jeannette Meyer Thurber (1850–1946): Music for a Democracy," in *Cultivating Music in America: Women Patrons and Activists since 1860*, ed. Ralph P. Locke and Cyrilla Barr (Berkeley: University of California Press, 1997), 134–63.

It was fortunate that Fanny had a companion with whom to spend her days, for as she reported in the same letter, she did not see much of her son: "As for Eddie, the day is not long enough for his work, and he has not a minute, and lately, even his Sundays are crowded almost as much as the week days, and as he says, if there were 24 hours of daylight, it would not be long enough to accomplish all they require of him. The Paris Conservatoire is no place for idle or lazy boys, and although Eddie is not a member, still he is obliged to do as the regular members do."[7] During his first year in Paris, Eddie was an auditor in the music theory class of Savard and a private piano student of Marmontel. These lessons were designed to prepare him for his entrance examination to the conservatory the following year, when he would attempt to gain admission to the most elite music school in the world.

The French conservatory system, like the French monarchy and the French transportation system, was and is highly centralized. The system consists of four levels of schools: the least selective are the Écoles Municipales de Musique Agréés (general municipal music schools); at the next level are the Écoles Nationales de Musique (the national music schools); and at the third level are the Conservatoires Nationaux de Région (the regional national conservatories). At the pinnacle is the Conservatoire National Supérieur de Musique de Paris, colloquially known as the Paris Conservatory. This school has offered advanced training in music since the late eighteenth century and has a long tradition of attracting some of the best and most talented students in the world. The number of students in each area of study is strictly limited, and thus the competition for admission is fierce. Admission and advancement are exam-driven, as each student's fate is determined by his or her performance in the annual *concours* (competition) in the summer. In order to be admitted as a regular student, McDowell would need to pass the entrance examination. Upon admission, the best students were eligible to compete for prizes in the annual *concours*.

As its name implies, the Conservatoire National was designed to be a training ground for French musicians. But a clause in the regulations allowed the director of the conservatory to make exceptions at his own discretion for foreigners who could pass the entrance examination. The rule was enforced inconsistently over the years: the Hungarian Franz Liszt was denied admission by director Luigi Cherubini in 1823, and the American Louis Moreau Gottschalk was denied admission in 1841 when Pierre Zimmerman refused to hear him. By the 1870s, however, the floodgates had opened, and Ambroise Thomas, who had become director in 1871, adopted the policy of admitting students on the basis of talent rather than denying them admission

7. Letter, Fanny McDowell to Walter McDowell, 5 October 1876, NYPL.

solely because of nationality. This policy proved to be contentious, because all students admitted to the conservatory received free tuition. State support of foreigners became the subject of complaints in the press, which seemed to intensify every year at the time of the *concours*. No matter how talented the students may have been, using tax dollars to give foreign students free instruction was perennially unpopular, and the feeling of injustice was only intensified when foreigners won prizes.[8]

Eddie knew without a doubt that he was a foreigner in France, as he told Mme. Aubert in June 1876:

> The other day I was sent on an errand to "Le Printemps" (A large dry goods store) when upon not finding it and thinking to air my French a little, I strutted up to a very digni-fied looking policeman and demanded of him in the most confident manner "where 'Le Printemps' was"? The policeman immediately pricked up his ears, inclined his head and said "Monsieur"? I repeated my question with a slight misgiving, upon which he began stroking his beard repeating to himself Prängtong-Prangtong—(Probably revolving in his mind what kind of an animal it was) I began to get decidedly discouraged and said with very little hope "Au Printemps" to which he responded "Au Prongtong" and then sank into a reverie. All at once I was seized with a brilliant thought. I got a pencil and wrote it for him. Oh! said he "Le Printemps["] (he said it <u>exactly</u> like I said it first) showed me the way and asked me whether I wasn't a <u>foreigner</u>. It was the last straw on the camel's back. I walked away in disgust from a man who didn't know how to speak his own language! Mamma is going to engage a teacher this week.[9]

As a concession to French (and later German) speakers, he began spelling his name "MacDowell" while in Paris. There is no evidence that he changed his name legally, but this was the spelling by which he became famous, and his parents followed suit after he was well known.

Perhaps as a consequence of his weak language skills, but more likely because of the influence of Buitrago, his closest friends during his Paris years were Latin Americans. The McDowells maintained contact with the Quesada family they had met on shipboard until they moved with their beautiful but sickly daughter to Costa Rica in August 1878.[10] Eddie also befriended a talented Cuban pianist named José Jimenes, who was admitted to the conservatory in October 1876 and won the first prize in piano the following summer, an almost unheard-of accomplishment. His best friend, though, was his former duet partner from New York, Michael Castellanos.

8. See for instance "Les Étrangers au Conservatoire," *Le Petit Journal,* 23 July 1889, 3.
9. Letter, Eddie McDowell to Madame Aubert, 18 June 1876, NYPL.
10. Letter, Fanny McDowell to Walter McDowell, 2 August 1878, NYPL.

Chichi, as Eddie always referred to him in his letters, had gained admission to the conservatory in 1875. They were almost immediately in contact after Eddie's arrival in Paris, as both were auditors in Savard's music theory class and piano students of Marmontel. Their friendship grew quickly, and MacDowell felt comfortable enough with the family that he could borrow money from them during his mother's vacation in Switzerland in November 1877.[11]

Their theory teacher Augustin Savard (1814–1881) had been appointed an instructor of solfège at the Conservatoire National in 1843, when he was not yet thirty years old, and he held this position for the rest of his life. His job was to drill students in the rudiments of music, and by the time Eddie entered his class as an auditor, Savard was nearing the end of his career. Eddie reported in November 1877, "Savard is getting sick—His eyes are giving out and he is irritable in consequence."[12] The drill was useful for MacDowell, both as a pianist and as a future composer. Among other things, he was forced to transpose Bach fugues into other keys and to read at sight melodies that changed clefs every measure or so.

His principal mentor in Paris was the piano teacher Antoine-François Marmontel (1816–1898), who taught solfège at the conservatory from 1837 to 1848 and piano from 1848 to 1887. The list of his students reads like a *Who's Who* of French music, including Bizet, d'Indy, Dubois, Pierné, and Debussy, of whom the last two were in MacDowell's class. But he also showed a genuine interest in his foreign students. Eddie described him shortly after beginning lessons:

> Mr. Marmontel is a nice old man and I like him very much. Every once in a while he puts his hands up to the side of his head, rolls up his eyes and says, "Oh! mon Dieu!" in the most helpless manner in the world. Sometimes I can not help laughing he says it so funnily—he does not come up to my shoulder—When he gets angry at his pupils, he throws their music at them and says, "Va! Polisson"! [get out of here, you scamp!] And they do "va" pretty quick too I tell you.[13]

As a private student, MacDowell paid for his lessons with the master teacher. According to Abbie Farwell Brown, he left a twenty-franc gold piece (four dollars) on the piano after every lesson. One day he forgot and was running down the stairs when the teacher called after him, "My boy! My boy! You have forgotten something!" an anecdote that Eddie remembered and enjoyed telling for years afterward.[14]

11. Letter, Eddie McDowell to Fanny McDowell, 5 November 1877, NYPL.

12. Ibid.

13. Letter, Eddie McDowell to Madame Aubert, 18 June 1876, NYPL.

14. Abbie Farwell Brown, *The Boyhood of Edward MacDowell* (New York: Frederick A. Stokes, 1924), 115–16.

Marmontel also allowed him to sit in on his conservatory classes, and on 5 October 1876 he was given the opportunity to play for the class, an unusual honor for a student who was not yet admitted. Fanny was afraid that he would be too nervous to play well, but Marmontel declared himself satisfied after the performance.[15]

MacDowell's parents had brought him to Paris to study piano, but he also tried his hand at composition. By May 1876 he had composed a set of *Improvisations*, op. 1, and a set of *Chansons Fugitives*, op. 2. By 18 June he reported that he had composed "a Nocturne, two Musettes, a Waltz, two more Nocturnes, a lot of little songs."[16] He continued to write a variety of short compositions during his two years in Paris. Among the pieces that he completed were a set of *Trois petits morceaux* [three short pieces], op. 5, dedicated to Mrs. Thurber, and *Deux Mélodies pour Piano et Violon*, op. 9, dedicated to Juan Buitrago.[17]

In the fall of 1876, Eddie began a correspondence with a New York boy named Henry Holden Huss (1862–1953). The two had been brought together by Elizabeth Phelps, a mutual acquaintance of their mothers, who had written to Henry, "I hope you and [Eddie] will correspond, it will be mutually helpful. Eddie is a good boy—has been carefully reared, and has I believe exceptional musical ability. I am quite sure you will like one another."[18] The opening of Eddie's first letter to his new pen pal reflects the stilted circumstances under which the two were brought together, and forms a striking contrast to his letters to Walter:

> Dear friend,
> Since you have so kindly given me the liberty of calling you friend, I gladly do so, and while thanking you for making the first overtures towards friendship and correspondence, I assure you I shall be happy to avail myself of both, and hope in good time to meet you, either on this or the other side of the Ocean, and to enjoy your society, for it seems to me that our music would be a bond of sympathy between us. I am very grateful to Miss Minnie Schaus and Mrs. Phelps, who must have spoken a good word; but then they are always doing nice things and so it does not surprise me.[19]

The first sentence sounds suspiciously like one of Fanny's run-on sentences, but it is written in Eddie's handwriting. Over the course of the next year, the two

---

15. Letter, Fanny McDowell to Walter McDowell, 5 October 1876, MacDowell Collection, NYPL.

16. Letter, Eddie McDowell to Madame Aubert, 18 June 1876, NYPL.

17. The *Trois petits morceaux*, op. 5, are in the NYPL, while the other juvenilia are in EMMC and the Columbia University Rare Book and Manuscript Library. None of these early works has been published.

18. Letter, Elizabeth B. Phelps to Henry Holden Huss, 23 October [1876], NYPL.

19. Letter, EAM to Henry H. Huss, 23 November 1876, NYPL.

boys shared their views on Wagner, Italian opera, musical conditions in New York, presidential politics, and other matters of mutual interest. Eddie was a great deal more advanced than Henry, and so their discussions of piano repertoire did not go far. He was also extremely busy, and as the year wore on, his responses became slower and slower. The surviving correspondence does not extend beyond the following summer, but in these guarded, formal letters may be found verification of MacDowell's concert attendance (Marmontel gave his students free tickets), his own piano repertoire, and other details of his first year in Paris. Huss eventually studied in Munich with Josef Rheinberger from 1882 to 1885, but the two New Yorkers were not close as adults.[20]

On 8 July 1877, MacDowell mentioned to Huss that this year's *morceau de concours* (required piano piece) for the upcoming annual conservatory competition would be the difficult Schumann Sonata No. 2, op. 22. As an auditor he was not eligible to play in the *concours*, but nonetheless he was caught up in the excitement surrounding the event. Only the best students from each class were allowed to compete, so earning the privilege of entering the *concours* in late July was an important rite of passage. The competitors (*concurrents*) were expected to be ready to play a composition of their own choosing as well as the assigned *morceau de concours* for that year's competition. In addition, they would have to read at sight a composition written especially for the competition, which would give no one an advantage. The judges consisted of a committee headed by the director and selected from among the faculty and outside experts. This committee would vote on the prizes of Premier prix, Second prix, Premier accessit, and Deuxième accessit, with the option of granting multiple awards in each category. The judges were informed before the competition of each competitor's results in previous competitions, as it was typical for a student who had received a lower prize in one year to move up to a higher prize.

Compounding the excitement was the fact that the competitors were drawn more or less equally from the studios of the two principal piano teachers: Marmontel and Georges Mathias (1826–1910), who was ten years younger than Marmontel but had the rare distinction of having studied with Chopin. It is typical in conservatories of music for students to develop intense loyalties to their teacher and fellow students, resulting in resentments and rivalries between studios. No matter how the administration and the teachers themselves try to downplay these rivalries, they seem to be inherent to a system of instruction that is so intensely personal. MacDowell was no doubt in the audience that heard Marmontel's students compete against those

---

20. For further information on Huss, see Gary A. Greene: *Henry Holden Huss: an American Composer's Life* (Metuchen, NJ: Scarecrow, 1995).

of Mathias, for the breathless report he sent home reflects the strong opinions of someone who heard the competition:

> I told you all about Chichi—Cast[ellanos]—and Marmontel. Jimenez, Rabaud—Trago & Belegue & Chichi played the best in the concours. Some of Mathias's pupils played hor-rably [sic] I don't see how they could have the face to play so—Jimenez play'd very well and read well Rabaud play'd very well and read pretty well Trago play'd and read well. Belegue play'd well and read splendidly Chichi play'd very well and read badly—(though not so badly as some of them) Marmontel told Chichi that it was an injustice and that he must study reading very much so as to be perfect next year. Indeed it was such an injustice that I am afraid for my self for next year[.] If I do get a prize it will have to be by hard work indeed—more so as Chichi was neglected from sheer injustice as they only gave one 2nd acc.[21]

The prizes awarded in the piano *concours* of 1877 were divided equally between the studios of Marmontel and Mathias. Premier prix: Jimenez, Trago, and Rabeau, of whom the last two were students of Mathias; Second prix: Bellaigue and Debussy, both students of Marmontel; Premier accessit: O'Kelly and Fournier, both students of Mathias; Deuxième accessit: Guiard, a student of Marmontel. Chichi had every right to feel that he had been dealt an injustice by being left off the list when the committee might have granted him a Deuxième accessit. Among the surprises was the second prize won by Achille [later known as Claude] Debussy, an indifferent student who did not stand out in Marmontel's studio; and the lack of a prize for Paul Aimé Braud, another of MacDowell's friends, who had earned a Deuxième accessit in 1876 but failed to advance in 1877.

A competition like this has a large subjective element, as there are many inter-locking skills and qualities that must complement each other in order to produce a successful audition. The judges must balance accuracy in rhythms, pitches, and dynamics against speed, power, tone quality, and musical expressivity while weighing the relative importance of the prepared piece versus the sight-reading. Ultimately, what sets the greatest musicians apart is a certain "je ne sais quoi" that appeals to listeners for reasons they do not fully understand. But what wins competitions—especially when all the competitors play the same repertoire—is the ability to play with a minimum of mistakes and without too much individuality of interpretation. The *concours* of July 1877 was controversial, as noted by Henry Cohen in *L'Art musical*: "But by one of those oddities to which those who frequent the conserva-tory *concours* are accustomed, the most-applauded student of all—M. Castellanos of Marmontel's class, whom public opinion balanced between the first and second

---

21. Undated letter on verso of a drawing of the view from his window, NYPL.

prize—received nothing at all."[22] This opinion was echoed by other reviewers, with Oscar Comettant hinting at a reason for the omission:

> *Havana is going to ruin*, says a popular Cuban song. If Havana goes to ruin, it will not be the fault of its pianists. Of the three first prizes, two fell to children of Cuba, MM. Trago and Jimenez. This last, dark as Othello, has excellent fingers certainly, but he shines especially in music demanding grace and sensibility....But how was it that the young Castellanos, student of Marmontel's class, did not figure among the chosen of this *concours*? Was it an oversight? I would almost be tempted to believe it, because this young pianist is one of those who obtained the most success before the public. His execution is sure, colored, interesting, and in my humble opinion in my notes, I designated him for the second prize. Fortunately he is only fourteen, and he can wait until next year for the prize he deserves and will certainly have.[23]

Given the unpopularity of foreign students, granting prizes to three Spanish-speakers in the same year would have opened the director to a barrage of external criticism. And given the rivalry between the two piano studios, granting more prizes to Marmontel students than to Mathias students would have opened that same director to internal complaints. Chichi and his friends knew he had been snubbed, but if the director influenced the decision, his reasons were clear. For justification, he could point to the New Yorker's weak sight-reading.

The entrance auditions were conducted after it was clear how many places in each class would be vacated by departing students. In 1877 they took place on Wednesday, 31 October. There were forty boys (not two hundred as reported elsewhere) selected to audition for a committee consisting of director Thomas and five piano professors. The *concurrents* ranged in age from nine years and one month to twenty-two years and six months, with Eddie in the middle of the age range. The students played a composition of their own selection (MacDowell's was the Schumann Sonata that had been the required piece at the July *concours*) and read another composition at sight. After hearing all forty competitors, the committee members voted by secret ballot and chose seven boys (not two) for admission. MacDowell was one of five who was selected by unanimous vote. Eddie was ecstatic, and wrote to his parents, who were both at home in New York:

> Well, the Concours is over at last. Now for a prize. I am quite proud of my examination, and so is Marmontel. He told me I ought to go and see Gen. Grant. He is all the time talking about it—in the class Friday, he said, "Ah! Ces americains, Ils font la conquête

22. Henry Cohen, "Concours du conservatoire," *L'Art musical* 16/31 (2 August 1877), 243.

23. Oscar Comettant, "Revue musicale," *Le Siècle,* 30 July 1877, 2.

du nouveau monde et pas encore content, ils viennent conquerir le vieux." [Ah! these Americans, they conquer the New World, and not yet satisfied, they are going to conquer the Old] He is very content. I was the 15th one to concourir....I wasn't frightened a bit, and read <u>without fault</u>. I am in high feather altogether.[24]

Once again, Marmontel had shown himself to be very supportive of his students, and MacDowell was understandably proud of his accomplishment. His acceptance meant that he could now enjoy instruction in piano, music theory, solfège, and other subjects for as long as he and his instructors deemed necessary, all at the expense of the French government. When Marmontel joked about conquering the Old World, he was struck by the coincidence of MacDowell's victory with the 1877 visit to Paris of General Ulysses S. Grant, a hero of the Civil War and former U.S. president.

Admission to the Conservatoire did not mean he could rest on his laurels, however, as he reported later in the same letter: "I am <u>terribly hurried</u> now when I have the Conservatoire. It is a continual scramble....You can't think how "pressét" I am—just 3 times more than last winter....Chichi and I read every day—4 hands. We take turns for the different parts. He has an "abbonnement" [subscription] at Flaxland's. We read <u>every day</u>."[25] The two friends understood that in order to earn prizes at the next year's *concours*, now less than nine months away, their sight-reading would need to be in top shape. In addition to piano classes with Marmontel, Eddie now had music theory classes with Savard and solfège classes with Marmontel's son, Antonin-Emile-Louis Corbaz (1850–1907).

In January 1878, Marmontel's class played midyear examinations, and the teacher wrote short evaluations of each student. These give a good sense of the progress each was making and also gave the professor the opportunity to send the director preliminary signals about prospects for the summer's *concours*. The evaluations of MacDowell and some of his classmates are models of subtle communication:

Debussy is studying much better. Less hot-headed than before. Intelligent[.] Will become an artist if he wants to tie himself down to more reflection.
Braud: very good student. Delicate and distinguished temperament.
Bellaigue: excellent student. Very good musician, has the authority of talent and the fine speaking of a mature man.
Castellanos: <u>Very good pianist</u>. Quite remarkable qualities of execution. I call his attention to the goodwill of my dear director.

24. Letter, EAM to Fanny McDowell, 5 November 1877, NYPL.
25. Ibid.

Pierné: Charming child, very studious. Will certainly be a distinguished musician.

Dowell [*sic*]: Good pupil, very studious. Has excellent pianistic qualities but lacks self-control.[26]

In a nutshell, the experienced teacher summarized each student's progress since the last evaluation, his inherent gifts and limitations, and his prospects for the future. At the end of the list of students he added a note to director Thomas stating that he was pleased with them all and could not rank them, asking instead for the consideration that they all deserved. On 25 January, the twelve members of Marmontel's piano class performed for a committee of seven judges, when MacDowell played a fugue by Mendelssohn.

On 20 June 1878, the class again played semester examinations, which this time also served as the qualifying round for the *concours*. MacDowell played a concerto by Carl Reinecke, the only selection in his class by a modern German composer. Marmontel again endorsed his favorite students in no uncertain terms. Regarding Chichi and Eddie he wrote:

Castellanos:Very brilliant pianist. Studious pupil, charming makeup and worthy of all the interest of the committee. Truly unlucky in last year's *concours*.

Dowell [*sic*]: Very good pupil, has real qualities of execution. I want to see him admitted to the concours. Auditor for eighteen months, has belonged to my class more than six months, and has been a student of the conservatory since December.[27]

The five judges selected nine of the class members to compete in the *concours*: Debussy, Loyer, Braud, Bellaigue, Castellanos, Pierné, René, and MacDowell were all unanimous selections, while a boy named Martinet squeaked into the competition with three votes. MacDowell was the only one of the seven piano students admitted the previous October who won the privilege of entering the *concours* during his first year.[28]

Fanny reported to Walter on preparations for the concours: "Isn't it strange that the concours is exactly on your birth-day? I do not think Eddie will get any thing this year but he has made enormous improvement[.] Did I tell you that Marmontel knew me when he saw me the first time after my return, what do you think of that? Eddie teased me about it."[29] The two played dominoes to pass the time, and seeing pictures of Walter and his father had made Eddie homesick.

26. Archives of the Conservatoire National, AJ[37] No. 286[2].
27. Ibid.
28. Archives of the Conservatoire National, AJ[37] No. 206[2].
29. Letter, Fanny McDowell to Walter McDowell, 15 July 1878, NYPL.

On Friday, 26 July 1878, the day of MacDowell's first *concours* finally arrived. This annual event was the focus of attention at the Paris Conservatory as it was in no other school of music. The competition was open to the public, and the panel of nine judges included several distinguished pianist/composers brought in just for the occasion: Stephen Heller, Émile Paladilhe, Henri Herz, and Camille Saint-Saëns; as well as the head of the Pleyel piano firm, Auguste Wolff. These outsiders, plus the director Thomas and three faculty members, heard nine students of Marmontel and eight of Mathias in an order selected at random, after which they voted for winners in the four categories. MacDowell drew the fourth position, which would not have been bad for him, except that the three previous contestants were Mathias students. When he stepped on the stage, he did not have the benefit of a whispered word from a classmate backstage, and the result was described by Henry Finck years later:

> He had plenty of applause for his playing of a Weber sonata, but his reading at sight of a manuscript composition by a member of the jury was disastrous for him. He had already played more than half of this piece when the increasing hilarity of the audience (there had been several victims before him) made him suddenly aware that he was playing the thing in minor instead of in major. Without transition, he jumped at once into major, "with the effect," as he remarked to the present writer, "of the sun suddenly shining from a coal-hole. It was like the coping-stone of a joke, and the audience's enthusiasm knew no bounds."[30]

His diligent practice at sight-reading with Chichi had not allowed him to avoid this humiliating experience before the musical cognoscenti of Paris. In this pressure cooker, each player had just one chance to get through the audition without making a mistake, and Eddie's first try at a *concours* was short and painful. All he could do now was to await the results of his friends.

The conservatory records are remarkably detailed on the subject of the *concours*, as befits the most important event of the year. The votes were tabulated for each prize, allowing us to see exactly how the final results came to be. The piano *concours* of 1878 was unusually contentious, and even those not privy to all the details could gather from newspaper reports that something was amiss. The nine-member jury awarded two of each prize, and the suspense mounted as multiple votes were required to reach a majority in several categories.

On the first ballot for the Premier prix, the mature, articulate Bellaigue received eight votes, Mathias's student Fournier received six votes, and the young Pierné

---

30. Henry T. Finck, "An American Composer: Edward A. MacDowell," *Century Magazine* 53/3 (January 1897): 449–50. The sight-reading example was written for the occasion by jury member Henri Fissot.

received two votes, giving the prize to the first two without a second ballot. On the first ballot for the Second prix, the future distinguished composer and organist Gabriel Pierné received votes from all nine judges, while Mathias's student O'Kelly, who had garnered a premier accessit in 1877 and was the son of a Parisian composer, received four votes. At this point Saint-Saëns resigned from the jury and left the room, leaving only eight voting members. Rumor had it that he refused to bow to pressure to vote for a candidate who had not warranted selection.[31] On the second ballot for the Second prix, there were five ballots marked for O'Kelly and three ballots left blank, giving another Mathias student the minimum number of votes to win a prize.

Four prize-winners had been chosen, but two categories remained. On the first ballot for the Premier accessit, Mathias's student Chevillard earned six votes, Braud earned three votes, Castellanos and Frène (Mathias's student) earned two each, and Debussy, Loyer, and Martinet earned one apiece. On the second ballot, with one vote per judge, Braud earned three, Frène earned two, and Chevillard [*sic*], Loyer, and Martinet earned one apiece, forcing a runoff between Braud and Frène. The former earned five votes, joining Chevillard as recipient of the Premier accessit. The most startling result came on the first ballot for the Deuxième accessit— Martinet (who had not earned more than one vote on any previous ballot) earned an absolute majority of seven votes, followed by Frène with four and Castellanos with two. On the runoff ballot, Frène earned five votes to Castellanos's three, giving him the other Deuxième accessit.

From the standpoint of the director, this awkward situation ended as well as could be expected. In each category, an award had been given to one student from each studio. Reversing the embarrassing trend of the previous year, all eight winners were French, including the young man with the Irish name. These were results that would draw the fewest complaints from the press and public, while neither teacher could claim to have been shortchanged. But from the standpoint of Marmontel's studio, Chichi had been robbed for the second year in a row. How had it happened that he had earned the third highest vote total for the Premier accessit and had not managed to place in the voting for the Deuxième accessit? How had Martinet—who had barely qualified to compete in the first place—come out of nowhere to win an absolute majority on the first vote for Deuxième accessit? Again, the injustice was noted by the critics, one of whom wrote: "Recognizing completely the reproof to M. Chevillard, to M. Braud and to M. Frène, I preferred M. Castellanos, whose colorful playing and solid fingerwork did not find favor with

31. Jean Bertrand, "Drame et musique," *La République française,* 5 August 1878, 2.

the jury. I would add that M. Martinet, second accessit, seemed to me especially weaker than M. Castellanos, and I would have postponed him to next year."[32]

Fanny wrote to Walter on 2 August, "The Castellanos go to the country to-morrow to remain the whole of the vacation. The Conservatoire begins in October (the first) so Chichi will have a long rest. They have hired a house there, and will stay until October. I wish we could afford to do so, but I think too, that the two weeks Eddie will spend in Switzerland will do him a world of good. He is very thin and pale & stoops over a little."[33] At the last minute, Thomas wrote to let Fanny know that he could afford to bring them both home to New York for the vacation. Eddie wanted to do this very much, but his mother decided to use the money to take a month's vacation in the French town of Émancé instead. This was the town near Chartres where the Braud family lived and where the Castellanos family had rented a home for the summer.

Three letters from Fanny document the rejuvenating time the boys enjoyed together. They spent their days outdoors in rain or shine, walking, catching frogs, and fishing for crayfish. She reported that Eddie "eats all I can manage to cook for him—so I have no fear of his suffering too much. He is much improved in every way & has grown taller, stouter and stronger. He looks forward to next summer [in America] with a great deal of anticipation."[34] The only musical activities took place when Eddie and Chichi played organ in a local Catholic church on Sundays. Fanny noted that they needed to hurry back to Paris by 24 September so that the boys could practice for the start of the new school year on 1 October. There is no hint in these three letters that she or her son knew about the surprise awaiting them on their return to Paris.

In September 1878, while the boys were vacationing in Émancé, the Conservatory enacted sweeping policy changes, the first major revision since 1850. Among the many rules that were tightened up was one intended to deal with underperforming students. This rule had been on the books since 1850 but had not been enforced in recent years. The rule stated that a student who competed in the *concours* for three consecutive years without winning a prize would be expelled from the conservatory, as would a student who earned a prize but failed to improve his standing in the two subsequent years.[35] The rolls of the conservatory show that this allowed the administration to expel dozens of students

32. "Piano," *L'Entr'acte.* 27 July 1878, 2.

33. Letter, Fanny McDowell to Walter McDowell, 2 August 1878, NYPL.

34. Letter, Fanny McDowell to Walter McDowell, 15 September 1878, NYPL.

35. For complete texts of both versions of the rules, see Constant Pierre, *Le Conservatoire national de musique et de declamation: documents historiques et administratifs* (Paris: Imprimerie Nationale, 1900).

who had been attending for years—including some since the 1860s—without winning prizes. Along with a host of deadbeats was one who was decidedly not— Chichi Castellanos. In 1876, the year before his first piano *concours*, Chichi had competed unsuccessfully in the solfège *concours*, meaning that after three tries and no prize, his career at the conservatory was over. Eddie's best friend, his duet partner from childhood who captured the hearts of the audience two years in a row, was dealt the final injustice. In solidarity with his friend, Edward withdrew from the conservatory.[36]

The story circulated in later years that MacDowell and his mother heard some music at the Exposition Universelle that convinced him he would prefer to study in Germany rather than in France. These stories were told decades later, and there is no hint of this rationale in any of the letters from 1878. In fact, Fanny was clear in her letter of 15 September that she expected Eddie to continue at the Conservatoire and compete in the *concours* of 1879. The legend that it was Nicolai Rubinstein's playing of the Tchaikovsky Piano Concerto that convinced him to switch is unlikely, since Rubinstein played on 9 September while they were in Émancé. There is a gap in the correspondence between the last Émancé letter of 15 September and a letter of 12 November stating that they had sold their furniture at auction and planned to travel to Stuttgart on 18 November, making it impossible to verify the decision-making sequence.

It is remarkable that MacDowell's parents allowed their son to go through with this. He had earned admission to the most exclusive music school in the world, where he studied free of charge. He had made excellent progress and had earned the respect and support of his teacher. Undoubtedly they felt that Chichi had been wronged in the *concours*, but they were leaving a very good situation in order to strike out for the unknown. Edward MacDowell was a strong-willed man who followed his principles even in the face of personal discomfort and uncertainty. His decision to leave France on principle was characteristic of the man he was becoming, and for better or worse, he would not retract that decision. When he boarded the train for Stuttgart on 18 November 1878, he had only a vague idea of what he would find.

36. There are four documents that verify this fact, each with a different date. The "Tableau des classes, 1877–1878" states that both were expelled (*rayé*) from Marmontel's class on 31 July, five days after the *concours*. The "Registre des sorties, 1878" lists them among twenty-eight conservatory students expelled on 30 September. The "Tableau des classes, 1876–1877" lists their expulsion from the solfège class of Marmontel's son on 1 October. The "Contrôle des Élèves" states that they resigned (*démissionné*) in October 1878. In all four cases, though, the two were grouped together, indicating that they reached a joint decision. There are no extant family letters that even broach the subject.

CHAPTER FOUR

A Fourth-Rate Conservatory and a
First-Rate Mentor

I F THE FRENCH SYSTEM OF MUSICAL TRAINING WAS CENTRALIZED AND HIERARCHICAL like the monarchy, the German "system" was more like a free-for-all that in its best aspects resembled a democracy and in its worst aspects anarchy. Felix Mendelssohn's founding of the Leipzig Conservatory in 1843 set a precedent for cities across central Europe to establish institutions for advanced musical training that combined practical study of an instrument with background in music history and theory. After the unification of the German Empire in 1871, the former kingdoms, principalities, dukedoms, and city-states still had a great deal of autonomy, reflected in the conservatories they established. There were royal music schools in Berlin, Leipzig, Dresden, Stuttgart, Würzburg, and Munich, a grand-ducal school in Weimar, a princely conservatory in Sondershausen, municipal conservatories in Berlin and Cologne, and a panoply of privately owned schools for beginners to aspiring professionals. Each school had its own rules, and the unique makeup of each faculty allowed for a rich variety of aesthetic orientations and disciplinary specialties. These schools were "consumer-oriented," giving a student with the necessary musical preparation— and the required tuition payment—a vast array of choices. For American students, these choices meant that practically anyone could find an appropriate place to study music and imbibe German culture. For German conservatories, foreign students paid their teachers' salaries and supported the local economy. By 1890 more than 50 percent of the student body at the Leipzig Conservatory consisted of foreigners, including a substantial number of Americans.[1]

1. For more on the German conservatory system, see E. Douglas Bomberger, *The German Musical Training of American Students, 1850–1900* (PhD diss., University of Maryland–College Park, 1991; UMI 92–25789).

Among the schools with a reputation for training pianists, none was more famous than the Stuttgart Conservatory. The school had been founded by Sigmund Lebert in 1857 and had obtained royal protection a decade later. Lebert's unique pedagogical method was outlined in his popular *Große theoretisch-praktische Clavierschule* [Grand theoretical and practical piano-school],[2] which achieved worldwide currency through English, Italian, and Spanish translations. The method emphasized slow practice, finger independence, and transposition, making it excellent for the mechanical training of the fingers. In order to take full advantage of the method, however, one needed to study with Lebert himself in Stuttgart, and with that end in view, Fanny and Edward sold their furniture and boarded the train from Paris on 18 November 1878.

The details of MacDowell's short time in Stuttgart are shrouded in mystery. The registration records of the Royal Conservatory in Stuttgart are no longer extant, but he may have simply taken private lessons with Lebert rather than immediately enrolling as a regular student. He alluded to their home in Stuttgart in a letter of several years later describing to his mother his new apartment in Frankfurt: "as nice a home as we were in Stuttgart only of course perfectly clean and nice inside."[3] Henry Finck summed up MacDowell's brief experience there: "That pedantic institution may be a good training-school for pedagogues, but it is no place for a young genius who needs elbow-room and personal freedom. It took him less than a month to find out that the Lebert method (which seemed to him 'to show up one's weakness through repose') was not what he had been looking for."[4]

But what was it that made him regret his decision to study in Stuttgart after such a short time? We can get a sense of what his piano studies might have been like by looking at the experience of another American, Edgar Stillman Kelley, who studied in Stuttgart from 1876 to 1880. Like MacDowell, Kelley was a piano student who was also interested in composition. Although he did not study with Lebert himself, he left extensive descriptions of the Lebert method, the only one used at the Royal Conservatory. As was the case with all students of the Lebert method, he was required to adopt a hand position that paired collapsed knuckles with sharply curved fingers, resulting in painful muscular tension. Kelley was also put off by

2. Sigmund Lebert and Ludwig Stark, *Große theoretisch-praktische Clavierschule für den systematischen Unterricht nach allen Richtungen des Clavierspiels vom ersten Anfang bis zur höchsten Ausbildung* (Grand theoretical and practical piano-school for systematic instruction in all branches of piano-playing from the first elements to the highest perfection), 4 vols. (Stuttgart, Cotta: 1858).

3. Letter to Fanny MacDowell, 3 August 1880, University of New Hampshire–Durham.

4. Henry T. Finck, "An American Composer: Edward A. MacDowell," *Century Magazine* 53/3 (January 1897): 450.

Lebert's personality, calling him "an old bully."[5] After a year and a half, Kelley summarized his experience: "[I]t was a fearful putback for me to go thro' Lebert's hideous 'Method.' It has done me no good, and has done me a great deal of harm for I play fearfully mechanical compared to what I used to. It is the most discouraging work for me and scores of others who have been thrown back."[6] MacDowell confirmed these aspects of the Lebert method in comments to Lawrence Gilman years later. He recalled that one student told him that Rubinstein himself would have been required to reform his technique had he studied at Stuttgart. He also remembered a student who had mastered the ascending scale but could not play the same scale descending.[7] After the high level of instruction he had enjoyed under Marmontel, he felt no need to go back to pianistic kindergarten.

There may have been another reason for his discomfort with Stuttgart, however. Whereas the Paris Conservatory reluctantly allowed talented foreigners to enroll in exceptional circumstances, the Stuttgart Conservatory accepted foreigners of all levels. The institution had begun as a private school, and the tuition money from foreign students was as welcome as that of local students. From its earliest years, the institution enrolled an unusually high number of English-speaking students, and in 1876 it had taken the additional step of hiring an American graduate of the conservatory, Percy Goetschius, to teach classes in music theory and history in English. He published a textbook expressly for use in these English-language theory classes that was reprinted well into the twentieth century.[8]

MacDowell could not fail to notice that the conservatory was overrun by English-speaking students with little incentive to immerse themselves in the culture. For a young man whose musical education had been cross-cultural from the beginning, this was not what he hoped to find. The prospect of tedious technical review at the piano along with theory and history classes in the company of English-speaking dilettantes must have been too much to countenance. We do not know whether he met Goetschius or Kelley during his short stay in Stuttgart, and we cannot confirm the reasons for his rapid departure, but as he had done several times before, he decided to cut his losses and try his luck elsewhere.

5. Letter, Edgar Stillman Kelley to his parents, 12 November 1876, Edgar Stillman Kelley Collection, Walter Havighurst Special Collections, King Library, Miami University of Ohio.

6. Letter, 8 January 1878, Kelley Collection, Miami University. For further details on Kelley's objections to the Lebert method, see E. Douglas Bomberger, "Kelley vs. Lebert: An American Confronts a German Piano Method," *American Music Teacher* 43/4 (February/March 1994): 14–17, 81.

7. Lawrence Gilman, *Edward MacDowell: A Study* (New York: John Lane, 1908), 7–8.

8. Percy Goetschius, *The Material used in Musical Composition: A System of Harmony Designed and Adopted for Use in English Harmony Classes of the Conservatory of Music, at Stuttgart* (Stuttgart: Zumsteeg, 1882).

When he wrote to tell Marmontel of his decision in January, his former teacher responded with a blistering letter that showed *his* view of the Stuttgart Conservatory:

My dear student,

I thank you for remembering me and for sharing with me your changes of direction. Without in any way criticizing the teaching and the methods of Lebert, etc., etc., I think very honestly that at the point where you and Castellanos have arrived it is stepping down several degrees to place yourself on the roll of a school that despite its popularity in Germany is a fourth-rate <u>provincial conservatory</u>. Lyon or Nantes hardly compare; Stuttgart, compared to Vienna, Berlin, Cologne, Leipzig, Prague, Moscow, Petersburg, Warsaw, [or] Naples is an estimable school but without radiance in Europe. In the end you have been very proud and succumbed to a movement of the spirit against injustice, but me, your sincere and devoted friend, I watched you go with veritable chagrin. Work, my dear and affectionate student, stay true to the memory of my advice and recommendations, and take a position in Wiesbaden at least for a time. Goodby[.] Offer my greetings to madame your mother and believe in my inestimable affection.

Marmontel[9]

Still stinging from the resignation of two of his best students, Marmontel gave a very strong warning about how the world would perceive their move. After years of training pianists and following their subsequent careers, he knew the importance of reputations and endorsements for establishing oneself in the cutthroat world of performance.

Ironically, his friend Chichi, who had moved to Stuttgart around the same time as the MacDowells, stayed and prospered: as part of the book commemorating its twentieth-fifth anniversary in 1882, the school published a list of outstanding alumni, among whom is Michael Castellanos.[10] After graduation at Stuttgart, Chichi returned to Paris for a brief time and then relocated to New York, where he was active as a performer and teacher until his death on 22 July 1940.[11] No evidence has been found of continued contact between MacDowell and Castellanos.

By early January 1879 Edward was established in Wiesbaden, a resort on the Rhine River known since Roman times for the curative properties of its hot

---

9. Undated letter, Marmontel to EAM, NYPL. The envelope is postmarked 4 January 1879, about the time MacDowell left Stuttgart for Wiesbaden.

10. "Verzeichniss von bedeutenderen früheren Zöglingen der Künstlerschule," *Festschrift für das fünfundzwanzigjährige Jubiläum des Konservatoriums für Musik in Stuttgart, den 30. Mai bis 2. Juni 1882* (Stuttgart: J. B. Metzler, [1882]), 14.

11. "Miguel Castellanos," *NYT,* 26 July 1940, 17.

springs. Written on 10 February 1879, his first letter to his brother, Walter, from his new home reflects his high spirits:

> My dear brother and male relation,
> It is so long since I have had the honor of conferring with you on paper that I can hardly find anything to confer about. Long before you receive this, Mamma and Mr. Buitrago will have told you all the news. After 18 years experience, I've come to the conclusion that I am a very smart boy. I now speak German fluently and gracefully. Sometimes however, the common class does not converse intelligibly—for instance the other day when I requested the servant girl to bring some more sugar for my coffee, she acted quite stupidly about it. She "spaziered" off and didn't return. I thought after a while, that it would be a good thing to reconnoiter a little, so I opened my door and saw to my astonishment a round bath tub which the girl evidently was struggling to bring through my doorway. I receiv'd it without hesitation (what was the use of discouraging her) but when she was about to go I tendered my original request again. A look of astonishment and exit Hebe. After a while I hear a short discussion outside my door, then comes a knock—I open—there is the proprietor of the boarding house—(the girl in the background seemed to be struggling with another tub.) he begs pardon and seems to explain (German—very bad) that he has no larger tubs in the house at which I proceed to explain accompanying myself with divers [sic] suggestive motions—He inclined a willing ear and I got my sugar in about ½ hour later.[12]

Edward's high spirits are understandable, for after nearly three years under the watchful eyes of his mother and Buitrago, he was living alone in a boarding house in Wiesbaden. What teenage boy would not brag to his brother about such an encounter with a servant girl in his independent new home? Fanny had left for America with Buitrago some weeks before, arriving in New York on 4 February.[13] From this point until his marriage in the summer of 1884, Edward would live alone in Germany.

It is instructive to compare this language episode with the earlier one in France. On that occasion, Eddie was at the mercy of an authority figure who could not understand his accent and was not inclined to be helpful; in this case, the youthful servant and the proprietor were doing their best to serve his needs, no matter how absurd they appeared to be. In both cases the difficulty arose from MacDowell's

12. Letter to "My dear brother and male relation," 10 February 1879, NYPL.
13. The ship's manifest of the SS *Canada*, filed with the port authority on 4 February 1879, lists Fannie MacDowell, age thirty-eight, as passenger no. 5 and John [sic] Buitrago, age forty-three, as passenger no. 10 [www.ancestry.com, accessed 13 October 2009]. It is not clear why Buitrago decided to leave Paris and accompany her on the trip home.

unfamiliarity with the language, but at eighteen he is much more confident and self-reliant than he was at fifteen, and the Germans appear more accommodating than the French.

The piano teacher with whom MacDowell intended to study was Carl Heymann (1851–1922). Mrs. McDowell had learned of the pianist through Emile Sauret, a violinist who had briefly been married to Teresa Carreño. The only child of their marriage, Emilita Sauret, was living with the James Bischoff family in Wiesbaden, and it was in the Bischoff home that the MacDowells first heard Heymann play.[14] Edward was sufficiently impressed that he agreed to live in Wiesbaden until Heymann could begin lessons later in the year. Presumably the proximity of the Bischoff family helped his mother feel more comfortable leaving him on his own in a strange land with few connections and minimal language skills.

Carl Heymann was one of the most gifted pianists of his generation and was called a "new Liszt" by Josef Schrattenholz.[15] MacDowell remembered his pianism:

> Heymann's teaching was inspiring to the last degree. He was the one pianist I have ever heard who, get as near the pianoforte as you could, remained a mystery as to how he did the things we heard. The simplest passage became a spray of flashing jewels in his hands. A melody seemed to have words when he played it. He produced tone colours that, like alpine sun-effects, were inexhaustible; yet, each one, fleeting as it was, more beautiful than the last. His technique, while always of the "convulsive" order in quick passages, seemed mysteriously capable of anything. He was a marvel; he had a poor wrist, and yet sometimes when he sat down to show me a wrist passage, a kind of quiver would run over him, then behold, the thing would be trilled off in the same supernatural way as all the rest.[16]

MacDowell's impressionistic description of his playing is, like so many of his images, highly visual: the flashing jewels, colors, and alpine sun-effects are evocative but musically imprecise, while the "quiver" that ran over him and made possible the supernatural overcoming of a physical limitation has an element of elusive mystery. Heymann's inscrutability to MacDowell may have derived in part from the teacher's tenuous grasp on his own sanity. After a brilliant early career, Heymann began to suffer from mental illness and withdrew from public life. His comeback began in 1872 with a brilliant performance as accompanist to August Wilhelmj and his appointment as music director of the town of Bingen-on-Rhein, not far from

14. Margery M. Lowens, "The New York Years of Edward MacDowell" (PhD diss., University of Michigan, 1971), 10–11.

15. *Illustrierte Zeitung,* 11 March 1882.

16. "Edward MacDowell: A Biographical Sketch," *Musical Times* 44 (1 April 1904): 222.

Wiesbaden.[17] Edward encountered Heymann during one of the best times of his life, as he was gaining confidence and returning to the public eye. He agreed to accept the young American as his student when he took a new position as piano instructor at the Hoch Conservatory in Frankfurt later in the year.

Another resident of Wiesbaden turned out to be an important connection for MacDowell and helped him to make fruitful use of the months he waited for Heymann's availability. Louis Ehlert (1825–1884) had studied with Mendelssohn and Schumann at the Leipzig Conservatory and later became an important composer, teacher, and writer. In 1873 he had left a prominent position in Berlin at the height of his career in order to move his ailing wife to Wiesbaden. The healing waters failed to restore her health, however, and she soon died. When Ehlert sought to return to his former position in Berlin, this did not prove possible, so he spent the rest of his life in Wiesbaden as a somewhat reclusive scholar and eccentric local authority on music.[18]

MacDowell's lessons with Ehlert were unconventional. He later recalled, "Ehlert was very kind to me, and when I asked him for 'lessons' he refused flatly, but said he would be glad for us to 'study together,' as he put it. This rather staggered me, as my idea in leaving Paris was to get a severe and regenerative overhauling. I worked hard all winter, however, and heard lots of new music at the *Cur Haus*[sic], which was like manna in the desert after my long French famine."[19] For a boy of MacDowell's independence, this approach was ideal, and the seasoned pedagogue Ehlert recognized that he would get more cooperation from his headstrong student by broaching the subject in this way. Ehlert also felt that MacDowell deserved a better piano teacher than Heymann, and he wrote to the eminent pianist Hans von Bülow asking him to consider taking on a talented young American as a student. Edward reported the results of these overtures in a letter to his mother:

> Ehlert wrote to Bülow asking to take a pupil[;] he also wrote in his letter something about musical matters which seems to have enraged Bülow for as Ehlert told me with a very meek expression, he wrote him a very rude answer and only spoke about the lessons in 2 lines saying that "He thought Ehlert knew he didn't take pupils." I am all right as my name was not mentioned—As for E. it was his own fault entirely. He didn't relish it though. Now of course it's Frankfort [sic].[20]

17. Hugo Riemann, *Musik-Lexicon*, 3rd ed. (Leipzig: Max Hesse's Verlag, 1887), 422.

18. There are many obituaries and dictionary articles with information on Ehlert's musical accomplishments, but this obituary was clearly written by someone who knew him well and understood the personal circumstances of his life: M. v. F., "Louis Ehlert," *Rheinischer Kurier*, erste Ausgabe, 6 January 1884, 1–2.

19. Quoted in Gilman, *Edward MacDowell: A Study*, 9.

20. Letter, EAM to his mother, 15 April 1879, NYPL.

After just a few months in the boarding house in Wiesbaden, MacDowell followed Heymann to Frankfurt, about twenty miles away. The teacher began his duties there earlier than expected, allowing MacDowell to enter the conservatory at the start of the second semester in early May.

Frankfurt was a town on the move in the 1870s and 1880s. Revered as the birthplace of Goethe, the city grew rapidly in the second half of the nineteenth century to become the business center of the German Empire. The population expanded from 80,000 in 1867 to 137,000 in 1880 and would reach 180,000 by 1890. Frankfurt was the second German city to install a modern sewage system, with only 49 flush toilets in 1870 but 27,500 by 1885. The giant Hauptbahnhof (central railroad station) was completed in 1888 just five hundred meters outside the former city walls, making travel to other European cities quicker and easier. Several of Frankfurt's most iconic landmarks were constructed at this time, including the Palm Garden, the Opera House, and the Stock Exchange. During the years Edward MacDowell lived there, construction was constantly underway as old neighborhoods were torn down to make way for beautiful new buildings.[21]

Among the new institutions in Frankfurt was a conservatory, which enrolled its first class just as MacDowell was leaving Paris. Dr. Joseph Hoch (1815–1874) had begun planning for a music school in his hometown as early as 1857, but it was his bequest of 900,000 Goldmarks that ensured the financial stability of the institution from its opening in the fall of 1878. The Hoch'sches Konservatorium, as it was known, hired as its first director the well-known composer Joachim Raff (1822–1882), whose works were among the most frequently performed of contemporary German compositions.

In hiring teachers for the new conservatory, Raff aimed to set the school apart from others by reflecting his own unique aesthetic goals. As a young man, Raff had lived in Weimar, where he was a student and personal assistant to Franz Liszt. He gained the reputation of being a highly analytical musician, which served him well as a teacher in later years. Along with this analytical ability came an unusual capacity for concentration. William Mason recalled that during their student days in Weimar Raff had already developed an impressive capacity for hard work, and his Frankfurt colleague Fritz Bassermann recalled that during his years at the conservatory Raff could compose undisturbed in his office despite the sounds of different instruments coming through the walls at the same time.[22]

21. This information was gathered from exhibits in the Frankfurt Historisches Museum in September 2009.

22. William Mason, *Memories of a Musical Life* (New York, 1901; repr. New York: AMS Press, 1970), 161; Peter Cahn, *Das Hoch'sche Konservatorium in Frankfurt am Main: 1879–1978* (Frankfurt am Main: Kramer, 1979), 80–82.

Raff had been present in Weimar during the time that Liszt was making his most important contributions to the "Music of the Future," or New German School. This group espoused "program music" that depicted extra-musical ideas or images as the culmination of historical development in music, contrasting themselves with so-called conservative composers like Brahms who persisted in writing absolute music with no such extra-musical connotations. They advocated radical experimentation in both form and harmony in order to sever ties with the Classical era. Finally, they used cyclical forms and thematic transformation to unify large works in the absence of traditional formal structures. In the decades since Raff's departure from Weimar, Liszt and Wagner had gathered a coterie of adherents who grew increasingly adamant in their denunciations of their enemies, but Raff was not a zealous follower of his mentor. Mason recalled that he loved nothing better than to argue the opposing viewpoint on any subject with his friends, and it may have been this propensity for disputation that kept him at arm's length from the Liszt/Wagner school. His own compositions strove for a middle ground between the progressive aesthetic orientation of the Liszt camp and the conservative orientation of Brahms and his followers.

Raff was determined to create a faculty that would reflect his eclectic aesthetic ideals. For the two piano teachers, he chose Joseph Rubinstein (1847–1884), an arch-Wagnerian, and Clara Schumann (1819–1896), a close friend of Brahms and ardent opponent of Liszt and Wagner. To these he added Bernhard Cossmann (1822–1910), the former principal cellist of Liszt's Weimar orchestra, and Julius Stockhausen (1826–1906), another close friend of Brahms. In the fall of 1880 he added the Liszt student Max Schwarz (1856–1923) and the soprano Malvina Schnorr von Carolsfeld (1825–1904), who had created the role of Isolde in Wagner's *Tristan und Isolde*. The early years of the school were characterized by constant strife among the faculty and numerous resignations.

This situation would not seem to present the most auspicious circumstances for a student who had been studying with the best piano teacher at the most renowned music school in the world. But the eighteen-year-old Edward was developing into an independent person who cared little for reputations and recoiled from following the crowd. For him, the *substance* of the teacher (as he perceived it) was more important than the reputation of the school, and thus the idea of casting his lot with a brilliant but unstable piano teacher in a brand new conservatory was not daunting.

On 5 May, Heymann and Sauret took Edward to meet Raff. Since he was seeking admission as a piano student, Edward reported in a letter to his mother that Heymann "blew me up to the skies as a pianist and as Raff began to look more propitious Heymann continued to swell and puff about me so that I began to be afraid for his soul."²³ Raff invited him to return two days later to be examined for admission to the composition classes as well. On 7 May he brought some of his compositions and exercises, which Raff examined for an hour. Edward reported that "he couldn't promise me that I would be a great composer, because one could never predict <u>those things</u> before hand, but that my future rested entirely with myself; that if I worked there would be no reason why I would not do all I wanted to." This was just what he wanted to hear and added a sentence to confirm Raff's credibility to his parents: "Now as Raff call'd Damrosch a poor wretch (D. is quite celebrated here as a composer) and runs down artists in a way to make one's hair stand on end—I am quite satisfied."²⁴ Leopold Damrosch (1832–1885) was a German conductor and composer who had immigrated to New York in 1871, quickly establishing himself as a leader in the city's musical life despite resentment from some native-born musicians. The teenaged MacDowell recognized in Raff's disregard for such a prominent figure a maverick attitude that was congenial to him.

The relationship with Raff would turn out to be the most important musical influence in MacDowell's life, and so it is worth considering what it meant for MacDowell. In many ways it signified the opposite of the established order to which he had grown accustomed in Paris. In their initial meeting, Raff opened the world to him by saying that anything was possible for a young man, and that even the persons with the greatest power and influence may be recognized as imperfect if one has the tools to assess them properly. Years later, MacDowell told his biographer Lawrence Gilman more about Raff's reactions to their first meeting:

> Heymann took me to him and told him, among other things, that, having studied for several years the "French School" of composition, I wished to study in Germany. Raff immediately flared up and declared that there was no such thing nowadays as "schools"—that music was eclectic nowadays; that if some French writers wrote flimsy music it arose simply from flimsy attainments, and such stuff could never form a "school." German and other writers were to be criticized from the same standpoint—their music was bad, middling, or good; but there was no such thing as cramping it into "schools" nowadays, when all national musical traits were common property.²⁵

Always ready for an argument, Raff was not about to accept diplomatically the assertions of his new piano instructor, even during an entrance interview with a prospective student. Arguing the point was more important than being cordial to his new acquaintances. This approach to relationships would be just as influential on the impressionable teenager as would Raff's ideal of eclecticism in musical style.

23. Letter, EAM to his mother, 8 May 1879, NYPL.
24. Ibid.
25. Gilman, *Edward MacDowell: A Study,* 9–10.

Like many German Conservatories, the Hoch Conservatory published *Jahresberichte* [annual reports] that list the students in attendance and provide information about the courses, public performances, and other events at the school. These show that MacDowell was very actively involved in the life of the school. In addition to the required examinations at the end of each semester known as *Prüfungen*, he played an important role in several public concerts, indicating that he was one of the best student performers in those early years. His repertoire consisted almost entirely of recent works.

MacDowell also had the opportunity to play several of Liszt's works for the composer himself when the eminent musician visited his old friend Raff at the conservatory. The first performance was on 9 June 1879, when the conservatory staged a concert of Liszt's works. The performers were mostly faculty, but MacDowell was one of three students invited to perform. He joined Theodor Müller-Reuter, a student from Dresden, in performing excerpts from a two-piano arrangement of Liszt's symphonic poem *Tasso*. On 18 June, nine days after the Liszt performance, MacDowell played the first two movements of the Saint-Saëns Concerto in G minor on an evening performance in the conservatory, and on 22 July he played the Andante and Finale of the Reinecke Concerto in F-sharp minor.[26]

Many decades later, MacDowell's classmate Frederic L. Abel, a longtime teacher at the Detroit Conservatory of Music, recalled some of their Frankfurt experiences in a talk delivered to a club in Detroit. He described Saturday nights spent in a cafe with fellow students from the conservatory:

> "Mac" was usually toast master and was full of jokes and tricks on the boys—one of the students, who afterwards became a famous violin teacher in the Frankfurt Conservatory, was remarkable for his lack of knowledge of the English language and "Mac" took keen delight in expatiating on his distorted sayings—in fact we all came in for our share of bantering....Often, while at our meals in a restaurant, he would write down themes at random, on the back of a menu card, then next morning would say "What did I do with that I wrote last night? Why didn't you save it for me?"—but in my student thoughtlessness, I am sorry now, I neglected to do so, and so these precious little sketches, which might have developed later into great compositions, were lost as he could never remember them next day....He was such a serious student he would work himself half sick at times, and was frequently almost overpowered with dejection and discouragement, then it was our turn to cheer him up.[27]

26. *Jahresbericht des Hoch'schen Conservatoriums zu Frankfurt am Main* (Frankfurt, 1879), 13, 15, 21.
27. Frederic L. Abel, "Personal reminiscences of Edward MacDowell written for the Musical Coterie of the Twentieth Century Club," typescript in EMMC. Abel's narrative is so full of factual

The companionship that Abel describes was a big change from previous years, when his mother watched him carefully and monitored his friendships. At the same time, it has a melancholy edge, as Abel describes the beginnings of mood swings that would become more severe in the years ahead. MacDowell had already adopted the pattern of overwork that continued throughout his professional career. In May 1880 he wrote to his parents that he had seen a doctor, who attributed certain physical problems to overwork and too little time outdoors. He resolved to do better, writing, "I guess he must be right and though I have an awful lot to do I am going to try to follow his advice."[28]

MacDowell's second year was even busier with performing, featuring public performances of a Karl Goldmark Suite for violin and piano with Fritz Bassermann on 11 February 1880, a Chopin berceuse and a Mendelssohn fugue on 21 April, the Schumann Quintet, op. 44 on 2 May, the accompaniment to a Bach Concerto for two violins on 23 June, a Suite for Violin and Piano of his own composition with Bassermann on 22 July, and Beethoven's "Emperor" Concerto on 23 July. The most memorable performance, though, was a second opportunity to play for Franz Liszt.

Liszt was again in Frankfurt in May 1880, and the conservatory presented a concert of his works on the 24th that included a solo performance of the Hungarian Rhapsody No. 14 by MacDowell as well as the "Offertorium" and "Benedictus" from the *Hungarian Coronation Mass* in an arrangement for violin and piano played by MacDowell and Bassermann. Abel recalled the performance from a unique vantage point:

> The hall in the Conservatory was small, and in the front row within five feet of me sat Liszt, C. Schumann, Raff, Sarasate, just then coming into prominence, and Raffael Joseffy. "Mac" made me turn the pages for him that day, and I well remember he was so nervous that perspiration literally dripped off his fingers on the keys, but he played beautifully and was highly complimented by Liszt for his performance. "Mac" then said, "Maestro...I have suffered so in playing before you, will you not play for us?" at which Liszt laughed, went to the piano and played several of his compositions ending up with his 12th Rhapsody. Needless to say the student body went wild with enthusiasm, the fellows, after the concert, nearly carried MacDowell out on their shoulders they were so proud of his success.[29]

Abel actually stated that this episode occurred after a performance of Schumann's Quintet, op. 44, but he seems to have conflated the two events in his memory. The

errors that it is not reliable for concrete information, but presumably at least some of his recollections about MacDowell's personality are reliable.

28. Letter to Fanny MacDowell, 13 May 1880, NYPL.

29. Abel, "Personal reminiscences of Edward MacDowell."

Jahresbericht described the request to Liszt on the occasion of the 24 May Liszt concert: "At the end of the performance a deputation of pupils asked the honored old master to play something. With friendly willingness he agreed to this request. Indescribable jubilation accompanied his entrance and exit."[30]

In addition to his performances at the conservatory, MacDowell made his debut with a professional orchestra in the Wiesbaden Curhaus on 23 January 1880. The concert was arranged by Ehlert, and although he did not receive remuneration, the opportunity to play in this setting was an auspicious one. He forgot to get a tuxedo with tails in advance, but Mr. Bischoff made arrangements to borrow one from his tailor in Wiesbaden. The Curhaus management sent a carriage to take him to the theater, and he reported that the conductor, Louis Lüstner, was very cordial to him. The orchestra members listened respectfully and applauded him with "ardour."[31]

MacDowell accomplished a great deal pianistically during his three semesters at the conservatory, but his lessons with Heymann were unconventional. He told Gilman that "Heymann let me do what I wanted; but in hearing him practice and play I learned more in a week than I ever had before."[32] It seems that Heymann allowed MacDowell to eavesdrop on his own practice sessions, thereby gaining insight into the mysteries to which Edward alluded earlier. Again, this seemed to be the right approach for the independent MacDowell at this point in his development. He had already done a great deal of routine drill in Paris, and Heymann's approach allowed him to become independent and to think for himself. MacDowell wrote to his mother in January 1880 that Heymann had predicted that "in his opinion I would surely be a great pianist. That I had an immense techniche [*sic*] already and I only needed polish. He is surely a good friend."[33]

In retrospect, the most important connection at the conservatory was not the piano teacher who had drawn him there in the first place, but the composition teacher whose classes were added almost as an afterthought. In addition to his piano lessons with Heymann, MacDowell's schedule included classes in composition and orchestration with Joachim Raff.[34] During his second year, the class did exercises that were less advanced than those he had covered in Paris, being three-voice rather than four-voice, and consisting entirely of species counterpoint with no rhythmic freedom. Raff recognized that these exercises were repetitious for MacDowell and

30. *Jahresbericht des Hoch'schen Conservatoriums 1879–1880*, 15.

31. Letter to Fanny McDowell, 24 January 1880, NYPL.

32. Gilman, *Edward MacDowell: A Study*, 10–11.

33. Letter to Fanny McDowell, 24 January 1880, NYPL.

34. This schedule was jotted on a manuscript copy of his op. 8 now in EMMC, box 6.

suggested that he work on an original composition in lieu of attending class for part of the year. The result of this assignment was the *Erste moderne Suite* [First Modern Suite], op. 10, completed in 1881.[35] This piece would eventually be crucial to establishing MacDowell's reputation. Like Heymann, Raff seems to have recognized that MacDowell had already completed a great deal of routine work in Paris, and that his personality was better suited to freedom than to more drill at this stage in his studies. After his withdrawal from the conservatory in July 1880, he continued to study privately with Raff for two years, but these lessons were not systematic or rigorous, consisting instead of work on compositions of MacDowell's choice.

In his history of the Hoch Conservatory, Peter Cahn notes that among the students of the early years were many who had already pursued studies elsewhere and came to Frankfurt for a few semesters of finishing rather than the normal three-year curriculum.[36] This describes MacDowell's situation precisely and explains his departure after only three semesters. It is also reflective, though, of a larger pattern in his schooling. Starting with P.S. 40 and continuing with the Charlier Institute, the Conservatoire National, the Stuttgart Conservatory, and the Hoch Conservatory, MacDowell had attended five schools without completing the specified program of study at any one of them. His schooling had presented him with many rich experiences, but it had also been highly unconventional. This flouting of procedure and willingness to abandon one course of action in pursuit of a better opportunity would characterize the rest of his life. At the same time, his creativity in circumventing obstacles and arbitrary timetables would serve him well as he set out to establish a career in the years after leaving the conservatory.

35. [Marian MacDowell], "The First Piano Suite by Edward MacDowell," typescript, EMMC, cited in Lowens, 17–18.

36. Cahn, *Das Hoch'sche Konservatorium*, 64.

CHAPTER FIVE

The Big Break

O NE OF THE ARCHETYPAL STORY LINES OF AMERICAN SHOW BUSINESS IS THE "Big Break." A chorus girl is thrust into the lead role of a Broadway musical at the eleventh hour and succeeds brilliantly. A midwestern farmer's daughter is "discovered" by a movie producer waiting tables in a Hollywood delicatessen. A young assistant conductor takes over the podium of the New York Philharmonic on short notice and establishes his reputation in one night. These stories reflect the fluid social mobility so vital to American culture, and they reinforce Americans' view of their nation as the land of opportunity.

MacDowell's story also includes a big break, when he had the opportunity to perform one of his own compositions before an audience of Germany's most influential connoisseurs of modern music. His brilliant performance on that occasion laid the foundation of his career in Germany and the United States. But his search for this break occupied the two years after his withdrawal from the Hoch Conservatory and required all of his creativity in negotiating the complex and insular German music world.

A six-page letter written to his mother on 3 August 1880—less than two weeks after his final performance as a student at the Hoch Conservatory—showed MacDowell in high spirits and supremely optimistic about the future. He had moved from his room in the Buchgasse ("really it was a little too much to stand, there, too much 'tenement' even for an Irishman") to a pair of rooms vacated by his friend Abel in the Friedenstrasse that was nicer and less expensive. He had agreed to give counterpoint lessons to "Miss Luckie (<u>pretty</u>) at the rate of 5 marks a lesson" and had plans to give concerts with the violinist Fritz Bassermann and a singer by the name of Eugenia Sessi. He had been forced to turn down an offer to accompany a French violinist in concert because of the Bassermann engagement, but he reported, "I'm going to give one in Berlin in October with Emile Sauret, who also will get my suite published. Hurrah." Raff had promised to play an overture he was writing when it was completed. He ended his letter with eight "hurrahs" and three "goodbyes."[1]

MacDowell was a young man with conspicuous talents in several areas, and he now hoped to turn these talents into a career that would earn a living. He had proven his skill as a piano soloist and accompanist at the conservatory, and he was already receiving engagements. Many of these engagements were for "honor" rather than money, however, like the Curhaus concert the previous January. In other cases, his take was dependent on the success of the concert giver. He did in fact go on tour with the Italian singer Sessi, but their concerts in Baden-Baden on 3 September and in Wildbad on 9 September were so unsuccessful financially that the tour was curtailed. Some of the promised engagements simply fell through—it is not clear whether the Sauret concert in Berlin ever took place, but his friend certainly did not arrange to have his suite published. MacDowell would experience many rejections and broken promises over the next several years, and his letters would contain fewer "hurrahs."

The one area that did offer real possibilities for remuneration was teaching. Though not as glamorous or artistically fulfilling as performance and composition, teaching provided steady income at a time when he needed it most. His brother, Walter, was already working with his father in the family milk business, and Edward could not help feeling that the allowance his parents continued to send was awkward. Many years later, after Edward died, his widow Marian recalled his financial situation in 1880:

Edward MacDowell resented bitterly, and I am not speaking too strongly, the statement sometimes made that his mother had made great sacrifices to give him his education....He was earning his own living when I met him in 1880, having lots of teaching—too much— Undoubtedly his Father and Mother were generous with extra presents— ...Seems to me what Edward MacDowell's Mother and I did for him (and certainly, with all humility, these last four years showed I did my share) should be our honour, our glory, and the word sacrifice should never be uttered or hinted at—but it was the blot on his Mother's devotion, she kept reminding him of it, and even as a boy it cut him cruelly.[2]

1. Letter to "my dear Mother," 3 August 1880, University of New Hampshire–Durham. MacDowell's farewell letter to Abel, in which he wrote "I envy your luck," is reprinted in May Leggett-Abel, *The Story of Frederic L. Abel: The Musician, The Soldier* (N.p., 1945), 5.

2. Undated letter, MM to W. H. Humiston, EMMC box 52/9. The letter indicates that it was written eleven months after MacDowell's death in January 1908.

Far from home, MacDowell was determined to make a name for himself in performance and composition, but for the time being, teaching would have to pay the bills.

Marian Griswold Nevins became MacDowell's student in October 1880. She had come from her home in Waterford, Connecticut, with the intention of studying with Clara Schumann at the Hoch Conservatory. When she arrived, however, she learned about the procedure that many of Germany's most famous teachers used to keep dilettantes at bay. Frau Schumann employed her two daughters, Marie and Eugenie, as assistants. New students began their studies with one of the daughters— often for years—until they had proven their seriousness and achieved a sufficient level of skill to make them worthy of study with the famous teacher. Miss Nevins was not willing to submit herself to this procedure and asked the advice of Raff, who recommended that she study with MacDowell. The situation was anything but auspicious, as she did not wish to study with an American teacher, and he did not have a favorable view of the typical American female student, but it did not take long for them both to warm to one another. When she wrote to tell her father of her decision later that month, he responded, "Am delighted to hear that you are so well pleased with the Music Teacher you have found and that you take such a sensible view of the mode of study you must pursue."[3] For Edward, the eight marks per week that she paid brought him closer to financial independence from his parents.

MacDowell continued to take private lessons with Raff and Heymann. The piano lessons did not last long, however, as Heymann's mental illness began to reappear, leading him to resign his position in September 1880. Before leaving the conservatory, he recommended to Raff that MacDowell be named as his successor. Only nineteen years old, MacDowell was an accomplished pianist, and Raff agreed that he would make a good replacement. The board did not approve the appointment, though, reportedly because of his age. This rejection must have been especially galling for MacDowell, as his fellow student Bassermann—the butt of his jokes in the cafe but also his partner for many chamber-music performances— was hired as a violin teacher at this time and remained there for his entire career. Bassermann was ten years older than MacDowell, but musically they must have considered each other equals.

The loss of Heymann was the first in a series of disappointments for MacDowell in the 1880s. Heymann had been his first and most important supporter in Germany, and it was through his influence that he had been accepted to the conservatory and had received so many performance opportunities there. MacDowell lost not just a

---

3. Letter, David H. Nevins to Marian Griswold Nevins, 18 October 1880, EMMC box 47/63. He states that he learned of her decision in her letter of 3 October, now presumably lost.

professional mentor but also a friend, as he told Henry Finck years later: "His people were very strict Jews, and, in deference to his father's wishes, he would never eat at a Christian's expense or in a Christian house. I told him I was a Quaker, which seemed to satisfy him completely, and we dined together often at an old restaurant in what I would now call a back slum."[4] Heymann moved back to Bingen after his resignation, and on 3 January 1881, he sent MacDowell a letter with some very useful advice on starting a performing career, recommending among other things that MacDowell always write in French, since his German was not very strong (advice that his student ignored). A few years later, Heymann was committed to a mental institution.

In November, Fanny McDowell paid a visit to her son, the first time they had seen each other in a year and a half. In a letter written from Frankfurt on Thanksgiving Day, Fanny told Walter that he had grown "tall and stout and German," and that he seemed very happy in his adopted home. She personally could not reconcile herself to the German way of life, preferring instead "our higher state of civilization in living in America," but she reported that Edward believed Germany offered many more advantages to a young artist than did the United States.[5]

Most importantly, Fanny wrote an extended description of Miss Nevins, with the astute observation that only a mother could provide:

> Well, I have just received a call from Miss Nevins, one of his pupils—American lady of New York I should think—She is very lady like—very intelligent very quiet and really seems a true lady. She has not a single trait of the harem-scarem American girl so disgusting to Eddie—but she is a sweet lady-like person. I fancy the English girl Miss Luckie whom he considered so pretty & wrote so much about is more like our American girls...I have not seen Miss Luckie yet—and as she is English—I suppose she will not feel that she must call and see Mr. McDowell's mother! At any rate, Miss Nevins is certainly excellent company for Eddie & in a friendly way they like each other. She is engaged to a New Yorker—but her health being poor I doubt if she ever marries. She is living at a hotel here with her maid to be doctored. She walks with a crutch, but has a very sweet bright face. Don't say anything of all I have written you if you ever write to Eddie because it would make him angry—as he only likes and respects Miss Nevins as a true American friend.[6]

4. Henry T. Finck, "An American Composer: Edward A. MacDowell," *Century Magazine* 53/3 (January 1897): 450.

5. Letter, Fanny McDowell to Walter McDowell, 24 November 1880, NYPL.

6. Ibid.

Fanny grasped immediately the calm intelligence that would later cause Edward to fall in love with her. She also hinted at their age difference—Miss Nevins was a "lady" more than three years older than her son. And Fanny may also have recognized that Marian had maturity beyond her years owing to the death of her mother when she was only eight years old and the resulting responsibilities that she had assumed as the oldest female in the home when her father did not remarry.[7] The health problems resulting from a severe fall would plague her for decades.

Spring 1881 brought two important performances for the aspiring pianist. On 14 March he played in the Saalbau in Darmstadt, and on 1 April he accompanied a male chorus conducted by Max Fleisch in Frankfurt. For the first concert he repeated the Reinecke Concerto that he had played in Wiesbaden a year earlier, along with solo works by Chopin and Saint-Saëns. On the second concert he had the opportunity to play solo works by Liszt, Chopin, and Saint-Saëns. His performance earned positive reviews in the Frankfurt papers and gave him his first exposure to the sound of a male chorus, which would later be important to his aesthetic development in the 1890s.

His continuing quest for financial stability led him to accept a position in March 1881 as piano instructor at the Darmstadt Conservatorium, founded three years earlier by the Frankfurt pianist Martin Wallenstein (1843–1896).[8] MacDowell's duties involved group lessons of three or four students at once, as was the practice in most German conservatories at this time. The promotional literature of these schools touted the method as a way for students to learn and gain inspiration from their peers. In practice, it allowed the administration to collect more tuition per hour than for private lessons and could easily result in one or two students receiving the majority of the attention from the harried teacher.

In addition to his classes in Darmstadt and his private students in Frankfurt, MacDowell now added a day of teaching in the medieval castle of the Count of Erbach-Fürstenau in Michelstadt. Because of poor train connections, this town southeast of Darmstadt required three hours' travel time in each direction, filling an entire day. MacDowell was hired to give music lessons to the children of this noble family, whose slow-witted complacency exasperated the impatient teacher. He could not remember their impressive titles and so resorted to addressing them

7. Robin Rausch, "The House that Marian Built: The MacDowell Colony of Peterborough, New Hampshire," *American Women: A Gateway to Library of Congress Resources for the Study of Women's History and Culture in the United States,* http://memory.loc.gov/ammem/awhhtml/awo8e/awo8e. html#ack, accessed 21 October 2009.

8. Email to the author from Dr. Peter Engels, director of the Stadtarchiv in Darmstadt, 20 October 2009.

as "monsieur" and "mademoiselle." During one lesson he recalled looking up to discover that they had fallen asleep in their seats.[9] He was inspired throughout his life by tales of medieval chivalry, but he preferred to imagine the castles and nobility of Germany in their original glory rather than in their modern state of decay.

The grueling teaching schedule and his decision to maintain Frankfurt as his home base meant that he spent many hours each week in transit, time which he used to read and compose. During this period he expanded his knowledge of German literature by reading the works of Goethe, Schiller, and Heine. He also read British poets like Byron, Keats, Shelley, and Tennyson. The most important musical work from this period of his life was his *Zweite moderne Suite*, op. 14, written during those long train rides. As with many of his later works, it was inspired by poetry, bearing a motto from Byron's *Manfred*. Other works that resulted directly from his reading were the five songs on texts by Heine, Geibel, and Klopstock, published later as opp. 11 and 12.

During the winter of 1881 MacDowell explored possibilities for wider exposure. He joined the Allgemeiner Deutscher Musikverein (ADMV) in January and inquired about the possibility of performing at the society's annual festival in Magdeburg in the summer of 1881. The ADMV had been founded through the efforts of Franz Liszt in 1861 and had presented festivals in various German cities nearly every year since. Although the presidents of the society had been Franz Brendel (1861 to his death in 1868) and Carl Riedel (1868 to his death in 1888), the unofficial leader of the organization was Liszt. The group strove to promote the New German ideals of Liszt and Wagner through the performance of new works by composers who shared their aesthetic views. The festivals in the early years included important premieres of works by Wagner, Liszt, Peter Cornelius, Felix Draeseke, and other protégés of Liszt.[10] Under the leadership of Riedel, a noted Leipzig choral conductor, the society gradually expanded its mandate by occasionally allowing the works of foreign composers to be performed in its festivals, but the process was painfully slow because of opposition within the membership. Liszt himself promoted the works of his friend Saint-Saëns and members of the Russian "Mighty Handful" (Mussorgsky, Balakirev, Borodin, Rimsky-Korsakov, and Cui), whose aesthetic goals were similar to his own. As Brahms became famous, his works were occasionally performed, and he eventually joined the ADMV after the death of Liszt. During the winter and spring of 1881, MacDowell corresponded with Riedel, who showed no interest in

9. Abbie Farwell Brown devotes an entire chapter to this colorful episode in MacDowell's life. See Brown, "Dull Pupils," chap. 18 of *The Boyhood of Edward MacDowell*, 155–62.

10. James Deaville, "Allgemeiner Deutscher Musikverein," *New Grove Dictionary of Music and Musicians*, 2nd ed. (London: Macmillan, 2001), vol. 1, 403–4.

programming the unknown American either as pianist or composer. Adding insult to injury, Riedel rebuked him for his late submission.[11]

One of the bright spots in his weekly schedule seems to have been his lessons with Miss Nevins. On 31 May 1881 he wrote a glowing letter of recommendation, noting "that she, by her unwavering perseverance and hard work has placed herself since last Autumn 1880 on a level but rarely obtained by musical students 'professional' or otherwise."[12] Her talent and capacity for work despite her physical limitations exceeded her father's expectations, who had urged her when she arrived in Germany not to take harmony lessons in addition to piano, because "that will tax your brain too much."[13]

As MacDowell settled back into the routine of teaching in fall 1881, he found that performances were not as plentiful as they had been earlier. On 7 November he had another opportunity to perform in the Frankfurt Saalbau, this time with the Philharmonic Society, playing Beethoven's "Emperor" Concerto and solo compositions by Chopin, Tchaikovsky, and Anton Rubinstein.[14] MacDowell continued to struggle with finding a balance between performing and composing while also teaching so much, and he needed advice on how best to proceed. Shortly after the Philharmonic Society concert, he sought Ehlert's advice on the question of publishing his compositions. The older man responded with a frank assessment of his chances along with some practical advice, which would guide his former student's efforts in the years ahead. This letter was so influential that it bears quotation in full:

> If a young composer whose manuscripts do not already have a definite reputation, as sometimes happens, wants to publish something, then he is usually in the position of needing to pay the printing costs of his work. There are two procedures for this. Either he undertakes the entire costs according to the amount contracted with the publisher, or he pledges to buy 30–50 copies of his work at the retail price, without the normal discount. 50 copies at these prices correspond approximately to the production costs. If you decide, therefore, to make this offer for one or more of your works, the question for the publisher is actually indifferent. I don't see, therefore, why you should deal with Schott, who lies so close to you geographically. Have him, even if you speak to him personally, put his demands in writing, since only written agreements have direct legal significance.

11. Letter from Carl Riedel to EAM, 8 June 1881, EMMC box 31/21.

12. Quoted in undated brochure, "Mrs. Edward MacDowell/Piano Recitals of MacDowell's Music," Margery Lowens private collection.

13. Letter, David H. Nevins to Marian Griswold Nevins, 23 October 1880, EMMC box 47/63.

14. Margery M. Lowens, "The New York Years of Edward MacDowell" (PhD diss., University of Michigan, 1971) 17.

Since you did not pose the question of whether you actually should publish, I don't need to comment, which I confess is good, since I am an avowed enemy of premature publication.

I would add that if you agree to the method of full printing costs, the publisher should present you with an account periodically. He then gives you on each copy sold a portion of the profits that you have both agreed upon.

With kind regards and the hope to hear from you soon again,

Yours truly,

Louis Ehlert[15]

In every profession, there are certain unwritten tricks of the trade that must be learned and mastered early in a career. A young man like MacDowell, living in a foreign country and beginning a career in a profession that no one in his family had ever pursued, needed the advice of a mentor. The wise Ehlert, who understood MacDowell's personality from the beginning, gave him practical advice on exactly how to proceed with finding a publisher for his works, while also warning him against undermining his future reputation by publishing too early. On a portion of the paper that Ehlert had left blank, there are calculations in MacDowell's hand (30 × 6 = 180; 50 × 5 = 250; etc.) as well as the name of Germany's most prominent music publisher, Breitkopf & Härtel, which MacDowell wrote three times to practice his penmanship.

As the long winter stretched through early 1882, MacDowell became increasingly disenchanted with his teaching in Darmstadt. The pay at German conservatories was notoriously low, and at a school like the Darmstadt Conservatory, which was more like a community music school than a professional training school, the pay was barely a living wage. MacDowell's personality did not allow him to bear up stoically under unrewarding circumstances, and in March 1882, a year after he had taken the position at Darmstadt, he resigned. With no prospects to replace this lost income, he faced the difficult decision of whether to go home to New York or to continue struggling in Germany. After talking things over with Raff, he swallowed his pride and wrote to his mother:

I have just been to see Raff about coming home and he is decidedly against it. He thinks it would spoil me "forever." Then besides he says that when I would come back I would have lost all the little name I have already and would have to begin all over again. He is a curious old fellow in some way[s]. I asked him point blank to take me in his conservatorium and he said that he hadn't enough scholars to admit his engaging a new teacher—and then he said that I should have stayed in Darmstadt and made opposition

---

15. Letter, Louis Ehlert to "Lieber Herr McDowell," 20 November 1881, EMMC box 30/35.

to Wallenstein, etc. So you see I am forced to ask you to continue my "salary"—I am really very sorry for after all at my age I ought to be earning my own living and more. It's awfully good of you and Papa to send me the money. I am glad however in one way that I left Darmstadt, the place was <u>so</u> unmusical and lonely that I couldn't hardly stand it at times. You know about coming home, that <u>if</u> I came home it would be for <u>good</u>. How many people do exactly the same and amount to nothing. If I <u>can</u> stay in Germany I will make a good name in a few years but in America I can't do anything as far as I can see.[16]

MacDowell's aspirations and his impatience had forced him into a difficult situation. Darmstadt was not fulfilling musically and barely remunerative financially, but leaving the position required him to go begging to Raff and his parents. As Marian later recalled, it hurt him deeply to be dependent on his parents, but his professional aspirations would not allow him to continue the drudgery of his job or to admit defeat and go home.

As he weathered this professional crisis, he may have turned to Marian for support. Her father could sense that Marian's feelings for her teacher had evolved to a new stage, and he expressed concern in March 1882. Marian wrote to him indignantly on 6 April accusing him of suspecting her of moral delinquency, a charge he denied in his next letter. He added, though, that he would be concerned about "the worth and capacity of the man," meaning his ability to earn a living.[17] Her father had not been completely honest with her about his own health, which was declining rapidly. Perhaps he feared that he would not be able to provide for her much longer, for in January he had written her that under no circumstances could she stay in Germany beyond May 1883.

As all these issues were coming to a head, MacDowell sent the manuscript of his *Erste moderne Suite*, op. 10, to Riedel for consideration at the 1882 ADMV festival. Riedel sent him a card on 9 April stating that he had looked over the suite several times. In his opinion the form was too archaic for the purposes of their festival, but he admitted that there were enough interesting parts that he would not stand in the way of its performance if Liszt voted for it.[18] MacDowell must have been disappointed with his reaction. This year he had followed the rules and submitted his manuscript early. Riedel did not say that the piece was poorly written, or that MacDowell was not a good enough performer to play it; rather, he implied that MacDowell should not have written a piece in this form in the first place! Since

16. Letter, EAM to "Mother," 26 March 1882, NYPL.

17. Letter, David H. Nevins to Marian Griswold Nevins, 23 April 1882, EMMC box 47/63. Although he mentions her letter of 6 April and his previous letter that prompted her response, both letters seem to be lost.

18. Letter, Carl Riedel to EAM, 9 April 1882, EMMC box 31/21.

Riedel was not able to make a definitive selection, he would have to wait for Liszt's response.

On 13 April, Franz Liszt wrote from Budapest: "Since the foundation of the Allgemeiner deutscher Tonkünstlerverein [*sic*], the definitive makeup of the programs is entrusted to me; it will be very agreeable to me to recommend the performance of your work. Please give your master, my old friend J. Raff, my constant feelings of highest esteem and admiration."[19] He promised to communicate his decision to Riedel when he returned to Weimar in eight days. With that letter, one of the most important communications of MacDowell's career, the venerable old man overrode Riedel's decision and endorsed a young American composer who was completely unknown in Germany. Why would he do this?

Liszt was notoriously capricious in his endorsements of young artists, but he had the reputation of being able to identify genius even in its early stages. Since the early 1850s, he had aided the careers of countless young performers and composers, giving the first recognition to Salomon Jadassohn, Joachim Raff, Hans von Bülow, Carl Tausig, William Mason, Peter Cornelius, and numerous others who were now household names. By the 1880s he showed no signs of slowing down, devoting much of his time to coaching young pianists and promoting young composers. In this case, MacDowell benefited from a unique situation in the history of the ADMV. The 1882 festival was to be held in Zürich, Switzerland, the first time it had met outside the borders of Germany. There was an internal dispute taking shape within the organization over whether its mission should continue to be the support of exclusively German music, or whether it should be broadened to include the music of foreign composers whose ideals were similar to those of Liszt and Wagner. The first tentative steps had already been taken in the new direction, and for the Zürich festival, Liszt clearly wanted to cast his vote for a more inclusive policy. The eventual program for the festival in Zürich on 8–12 July 1882 included three Swiss composers, two Russians (Tchaikovsky and Balakirev), Saint-Saëns, the Polish Wieniawski, and the American MacDowell.[20] The presence of a non-European composer on the program was an important symbolic gesture.

When Raff heard of Liszt's response, he advised MacDowell to go to Weimar to see Liszt personally to confirm it, and MacDowell wrote to his mother on 23 April that he had heard nothing further from Riedel and Liszt, but "one can't be

19. The facsimile of this letter is reproduced in a plate opposite page 18 in Lawrence Gilman, *Edward MacDowell: A Study* (New York: John Lane, 1908).

20. "Bekanntmachung des Allgemeinen Deutschen Musikvereins. Tonkünstler-Versammlung in Zürich, 8. bis 12. Juli 1882," *Neue Zeitschrift für Musik* 78/28 (7 July 1882): 311.

too sure of anything you know."[21] He went on to say that he had visited Ehlert in Wiesbaden:

> Ehlert is a hard case and is perfectly delighted with my compositions. He told me along with a lot of other things that I had "genius" of the first order and that my music was "poetry" throughout. He said that I was exactly like Schumann when he was young and that in a few years I would be astonishing people. All this is very encouraging but "many a slip" you know is my motto now and I don't "take stock" in all the wind which passes through the youthful ears.

His spirits had clearly been restored, and the last part of his letter is filled with silly joking about switching from beer to wine. He alluded to Ehlert's compliments by signing his letter "Your thirsty son E. A. McDowell. G. 1st O."[22]

The acceptance of his work for the ADMV festival was undoubtedly a momentous event for the young composer, but his mood shift reflects a pattern that would become more pronounced in the years ahead. During the winter months, MacDowell had grown more and more despondent, leading him to take drastic action to change his situation, in this case resigning his position at Darmstadt. With the arrival of spring, his spirits were restored. When Ehlert said that he was "exactly like Schumann when he was young," he may have been referring not only to the poetry of his music but to the severity of his mood swings. Ehlert had studied with Schumann as a young man and no doubt remembered his manic-depressive illness, which was akin to MacDowell's seasonal patterns. Perhaps without realizing why, he recognized a correlation between the two men. MacDowell's pattern would be repeated often, and whenever he allowed his winter blues to affect an important professional decision, he ran the danger of acting rashly.

The other side of the equation was the manic energy that MacDowell developed after the arrival of spring, illustrated in the compositional history of his first concerto, written in the spring of 1882. According to Gilman:

> One day while he was sitting aimlessly before his piano there came a knock at his door, and in walked, to his startled confusion, his master, Raff, of whom MacDowell stood in unmitigated awe. "The honor," he relates, "simply overwhelmed me. He looked rather quizzically around at my untidy room, and ... then he abruptly asked me what I had been writing. I, scarcely realising what I was saying, stammered out that I had a concerto. He walked out on the landing and turned back, telling me to bring it to him the next Sunday. In desperation, not having the remotest idea how I was to accomplish such a task, I worked like a beaver, evolving the music from some ideas upon which I had

21. Letter, EAM to "my dear Mother," 23 April 1882, NYPL.
22. Ibid.

planned at some time to base a concerto. Sunday came, and I had only the first movement composed. I wrote him a note making some wretched excuse, and he put it off
until the Sunday after. Something happened then, and he put it off two days more; by
that time I had the concerto ready."[23]

The draft of the concerto shows dates ranging from "März 1882" to "6 Mai," a bit
more than the two weeks remembered by MacDowell, but nonetheless a remarkably
short gestation period. The composer had a tremendous capacity for hard work, and
in this case his pride drove him to frantic efforts to avoid admitting his falsehood,
while the return of spring gave him the stamina to follow through.

The first concerto, eventually published as op. 15, is one of MacDowell's most
tightly constructed works. Perhaps because of the speed with which he wrote it,
the work eschews the contrapuntal complexity of the two piano suites in favor of
direct, homophonic textures and memorable melodies that are treated sequentially.
The first movement opens with a twelve-measure maestoso cadenza containing the
rhythmic motive that will form the basis of the work:

5.1 First Piano Concerto, op. 15: I, mm. 1–6

At the beginning of the Allegro con fuoco that follows, this germ is transformed
into a theme that permeates the rest of the movement:

5.2 First Piano Concerto, op. 15: I, principal theme, mm. 13–14

23. Gilman, *Edward MacDowell: A Study,* 16–17.

MacDowell tosses this energetic theme from instrument to instrument, allow-ing its rhythm to drive the forward motion of the movement. A contrasting second theme is presented in the relative major:

5.3 First Piano Concerto, op. 15: I, second theme, rehearsal D

Fragments of the first theme appear as countermelodies to the second theme, while the development is built largely on the first theme. The two are again com-bined contrapuntally in the recapitulation, and the movement closes with a rhap-sodic cadenza based on the second theme followed by a frantic rush to the triple fortissimo close with the orchestra playing the first theme and the piano embel-lishing with Lisztian blind octaves, an alternating-hand technique that creates a thunderous rush of sound.

The tranquil second movement is based entirely on one melody, developed tex-turally rather than thematically through a succession of piano and orchestral timbres. The piano primarily plays a coloristic role in the orchestra rather than taking the soloistic lead. The third movement is a sparkling rondo that features the glittering passagework for which MacDowell the pianist later became famous. An extended section near the end brings back the main theme from the first movement, initially in augmentation and then developed in rhythmic fragments.

The overall effect of the work is of a few memorable themes repeated in differ-ent coloristic combinations and developed motivically. The young composer's need to produce a piece quickly forced him to condense his ideas and use them sparingly, resulting in a work of emotional power and directness. It owes much to Lisztian virtuosity, but more importantly it is heir to the tradition of motivic development that Liszt admired in the works of Beethoven and used so extensively in his own works.

When the concerto was complete, Raff was pleased and recommended that he play it for Liszt. MacDowell took the train to Weimar on 18 June[24] and had an attack

24. This date is found in Carl V. Lachmund's diary from the period. He states that MacDowell sat in on the masterclass but was granted a private session to allow Liszt more time to look at his

of nerves sitting on the doorstep of the Hofgärtnerei, the house on the edge of Weimar's park where Liszt occupied the second floor. Eventually he was invited to enter, and after he played his concerto (accompanied on a second piano by Eugen d'Albert, who happened to be there), Liszt reportedly told d'Albert, "You must bestir yourself if you do not wish to be outdone by our young American."[25]

The following weeks were spent practicing his *Erste moderne Suite*, op. 10, for the ADMV performance. The work had been composed during his days at the Hoch Conservatory, when Raff asked him to write an original composition rather than submit himself to the review of rudiments that he had already learned in previous years. By the late nineteenth century, the term "suite" was used much more broadly than the traditional Baroque suite of dances. None of the five movements of MacDowell's suite has a dance title, and in fact they all tend toward rhapsodic rather than dancelike rhythms. The work as a whole is highly virtuosic, and as one reviewer commented after its publication the following year, "unconcerned about the great crowd of tinkling piano players, his creation has only the musicians and the more discriminating musical audiences in mind, and he wants to give something to them only." The reviewer added, however, that it was cloaked in modern garb, as the title suggests, and therefore could be quite effective as a concert piece for a sensitive, accomplished pianist.[26]

The second and fifth movements are polyphonic, though in the free manner of nineteenth-century fugato movements rather than in strict eighteenth-century style. The opening prelude, which was the most frequently played in years after, features a flowing melody surrounded by feathery figuration. The third movement, Andantino and Allegretto, is the longest and most lyrical, foreshadowing some of MacDowell's haunting melodies from later years and employing a chromatic accompaniment closely modeled on Chopin's Prelude in E minor, op. 28, no. 4. The harmonies clearly show the influence of Wagner and Liszt, but MacDowell here has not yet achieved the subtlety of his mature works.

As the big event, scheduled for 11 July, drew closer, MacDowell stayed in touch with Raff, who continued to be supportive despite signs of physical weakness that

compositions. Lachmund stated that he and MacDowell spent an hour together in a Bierstube that evening, but "owing to his natural reticence and that he left sooner than expected, I did not hear any of his compositions; neither did I hear anything about them through the usual gossip-channels or from the Master direct." Carl V. Lachmund, *Living with Liszt: from the Diary of Carl Lachmund, An American pupil of Liszt, 1882–1884*, ed., annot., and intro. by Alan Walker, Franz Liszt Studies Series No. 4 (Stuyvesant, NY: Pendragon Press, 1994), 85.

25. Gilman, *Edward MacDowell: A Study*, 17; and Finck, "An American Composer," 451.

26. W. Irgang, "E. A. MacDowell, Op. 10 und Op. 14, Erste und zweite moderne Suite für Pianoforte," *Neue Zeitschrift für Musik* 79/31 (27 July 1883): 350.

his student had not noticed before. He told his mother that another visit to his third-floor walk-up apartment had tired the older man significantly, adding that he had given him a box of cigars for his birthday on 27 May and a second box five days later.[27] On the afternoon of 24 June, he walked part way home with Raff, and he later recalled that when he shook his hand it seemed "very hot and dry, and his eyes were unusually bright."[28] The next morning, the barber who came to shave Raff found him lying in bed, dead of a heart attack. MacDowell was devastated, and when Marian came for her lesson later that day, he gave her all the money he had and asked her to buy flowers to be placed on his casket. The funeral, which featured music by the orchestra and male chorus, moved MacDowell deeply. The widow Raff and her daughter did not attend, so he paid them a visit on 30 June. She told him of Raff's high regard for him, and he asked permission to dedicate his suite to her, as he had intended to dedicate it to her husband.[29] The death of Raff, like the departure of Heymann earlier, signified the loss not only of a friend but also of an important mentor who MacDowell had been expecting to guide and open doors for him in the years ahead. His immediate reaction was to consider relocating to Berlin, but he thought better of that and remained in Frankfurt.[30]

A week after his visit to Frau Raff, he boarded the train for Zürich, just over the border in the German-speaking sector of Switzerland. He wrote a short letter home on 10 July reporting on his safe arrival and his days spent practicing in a music store as well as the constant rain that had soaked him every day. He noted that he had received an invitation to stay with some acquaintances, but "owing to my extreme bashfullness [sic] I declined; very sorry, but it is my way." He added, "fingers in good order and am very hopeful."[31]

For any musician, the preparations for a big performance are daunting; for an aspiring performer about to step onto the biggest stage of his life, the pressure can be overwhelming. MacDowell must have known that this performance could make or break his reputation, not only as a performer but as a composer. Like many sensitive musicians, he was introverted and needed time alone to concentrate before the performance. When he stepped on the stage on the evening of 11 July 1882, he would be greeted by glaring lights and the thunderous noise of a crowd of strangers. In order to play the long and technically difficult piece on an unfamiliar piano, his arms and hands needed to be physically ready: warm but not tired, strong but not

---

27. Letter, EAM to "Mother," 29 May 1882, NYPL.

28. Finck, "An American Composer," 452.

29. Letter, EAM to "Mother," 1 July 1882, NYPL.

30. Letter, EAM to "Mother," 25 June 1882, personal collection of Margery Morgan Lowens.

31. Letter, EAM to "Mother," 10 July 1882, University of New Hampshire–Durham.

clumsy, supple but not flaccid. His concentration needed to be so focused that he could block out all the distractions in the room while anticipating every nuance in his score. His emotions needed to be at their most sensitive to express the mercurial moods of the music, but he could not give in to fear or anxiety about the outcome. And as a piano soloist, he would be on stage absolutely alone, with no supporting musicians to cover for him or give him a breather. This was the moment for which he had prepared since leaving New York six years earlier.

When a performer has given his best performance, when he is "in the zone," it is hard to remember the details of that performance, but he knows the effect he has achieved. To his family MacDowell reported, "Last night I played with great success, and got recalled with any amount of 'bravos.' I felt well and play'd well and am very well satisfied in every way." He listed the famous musicians who had warmly congratulated him on both his playing and his composition, including Saint-Saëns, whom he had last seen as a jury member at the ill-fated *concours* four years earlier. Liszt was so beset with admirers that Edward did not have the courage to approach him.[32] His positive feelings were confirmed by the reviews, among which was this assessment from the *Musikalisches Wochenblatt*:

> The appearance of Herr E. A. MacDowell from Darmstadt was also of great interest. He introduced himself to the audience here not only as pianist, but at the same time as composer, and turned out to be an artist of importance in each direction. His suite, consisting of five movements, is a work that documents the singular and outstanding compositional gift of the above-mentioned. If perhaps the winged steed [Flügelpferd] of the tone poet gallops somewhat unbridled here and there, his healthy originality and abundant inventiveness allow the best hope for the future with greater mastery of his innate strength.[33]

In his ecstatic letter to his family, MacDowell commented further, "By the way I got immensely applauded when I first came on the platform—why I do not know—very pleasant however. I got also much applauded after every movement."[34] True to form, the young man was so focused on his performance that he missed the broader political significance of the occasion. Even before he played a note, the partisan crowd was cheering the presence of a non-European on the program, a development that represented a turning point for the ADMV. For those who knew that his teacher and Liszt's friend Raff had died unexpectedly just two weeks earlier, his appearance on stage had additional sentimental meaning. MacDowell, though perhaps oblivious to

32. Letter, EAM to "Mother," 12 July 1882, NYPL.

33. "Die neunzehnte Tonkünstler-Versammlung des Allgemeinen deutschen Musikvereins. Vom 9. Bis 12. Juli 1882 (Fortsetzung)," *Musikalisches Wochenblatt* 13/33 (10 August 1882): 386–87.

34. Letter, EAM to "Mother," 12 July 1882, NYPL.

the backstory, had the good fortune to be in the right place at the right time, and he seized the opportunity with both hands.

The legend of the big break centers on two related components. First is an opportunity that is suddenly and unexpectedly thrust upon the aspiring artist. Second is the necessary preparation and courage to succeed on the big stage. MacDowell's performance in Zürich shows that he rose to the occasion by turning in a brilliant performance that impressed his audience with his skills as both composer and performer. The story does not end here, though, for there is a third component to a real-life big-break story that is just as important as the other two. In order to convert the break from a flash in the pan into a career, the artist must have the tenacity and connections to build on that break and establish himself on a long-term basis. In MacDowell's case, his quest to become established would require unusual persistence and the ability to weather disappointment and rejection in the years ahead.

CHAPTER SIX

Establishing a Career in Germany

CAREER DOES NOT HAPPEN BY ITSELF. IN THE YEARS FOLLOWING HIS 11 JULY 1882 performance in Zürich, MacDowell worked incessantly to capitalize on this opportunity and thus establish himself as an artist. By the time he returned to the United States in late 1888, he would bring a strong reputation and an enviable list of publications with German publishers. But achieving this reputation required hard work and personal sacrifices. The events of these years and the tedious process of self-promotion show us a great deal about his character and the development of his mature compositional style.

In June 1882, MacDowell began keeping letter books, in which he wrote rough drafts of business letters and pasted in the replies he received. Writing in a foreign language, he needed to revise his communications in order to correct grammatical errors. These books, containing hundreds of letters to and from MacDowell, chronicle his developing career and provide a window into musical conditions in the German Empire at this time. They have been largely ignored by previous biographers, perhaps because of the difficulty in deciphering them. German orthography and penmanship were in transition at this time, compounding the normal difficulties of reading handwritten notes with alternate spellings, archaic vocabulary, and wildly varying styles of penmanship. Furthermore, the contracts and letters from publishers contain a dizzying array of legal terms that would eventually have serious implications for his financial stability. Only after achieving fame in the 1890s did he understand some of the mistakes he had made as a young man during this crucial phase of his career.

MacDowell had prepared for years for a career as a concert pianist, but the success of his composition in Zürich was new. He later recalled his decision to rethink his career aspirations:

At this Zürich concert, I played my suite with my notes before me, as, until then, I had never waked up to the idea that my compositions could be worth actual study or memorizing. I would not have changed a note in one of them for untold gold, and *inside* I had the greatest love for them; but the idea that any one else might take them seriously never occurred to me. I had acquired the idea from early boyhood that it was expected of me to become a pianist, and every moment scribbling seemed to be stolen from the more legitimate work of piano practice.[1]

The composer was perhaps a bit disingenuous in this statement, as we know that he had written to Ehlert nearly a year earlier about publishing his works and had thought enough of his compositions to show them to Liszt. But the event was undoubtedly a watershed for him. Not only had the ADMV performance demonstrated that his compositions could generate serious interest among knowledgeable musicians, but the death of his composition teacher gave it added significance. Now that Raff was gone, he was no longer a student, and he could legitimately present himself as a professional composer.

In the years ahead, MacDowell would continue to pursue both careers, and it is worthwhile to consider the personal qualities that he brought to each. Composition is a solitary pursuit requiring persistence, self-discipline, and a sensitive awareness of one's innermost inspiration. In a sense, the personal qualities needed by a composer were those cultivated by the Society of Friends during his childhood, despite the lack of music in the Quaker meetings. A performer, on the other hand, needs to be able to work with other performers and meet the demands of concert promoters. A free-lance performer must cultivate every relationship and cannot afford to burn any bridges. Even the best performer must swallow his pride daily to stay on the good side of anyone who could possibly help him. MacDowell may have begun to realize at this time that his personality was better suited to the solitary pursuit of composition than the collaborative world of performance. He was already developing an unfortunate habit of burning his bridges, even those that could have been professionally profitable. On 1 July 1882, before leaving for Zürich, he had reported to his parents on a visit to Wiesbaden: "I saw Mrs. Bischoff and Sauret at Wiesbaden. I had the pleasure of telling S̲ what I thought of him and also of rather astonishing him with my playing. He invited me to s̲t̲a̲y̲ with h̲i̲m̲ in Berlin and I laughed in his face. I have the 'bulge' [advantage] on him at last."[2] It may have given Edward

---

1. Henry T. Finck, "An American Composer: Edward A. MacDowell," *Century Magazine* 53/3 (January 1897): 451–52.

2. Letter, EAM to "Mother," 1 July 1882, NYPL.

pleasure to insult Teresa Carreño's ex-husband and refuse his offer of hospitality, but it was a reckless choice for a young man who would need every possible friend in his pursuit of a career.

Wasting no time after his return from Zürich, MacDowell wrote to B. Schott's Söhne in Mainz on 31 July, as Ehlert had recommended. This publisher had come to prominence early in the nineteenth century, gaining renown for first editions of Beethoven's *Missa Solemnis*, Ninth Symphony, and several of the late string quartets. MacDowell probably knew of Schott's first editions of Wagner's *Der Ring des Nibelungen* cycle and other works by composers of the New German school. MacDowell offered to send manuscripts for their consideration, but they replied on 5 August that they were too busy with "the imminent publication of the full score of *Parsifal*, besides two symphonies, not to mention a number of other works" to consider his compositions.[3]

MacDowell immediately approached another publisher, this time the eminent Leipzig firm of Breitkopf & Härtel. This company had played an important role in German publishing since the early eighteenth century, and its technological innovations in music printing had revolutionized the industry in the 1750s. The firm had published works by nearly every significant composer of the Classical era and continued to be an industry leader in the late nineteenth century with its monumental complete works editions of Bach, Beethoven, Mozart, Mendelssohn, and other composers. On the day that Schott refused to look at his works, he wrote to Breitkopf & Härtel offering to send his works for their consideration. They expressed their willingness to look at his works in a letter of 8 August, and on 15 August he sent them not only the first but also his second modern suite.[4] On 31 August, he received a response that would have a profound impact on his future career:

Most honored sir!
We have made the acquaintance of both modern suites for pianoforte, sent to us as promised in your esteemed letter of 15 August. These caught our interest, and we would

3. Letter, B. Schott's Söhne to EAM, 5 August 1882, "Business Letters from 8 June 1882 till 1 March 1884," EMMC box 32.

4. MacDowell saved nearly all the letters he received from Breitkopf & Härtel over the years, and they are now in the MacDowell Collection in the Library of Congress. The publisher lost many important archives during the World War II bombing raids on Leipzig, but among the materials that did survive and are now housed in the Sächsisches Landesarchiv in Leipzig are six important letters from MacDowell, which will be discussed in later chapters, as well as hundreds of *Copirbücher* containing copies of all outgoing letters from the firm. These copies are useful for cross-checking the information in MacDowell's letters, for copies of the occasional letter that MacDowell did not

gladly be ready to let these works be released under our firm, if we were not, through the various sacrifices which the great complete works editions and such currently demand, required to limit the venture publication of new works as much as possible. We would, however, if you consider the publication to be important, make the proposal to share the possible profit as well as the costs of production. To our sorrow, we cannot at this time promise the acceptance at our risk alone; but should a settlement proposal like the above be welcome to you, we find ourselves most ready.[5]

What was a young composer to do? It was bad enough to compete with Wagner, Brahms, and other contemporaries, but how could he ever hope to compete with Bach, Beethoven, and other ghosts of the past? He recalled Ehlert's advice, though, and asked the publisher for the price of sharing the production costs.

MacDowell had sent his two longest and most substantial solo works to date, probably thinking that these were his most impressive compositions. From the publisher's point of view, however, a longer work requires more paper and more engraved plates. Breitkopf & Härtel informed him that the total production costs were Mk. 434, making his share Mk. 217. MacDowell's monthly rent for his first apartment in Frankfurt had been Mk. 90, while the second had been Mk. 38. His earnings for private lessons were 4 or 5 marks per hour. This represented a significant outlay of money in advance. Since leaving his position in Darmstadt his income had been limited, and there was only one way to come up with that kind of money—his parents. On 10 September, he accepted the publisher's offer.

Over the course of the next month the plates were engraved, and he received proofs in October. He made a miscalculation owing to inexperience, however, for after the first proofs, he wrote to the publisher on 18 October requesting another change. They responded the next day to inform him that since they normally did not prepare two proofs, his requested change would result in an extra charge. In the margin of the firm's *Copirbuch* copy of this letter is a handwritten note: "Der Titel der 2n Suite erhält <u>wohl</u> keine Dedikation!" [The title page of the second suite contains <u>no</u> dedication!].[6] The dedication of the second suite to Camille Saint-Saëns was thus a very late afterthought.

On the same day that Breitkopf & Härtel sent him the corrected title page, Edward had to write a very difficult letter to Marian. He had received word that her

---

save (e.g., the 8 August 1882 letter inviting him to submit his manuscripts, found in *Copirbuch* 260, 312), and for occasional marginal notes that were added to the copies in the books.

5. Letter, Breitkopf & Härtel [B&H] to EAM, 31 August 1882, "Business Letters," EMMC box 32.

6. Copy of letter, B&H to EAM, 19 October 1882, *Copirbuch* 261, 123.

father had died on 2 November, and his letter reflects the intensity of his feelings and his insecurity about his role:

> Dear Miss Nevins:
>
> Please excuse my not coming to see you today. In the first place I don't want to trouble you—Secondly I am sure you are having many people to see you and wouldn't want me: I only hope you won't be "foolish" and get ill. If you wish to see me or would like to have me come just write a line and I'll appear—only please don't think it is want of "sympathy" that makes me stay away. It is simply because I don't want to trouble you with my stupid talk. If I can be in any way of use, of course you know I am always ready.
>
> Yrs
> E. A. McDowell[7]

An undated letter on mourning paper that may have been her response to this expression of sympathy shows how much he meant to her immediately after her father's death:

> Dear Mr. McDowell
>
> Thank you very very much. As for paying I will talk about that when I see you.
>
> I want to say something which you may think stupid. If sometimes I let you see I am unnecissarily [*sic*] hurt by something you have said, forgive me, and remember you are the only one who has the power of giving me much pain or pleasure. Ever yours
>
> MGN[8]

Marian had not seen her father for more than two years, and he had done his best to hide the severity of his illness from her. The letter that he dictated on his deathbed, telling her he loved her and urging her to find good financial advisors, must have come as a shock. Clearly she could not stay much longer in Europe, and this impending departure would make her and Edward reevaluate their relationship over the coming months.

On 21 December 1882, Breitkopf & Härtel sent MacDowell the much-anticipated news that his First and Second Modern Suites, opp. 10 and 14, had been printed. They sent him "the usual six free copies," assured him that the general shipping to music stores would probably take place after the first of the year, and closed the letter, "May the publication of these two works be accompanied by the best success."[9] Three days after his twenty-second birthday, MacDowell was a published composer.

---

7. EAM to Miss Nevins, 11 November 1882, EMMC box 31/49.

8. Undated letter on mourning paper, MacDowell Collection, Library of Congress Manuscript Division, Box 6.

9. Letter from B&H to "E. A. MacDowell, Tonkünstler," 21 December 1882, "Business Letters," EMMC box 32.

The copies that the composer received were beautiful. Published in large format, they featured ornately lithographed title pages, ample margins, and well-spaced musical notation. Breitkopf & Härtel had earned its reputation honestly with elegant, readable scores and a reputation for accuracy. MacDowell must have felt that these attractive editions were an auspicious start and well worth the price he had paid. Legend has it that it was through Liszt's influence that Breitkopf agreed to publish MacDowell's suites, but there is no evidence in the surviving correspondence that this was the case; rather, it seems that the publisher was willing to print the compositions as long as they did not entail a financial risk.

In February he sent copies of the two works to Liszt in Budapest. At the same time he thanked Liszt for his suggestions on the concerto he had played for him in Weimar the previous summer, noting that he had completely revised it in the meantime. He asked permission to dedicate it to Liszt, writing, "although it still remains unworthy of you, it is, thanks to your inestimable comments, much more respectable." Liszt replied twelve days later with a brief congratulatory note that MacDowell treasured long afterward: "Your 2 Pianoforte Suites are excellent. With sincere pleasure and thanks I accept the dedication of your concerto."[10]

As the winter stretched on, MacDowell became impatient not only for the spring but also for results from his publications. On 10 February 1883 he wrote to Breitkopf & Härtel asking why his pieces were not included in the publisher's annual announcement of new repertoire. They responded on 15 February that the announcements had been sent to the house periodicals of book and music stores earlier, and that they would be sent to music journals within the next week. Review copies had been sent to editors who had requested them.[11] MacDowell was learning that the process of publication could be painfully slow.

Meanwhile, he took steps to build on his initial success by sending other works to different publishers. On 10 March he wrote a follow-up letter to E. W. Fritzsch of Leipzig asking why he had not received a response to the manuscripts of his *Prelude and Fugue*, op. 13 and his *Serenade* for pianoforte, op. 16, for which he had been waiting for several weeks. Fritzsch, a much smaller publisher than Breitkopf, responded ten days later that he was so overwhelmed with work that he had not been able to make a decision yet. On 31 March he wrote that he would accept both pieces,

10. Draft letter, EAM to Franz Liszt, 10 February 1883, "Business Letters," 16–17; facsimile letter, Franz Liszt to EAM, 22 February 1883, plate opposite page 22 of Lawrence Gilman, *Edward MacDowell: A Study* (New York: John Lane, 1908). MacDowell's letter contradicts the assertion by Gilman (17) that he had changed only three lines of passage work after completing this concerto for Raff in spring 1882.

11. Letter, B&H to EAM, 15 February 1883, "Business Letters," EMMC box 32.

asking if the composer wanted to make any changes before they went to press. MacDowell responded on 2 April with a small change in the pedal markings and a request to dedicate the *Serenade*, op. 16, to Hans Huber, one of the Basel composers whose works had been performed at the festival in July 1882.[12]

The *Serenade*, op. 16, is a pleasant-sounding work in a gently rocking moderato tempo that builds to a *fortissimo* climax in the middle section before returning to the rocking motion of the opening. It is reminiscent of the popular *Liebestraum* No. 3 of Liszt, a staple of American parlor pianists. Like that work, MacDowell's *Serenade* features a tuneful melody sung over a block-chord accompaniment. There is a dramatic key change (in MacDowell's case from B-flat major to F-sharp major). Like the famous Liszt work, it features a free cadenza with very high figuration for both hands leading to the return of the main theme. Though technically more difficult than most parlor music, MacDowell's *Serenade* lies comfortably under the hands, except for an extended passage combining trills and octaves in the right hand playable only by someone with large hands.

The *Prelude and Fugue*, op. 13 is one of the few works to bear a French title page, which reads "Prélude et fugue pour pianoforte par E. A. Mac-Dowell, Oeuvre 13, à Monsieur Marmontel, professeur de piano au Conservatoire de Paris."[13] In the key of D minor, the work is severe, both in the unrelentingly somber mood that does not lift until the final cadences and in the complexity of the contrapuntal textures. His friend Templeton Strong recalled that within a few years he came to regret this composition:

> Already at this time (winter of 1886–1887) he was dissatisfied with all that was contrapuntal in his earlier compositions, the Modern Suites and Prelude and Fugue, as not possessing that particular sonority of which he was gradually becoming such an exceptional exponent. The contrapuntal manner seemed to be opposed to the euphonious sonority his whole being craved for, and it may be that in some ways this passion became somewhat restrictive with regard to the development of his possibilities; I have reason to believe that he felt this later on in life, and that it was a source of some regret to him.[14]

Ehlert had advised him against premature publication of his early works, but in his eagerness to establish his reputation, he had ignored his mentor's advice.

MacDowell realized during the winter of 1883 that he could not ignore his pianistic career, and he placed ads in several of the leading music journals that

---

12. Fritzsch's letters are in EMMC box 30/39, and MacDowell's drafts are found in the book "Business Letters," box 32.

13. O. G. Sonneck, *Catalogue of First Editions of Edward MacDowell (1861 [sic]–1908)* (Washington: Government Printing Office, 1917), 12.

14. TS, "Edward MacDowell as I Knew Him, second paper," *Music Student* 8/1 (September 1915): 7.

read simply "E. A. Mac-Dowell, Pianist, 72 Zeil, Frankfurt/M." At the same time he wrote to a number of conductors inquiring about engagements, but the results of these inquiries were mostly disappointing. In early May, Edward attended the ADMV festival in Leipzig, which encouraged him greatly. He heard concerts by Eugen d'Albert (the pianist who had accompanied his piano concerto in Weimar a year earlier), Alfred Reisenauer, and Marie Jaëll, all young students of Liszt whose playing was on a level with his own. He made the acquaintance of the Polish pianist Moritz Moszkowski when they sat together at one of the concerts, and he met a Dr. Meissner who promised to arrange a concert in Berlin.

This flurry of activity was described in a letter to his mother written on 13 May 1883. His parents had paid for the trip to Leipzig, and the letter listed all the avenues he was pursuing to try to establish his concert career. He even toyed with the idea of returning to the United States, although it is not clear whether this was a serious idea or just a way of placating his mother. He asked her, "By the way if I came to America could I get a chance to play right away ('debut' I mean) with orchestra? I must get my 'hand in' some way this winter....The fact is that I can't stand doing 'nothing.' If it's 'no go' why I'll have to try New York that's all."[15] This letter and his efforts of the previous months reflect a new urgency that originated in February 1883 and intensified during the following months. His letter seems calculated to prove to his parents that he was doing everything within his power to establish himself as a concert artist following a fall and winter devoted primarily to composition. What was the reason for this sudden change?

There are no extant letters from his family during this crucial period, but an examination of contemporary news reports verifies that his father's business endured a crisis during the winter and spring of 1883. Thomas F. McDowell had participated in the growth of a new industry during the previous decades, as Manhattan became too crowded to supply its own milk locally. With the help of the expanding rail system, McDowell and other milk distributors had arranged for the shipment of fresh country milk from surrounding rural areas, especially Orange County just northwest of the city. The milk was shipped to Manhattan, where McDowell supplied it to restaurants, bakeries, and private homes. Starting on the ground floor of a new industry in the 1850s, McDowell had been able to provide a good income for his family and eventually to take his son Walter into the business.

As the new system became established, though, farmers and distributors came into conflict over prices. According to the *Rural New-Yorker*, the average prices that farmers received for their milk declined steadily from 1870 to 1895, despite rising

15. Letter from "E" to "Mother," 13 May 1883, NYPL.

feed costs.[16] Distributors, on the other hand, were frustrated by seasonal fluctuations in milk supplies as well as increasing regulation from the Board of Health.[17] The question of who would establish the price of milk came to a head in March 1883, when the two sides reached an impasse.[18] On 14 March, Orange County farmers voted to stop shipping milk to the city until they received their desired price. Milk dealers initially scoffed at this action, but a week later, the city was feeling the impact of the strike, as the farmers had timed their strike to coincide with increased demand by bakers preparing hot cross buns for Easter. There were widespread reports of "spilling committees," gangs of ruffians who accosted farmers attempting to circumvent the strike and emptied their cans of milk on the road to prevent its reaching the station.

On 24 March, a conference committee representing producers and distributors reached an agreement that fixed prices for the coming year.[19] For large dealers, the impact on their business was negligible, but for a smaller dealer like McDowell, his profit margins were reduced and he could no longer expect the rapid expansion he had enjoyed previously. It cannot be a coincidence that Edward's letter book shows a sudden increase in efforts to secure performing engagements and that his 13 May letter to his mother lists these efforts in such detail. He must have realized that he could not rely on continued support from home indefinitely.

There was a second event that changed Edward's life that winter. As we saw in 1882, the winter blues could cause Edward to make drastic decisions in an effort to change his situation. In 1883 he made one of the happiest changes of his life, but one that would bring new anxieties and responsibilities—he proposed marriage to Marian Nevins.

After the death of her father in November 1882, Marian recognized that her days in Germany were numbered. Her father had estimated her annual expenses at $1,500, which included salary and living expenses for her nurse, "Sister" Kathleen Collis, as well as her own living expenses and music lessons.[20] Her precarious health—sciatic nerve

16. Cited in John J. Dillon, *Seven Decades of Milk: A History of New York's Dairy Industry* (New York: Orange Judd, 1941), 17.

17. "The Milkmen's Protest," *NYT,* 17 August 1882, 8. In articles published on 5 October, 7 October, and 19 October, the *New York Times* listed the names and addresses of dozens of New York milk dealers who had been fined for selling adulterated milk. Thomas McDowell was not among them.

18. "Who Will Fix the Price: A Milk-Rate War Threatened by the Producers," *NYT,* 11 March 1883, 7.

19. "End of the Milk Strike: Producers Make Terms with Independent City Dealers," *NYT,* 25 March 1883, 2.

20. Letter, David H. Nevins to Marian Griswold Nevins, 23 October 1880, EMMC box 49/63.

problems resulting from a fall and recurring respiratory problems—required periodic travel to healthful climates for recovery. All these expenses stretched her father's resources, and he had set the spring of 1883 as the outside limit on her stay in Europe. After his death, she was living on her inheritance, which was generous but not unlimited.

During the winter of 1882/1883, she became ill with pneumonia and asked Edward to make arrangements for her to travel first to Switzerland and Italy to recover and then home.[21] Their impending separation after two and a half years of friendship spurred him to propose marriage on the eve of her departure in mid-February. A letter written later that day reflects his powerful emotions combined of love and concern for her health:

> My dearest
> Sister's a brick. She's going to telegraph me as soon as you get to Basel so when you are getting this I will be singing Hallelujah's for your safe arrival. For of <u>course</u> you have been good on the way, God bless you darling and keep you from harm, it seems horribly bitter to be separated from you till summer, but it is for the very best. Now <u>do, do</u> be good and take care. You know you <u>promised</u>....Now dearest if you get this in the evening—just give me one kiss and be a good girl and go to <u>sleep</u>. How horribly black & white it seems on paper, but dearest, I know you understand it all. I am thinking of today when I held you fast in my arms, Darling, love <u>can't</u> be more than I feel. I would give anything to come to you again tomorrow, only I can't bear to give you pain and it would seem as if you were <u>really</u> going. Well my dearest my first "Liebesbrief" [love letter] must be short, but it looks <u>too ghastly</u>. But you <u>do</u> know all. If I ever held you again in my arms I could not <u>say</u> it all, as for writing it, it is impossible. Dearest, my dearest you <u>can't</u> love me more than I do you. Darling, now be a good girl and go to bed and <u>sleep</u>—take care of yourself as if it were <u>myself</u> that were ill,—you <u>must</u> get well. Dearest if I had wings I would have told you all this insane letter in one kiss, Good night, good night, God how I love you darling
>
> > forever your
> > Eddie (or <u>Ned</u>)
> > I hate 'em both[22]

This anxiety over the welfare of another was something new for Edward, whose life had been self-centered to this point. There is no evidence of any serious romantic attachments prior to this time, and his commitment to Marian was thus a major change for him. His introspective, sometimes brooding personality fed his anxiety when they were apart. Marian recalled many years later that she had accepted his

21. Drafts of a telegram requesting housing in Basel on 13 February 1883 and a letter requesting tickets to America on 19 April were written in his "Business Letters," 21 and 43, EMMC box 32.
22. [EAM] to [MM], Monday night "*late*," EMMC box 31/52.

proposal of marriage on condition that they live apart for a year to test their love.[23] For a man of Edward's sensitive nature, it was truly a test, and his letters show that the suspense was excruciating.

After spending the winter and spring of 1883 in the south, Marian was still not fully recovered, and she and Kathleen returned to America in July.[24] Rather than move in with her family in Waterford, Connecticut, she chose to live with MacDowell's parents in New York until their planned marriage the following summer. On 20 July he wrote to her, "Dearest, I think of you always and am <u>so</u> anxious for you to take care of yourself. Please do. You will have seen my mother by this time. I hope all goes well."[25] Knowing Fanny's volatile personality, it is easy to imagine Edward's apprehension, but she was on her best behavior and welcomed her future daughter-in-law into the family. Marian later recalled: "I returned home in 1883, lived a Winter with the MacDowells, paying my board, naturally. They were in a large comfortable house with every comfort and two servants—That Winter was a hard one for Edward, and they sent him fifty dollars a month, which represented practically my board—They were kindness itself to me and I imagined they were fond of me."[26]

Back in Germany, MacDowell was not only worried about Marian's health, he also had an urgent need to establish his musical career. He confirmed in a letter of 30 June 1883 that his parents were sending him fifty dollars (Mk. 200) per month but confided that he was afraid his mother would withdraw the allowance if he did not come up with something soon. He was frustrated at not being able to stay out of debt, he could not afford to bring Marian to Germany to live with him yet, but he was unwilling to consider returning to the United States without having established a solid record of accomplishments.[27] This dilemma led him to take unprecedented steps to find something—anything—in Germany.

Ehlert had warned MacDowell that an unknown composer would need to pay some or all of the production costs in order to get his first works in print. Raff had advised him to offer his services as a concert artist, even if he did not cover his costs. The problem for MacDowell in the summer of 1883 was that his rent alone used more than a fourth of the 200 marks he received each month, leaving insufficient money for food, travel expenses, and costs associated with his career. Any students he was able to secure took time away from his practicing and composing.

---

23. MM, "Childhood and Early Years of my Life," typescript, 30–32, EMMC box 39.

24. Passenger records indicate that Marian Nevins, age twenty-six, and Kath Colliss, age nineteen, arrived in New York on 9 July 1883 aboard the *Servia*. www.ancestry.com, accessed 31 October 2009.

25. Letter, "E" to "My Darling Marian," 20 July 1883, EMMC box 31/50.

26. Undated letter, MM to W. H. Humiston, EMMC box 52/9. The letter indicates that it was written eleven months after his death in January 1908.

27. Letter, "Edward" to "Dearest Marian," 30 July 1883, EMMC box 31.

During the summer of 1883, as Marian returned to New York and settled in with his parents, MacDowell wrote a barrage of letters to concert agents and con-ductors asking for engagements. All of the agents turned him down, and the Dr. Meissner who had been so encouraging about concerts in Berlin turned out to be no help. His old friend Teresa Carreño wrote a strong letter of support to a concert agent in London, which also led to nothing. He received repeated rejections from conductors for high-profile concerts, but he did manage to arrange for several run-throughs of his concerto by smaller orchestras during rehearsals and also for a performance in November. This was crucial for him, because it would soon be published, and he wished to verify that the orchestral parts were correct.

The publication history of the Piano Concerto, op. 15, is among the most impor-tant of his career, not only because it was his first published orchestral work, but because of the contractual ramifications that would only become clear years later. Recognizing the value of the Breitkopf & Härtel reputation, he sent his score to them for consideration late in the spring of 1883. On 4 June, they responded posi-tively but were again unwilling to accept the complete financial risk and offered to publish it if he would pay a Mk. 300 subvention. Since this would present a substantial hardship financially at a time when he was hesitant to ask his parents for even more money, he wrote back to the publisher the next day asking for a state-ment of financial returns from the publication of the two suites the previous year. They responded that it was too early to give such a statement, since the works had only been sent to dealers in January. On 29 June he asked for an extension until 15 August to consider their offer.

The decision must have been a difficult one. He did not want to ask for help from home, and his allowance was barely enough for his living expenses, yet the publication of his concerto by Breitkopf would be an important honor. Finally on 25 July he was able to send them Mk. 200, agreeing to send the remaining Mk. 100 in three to five months. The contract for his First Piano Concerto, op. 15, sent on 27 July, was a complicated one, and before signing it he wrote to question the meaning of §2, which concerned the payment of the remainder of the subvention and the timing of the printing. The publisher answered to his satisfaction, and he signed the contract, without bothering to question the meaning of the much more important §1 of the contract: "The publishers Breitkopf & Härtel will produce the above-named work in the manner of similar published works and communicate the same in the usual manner of their business."[28]

28. Die Verleger Breitkopf & Härtel stellen genanntes Werk nach Art ihrer ähnlicher Verlagswerke her und mitteilen derselbe in der in ihrem Geschäfte üblichen Weise. "Verlags-Vertrag," 27 July 1883, "Business Letters," EMMC box 32.

A piano concerto is a complicated work that combines a solo pianist with an orchestra. In order to play it successfully, the performers need three different versions of the score: The "Klavierauszug" contains the solo piano part with the orchestral parts in a piano reduction, allowing it to be performed on two pianos during rehearsals. The "Partitur" is the full score with all orchestral parts and the piano part incorporated for the use of the conductor. The "Stimmen" are the individual orchestral parts for each player in the orchestra. When MacDowell envisioned the publication of his concerto, he had in mind the printing of all three components. When Breitkopf & Härtel agreed to publish the work "in the usual manner of their business," this was a coded way of saying that they would print and sell the two-piano version. The full score and orchestral parts would be kept in *Abschrift* (manuscript copy) in their rental library; if the piece received a performance with orchestra, they would send handwritten copies of score and parts on a rental basis. Edward had just agreed to pay a sum equivalent to six months' rent, and he would not find out until later that he was getting only a third of what he thought he had paid for.

Also on 27 July, the *Neue Zeitschrift für Musik* published a review of his suites, opp. 10 and 14. This journal had been founded by Robert Schumann in 1834 and had become one of the most important musical journals in Germany. Its direction had shifted since its early days under Schumann's editorship, and by this time it was known for its support of the New German School of Liszt, Wagner, and their followers. This ideological direction may have been the motivation behind the editor's decision to print a two-page review of the piece that had scored such a success on the previous year's ADMV festival. W. Irgang wrote detailed descriptions of the suites, describing each in the most complimentary terms. Comparing the two suites, of which the first was naturally better known, he wrote, "It is difficult to say which of these should have preference, for as far as I am concerned, they are both equally valuable and neither can be placed behind the other; concert artists will perhaps decide in favor of the second, if they do not wish to incorporate both in their program."[29]

Buoyed by this positive review and the publication arrangements for the concerto, he sent two additional sets of piano works to "his" publisher: the *Barcarolle* and *Humoreske*, op. 18, and the *Wald-Idyllen*, op. 19. Breitkopf & Härtel responded on 4 August that they would accept the works under the same conditions as the previous ones, this time for a subvention of Mk. 150. His finances stretched to the breaking point already, MacDowell sent a counteroffer on 5 August proposing the

29. W. Irgang, "E. A. MacDowell, Op. 10 und Op. 14, Erste und zweite moderne Suite für Pianoforte," *Neue Zeitschrift für Musik* 79/31 (27 July 1883): 350.

second option Ehlert had described to him: no money up front, but if the pub-lisher did not sell one hundred copies in two years, he would buy the remainder. The publisher must have guessed that this young man's funds were too unstable to guarantee such an agreement, and they responded on 6 August that because of the costs of the critical complete works editions they were preparing, they could not shoulder the entire risk, especially as they did not yet have a sense of how success-ful his previous works were going to be.[30] This response made the composer so irate that he scribbled across the top of the letter the reply he must have fantasized about sending: "Schweinerei! Wie? Bitte schicken Sie es retour" [Screw you! What? Please send it back]. After this disappointment, MacDowell again wrote to Schott in Mainz. After what seemed to the composer too long a wait, he wrote a peevish letter demanding to know why they had not responded to his offer. They replied that they were not interested in his works.

At this point MacDowell's search for a publisher took an unusual turn. He con-tacted the Frankfurt music dealer André to offer him an exclusive two-year contract for the publication of his works, "since I am very anxious that my name be made known in the musical world." In exchange for these publications he requested no payment, he offered to pay for all advertising, he promised to pay all costs that were not covered after two years, he offered complete ownership of copyrights during the two years, and he promised not to make contracts with any other publisher dur-ing this period.[31] André replied promptly that he would need to see the pieces first. MacDowell sent his piano pieces, opp. 17 and 18, on 5 September, and by the 21st, he could wait no longer: "Dear sir: I take the liberty of asking about my publication offer. I wish very much, for different reasons, to receive your conclusion in a few days." Four days later, André offered to print one hundred copies of these works for the price of Mk. 212. MacDowell rejected the offer, informing André that he wanted a *publisher*, not a printer.[32]

After wasting nearly a month on this gambit, it was late September, and MacDowell was desperate. Rather than send his works to one publisher and wait impatiently for a rejection, he wrote to four publishers simultaneously, listing works that he could send them for consideration if they were interested. These publishers—Bote & Bock, Ries & Erler, Rahter, and Hainauer—were not as renowned as Breitkopf & Härtel or Schott, but MacDowell was determined to get his music in print as soon as possible, and he sweetened his offer with a proposal to grant full copyright

---

30. "Business Letters," 98, EMMC box 32.

31. Undated draft letter to Joh. André, "Business Letters," 108–9, EMMC box 32.

32. The whole exchange of letters is found in "Business Letters," 111, 128, 129, and 135, EMMC box 32.

to the publisher without an honorarium. One of the publishers recognized an opportunity and was able to take advantage of MacDowell's urgency to work out a business arrangement that would prove very lucrative in the years ahead.

Julius Hainauer was located in Breslau (now Wrocław), in the eastern part of the German Empire in present-day Poland. The publisher specialized in the music of eastern European composers, and he had published noteworthy editions of works by Antonín Dvořák and Moritz Moszkowski. He replied promptly to request the manuscripts of opp. 17 and 18, and responded equally promptly with a contract for their publication. On 19 October 1883 MacDowell signed and returned the contract, making a copy in his letter book. His cover letter reflects his hopes for the relationship: "I hope in any case that my compositions may result in our mutual satisfaction, and that it will lead to a long business relationship."[33] Hainauer recognized MacDowell's urgency, and exactly two months after the composer returned the contract, he was able to send printed copies of the four piano pieces, opp. 17 and 18. Edward wrote a grateful letter on 23 December to thank him for the Christmas present.

With these two works, MacDowell achieved his first genuine success. These works have a charm that made them very popular in their day, and one of them, *Hexentanz* [Witches' Dance], op. 17, no. 2, remained among his best sellers throughout the twentieth century. Marian MacDowell explained that the witches in this dance are not the frightening variety but are instead water nymphs or tree nymphs of German folklore.[34] The piece is virtuosic, featuring light passagework in the treble that seems indebted to Mendelssohn's elfin pieces, but with a harmonic coloring that reflects French influence. The middle section switches to a broad, tuneful melody in the tenor register that was completely new for the time. Such melodies, which later commentators attributed to MacDowell's Celtic heritage, would help define his signature style in his mature works. The ending, in which the passagework rises to the top of the keyboard and seems about to fly off into the air, is particularly effective in performance. The piece offers pianists the advantage of sounding harder than it is—this is not to say that it is an easy piece, but the patterns lie so comfortably under the hands that the brilliant effects are achieved with physical efficiency rather than sheer effort. This is one of the earliest pieces that sounds unmistakably like MacDowell, helping to explain why the composer had such a hard time finding a publisher who would take a risk on such an unconventional and distinctive composition.

33. Draft letter, EAM to Julius Hainauer, 19 October 1883, "Business Letters," 162, EMMC box 32.
34. MM, *Random Notes on Edward MacDowell and his Music* (Boston: A. P. Schmidt, 1950), 7.

The other piece in this group that achieved early success was the *Barcarolle*, op. 18, no. 1. Teresa Carreño recalled that the composer sent her a copy of this work in manuscript, asking her professional opinion on whether he had any potential as a composer. In describing what impressed her about the *Barcarolle*, one of her favorite compositions, she noted that it had an element of individuality that was highly unusual:

> Every one with the habit of composition has tried his hand at a barcarolle. The music catalogues are crowded with the results—rococo, saccharine, banal. The form in itself is an incentive to mediocrity. It is so easy to be merely pretty and popular. But the youthful genius of MacDowell escaped this. Working with the simplest thematic material, he succeeded in being unconventional within the most conventional lines. He had an old story to tell, but he told it in his own way and in a manner to indicate that whatever he might have to say in music would be said in a way that was unmistakably his....Instinctively I felt that the boy who wrote it was destined for great things.[35]

With these two works, Hainauer had obtained the rights to a bona fide hit that would be among his biggest sellers. As MacDowell had no money to spare, he asked only for a few free copies of each piece, with no fee or royalties, in exchange for the publication rights. This is the agreement that Edward signed:

> The royal court music- and book-dealership of Herr Julius Hainauer in Breslau has obtained and acquired from me the sole legal, unlimited, and exclusive publication and distribution rights to the following musical works composed by me:
>
>> Op. 17 Zwei Fantasiestücke zum Concertgebrauch für das Pianoforte No. 1. Erzählung No. 2. Hexentanz
>> Op. 18 Zwei Stücke für das Pianoforte I. Barcarolle II. Humoreske
>> in any editions and for all countries and [all] times. It is accordingly only the
> above-named publishing house that is entitled to print, to edit, to sell, to distribute, or to allow to be sold and distributed these compositions in the original or in any arrangements; any printing, any edition, and any sales that take place without the consent of this sole authorized business are to be considered unlawful reprints.
>
> I hereby acknowledge at the same time the correct receipt of a predetermined honorarium of—[blank space]—for the above compositions, confirm all of the previous through my personal signature, and bind myself legally to the same on demand.
>
> (signed) E. A. MacDowell

Why would MacDowell sign such a contract, which would turn out to be one of the costliest mistakes of his career? He needed to prove to his parents, to his

35. Teresa Carreño, "My Interpretation of MacDowell's Barcarolle," *Delineator* 75 (January 1910): 47.

future wife, and most of all to himself that he could make a living as a musician, and getting his works in print quickly was more important at this stage than earning a fair wage for his creativity. Hainauer was able to take advantage of a young man driven to desperation by the need to prove the viability of his chosen career before he married. To his credit, Hainauer recognized the potential of these pieces that had already been rejected by several publishers. To his shame, he refused in later years to share the profits or relinquish any of the rights the young composer had naively signed away. MacDowell later admitted to Arthur P. Schmidt, his principal American publisher, that he had been crazy when he signed those early German contracts.[36] But in December 1883, what mattered most was that he could send his new publications home as Christmas presents.

Under similar contractual conditions, he arranged to have three additional opuses published by C. F. Kahnt of Leipzig: opp. 11 and 12 consisted of five songs for solo voice and piano accompaniment; op. 19 was a set of four piano works titled *Wald Idyllen* [Forest Idylls], dedicated to Marian Nevins. The publisher accepted the songs—which had limited commercial appeal—on condition that he receive some piano music to offset his losses. The composer signed away the rights to all three works in exchange for ten free copies of each. MacDowell's relations with Christian Friedrich Kahnt (1823–1897) demonstrate the insularity of the German music world at this time. Kahnt was not only a publisher, he was also editor of the *Neue Zeitschrift für Musik*, and the secretary of the ADMV. MacDowell dealt with Kahnt in all three roles.

MacDowell reported in a letter to Marian in May that he was practicing the *Wald Idyllen*, op. 19, in case he received a last-minute invitation to attend the ADMV festival in Weimar. Despite their thoroughly German title, the composer described them as "Frenchy."[37] He added that they were not easy to play, and that some of the stretches would be too much for her. This is one of the few instances when MacDowell acknowledged this aspect of his piano writing: even in the simplest pieces, he favors the open sound of the tenth, making them difficult to play for most amateur pianists.[38]

After much delay (and the payment of the final Mk. 100 of his subvention on 24 January), Breitkopf & Härtel prepared the two-piano version of the concerto, op. 15, which was released in late winter 1884. MacDowell wasted no time

---

36. Letter, EAM to Arthur P. Schmidt, 22 July 1902, EMMC.

37. Letter, "E" to "My Dearest Marian," 12 May 1884, EMMC box 31/51.

38. In 1904 he received a letter from a British pianist asking which of his pieces would be appropriate for pianists with smaller hands. Letter, Evelyn Simms to EAM, 21 April 1904, MacDowell Collection, Library of Congress Manuscript Division, Box 6.

sending copies to potential performers, as he did with all his new works. In a letter to Hainauer in February 1884, he requested that sixteen copies each of the four piano pieces, opp. 17 and 18 (sixty-four copies total), be sent to a list of persons, with the bill to be sent to him. In order to promote the performance of his works, he needed to purchase copies of the scores, for which he would receive no royalties.[39]

MacDowell pinned many of his hopes on the upcoming ADMV festival in Weimar, the epicenter of the New German school and Liszt's summer home. He sent the newly printed concerto to Riedel, Liszt, and Kahnt with the request to perform it with orchestra at the festival. Although Liszt had accepted the dedication of this work, there is no indication that he responded to MacDowell's submission for the festival; Riedel also did not reply, perhaps still piqued about MacDowell's going over his head in 1882. Kahnt wrote on 30 April that the piece could not be programmed, as they had already scheduled four symphonies and two concertos. Despite this refusal, he still wished to attend the Weimar festival. He wrote cynically to Marian, "I expect [Carl] Dierich [dedicatee of op. 11] to sing some of my songs; if he doesn't it will only be another promise broken."[40]

Throughout this frantic year of successes and disappointments, MacDowell's moods continued to vacillate. After a successful performance in November 1883 he wrote to Marian:

> My dearest girl I am just delighted and would have given anything to have you here to [sic] in time to hear my symphony. It sounded splendidly and I see everything "couleur de Rose" again. You mustn't mind dear that I am so upset and "ugly" sometimes I can't help it[;] do what I will everything seems black to me sometimes. Now however it's all "blanc Himmel" again and I would give anything for a kiss from you darling. It isn't long til next Summer and then we'll make up for lost time.[41]

Such joy would usually give way to despair. He worried when her letters were slow in coming, he worried about how things were going with his mother, and he even worried that she would change her mind and marry Walter instead.[42] Most of all, he worried about the health of Marian and his parents. On 24 January 1884 he wrote, "I hope that Papa has not been ill any more, I can't imagine why you didn't write me about it at the time. I would rather a hundred times hear of such things

39. Draft letter, EAM to Julius Hainauer, 6 February 1884, "Business Letters," 201, EMMC box 32.

40. Letter, "E" to "Dearest Marian," 5 May 1884, EMMC box 31/51.

41. Letter, "E" to "Dearest Marian," 22 November 1883, EMMC box 31/50.

42. Letter, "E" to "My Dearest Marian," 2 January 1884, EMMC box 31/51.

at once, other wise I am never <u>certain</u> about anything. You know I don't like hiding any thing of that kind."[43]

MacDowell's anxiety over sickness was intensified by yet another death of one of his close mentors. On 4 January 1884, Ehlert had attended a concert by the violinist August Wilhelmj at the Wiesbaden Curhaus. Just before the overture, he felt unwell and left the auditorium. Within minutes he was dead of a heart attack. This latest brush with mortality was compounded by a memorial concert for Raff that took place four days later. Hans von Bülow and his orchestra from Meiningen played Beethoven's funeral march and a program of Raff's composi-tions on a stage set with a bust of Raff surrounded by laurels. Edward reported to his mother that von Bülow attempted to make a speech "but looked as if he could hardly keep from crying & then put the wreaths over Raff's bust. It was very affecting." These events indeed affected him physically as well as emotionally. In the same letter, he told his mother, "I am having very much trouble…I <u>feel</u> pretty well and sleep well, but <u>look</u> as if I was going to skip into the 'silent tomb' in less than no time. I dare say a couple of pills or something will make me look all right again." He flippantly signed his letter "your affectionate luxury Edwardus (Pianist und Componist)."[44]

Though clearly discouraged, he stubbornly refused to consider moving back to the United States. He alluded in his letter of 24 January 1884 to an offer he had received in America, but he felt it was too tentative to consider, since similar offers in Germany had fallen through. He reiterated his assertion that he would not return permanently until all his opportunities in Germany had been exhausted. This dis-cussion continued through the winter and spring, as these lines from a 25 May letter to Marian indicate:

> I hope now everything is plain about my coming home. I certainly will come as soon as I find no more chance here, only, as I have said always, I don't like the idea of staying there. It will certainly knock my composition in the head. I do hope we might be able to live at least for the next few years in Germany. Besides I have kind of an idea that when I am with you things may go better, that is to say that I may have better luck. I certainly couldn't have worse. I hope at all events we will be able to get something to authorize our getting married before long.[45]

43. Letter, "Eddie" to "My dearest Marian," 24 January 1884, EMMC box 31/51.

44. Letter, "your affectionate luxury Edwardus (Pianist und Componist)" to "Mother," 10 January 1884, NYPL.

45. Letter to "My dearest Marian," 25 May 1884, EMMC box 31/51.

Despite his growing list of contacts and publications, MacDowell's discouraging words reflect a new attitude about his career. It seems likely that anxiety over his impending marriage and his first visit to the United States in eight years colored his views. At the same time, the winter of 1883/1884 marked a noticeable change in Edward's outlook. From this point on, he would approach new opportunities and successes skeptically, as if he assumed that things would not work out. His dealings with professional contacts would also reflect this newfound pessimism, exacerbating his natural introversion into an aloofness that would often be interpreted as disdain. During this long winter alone in Germany desperately trying to establish his career before his marriage, Edward MacDowell had reached his quota of disappointment and broken promises. His personality would never be quite the same.

CHAPTER SEVEN

Married Life

A FTER TYING UP LOOSE ENDS IN FRANKFURT, EDWARD SET SAIL FOR NEW YORK aboard the SS *Elbe*, arriving on 28 June 1884.[1] As he crossed the ocean, he must have had time to reflect on the past eight years and all that had transpired to bring him to this moment. He would soon be reunited with Marian after a separation of a year and a half; he would see his father and brother for the first time in eight years; and he would see his mother for the first time since her visit to Frankfurt nearly four years earlier. Marian had lived with his family for nearly a year. What sort of familiarities had they developed in his absence? He had left New York as a boy—would he be accepted as a man when he arrived?

Edward was prone to anxiety under the best of circumstances; in this situation he must have been especially anxious. Since the family was together during their month in America, we have few letters as evidence of his feelings, but one incident illustrates his state of mind at this time. Marian reported years later that he became apprehensive as she prepared to travel from New York to her family home in Waterford to finalize the wedding plans. He asked her to marry him before leaving, to which she agreed.[2] This first marriage took place before Chief Justice David

---

1. A draft letter from 14 June 1884 booking passage on the SS *Elbe* is found in "Business letters & Answers, 1884–1885," EMMC box 33. The ship arrived in the port of New York City on 28 June 1884. The list of the ship's passengers includes one "E. A. Dowell," misidentified as a thirty-seven-year-old tailor of German citizenship. *New York Passenger Lists, 1820–1957*, www.ancestry.com, accessed 5 November 2009.

2. Marian MacDowell, "Childhood [and] Early Years," 38–39, EMMC box 39; cited in Margery M. Lowens, "The New York Years of Edward MacDowell" (PhD diss., University of Michigan, 1971), 24.

McAdam of the City Court on 9 July 1884, twelve days after his arrival in New York and twelve days before their marriage in Waterford.[3] The curious incident corresponds with other reports of MacDowell's anxious nature, but it does not fully explain why he was so insistent on this extra ceremony. He may have been worried about meeting her relatives, but he may also have been a victim of other anxieties going all the way back to his childhood. Among the many rules of the Quaker Discipline was one forbidding marriage by a "hireling minister," or paid clergyman. When Edward's parents were married a generation earlier, the ceremony had been performed by a city alderman, not a minister. As curious as it seems, he—or his parents—may have been apprehensive about flaunting Quaker Discipline at the wedding in Waterford, and thus arranged for an acceptable marriage in advance, even though he was not a member of the Society of Friends and did not have to worry about disownment.

Even though they had written weekly letters to each other during his years in Europe, Edward and his family had a lot of catching up to do. Changes in their home, Walter's work in his father's business, their impressions of Marian: all these must have entered into their conversations. They were undoubtedly struck by the changes in Edward. Did they tease him about his clothing and hairstyle? Did he allow stray German words to slip into his conversation? Did he play his music for them? Did he talk of the famous people he had met? When a family member returns for a visit after a long absence, one is tangibly reminded of bygone times but also reminded of the incremental changes that have accumulated during the intervening years. Were Fanny and Thomas made aware of changes in their relationship? Did Walter resent being the son who had not traveled? Did Edward smile stiffly as Fanny reminded him yet again of the sacrifices she had made for him?

A letter from Edward to Marian dated only "Friday" (most likely 18 July) contained final details about what he would bring when he came on Sunday night before the wedding. He was worried because she had again fallen ill: "I will be anxious till I know you are alright again. I think of you all day & dreamt of you last night—Darling you can't tell how I love you and think of you every second. It'll only be a few days now. Dearest forgive these few words. If I could only say what I feel t'would have been longer. Until Monday darling; have courage."[4]

The wedding took place at 4:00 pm on Monday, 21 July 1884, in the family home at Shaw Farm in Waterford, Connecticut. According to her sister's diary entry, the house was filled with flowering plants, and the bride stood beneath an arch of

3. "A Transcript from the Record of Marriages in the City of New York," prepared 7 April 1885, NYPL.

4. Letter, "Edd" to "My dearest Marian," Friday [18 July 1884], EMMC box 31/52.

climbing ferns and white flowers. There were about sixty persons in attendance, mostly friends and family on the Nevins side. Marian's sisters Anna and Nina, along with two cousins, served as bridesmaids. Nina later recalled, "It was a charming wedding—we liked Edward and he behaved like an angel."[5]

The wedding day makes a bride look radiant, as the joyful gathering of family and friends filled with hope for the future casts everything in the best light. One wonders, though, if any of the guests were struck by the incongruity of the visual picture of the couple. Edward MacDowell was tall and strikingly handsome, with European clothes and hairstyle. Marian was not. Teresa Carreño, who could always be counted on for a frank opinion, had expressed surprise on meeting Marian that she was not more beautiful.[6] In later years Edward used the pet name "Toddles" because she still limped from her back injuries. Of all those present, the gifted portrait artist Edward would have been the most sensitive to her physical appearance, but he was deeply devoted to her, and their separation had only intensified his feelings.

Two days after the wedding, the couple sailed to England for a brief honeymoon. After visiting Exeter and Bath, they traveled to London, where the highlight was attending performances of Shakespeare.[7] This blissful time awakened Edward's creativity, and the recollections of Marian and the evidence of a sketchbook from the period allow us to re-create his creative process. They attended at least three plays: *Hamlet*, *Othello*, and *Much Ado about Nothing*, and he set about planning some two-piano works based on the characters of these plays. His initial concept for these works was segregated by gender: op. 22 was to consist of three movements "Hamlet," "Benedick," and "Othello," while op. 23 would bear the titles "Ophelia," "Beatrice," and "Desdemona." Eventually these works were realigned into three pairs, but "Hamlet" and "Ophelia" were the only two that were completed and published.[8] The sketch for the "Benedick" movement was saved by Marian and published in a facsimile edition in 1947; portions of the music were later transformed into the scherzo of the Second Concerto.[9]

The reasons for their enchantment with Shakespeare were the actors in the leading roles, Henry Irving (1838–1905) and Ellen Terry (1847–1928). Irving had opened the Lyceum Theatre in 1878 with Terry as his leading lady, inaugurating

---

5. Unsigned paper that seems to have been torn from a diary, 23 July 1884, EMMC.

6. Marian MacDowell, "Celebrated People I have Known," EMMC.

7. M. M. Lowens, "The New York Years," 24.

8. Ibid., 24–25.

9. Edward MacDowell, *Benedick: A Sketch for the Scherzo from the Second Concerto for Pianoforte*, intro. by John Erskine (New York: The Edward MacDowell Association, Inc., 1947).

a twenty-year reign as England's preeminent Shakespearean actors. Both had been successful prior to their partnership, but together they achieved a rare artistic synergy. Rumors swirled about their possible romantic attachment (he was separated from his wife and she was separated from the second of three husbands when the MacDowells saw them), which only added to the intensity of their onstage chemistry. Small wonder that Edward's creativity was inspired by their performances.

Marian also recalled these performances with pleasure. In 1937 she wrote to John Erskine, "That was in 1884, the summer we were in London, when we sold the family silver, and gorged ourselves on Irving and Ellen Terry."[10] In order to pay for their honeymoon, the impecunious couple had indeed sold the silver they had received as wedding presents. Further evidence of this is found in a drawing and note in the MacDowell Collection in the Library of Congress. On the address side of an envelope embossed with the maker's mark "C. S. Brown, Stationer &c, 196, Strand" is a pen-and-ink drawing of a squat teapot, above which Marian wrote in pencil, "Sketch made of Tea Pot we sold with the rest of the silver in London! Made with the idea of replacing, when we got rich!"[11]

Edward had written to Marian in late May, "I have kind of an idea that when I am with you things may go better, that is to say that I may have better luck," and he put this idea to the test after their return to Frankfurt. His daily record book includes a list of thirty-one cities and conductors to whom he wrote between 22 and 25 August 1884 in his quest for performing engagements. Shortly after, he learned of an opening at the Würzburg Conservatory, and he called on Frau Raff, Marmontel, and Sauret for letters to support his application.[12] These letters were not enough to win the position, however, and the response from his performance inquiries was also disappointing. MacDowell had four students, including the reliable Miss Luckie and a young man from South America named Hilario Machado, but these would hardly pay the rent for the couple.

Their financial woes led to the first serious fight of their marriage, but this argument was with his parents. During the fall there were financial problems in the McDowell home in New York, undoubtedly from the aftereffects of the milk strike. According to a letter from Marian to her sisters the following spring, Edward's parents had agreed to send them fifty dollars a month for a year but no longer. After three months, Edward and Marian realized that his parents were under extreme

10. Quoted in Erskine's introduction to *Benedick*, 4.

11. EMMC box 28. Marian also recounted this story in a letter to Nina Maud Richardson, 27 November 1930, EMMC box 53/21.

12. M. M. Lowens, "The New York Years," 25.

financial duress; they decided not to accept the allowance they had been sending and instead to begin cashing the railroad bonds she had inherited from her father.[13] Fanny and Thomas disagreed with this decision and wrote strong words to that effect in December; the issue was further complicated by the fact that the bonds were on deposit with Thomas's broker.[14] The disagreement dragged on into January 1885, causing a miserable holiday season for Edward and Marian, who had returned the December allowance check but did not receive the money from the first railroad bond until 2 January. On that day, Marian wrote to Thomas apologizing again for the misunderstanding:

> Our letter which has caused all this trouble was written entirely from a sense of duty to you, Mother & ourselves—and with but one idea, that of relieving you of all expense. We know from Mother's letters what great expenses you were having—and under the existing circumstances we spoke of in our letter, there was absolutely nothing else for us to do. However we must accept your decision, and in doing it we only repeat what we said before—that we said nothing that was meant unlovingly or undutifully, nor did we for a moment dream of or wish for any such result. It hurts us terribly that you should have so entirely misunderstood us.[15]

The realignment of family relationships is a necessary but painful part of starting a marriage, and in this case the new relationships (Thomas addressed Marian as daughter, and she addressed him as father) were strained by financial difficulties on both sides. We can only guess at what Thomas may have said in his letter to the newlyweds, but we have a much better idea of what Fanny wrote to them. In a draft letter written a week after Marian's letter to Thomas, Edward wrote to his mother in terms not duplicated in any of the surviving correspondence:

> Dear Mother,
> Though I am afraid my letter may not be a very welcome one, still I cannot refrain from writing you a few words. In fact I fear I must ask you to please discontinue speaking of me in such terms as you have in your letters to Marian, for, in the first place, my duty to her is to shield her from all such hard accusations, which, though directed against me, affect her equally, and in the second place, it is her duty to me not to listen to any such awful charges as you bring against me. Nobody, not even my own Mother, has the right to write to my

---

13. Letter, Marian MacDowell to "Dearest sisters," 21 May 1885, EMMC.

14. Letter, T. F. McDowell to Marian MacDowell, 17 December 1884, "Business letters & Answers, 1884–1885," EMMC box 33.

15. Draft letter to Mr. T. F. McDowell, 2 January 1885, "Business letters & Answers, 1884–1885," EMMC box 33.

wife that I am utterly wanting in religion, undutiful, heartless, cruel, not thankful, and that I have broken my Mother's heart and will break hers too.

Ever your son

E A MacDowell[16]

After years of chafing under his mother's controlling thumb, Edward had finally told her off. Moreover, he and Marian had declared their financial independence in the only way they could. Thomas made it clear that he did not agree with this course of action, and as a businessman, he must have felt that by spending her inheritance they were trading their future security for present comfort. The letters that passed between them as the bonds were transferred are cold and businesslike, but there is tension just beneath the surface. The story Marian told in later years was that she insisted before their marriage that Edward allow her to support him with her inheritance for several years so that he could devote himself to composition. These letters indicate a different timeline, necessitated by the deterioration of his parents' financial situation and his own inability to find paying work in Germany. This would not be the last time that Marian tidied up the details of their life story for the benefit of biographers and publicity men, but who could blame her for wanting to bury this unhappy episode in their family life?

With few students and fewer performances, Edward had time in the winter of 1884/85 to devote himself to Marian and to composition. His principal preoccupation during this time was with orchestral works. To date, his only completed orchestral composition had been the Piano Concerto, op. 15, but in the year following his marriage he began and abandoned several large-scale orchestral works, including a scene for tenor, baritone, and orchestra based on Goethe's *Faust* and an overture on *Parisina* after Byron. He also wrote a set of *Mondbilder*, op. 21 [Moon pictures] that were originally intended for orchestra but rewritten as piano duets. The "Erste Symphonie in G moll, op. 24" [First Symphony in G minor], of which only the cover survives, probably also dates from this period.[17]

Along with these abortive attempts, MacDowell completed his first large-scale orchestral work, *Hamlet and Ophelia*, op. 22. The image of Henry Irving and Ellen Terry playing the roles of the doomed lovers in London remained in his mind after his return to Frankfurt, and he completed the score during his first winter with Marian. By early November, the composer was sufficiently confident of the work's completion that he could write to Irving and Terry to request their permission

16. Draft letter to Mrs. T. F. MacDowell, 9 January 1885, "Business letters & Answers, 1884–1885," EMMC box 33.

17. The title is found on the cover of an early sketchbook now in the collection of the University of New Hampshire Library.

to dedicate the two parts of the work to them. The scores and correspondence show that he was indecisive about whether it was actually one piece or two; the letter to Irving requests permission to dedicate *Hamlet*, op. 22, to him and *Ophelia*, op. 23, to her. Upon publication by Hainauer in 1885, the title page read *Hamlet. Ophelia. Zwei gedichte für grosses orchester*, op. 22 [Hamlet. Ophelia. Two poems for large orchestra], but according to Gilman, MacDowell preferred the designation *First Symphonic Poem ("a. Hamlet"; "b. Ophelia")*, and he designated *Lancelot and Elaine*, op. 25, his "second symphonic poem."[18] Because of the expense of printing orchestral scores, he was forced to pay part of the production costs. In order to make it as marketable as possible, MacDowell requested the publication of a four-hand piano arrangement first, which was completed in June 1885, followed by orchestral parts and full score the following fall.[19] Like Breitkopf & Härtel, Hainauer had been hesitant to print the full score and orchestral parts of *Hamlet & Ophelia*, op. 22. In addition to the production costs he had paid for the two-piano score, the composer eventually paid Mk. 325.40 toward the printing of the full score and parts.[20] The availability of printed parts made it more attractive to conductors, though, and thus facilitated more performances.

The symphonic poem *Hamlet & Ophelia*, op. 22 (it is almost always performed as one unit), is relatively short at just over thirteen minutes. It clearly reflects the influence of the Liszt symphonic poems, beginning low and soft before working up to several dramatic climaxes in the course of the two movements. As Liszt often does, MacDowell concentrates more on the development of the characters than on telling a coherent narrative. The Hamlet theme is bold and assertive with effusive orchestral flourishes and much chromaticism. The Ophelia theme is languid and flowing, with diatonic harmonies that eventually give way to more fervent expression and echoes of Wagnerian harmony. The "Tristan" chord, which by this time was so well known as to be a cliché, puts in an appearance in the Ophelia movement. MacDowell hurriedly arranged to hear the score in rehearsals at the Palmengarten in Frankfurt and also with the orchestra in the resort town of Bad Homburg in order to check the accuracy of parts.

Hamlet & Ophelia received serious attention in Germany, as Hainauer took out large display ads in music journals to promote the work. The two-piano score

---

18. The publication history of this work, like so many others, is ably chronicled in O. G. Sonneck, *Catalogue of First Editions of Edward MacDowell* (Washington: Government Printing Office, 1917), 18–19.

19. Draft letters from EAM to Julius Hainauer, 9 April 1885 and 16 April 1885, "Business letters & Answers, 1884–1885," EMMC box 33.

20. Letter and bill from Julius Hainauer, 26 March 1886, EMMC box 30.

received a brief notice in the *Neue Berliner Musikzeitung* shortly after its publication, while the full score was given a much longer and more thoughtful review in the *Musikalisches Wochenblatt* in 1890.[21] More importantly, the work was played by orchestras in Sondershausen, Wiesbaden, and Berlin within a year of the publication of the orchestral score.

Though his primary attention went into orchestral music during the first year of his marriage, he continued to produce piano works as well, and he was becoming more adept at arranging for their prompt publication. In October 1884 he offered two sets of piano duets, opp. 20 and 21, to Hainauer, and within two months they were in print. This rapid turnaround, which was more characteristic of Hainauer than the other publishers, could lead to errors and left little time for corrections. The first proof copy of *Mondbilder*, op. 21, had the title of the first number as "Kindermädchen" [nursemaid] rather than "Hindumädchen" [Hindu girl]. In addition, the publisher's inattention to detail had caused the envelope to be misaddressed, and MacDowell did not receive the proofs of *Drei Poesien*, op. 20, in a timely manner. This edition gave rise to another last-minute change, when he sent an urgent request to alter the dedication from "Frl. H. O. Luckie" to "Frl. S. L. Pettee."[22]

The dedications of MacDowell's publications fall into two general categories. On the one hand are dedications to persons who had been or could be professionally useful to him: Franz Liszt (op. 15), Camille Saint-Saëns (op. 14), Carl Dierich (op. 11), Emilio Agramonte (op. 26), and Hans Huber (opp. 16, 17), for instance. On the other hand are purely personal dedications: Frau Doris Raff (op. 10), Marian Nevins (op. 19), Frl. S. L. Pettee (op. 20), Frl. L. E. Nevins (op. 21), Mrs. James Bischoff (op. 12), and Templeton Strong (op. 25). A few of MacDowell's dedications fit both categories, for instance, those to Marmontel (op. 13), Carreño (op. 23), and Desvernine (op. 18). Nearly all of his early works carry dedications, but the practice became increasingly rare in his later works, especially after his move to the United States in 1888. Significantly, among the dozens of persons honored with dedications is not one member of his own family.

As MacDowell struggled to find publishers for his works and performers willing to present them in Germany, he began to hear reports from America of performances there. Among the first to program his works was his old friend Teresa Carreño, who had played a movement from the *Erste moderne Suite* in Saratoga on 4 August 1883 and the entire *Zweite moderne Suite* in Chicago on 8 March 1884 and

---

21. "Recensionen," *Neue Berliner Musikzeitung* 40/7 (18 February 1886):49; Georg Riemenschneider, *Musikalisches Wochenblatt* 21/1 (26 December 1889): 3.

22. Draft letters from E. A. MacDowell to Julius Hainauer, 26 November 1884 and 2 December 1884, "Business letters & Answers, 1884–1885," EMMC box 33.

in Detroit shortly after.[23] Carreño played his music regularly on her concert tour in spring 1885, introducing it to audiences in smaller towns throughout the eastern United States. Her performances of the *Zweite moderne Suite* in New York on 16 March 1885 and *Hexentanz* at the Worcester Festival and in New York in September 1885 were important milestones in his US reception.[24]

MacDowell probably was not aware of it yet, but his compositions were benefiting from a trend in the United States that would gain momentum over the next decade. Many American composers felt that their works had not received the respect they deserved in their native country, in part because of prejudice against American musicians but also because of inequities in the US Copyright Law. At this time, only American composers could obtain copyrights for their work in the United States. This law was designed to protect American authors, but it inadvertently provided an incentive to publishers to favor foreign composers, whose works could be printed and distributed in the United States without paying royalties. Beginning in July 1884, when the pianist Calixa Lavallée played an entire program of American works at the MTNA convention in Cleveland, there was a groundswell of support for American composers that led to hundreds of all-American concerts and the inclusion of more American works in mixed concerts as well. MacDowell's compositions began appearing in print just as concert organizations were searching for new American music to meet the demand for American Composers' Concerts, allowing his music to find an audience while he still lived in Europe.[25]

The most influential of the American Composers' Concerts during this era were large-scale orchestral concerts. It was relatively easy to find an audience for one's solo piano works or songs with piano accompaniment, especially with a friend like Teresa Carreño. Achieving a performance of a symphony or a concerto was a different matter altogether, because of the cost involved in such a concert and the small number of American orchestras. MacDowell reported to Breitkopf & Härtel on 13 November 1884 that no fewer than three American conductors were interested in programming his concerto.[26] One of these, a young Texan by the name of Frank Van der Stucken, presented the American premiere of the work on 31 March 1885.

---

23. M. M. Lowens, "The New York Years," 21–22.

24. The most thorough discussion of Carreño's patronage of MacDowell is Laura Pita, "Presencia de la Obra de Edward MacDowell en el Repertorio de Teresa Carreño" (master's thesis, Universidad Central de Venezuela, 1999).

25. For a discussion of American Composers' Concerts in this era, see E. Douglas Bomberger, *"A Tidal Wave of Encouragement": American Composers' Concerts in the Gilded Age* (Westport, CT: Praeger, 2002).

26. Draft letter, EAM to B&H, 13 November 1884, "Business letters & Answers, 1884–1885," EMMC box 33.

Frank Van der Stucken (1858–1929) was born in the German-speaking enclave of Fredericksburg, Texas, to a Belgian father and a German mother. He had been taken as a child to Belgium, where he studied with Pierre Benoit. He later pursued advanced studies with Carl Reinecke in Leipzig and eventually won a position as conductor of the Breslau municipal theater from 1881 to 1882. His reputation and talent were such that Franz Liszt helped arrange a concert of his works with the Weimar court orchestra and chorus in 1883. Although he was a gifted composer, his chief contribution to American musical life would be as a conductor. His long and varied career was the most successful by a native-born American conductor before the appearance of Leonard Bernstein. Van der Stucken settled in New York in 1884, succeeding Leopold Damrosch as conductor of the German singing society Arion. During the 1884/1885 concert season, he presented four "Novelty Concerts" that introduced new orchestral works by Grieg, Chabrier, Dvořák, Tchaikovsky, and others, a risky venture that could only have succeeded with generous backing from the Arion Society members.

The final concert of the series on 31 March 1885 was by far the riskiest, as Van der Stucken devoted an entire evening to works by American composers. This event took the American Composers' Concert movement from the relatively safe territory of piano and vocal concerts into large-scale orchestral concerts. The reviewers of this first all-American orchestral concert applauded the auspicious event, but most were wary of the music itself because there was so much that was new. The Prelude to *Oedipus Tyrannus* by the Harvard professor John Knowles Paine was considered by most critics to be the strongest work, although there was also significant interest in the symphonic poem *Undine* by Templeton Strong. The second and third movements of MacDowell's *Concerto in A minor*, op. 15, with the solo part played by the pianist Adele Margulies, appeared second on the program.

MacDowell was thrilled to have his work performed with orchestra in New York, but in a draft letter to Van der Stucken dated 19 April he expressed surprise that the score and parts had been sent by Breitkopf & Härtel in manuscript form. He stated that he had assumed the scores would be lithographically reproduced in the manner of Wagner's *Lohengrin* score, which had introduced an innovative technology using transfer paper to speed the process of preparing the printing plates. More than a year after the publication of his concerto at great personal expense, he finally realized that he had been duped by the publisher.

MacDowell's ongoing correspondence with Breitkopf & Härtel illustrates the difficulty of an expatriate composer attempting to do business in a foreign language. Before leaving for home the previous spring, he had requested a royalty statement for the second time, but again he had received no answer. In November he had written to confirm that the parts and full score to his concerto would be published, to which they had promptly replied that they would be included in their catalog and sent in manuscript copy (Abschrift) from their stock (auf Lager führen). MacDowell had still not fully grasped that their understanding of this ambiguous phrase was different from his understanding. He assumed that even if the parts and full score were not engraved they would be lithographically reproduced rather than copied by hand for each order. The issue was not just an aesthetic one but rather a matter of the accuracy of the parts, which could be compromised every time they were recopied. He finally seems to have realized his error when the parts were sent to New York for the Novelty Concert, and on 15 March he sent Breitkopf & Härtel a blistering letter accusing the publisher of contract violations both for neglecting to send an annual statement and for failing to print the score and parts.

It is difficult not to read a certain smugness in the publisher's reply: "What we already wrote to you earlier, that the score and parts of your A-minor Concerto will be retained in stock to be copied [abschriftlich vorräthig gehalten werden] is still true today. Of course with such works only a few copies, sometimes just one or two, can be set aside, since the publisher has to reckon with the fact that the demand for such is very modest. As long as the original is available, copies can be prepared at any time."[27] MacDowell had misunderstood the meaning of the German terms, and he had been giving his English-speaking contacts incorrect information on the basis of his misunderstanding. Regarding the royalty statements, they noted that it was too early to give returns for the concerto, but they enclosed statements for the two suites. They denied any wrongdoing but said that they didn't want to set up a royalty account for him, since there had not been any actual profit yet. They commented, "As you will see, the sales were in general very encouraging, so that probably in this year they will produce a net profit."[28] The enclosed royalty statements show that the publisher had printed 250 copies of each suite, had sent ten copies of each suite to editors, and had sold ninety-one copies of op. 10 and eighty-four copies of op. 14. The reason for the lack of net profit was that the earnings from sales were being applied to the publisher's half of the production costs, meaning that MacDowell still had not earned a cent. In the summer of 1885 he would finally receive a check for Mk. 37.15, while 1886 would bring Mk. 92.22, and 1887 would bring Mk. 84.21. Whenever he complained, as he did in the summer of 1886, the publisher promptly explained that he had miscalculated or misunderstood. The composer was learning a hard lesson about the economics of publishing.

The money that he received from Breitkopf & Härtel was next to nothing, but clearly someone recognized the sales potential of his music. In the spring of 1885 MacDowell learned of an illegal reprint of the "Praeludium" from the *Erste moderne*

27. Letter, B&H to EAM, 17 March 1885, EMMC box 30/14.
28. Ibid.

Suite, op. 10, by J. O. Prochazka of New York. He purchased copies himself and then informed Breitkopf & Härtel so that they could prosecute the matter, thereby protecting his publisher's income while compounding his own losses. Prochazka proposed publishing some of MacDowell's future works, but the composer refused to have anything to do with him.

With performing opportunities scarce, and earnings from his growing list of publications so negligible, the MacDowells were pleased when an opportunity for a teaching position in Scotland became available. The pay at German schools like the Darmstadt Conservatory was barely a living wage. As Marian explained to her sisters: "In Germany the good ones (so far as salary goes) are very rare—He has had two or three chances for places where they only pay something like five or six hundred dollars—which is really the average sum, but that is for very much work, and would take up all most all his time, and he would have little left for his Composition which is of course very important."[29] Lindsay Deas, a British classmate of MacDowell's from the Hoch Conservatory, died late in the spring of 1885, leaving vacant his position as Edinburgh examiner for the Royal Academy of Music. The family nominated MacDowell for the position, and he and Marian spent several weeks in England during June in an attempt to secure the position. According to Gilman, his candidacy was sabotaged by Lady Macfarren, who objected to his connections with Liszt and the New German School.[30] A draft letter to Mrs. Deas, however, indicates that he was also concerned about the number of students and the conditions of the appointment.[31] Teresa Carreño urged him to keep up his courage: "I am very sorry that you should have been brought to London to meet with a disappointment, but do not loose [sic] courage. We all have to go through all these 'nasty' drawbacks until we find a little good wind and sail on clearly and brightly, as I know you will."[32]

The couple had already adopted a pattern of frequent moves, which Edward had witnessed in his parents and which would characterize their life together. In the fall of 1884 they had started out in a very small apartment on Praunheimer Strasse in Frankfurt, but they had moved to more comfortable quarters in the Hotel du Nord after they began cashing Marian's inheritance. They placed all their things in storage during the summer in England, and then they settled in Wiesbaden in the fall of 1885. The relocation from Frankfurt to Wiesbaden took them from a bustling

29. Letter, MM to "Dearest sisters," 21 May 1885, EMMC.

30. Lawrence Gilman, *Edward MacDowell: A Study* (New York: John Lane, 1908), 24–25.

31. Draft letter from EAM to Mrs. Deas, 16 June 1885, "Business letters & Answers, 1884–1885," EMMC box 33.

32. Letter, "Your old 'granny' Teresita" to "Eddie," 18 August 1885, EMMC box 30/22.

metropolis back to the resort town known for its hot-water baths. The spa attracted many tourists, including a large contingent of British and American expatriates. Central to the city's cultural life was the Curhaus, whose giant neo-Classical façade welcomed guests who came to enjoy concerts in the auditorium as well as other diversions in the casino. An orchestra played regular concerts there, and guest artists put in frequent appearances in the comfortable town. The MacDowells lived initially in the Pension Quisisana at 3 Parkstrasse, a wooded street in close proximity to the Curhaus.

One of the attractions of Wiesbaden was the opportunity to be close to the James Bischoff family, whom Edward had known since his arrival in Germany six years earlier. Mrs. Bischoff had been a close friend of Carreño in the 1870s, which allowed Fanny to make contact with the wealthy woman while she still lived in England and to arrange for her son to move to Wiesbaden after the Stuttgart plans fell through. The two songs, op. 12, were dedicated to Mrs. Bischoff when they were published in February 1884, and in late November of that year, he requested an "extra-schön Titel" (extra-pretty title page) to be prepared at his own expense as a Christmas present for Mrs. Bischoff.[33] Clearly she and her husband were persons that MacDowell valued. On 4 September 1885, he wrote to inform them of the impending relocation to Wiesbaden.[34]

Before long, though, Edward and Marian found themselves in the middle of a conflict with Mrs. Bischoff. In 1876, after caring for Carreño's daughter Emilita for several years, Mrs. Bischoff had proposed to adopt the child, on condition that Carreño relinquish all rights to contact her in the future. The pianist reluctantly signed the agreement in the interest of her daughter's security and kept her promise to stay away from the Bischoffs.[35] But Edward was in touch with Carreño, and he received at least two letters from her during the fall of 1885.[36] After sharing his own

33. Draft letter from EAM to C. F. Kahnt, 30 November 1884 and postcard from C. F. Kahnt to MacDowell, 9 December 1884, "Business letters & Answers, 1884–1885," EMMC box 33.

34. Draft letter from EAM to Mrs. Bischoff, 4 September 1885, "Business letters & Answers, 1884–1885," EMMC box 33.

35. For an account of the agreement and Carreño's attempts to reestablish contact with her daughter in later years, see Marta Milinowski, *Teresa CarreñNewo "by the grace of God"* (New Haven: Yale University Press, 1940; repr. New York: Da Capo, 1977), 116–17, 198–200, 343–44.

36. A letter of 18 August is in the EMMC box 30/22; a letter of 23 November is in the MacDowell Collection, Library of Congress Manuscript Division, box 6; in a draft letter to Mrs. Bischoff of 15 December, "Business letters & Answers, 1884–1885," EMMC box 33, he offers to let her see a letter he received from Carreño in Venezuela, which may be the letter of 23 November or a different one.

family problems during a long private talk with Mrs. Bischoff on 14 December, he begged her not to speak about them to anyone. The following week, he and Marian declined an invitation to spend Christmas with the Bischoffs, explaining, "I hope you will not be angry at our excusing ourselves for Christmas day. Under the circumstances we think it best. You would surely not miss us—and we would infinitely prefer coming at some future time when we would be surer that your suspicions about us in connection with Teresita had entirely vanished. Our presence on that day would only remind you of very disagreeable things."[37] Once again, Edward had broken off a friendship at the darkest time of the year, and there is no evidence that he renewed it afterward.

During the winter of 1885/86, MacDowell began a correspondence with Carl V. Lachmund (1857–1928), an American pianist whom he had first met in 1882 during his visit to Weimar. Lachmund and his wife, Carrie, a harpist, had lived in Weimar from 1882 to 1884, during which time they became close to Liszt. Carrie's letters about their experiences were published in Chicago newspapers, and Lachmund's extensive diary is a valuable eyewitness account of the Weimar masterclasses.[38] Liszt provided him with a letter of reference when he moved to Minneapolis in 1885, an honor that he rarely bestowed on his students. MacDowell and Lachmund exchanged letters starting in October 1885, and Edward enclosed copies of German musical papers to help his friend stay up to date. On 29 May 1886, he sent Lachmund an extensive biographical sketch and list of publications that formed the basis of an article published in the 6 November issue of the *American Art Journal*.[39] The friendship with Lachmund, like his earlier relationship with Huss as a teenager, was easier because of the ocean that separated them. By nature a shy, reserved person, Edward found it uncomfortable to maintain close friendships; a "pen-pal" relationship was less threatening. MacDowell had much to report to Lachmund, as that winter had brought some notable successes and had also given him time to produce several new compositions. The list prepared for Lachmund includes three orchestral works in manuscript: a Second Piano Concerto, op. 23, a Roland Symphonie for large orchestra, and *Lancelot & Elaine* for large orchestra. In summarizing his recent career for the biographical article, he frankly admitted, "I have had no trouble to find

37. Draft letter, EAM to Mrs. Bischoff, 23 December 1885, "Business letters & Answers, 1884–1885," EMMC box 33.

38. Carl V. Lachmund, *Living with Liszt: from the Diary of Carl Lachmund, An American pupil of Liszt, 1882–1884*, ed., annot., and intro. by Alan Walker, Franz Liszt Studies Series No. 4 (Stuyvesant, NY: Pendragon Press, 1994).

39. Carl V. Lachmund, "E. A. MacDowell and other Americans in Europe," *American Art Journal* 46/3 (6 November 1886): 37.

publishers willing to accept my things, however the little success I have had with my compositions has caused me to neglect my piano playing."[40]

In December 1885 MacDowell began investigating the possibility of having their remaining possessions shipped from New York to Wiesbaden. Ostensibly, this was a cost-saving move, as their accommodations in a furnished *Pension* were more expensive than an unfurnished apartment. At the same time, it reflected the ongoing tension with his parents, who were not only storing their furniture and other things but were also serving as custodians of Marian's railroad bonds. After six months of correspondence, Edward wrote to his father in May 1886 that arrangements for shipping had been finalized: "I herewith acknowledge receipt of £. 102/10 which you sent my wife in payment of debt and will see that our bonds and other belongings are removed from your keeping at the earliest opportunity."[41] Later that summer, professional movers packed up Edward and Marian's things in the McDowell home in New York, and Thomas transferred eight $1,000 bonds to a London bank for the young couple.

Edward and Marian made their third visit to London in as many years during the summer of 1886. While there, they met Marian's sisters Anna and Nina, who would be joining them in Wiesbaden in September for an extended stay. Anna wrote to her cousins in America that Marian had not been sick once since her marriage two years ago. She reported that the MacDowells were trying very hard to live within their means, adding, "The more we see of Edward, the more impressed we are with his fine qualities and are perfectly sure of his deep affection for Marian."[42] The following winter in Wiesbaden they would have the opportunity to learn to know him much better and also to care for Marian during the first major health crisis of their marriage.

40. Letter, EAM to Carl V. Lachmund, 29 May 1886, NYPL; the draft of this letter is found in "Business letters & Answers, 1884–1885," EMMC box 33.

41. Draft letter, E. A. MacDowell to T. F. McDowell [*sic*], 26 May 1886, "Business letters & Answers, 1884–1885," EMMC box 33.

42. Two letters from Anna L. Nevins to "Dear cousins," one undated but written either 17 or 18 June 1886, the other dated 21 June 1886, EMMC box 60.

CHAPTER EIGHT

Templeton Strong, Loyal Friend

VEN THE MOST HAPPILY MARRIED MAN NEEDS MALE COMPANIONSHIP. AS EDWARD and Marian were establishing their home, he may not have realized that anything was missing. But at the most opportune time, he forged a close personal bond with a fellow American composer that would last for the rest of his life.

MacDowell was painfully shy, making it difficult for him to become friends with strangers. Upon returning to their rooms in the Parkstrasse one day in spring 1886, the MacDowells found a small and neatly printed visiting card inscribed with the name of Templeton Strong Jr. Such cards were highly fashionable, signifying the user as a stylish young man who would not be agreeable to Edward. When the visitor returned, Edward treated him coolly because of his preconceptions about the sort of person who would leave such a card. The meeting was awkward, for Strong was also shy, and it took the intervention of Marian to help them realize that they were compatible. When the ice was broken, they discovered they had much in common and that each had been urged for some time to make the acquaintance of the other.[1]

George Templeton Strong Jr. (1856–1948), four and one-half years older than MacDowell, had grown up in a completely different world only a few blocks from the childhood home of his new friend. Strong's father was a prominent Manhattan lawyer who was also an avid music lover. He used his sizable fortune and personal influence to support cultural and educational organizations in the city, serving as trustee of Columbia College and Trinity Church Wall Street as well as president

---

1. TS, "Edward MacDowell as I Knew Him," *Music Student* 7/12 (August 1915): 240.

of the New York Church Music Society and (for four years) of the New York Philharmonic Society. His private life was devoted to music, as verified in his voluminous diary of concert attendance and home music making. He insisted that his children learn to play musical instruments and share his love of classical music.[2]

G. T. Strong Sr. recognized early that his son "Temple" had unusual gifts for music, and he watched with pride as he mastered the oboe and played chamber music with friends. The father disapproved of his son's rebellious teenage behavior, though, and in punishment for some undisclosed offense, the young man was locked out of the family home near the end of his eighteenth year. Strong Sr. died three months later, before the two could reconcile, and Strong Jr. never followed his father's path into the law firm, choosing instead to work as an orchestral musician in New York before leaving to spend most of his life in Europe. He studied music in Leipzig from 1879 to 1886, but he and his wife grew tired of the flat, gray countryside surrounding Leipzig, and in the spring of 1886 decided to relocate to Wiesbaden in search of more attractive scenery and a more healthful climate.

The comparative paths of the two men reflect the vagaries of American social mobility. Strong was born to a life of privilege but had walked away from it to follow his dream. MacDowell was born in modest surroundings with a mother who pushed him to better his station in life. Despite their differences, they shared a New York childhood, a European youth, and a commitment to the New German aesthetic of Liszt and Wagner. Most importantly, they knew what it meant to be outsiders.[3] The two were unusually sympathetic, both in personality and musical views. They enjoyed making puns, drinking beer, hiking, and talking about a broad range of serious and trivial topics. Regarding their musical discussions, Strong reported that since they agreed on practically every aesthetic question, there were no debates and little technical discussion. For MacDowell, who had been disappointed so many times by broken promises and fickle professional friendships, this newfound intimacy and trust would be a source of stability and reassurance in the years ahead.

Marian described their daily routine in Wiesbaden: "MacDowell looked up to Strong with great admiration for his talent. Every day they met—either to take long

2. Three volumes of excerpts from these diaries have been published as *Strong on Music: The New York Music Scene in the Days of George Templeton Strong, 1836–1862*, 3 vols., ed. Vera Brodsky Lawrence (Chicago: University of Chicago Press, 1988–1999).

3. Strong's life is chronicled in William C. Loring, Jr., *An American Romantic-Realist Abroad: Templeton Strong and his Music*, Composers of North America, No. 4 (Lanham, MD: Scarecrow, 1996). Strong recalled his early friendship with MacDowell in TS, "Edward MacDowell as I Knew Him," *Music Student* 7/12 (August 1915): 239–42. The essay was published in twelve installments during the following year.

walks or to come to me for afternoon tea and some American form of cooking—they were particularly fond of little light buscuits [*sic*] with jelly or jam—American cookies & cake—for I had learned to be a really good cook. Strong was very lovable and delightful as a companion."[4] Since boyhood, MacDowell's friendships with other men his own age—Chichi, Huss, Abel, Lachmund—had all been relatively short-lived. Here at last was a close friend who was also loyal, providing a stability that Edward had been missing.

MacDowell quickly came to rely on Strong not only as a friend and artistic confidant but also as something of an errand boy. One of the curious things about their relationship is that MacDowell asked Strong to do all sorts of menial tasks for him, to which the latter raised no objections. Already in the summer of 1886, when they had recently met, MacDowell wrote from London to ask Strong to dispose of some items that he had left in the Pension Quisisana, and later to place ads in the papers for him and to make a hotel reservation in advance of their arrival. Upon returning from an extended trip in 1887, Marian's sister Anna reported to her cousins, "We reached Wiesbaden Saturday night. Edward and Mr. Strong met us at the Station and we were delighted to see them. Mr. Strong appears to belong to the family, and carried our wraps meekly up to the house, and assisted at our cup of afternoon tea."[5]

Edward no doubt felt the need of Strong's companionship in the fall of 1886, when Marian's two sisters arrived to share their spacious new apartment in the Jahnstrasse. Anna and Cornelia (Nina) Nevins had spent the previous winter in France and the summer in England. They stayed in Wiesbaden from 12 September 1886 to 14 January 1887, at which point they left to travel in Switzerland and Italy. They spent their time practicing piano and studying German with the help of the MacDowells. Their letters to their cousins back home give a good sense of what they were doing and also of their impressions of the married couple. Anna reported that she and Nina had vigorous debates about music with Edward, stating "he ruthlessly slaughters Beethoven's reputation, and proves to us that he was an imperfect artist, and that most of his music is poor stuff—Is not that a hard doctrine? We go every week to concerts at the Curhaus and are told pityingly what to admire and what not."[6] The sisters did their best to defend the Classic school but with little success against their opinionated brother-in-law.

Almost as soon as her sisters arrived, Marian fell ill. On 7 October, her sister reported that she had dressed for the first time in six weeks. The illness may have

4. MM, "Celebrated People I Have Known," manuscript, EMMC box 39/5.
5. Letter, Anna Nevins to "Dear cousins," 6 May 1887, EMMC box 60/17.
6. Letter, Anna Nevins to Judith, 2 December 1886, EMMC box 60/17.

been appendicitis, as a letter of 11 October seems to indicate: "the doctor said if it had not been taken in time it might have developed into Peritonitis."[7] By Thanksgiving the family was able to prepare a real American feast, and Edward ate so much that he "needed a great deal of mineral water to enliven him."[8] Nina mentioned in this same letter that he had been feeling discouraged about his lack of success but was cheered by some clippings the cousins had sent about performances in the United States.

The new apartment had five rooms plus a kitchen and maid's room. Anna noted that they had sent everything Marian owned from America, which filled the apartment. They were very comfortable, and Edward finally had a music room that was conducive to work: "The music room at present contains a grand piano, big table and two chairs, cool parquet floor, two pretty rugs, and one or two nice pictures, and a pretty screen hiding the stove in the corner. That is where Edward works five or six hours in the day at the table by the piano, with his pen and paper, getting up every now and then to strike a few chords that sound cheerful and soothing to us as we are busy in the other part of the house."[9] Strong confirmed that his daily routine went something like this: "He was not a very early riser, generally breakfasting at 8 a.m., and thereafter working until mid-day, when he dined; then he continued working until nearly 4 p.m., when we would meet either at his house or at mine, or somewhere between the two. His evenings were usually spent in reading."[10]

The project that Edward was working on was a new symphonic poem titled *Lancelot and Elaine*, op. 25. The work was inspired by Tennyson's *Idylls of the King*, of which Strong owned a first edition with engravings by Gustave Doré.[11] This orchestral composition took the better part of fall 1886 to complete. By early October, Marian was enlisted to help him complete the project, as she reported to her cousins: "I am very busy just now helping Eddie copy the Orchestral parts of his Elaine—My share is about one hundred and twenty pages."[12]

The genesis of this major work illustrates the commitment required in writing an orchestral composition. Not only is it much more time-consuming to write and copy than a piano piece or song, but the expenses of publishing and performing the work make its chances of success much smaller. Edward

7. Letters, 7 October 1886 and 11 October 1886, EMMC box 60/17.

8. Letter, Nina Nevins to Cousins, 28 November 1886, EMMC box 60/19.

9. Letter, Anna Nevins to Cousins, 13 September 1886, EMMC box 60/17.

10. TS, "Edward MacDowell as I Knew Him, third paper," *Music Student* 8/2 (October 1915): 29.

11. TS, "Edward MacDowell as I Knew Him, fifth paper," *Music Student* 8/4 (December 1915): 81.

12. Letter, MM to Cousins, 10 December [1886], EMMC box 51/1.

knew before he started the piece that it would be a challenge to find a publisher. He knew that it was not likely to receive many performances nor would he recoup his investment of time or money; the sole reason to write it was to enhance his reputation as a serious composer. After much effort and a subvention of $100 supplied by Marian's cousins, MacDowell saw the work published by Hainauer in 1888. He later came to regret some of the choices he made in the work, noting on his copy that it was "too full of horns."[13] This work, his most ambitious of 1886 and one that reflected the aesthetics of Liszt, was dedicated to his friend Templeton Strong.

His first symphonic poem, *Hamlet and Ophelia*, op. 22, was performed at the Curhaus in Wiesbaden on 26 December 1886. The MacDowells and the Nevins sisters had celebrated Christmas with inexpensive gifts: Marian gave linen and lace, while Edward gave a photograph of a scene from the Nibelungen Lied and some of Heine's songs. On the morning of 26 December, a Sunday, the conductor Louis Lüstner visited him in advance of the performance. In Marian's words, "The Capellmeister here saw Eddie this morning and gave him such warm kind praise—perhaps the best praise was that the Orchestra itself liked it very much—They are so hard to please."[14] That afternoon they attended the Curhaus performance that included his symphonic poem. Orchestral musicians are among the most disciplined of professionals, but the day after a holiday is perhaps not the most opportune time for them. There may have been a few *Katzenjammer* (hangovers) among the players, for Edward was in despair afterward about the poor performance. It cannot have helped that because of the 4:00 p.m. start time, he entered the Curhaus in the light and left in darkness. The work had been played a week earlier in Baden-Baden, and he had hopes for performances in Frankfurt and Berlin as well, but an inadequate performance at the darkest time of year only fed his discouragement about the reception of his works in Germany.

Deepening his gloom about his prospects was the death of Franz Liszt on 31 July 1886. With this latest loss, MacDowell felt that his allies in the German musical establishment were disappearing too fast to be replaced. Heymann had resigned from the Hoch Conservatory because of mental illness in 1880; Raff had died in 1882; Ehlert had died in 1884, and now Liszt passed away in the summer of 1886. Even though the latter had not helped him as much in recent years as he had during his early career, MacDowell could not help feeling that this was an important loss.

As MacDowell struggled with few signs of encouragement, his reputation was growing in the United States. Lachmund's promised biographical article, for which

---

13. Oscar George Theodore Sonneck, *Catalogue of First Editions of Edward MacDowell* (Washington: Government Printing Office, 1917), 21.

14. Letter, MM to Cousins, 26 December [1886], EMMC box 51/1.

he had sent information in May, finally appeared in the 6 November 1886 issue of the *American Art Journal*. The article mentioned four expatriate composers— Arthur Bird, W. Dayas, Strong, and MacDowell—but it was devoted almost entirely to accolades for MacDowell. In summarizing his compositional style, Lachmund wrote, "MacDowell's compositions show him the possessor of genuine feeling and spontaneous ideas, combined with deep and clear thought, also as being thoroughly familiar with musical form and orchestral devices, such familiarity being, no doubt the result of careful study of the great masters of the classic, romantic and modern schools. He shows a special tendency toward the last-named both in thought and development."[15]

Performances were more important than publicity, though, and these also began to snowball. Frank Van der Stucken played *Ophelia* in New York on 4 November 1886, earning praise from the influential critics Henry E. Krehbiel of the *Tribune* and Henry T. Finck of the *Evening Post*.[16] MacDowell's most faithful advocate continued to be Teresa Carreño, who toured her homeland of Venezuela in 1885–1886 for the first time since leaving the country in 1862. Here she introduced MacDowell's music on several concerts. On her North American tour of the following year, she continued to feature his works.[17] Looking for a suitable way to acknowledge her support, he toyed with the idea of dedicating to her the *Vier Stücke*, op. 24, published in 1887 by Hainauer. These four works—"Humoreske," "Marsch," "Wiegenlied," and "Csardas"—were short, appealing pieces that became staples of her repertoire, but in the end they were published without dedication. Edward had other plans for a more worthy piece to bear her dedication, a concerto that he would turn to later in 1887.

At about this time, Edward made a curious decision: he changed the year of his birth. MacDowell's birth in New York on 18 December 1860 was recorded in the register of births now housed in the Municipal Archives and Records Center of New York City, but the child's sex was incorrectly given as female, and no name was recorded.[18] His mother Fanny entered the correct date of birth into a family Bible some time later.[19] A photo now in the Library of Congress (Plate 1) is

15. Carl V. Lachmund, "E. A. MacDowell and other Americans in Europe," *American Art Journal* 46/3 (6 November 1886): 37.

16. Margery M. Lowens, "The New York Years of Edward MacDowell" (PhD diss., University of Michigan, 1971), 33. H. E. Krehbiel, *Review of the New York Musical Season 1886–87* (New York: Novello, Ewer & Co., 1887), 16–17.

17. Laura Pita, "Presencia de la Obra de Edward MacDowell," 43–48.

18. The discovery of this entry in 1972 is detailed in Arnold T. Schwab, "Edward MacDowell's Birthdate: A Correction," *MQ* 61/2 (April 1975): 234–35.

19. A transcription of the entry by her grandson is described in ibid., 234.

labeled "For Grandmother. Eddie Alex. McDowell (3½ years old) July 18th 1864 born Dec. 18, 1860."[20] The 1870 census, enumerated on 30 June 1870, listed his age as nine, which was correct.[21] The 1880 census, enumerated on 8 June 1880, listed his age as nineteen.[22] His birthdate was also correctly recorded in the admission rolls [Contrôle des Élèves] of the Paris Conservatory when he was admitted in 1877. The composer clearly knew this to be his correct birthdate, as he gave it to Lachmund for the *American Art Journal* article in 1886. Both the draft of his letter to Lachmund in his letter book and the actual letter preserved in the Lachmund Collection of the New York Public Library contain the correct date.[23] At about the same time, he supplied biographical information, including the correct year of birth, for the third edition of Hugo Riemann's *Musik-Lexicon*, which bears the publication date of 1887.[24]

Curiously, though, on 7 January 1888, MacDowell listed his date of birth as "18. Dec. 1861" when he wrote to J. D. Champlin Jr. with answers to biographical questions for an upcoming reference book.[25] The book took several years to appear in print, so the first known appearance of the incorrect date was in James Huneker's article in the 10 April 1889 issue of the *Musical Courier*, for which the author wrote to MacDowell requesting biographical information on 3 April 1889.[26] For the rest of his life, the composer allowed the incorrect birthdate to be perpetuated, until it gained the authority of repetition. In the fourth edition of *Riemann's Musik-Lexicon*, published in 1894, the date was changed to 1861.[27] This was the date in every

20. EMMC box 37/6.

21. In the entry for the 8th District, 18th Ward, 53, the enumerator incorrectly listed the family name as "McDonnell." Reproduced on www.ancestry.com, accessed 7 February 2010.

22. Supervisor's District 1, Enumerator's District 70, p. 32, reproduced on www.ancestry.com, accessed 7 February 2010.

23. Letter, EAM to Carl V. Lachmund, 29 May 1886, NYPL; the draft of this letter is found in "Business letters & Answers, 1884–1885," EMMC box 33.

24. Hugo Riemann, *Musik-Lexicon*, 3rd ed. (Leipzig: Max Hesse's Verlag, 1887), 582. The letter to Lachmund states that he supplied the information to Riemann shortly before sending it to Lachmund.

25. Letterpress copy, EAM to J. D. Champlin Jr., 7 January 1888, EMMC box 29/4. *Cyclopedia of music and musicians*, 3 vols., ed. John Denison Champlin and William Foster Apthorp (New York: Charles Scribner's Sons, 1888–1890).

26. Letter, James G. Huneker to EAM, 3 April 1889, EMMC box 30/61. "Personals: E. A. MacDowell," *MC* 18/15 (10 April 1889): 284.

27. Hugo Riemann, *Musik-Lexicon*, vierte vollständig umgearbeitete Auflage [4th fully rev. ed.] (Leipzig: Max Hesse's Verlag, 1894), 638.

dictionary of music until Margery Lowens's entry in the 1980 *New Grove Dictionary of Music and Musicians.*[28]

Why did MacDowell give false information to Champlin and Huneker? He may have believed that his professional chances in America would be better if he were younger. He had never been a prodigy, but he may have felt that even an extra year of youth gave him a professional advantage. Second, as his thirtieth birthday loomed, he may have experienced a so-called midlife crisis. Granting himself an extra year in his twenties could have helped to assuage the personal sense of his advancing age. Third, it may have been a practical joke in collusion with Strong. Both men loved high-spirited banter, and they relished the confidences shared only with each other. This might have been the ultimate inside joke by the man who, as his student Henry Gilbert recalled, "usually looked as if he'd just seen something funny (perhaps he had) and only kept himself from laughing by main strength of will."[29] Whatever the reasons, we can be sure that he was intentional about it. On a piece of manuscript paper in a sketchbook from this time, MacDowell wrote out a series of dates and numbers showing how old he was at each stage of his life. The makeshift reference chart correlates his correct age from birth through age twenty-six, with the date 1860 underlined at the end. No doubt this chart helped him verify his deception in responding to requests for information.[30]

In December 1886, as a break from the challenges of *Lancelot and Elaine* and the disappointing performance of *Hamlet and Ophelia*, MacDowell wrote a set of six songs on texts by Margaret Deland that he called *From an Old Garden*, op. 26. Deland (1857–1945) would go on to become a prominent novelist and short story writer, and had published her first book, a collection of poems titled *The Old Garden*, in 1886. Edward set six of these poems to music in a matter of a few days after Christmas. On 17 January 1887, three days after putting his sisters-in-law on the train for Switzerland, he sent two manuscript copies of the songs to America. The first copy was to the Cuban choral director Emilio Agramonte, thanking him for programming some of his earlier songs in a concert in New York and asking him for the privilege of dedicating *From an Old Garden* to him. On the same day, he sent another copy of the songs to the publisher G. Schirmer in New York.[31] This

---

28. Credit for the discovery goes to Arnold Schwab, who had earlier exposed Huneker's change of his own birthdate: Arnold T. Schwab, "Huneker's Hidden Birthdate," *American Literature* 23/3 (November 1951): 351–54.

29. Henry F. Gilbert, "Personal Recollections of Edward MacDowell," *New Music Review* 11 (1912): 494.

30. "Sketches of op 23 and of the 'Marionettes,'" EMMC box 6/11.

31. Drafts of both letters are found in "Letters & Answers 20 März 1885," 67–68, EMMC box 32.

was the first time he had offered his compositions to an American publisher, and his request was very simple: he asked for no remuneration but specified that the title page of the publication should have the same design as the original book of poems. MacDowell was very sensitive to the visual impact of his publications, and he considered it his right to suggest pictorial images.

Over the next several months, the negotiations with Schirmer became complicated, first because the publisher contacted Carreño as an intermediary, next because there were issues about how the copyright notation should be worded, and most importantly because the final publication was not printed according to the composer's specifications. The format was octavo, a smaller size normally used for choral music, and the title page was plain rather than ornate as he had requested. He apologized to Agramonte in a letter of 2 July 1887: "It annoys me doubly as I also intended the handsome edition as a compliment to you; it makes me mortified to see your name at the head of such an ugly piece of printing. At any rate you will see from the design I made for the title page (which I have directed Schirmer to send you and which he *must* do) what I intended—and I hope you will take the will for the deed."[32] He wrote a very strong letter to the publisher on 14 August outlining his grievances in nine points, stating that he had been advised by musicians and businessmen that he was in the right.[33] Schirmer offered to reprint the title page, but MacDowell refused, preferring to nurse his grudge instead. Eventually the publisher sent him $50 in compensation for the error, but MacDowell refused their offer to share the copyright. A letter of 17 October 1887 indicates that the matter had been resolved to his satisfaction.[34]

This was an early instance of a pattern that came to characterize MacDowell's business dealings in later years. He would become so angry at what he considered the dirty dealings of publishers and other associates that he would refuse to seek a compromise. It seems that on some emotional level he preferred the satisfaction of knowing he had been wronged to accepting a compromise that was in any way less than he had originally bargained for. In this case, his obstinacy hurt him financially, as indicated in a letter from G. Schirmer to Marian written nearly two decades later:

New York, Jan 30, 1906

Dear Mrs. MacDowell,

A number of years ago we published a little volume of Mr. MacDowell's songs entitled "Songs from an old Garden", the copyright of which he ceded to us at a nominal price.

32. Letter, EAM to Emilio Agramonte, 2 July 1887, EMMC box 33.
33. Letter, EAM to G. Schirmer, 14 August 1887, EMMC box 29/4.
34. Draft letter, EAM to G. Schirmer, 17 October 1887, EMMC box 29/4.

Since that time we proposed to him to annul that contract and initiate a royalty agreement. He declined our proposition, however, preferring to treat the matter as a business transaction that was closed. We appreciated his attitude & point of view. But we should like at this time to renew the proposition asking you to look at it from *our* point of view. We find on examining our records that the little volume has enjoyed a considerably larger sale than we were aware of and we should feel much more comfortable if the composer were to participate with us in the profits. We therefore address you, as we understand that you are managing Mr. MacDowell's affairs during his regrettable illness and ask you to let us account to you for all sales up to date, by sending you our check for $497.50 being 10% on the price of all copies sold less the amount originally paid, & to let us account to you regularly hereafter.[35]

At the time of publication, MacDowell had grown accustomed to giving away the financial claim to his compositions (which his dealings with Breitkopf & Härtel showed were too negligible to worry about) in exchange for accommodations that he felt would help his reputation. He was pleased when Agramonte included the songs on a concert in New York's Chickering Hall on 12 April 1887.

MacDowell's irrational anger at the publisher may have been an extension of a much more serious disappointment that happened at about the same time. That spring, while her sisters were traveling in Italy, Marian suffered an accident that led to the stillbirth of their only child. Years later she recalled that they could not afford the proper medical care, and that when they sent a telegram home to ask for money to be cabled, it did not arrive for weeks. In her words, "The delay in the money coming from New York showed a curious twist in MacDowell's nature which was exhibited two or three times during his life; a rather dreadful feeling of unforgivingness towards those who had ignored the real cry for help our cable had expressed. The money did come, but it was too late."[36]

From the perspective of old age, Marian could look back and recognize how her life would have been altered by caring for a child; at the time, though, she was devastated and her husband was bitter. When the sisters returned to Wiesbaden late in the spring, they found her still weak, and they spent the rest of the summer nursing her back to health. For herself, she cherished the memory of Edward's attentiveness before they returned: "The memory of that week when my young husband took entire care of me, with all the tenderness and even cleverness of a trained person is something I could never forget."[37]

---

35. Letter, G. Schirmer to MM, MacDowell Collection, Library of Congress Manuscript Division, box 6.

36. MM Notebook No. 4, 84–85, EMMC box 39/5.

37. MM Notebook No. 4, 84–85, EMMC box 39/5. Strong was also impressed by his friend's care during Marian's illness [Strong, "Edward MacDowell as I Knew Him, third paper," 29]. Ironically,

As Marian recovered, the MacDowells waited impatiently for another change in their lives. That spring, Edward and Templeton had been on one of their daily walks when they came upon a run-down cottage on the hill north of Wiesbaden known as the Neroberg. Throwing caution to the wind, Edward and Marian cashed more bonds, took out a mortgage to buy it, and hired workers to make extensive repairs that required months. The Neroberg section of Wiesbaden is among the most picturesque sections of a picturesque city. The Grubweg, which was renamed Nerobergstrasse in the early 1890s, traversed the side of a hill in close proximity to birch forests and vineyards. Above their home was a Greek chapel that is still standing today. The hill was popular with walkers, and Marian's sister noted that there was more foot traffic past their new home on the edge of town than there had been in the Jahnstrasse in the center of town. On 7 August, Nina wrote that Marian was "improving steadily, and feels so well, that it is a constant struggle to keep her under control, and not to allow her to do too much. The repairs in her little house are not finished yet, as we had hoped they would be by this time. The deliberation of a German workman is past belief to anyone who has not witnessed it."[38] In late August, right before the sisters returned to the United States, they moved into their new home at 21 Grubweg, where they would spend some of the happiest days of their lives.

By this time MacDowell had set aside his performing career in order to concentrate full time on composition. The years 1887 and 1888 were remarkably prolific for him, as he produced a string of compositions that were published almost immediately. For piano, he wrote *Sechs Idyllen*, op. 28 (Hainauer, 1887), *Sechs Gedichte nach Heinrich Heine*, op. 31 (Hainauer, 1887), *Vier kleine Poesien*, op. 32 (Breitkopf & Härtel, 1888), *Etude de Concert*, op. 36 (Schmidt, 1889), *Les Orientales*, op. 37 (Schmidt, 1889), and *Marionetten*, op. 38 (Hainauer, 1888); for men's chorus, *Drei Lieder*, op. 27 (Schmidt, 1890); for solo voice, *Drei Lieder*, op. 33 (Hainauer, 1889), and *Two Songs*, op. 34 (Schmidt, 1889). He also wrote the *Romanze*, op. 35, for cello with accompaniment of orchestra or piano (Hainauer, 1888) as well as portions of the symphonic poem *Lamia*, op. 29, and a "Roland" Symphony that eventually was published as *Die Sarazenen* and *Die schöne Alda*, op. 30.[39] Most important for his future was the Second Piano Concerto in D Minor, op. 23 (see chapter 9).

Germany was the first country to adopt a system of universal health care, when Bismarck included it as part of his package of social reforms in the 1880s. Had they been German citizens, they would have been entitled to coverage.

38. Letter, Nina Nevins to Cousins, 7 August 1887, EMMC box 60/19. For an entertaining account of the extensive repairs and MacDowell's exasperation with the workmen, see Strong, "Edward MacDowell as I Knew Him, fourth paper," 51.

39. M. M. Lowens, "The New York Years," 34–35 and 373–75; Sonneck, *Catalogue of First Editions*, 22–30.

Fall 1887 brought an important event in the history of American music that helped both MacDowell and Strong. Following up on the success of his Novelty Concerts, Van der Stucken presented the most ambitious series of American concerts to date, a series of five evenings of American music in November 1887.[40] The first concert on Tuesday, 15 November, included MacDowell's *Hamlet*, which W. J. Henderson of the *New York Times* identified as the most striking composition of the evening: "The purpose is clear and is distinctly exposed. The stormy character of the opening bars fittingly portrays the conflict of emotions in the princely Dane, and the frequent passionate bursts ending in abrupt and suddenly suspended fortissimi are admirably expressive, while the cantabile music in melody and movement signifies clearly the melancholy and love of Hamlet. The scoring is strong and richly colored, and on the whole the composition is one of no small merit."[41] Strong's First Symphony in F was the featured work of the final concert on Thursday, 24 November. The work merited a long and thoughtful analysis from Henry E. Krehbiel, who called it one of the "half-dozen best compositions performed at the concerts." The majority of his critique, however, consisted of "reminiscence-hunting": identifying echoes of Raff and Wagner in the work. Krehbiel took the composer to task for failing to cull these reminiscences during the revision process. The critic, who was among the most respected in America, stated, "For Mr. Strong's talent we have heretofore expressed much admiration. We believe that he will be a credit to the art of his native land, but before then he must become more original in his manner of expressing his musical thoughts."[42] Both composers were becoming well known in New York through Van der Stucken's advocacy and the attention of America's most prominent critics.

Originality and influence may have been among the topics discussed by the two composers on their daily walks through the hills above Wiesbaden. During this time, MacDowell's ideas about American music were beginning to solidify, no doubt helped by the opportunity to discuss his thoughts with a like-minded American composer. His conclusions, articulated in a 22 December 1887 letter to Lachmund, reflect the ideas of Raff and the indirect influence of Liszt. After stating that nationalism in music had been eliminated because of inexpensive musical scores and larger orchestras—citing Meyerbeer, Verdi, and Giovanni Sgambati as proof that nationalism was dead—MacDowell turned to American music:

> As for Americans expecting, striving, or even wishing to create an <u>American</u> school of composing, it is utter nonsense. What they strive after, is to write good music and if they

---

40. For a discussion of this series of concerts, see E. Douglas Bomberger, "Frank Van der Stucken's Novelty Concerts," chap. 4 of *"A Tidal Wave of Encouragement,"* 29–43.

41. [W. J. Henderson], "Music by Americans," *NYT,* 16 November 1887, 5.

42. [Henry E. Krehbiel], "The Last American Concert," *New York Tribune,* 25 November 1887, 5.

<u>do</u> succeed they want recognition for it, and <u>not</u> reproaches because they have not given American color (<u>what</u> that can mean in a land which possesses no Volkslied, I fail to see) to their works. The few criticisms I read [of Van der Stucken's concerts] made me very angry when I saw that reproach in them. Van der Stucken has been kindness itself, and it seems almost an unthankful act to criticise the scheme of "American" Concerts. However I have always thought that "Particularismus" was a bad thing for music—and "<u>American</u>" Concerts suggest to my mind that people wish that American music should stand by itself and have its own standard of criticism—All that American art wishes and <u>needs</u> is the fair criticism that ought to be meted out to the productions of other Nations.[43]

McDowell's advocacy of a universal aesthetic was out of step, not only with American thinking, but also with recent European trends. In the years ahead, his assertions in favor of cosmopolitan style and against American Composers' Concerts would become more and more strident, to the dismay of many of his American colleagues. True to his personality—and his Quaker roots—he refused to waver from a principle that he valued.

That fall, Fanny McDowell began a concerted campaign to convince Edward and Marian to return to New York. On 23 October 1887, she wrote to Marian with a specific plan for them to return to America. She proposed that they could live with Edward's parents, which they would arrange on a strictly businesslike basis, allowing him to teach, perform, and promote his works in the United States.[44] When Edward and Marian refused this suggestion, she found other strings to pull. On 7 March 1888, Edward received a telegram from Fanny's old friend Jeannette Meyer Thurber inviting him to join her National Conservatory of Music in New York as professor of harmony and composition. He considered this offer at length, and finally responded on 21 April with a telegram that read simply "Thanks no / no sig."[45]

If Edward would not go to America, then America began to come to him. His reputation was growing on the other side of the Atlantic thanks to his steadily expanding list of publications, the well-reviewed performances of his works, and the biographical notices in the *American Art Journal* and the third edition of Riemann's music dictionary. In the summer of 1887 he received a visit from B. J. Lang, a prominent Boston organist and conductor who went out of his way to visit Wiesbaden during a trip to Europe with his family. Nina reported on his visit to Wiesbaden in July 1887:

A Mr. Lang, who is a leader of both instrumental and choral societies in Boston, came to see Edward. He had known nothing of him personally, but had been attracted by his

43. Letter, EAM to Carl V. Lachmund, 22 December 1887, Lachmund Collection, NYPL.
44. M. M. Lowens, "The New York Years," 39.
45. EMMC box 37/15.

music, and wished to meet him. He was very complimentary; said he had already played some of his music in public, and wished to do so again. He said with pride, that he was a man of no vices—and drank neither wine, beer, tea or coffee, nor did he smoke, so all Edward could do for him was to take him to drive in the woods.[46]

Later in the year, MacDowell received a visit from another Boston musician, George Whitefield Chadwick, and his wife. The organist and composer had studied in Leipzig and Munich in 1877–1879, making a splash with the performance of his overture *Rip Van Winkle* in the Leipzig Gewandhaus. He spent the rest of his life in Boston, but he retained a sentimental fondness for Germany, visiting as often as he could and re-creating German *Gemütlichkeit* through his parties in Boston. Chadwick was outgoing and jovial, very much the opposite of MacDowell and Strong, but they had a cordial visit on their first meeting. Later in the year, a third Boston musician, Arthur Foote, visited the two expatriates in Wiesbaden.[47]

On 15 February 1888, Carreño premiered a new composition, the *Etude de Concert*, op. 36, in Chicago's Weber Music Hall. Written in response to her request for a brilliant concert piece, the etude has a big-boned virtuosity reminiscent of Liszt. It opens with an arresting octave passage and then spins out a lyrical melody that is embellished with a variety of keyboard figurations. Like the concert etudes of Liszt, there is virtually no development of the melody, but the interest lies rather in the imaginative ways that the composer surrounds it with brilliant and varied figuration. The short piece is dazzling in performance and went on to become one of his most frequently performed works.

During this period, Edward's sedentary lifestyle began to take a toll on his waistline, prompting Marian to urge him to exercise more. He continued to take daily walks with Strong, and they experimented with baseball and boomerang throwing in a meadow in the hills. When the weather prohibited outdoor exercise, they would meet in Edward's music room to play for each other and discuss music. Strong was not an accomplished pianist, but MacDowell insisted on playing four-hand music together to his friend's chagrin. Strong remembered this as the happiest time of his life thus far: "There was never the slightest disagreement, never the slightest cloud between us, our feelings for each other being those of a loyal and affectionate *cama-raderie*, coupled with a very sincere admiration on my part....Rarely, if ever, did a day pass of which we did not spend the afternoon together, its having become an understood thing, virtually from the beginning of our intimacy, that we should do so."[48]

46. Letter, Nina Nevins to Cousins, 24 July 1887, EMMC box 60/19.

47. Nicholas E. Tawa, *Arthur Foote: a Musician in the Frame of Time and Place* (Lanham, MD: Scarecrow, 1997), 78.

48. Strong, "Edward MacDowell as I Knew Him, seventh paper," 151, 152.

Strong was impressed with the intimacy between Edward and Marian. Her intellect was a match for her husband's, and their friend recalled being afraid to join in the conversation at times because the two of them were so quick-witted. More importantly, the couple was comfortable and happy together: "When we were all together, and he was making most dreadful jokes, I can still hear Mrs. MacDowell say: 'Eddy, shut up!' Which was but adding fuel to the unquenchable fire, so full of buoyant life was he."[49] His friend's marital bliss was in contrast to his own. Anna Nevins opined that Strong's wife, Veronica, was "beneath him in education and family," and she did not often join her husband's conviviality.[50] The two were divorced in 1892, and Strong remarried in 1894. In June 1888, the MacDowells and Strong (without Veronica) vacationed briefly in Chamounix, Switzerland, playing on glaciers and gazing in awe at the towering mountains. Edward found the Alps oppressive, but Templeton was becoming more enamored of them with each visit.[51]

Later that summer, the MacDowells heard from Lang, who was again in Europe to attend the Bayreuth Festival, an annual gala of Wagner opera performances under the direction of his widow Cosima. The older man paid them a visit in late July or early August, but this time he came with a purpose. In no uncertain terms, he urged them to return to the United States and make their home in Boston. Marian recalled that he "rubbed it in so hard and so vividly that it was MacDowell's duty to come back to his own country and not become an American foreigner of which there were too many."[52] The couple had been investigating possibilities to return to the United States all winter with the help of Fanny, but he had turned down a good offer to teach at the National Conservatory in New York. Somehow, Lang convinced him to move to Boston, where he would need to rely on private teaching and performance to make a living in a town where he had few connections. Once his mind was made up, he tried to convince Strong to accompany him, but his friend felt the risk would be too great. The two had become inseparable over the previous two years, but nothing Edward said could convince Templeton to join him in moving to the States. In a matter of weeks the MacDowells sold their furniture at auction, packed their trunks, and sailed for New York on 21 September. Their friend was left to clean up the mess.

Strong returned to the Grubweg house every day for the next several weeks, disposing of their kitchen utensils and other odds and ends. He sent detailed reports to MacDowell on the earnings and on his difficulties, particularly in finding a

49. Strong, "Edward MacDowell as I Knew Him, third paper," 29.
50. Letter, Anna Nevins to Cousins, 3 January 1887, EMMC box 60/17.
51. Strong, "Edward MacDowell as I Knew Him, seventh paper," 152.
52. MM, typescript, vol. I, EMMC box 39/5, quoted in M. M. Lowens, "The New York Years," 41.

buyer for the bathtub. Among the detritus that he found strewn about the house were draft scores to MacDowell's compositions, including the invaluable draft of the Second Piano Concerto, and the book of business letters and contracts that chronicled MacDowell's early career in Germany. MacDowell wrote that he should destroy them, but Strong saved them, preserving a crucial part of the documentary evidence for this biography. The house was sold in December at a profit of $200.[53] For Strong, the hardest day was when the piano was removed: "It was an exceedingly and almost unbearably depressing and sad period, and I can never forget my feelings when, having at last sold the piano, I saw it carried out of the house. I felt like a chief and sole mourner at a lonely funeral. I never again saw the house, nor passed near it."[54]

After twelve years in Europe, MacDowell's decision to leave was abrupt. Strong felt that his friend was on the brink of real fame and could before long have established a situation in Wiesbaden similar to that of Liszt in Weimar, where students came from around the world to benefit from his teaching, and he had time and solitude to compose.[55] Instead, Strong could only imagine what he was doing thousands of miles across the ocean, grieving for what they had both lost:

> Nov. 24/88. Wiesbaden.
>
> 12:30 a.m.
>
> Dear old Man: I closed up a letter to you this ev'g and now begin another, for I feel as though I were near you when I write to you. Have just finished reading the London World (Yates) and Punch with a whiskey accomp. and after walking about the room here five minutes, I began thinking of you,—looked at the clock,—saw 12 ½ a.m.,—thought of you this Saturday ev'g in Boston, time about 6:30 p.m.,—and wondered what you were doing,—wondered if the wind was screaming and if the night was as wild in Boston as it now is here, for blasts of wind come down now from the Taunus mountains, that seem to threaten the windows with destruction: the tree outside my window seems to be in a state of terror,—it fairly yells every moment or two. A ghostly night it is, and thank God you are not on the sea! And now, just as I begin writing, my lamp is going out: well, I must forgive it, for it has been lit ever since four o'clock, so dark was it. Tomorrow I shall answer your A1 letter, or begin it anyhow. Good night, old truepenny! When don't I think of you, old rascal! with your jokes and general air of innate cheerfulness. Old man, it was a sorry day for me when you left here. And now I think of the little house up on the

53. Letters, J. Chr. Glücklich, real estate agent, to EAM, 14 December 1888 and 18 March 1889, MacDowell Collection, Library of Congress Manuscript Division, box 6.

54. Strong, "Edward MacDowell as I Knew Him, eighth paper," 190.

55. Ibid., 189–90.

hill, all alone and empty, deserted this wild night, and from that my thoughts travel off to spring mornings when I came up at six, and inspected the vegetable garden and listened to the bees and awaited the appearance of your head at the little front window, up under the eaves. Well well,—it's all vorbei—good night, old boy.[56]

56. Letter, TS to EAM, 24 November 1888, EMMC box 31/30.

BOOK TWO

Edward MacDowell in Boston

CHAPTER NINE

The Prodigal Returns

O N 21 SEPTEMBER 1888, EDWARD AND MARIAN MACDOWELL SAILED FOR THE United States, after a hasty decision and frantic packing. In his last letter to Strong before leaving the German port of Bremen, he wrote, "Arrived safely—beefsteak and wine revived us. Bremen is a swindling hole—<u>Sure</u> cure for any doubts about staying in Germany—I shudder to think of your staying here—even until next spring."[1] The Grubweg house was only partially emptied, as Strong would need months to dispose of their things. His friends, meanwhile, had set their sights on America and did not look back.

Upon arrival in New York, the MacDowells stayed with Edward's parents for a week. It was probably during this time that he saw Teresa Carreño for the first time since his childhood. In addition to giving him lessons, she had encouraged his compositional efforts and played his works in concerts all over the country. If he owed his modest reputation to anyone, it was to her. But his indebtedness did not stop him from speaking frankly. When she played for him, he was shocked at her sloppy technique, and he urged her to take a year away from performing to fix her problems before she lost her audience. Clearly MacDowell did not intend to fit unobtrusively into the American musical scene; he would be fearless in speaking his mind and unwavering in his principles, even to persons whose goodwill was crucial to his success.

On Saturday, 6 October, the couple headed north to Boston. Neither of them knew the city, and so their initial task was simply to set up housekeeping. MacDowell reported to Strong that B. J. Lang showed unexpected hospitality on their arrival:

1. Undated letter, EAM to TS, EMMC box 29/27.

Mr. Lang met us at the Station and told me he had a "boarding house" engaged for us, for which we blessed him all in our power, but when the carriage "fetched up" at <u>his</u> house—and we saw Mrs. Lang & her daughter standing in the open doorway to welcome us I came to, with a start and tried to run but it was too late. So here we are occupying the spare room and feeling like criminals. It was really too kind and good of them and I only hope some time to be able to show my appreciation some way.[2]

He wrote under the date of his letter, "Mr. Lang's house. Swellest part of <u>Boston</u>," and raved about the "rooms fit for a prince," the "oriental magnificence" of American breakfasts, and the four pianos in the Langs' house. Continuing his campaign to convince Strong to join him, he wrote, "America is simply <u>paradise</u>—and there's no place like it in my mind."

Lang's twenty-year-old daughter Margaret (1867–1972) was living with her parents when the MacDowells arrived. She told Marian years later about the excitement she felt over their presence in the family home:

Have I ever told you of a morning at our house in Boston—when you and Mr. MacDowell were staying while looking for a house?? I was upstairs in my room, & everybody had, I thought, gone out,—when I heard the piano in our music room. Superb, thrilling playing. And I thought "MacDowell himself! How wonderful; he thinks he is alone." I crept down the hard-wood stairs in my stocking feet,—sat down on the stairs outside the door & listened. At last it stopped, & before I could escape—<u>you</u> came out of the music room!"[3]

Marian MacDowell did not pursue a professional career, but she maintained her skills as a pianist, which would become important in later years to promote her husband's works. The admiration was mutual, as MacDowell wrote in a letter of 19 October to Strong, "By the way, his daughter Miss Lang composes awfully pretty songs and is going to print soon. I'll send you a copy as soon as out. You will like them immensely. I do."[4]

The decision to locate in Boston is surprising in some ways but reflective of the couple's personal tastes and their perceptions of America. New York was where Edward had grown up, where his parents lived and had many connections, and where he had been offered a conservatory teaching position by his mother's old friend Jeannette Meyer Thurber. The city had many musical organizations, along with a large German-speaking population, and would have provided ample opportunities for MacDowell to earn a living. But it was also a much larger city than Boston. New York had grown dramatically since Edward's childhood, evolving into

2. Letter, EAM to TS, 7 October 1888, EMMC box 29/27.
3. Letter, Margaret Ruthven Lang to MM, 5 June 1955, EMMC box 46/36.
4. Letter, EAM to TS, 19 October 1888, EMMC box 29/27.

the commercial center of the country and the destination of choice for immigrants. The hectic pace of life in New York and the cramped quarters among the ever-taller buildings in Manhattan were not to Edward and Marian's liking. After the couple visited his parents during their first Christmas holiday in America, he confided to Strong that the visit had tired him: "We just returned from N.Y. where we went to spend three days—considering it 'rest' for me! We are almost dead from the fatigue of the journey and the everlasting go of paying calls etc."[5]

Lang no doubt had a large role in convincing them to choose Boston. As a leader in the city's cultural life, he took pride in the "Athens of America," home to Harvard University, the Boston Symphony, the Boston Public Library, the Museum of Fine Arts, and other havens of high culture. Here the wealthy descendants of New England's first European settlers came closest to establishing a class of hereditary aristocracy. Boston was not the largest, richest, or most progressive city in America, but it worked hard at being the most cultivated. Its size and ambience were also much closer to the German cities the MacDowells had known.

Within a short time, the couple found lodgings at 86 Mount Vernon Street, in the Beacon Hill neighborhood of Boston. This was one of the wealthiest sections of the city, making it a good location for attracting students. They rented an entire floor with bathroom, heat, lights, and meals served in their rooms for $30 a week—an extravagance of the first order for a couple with no income. The Chickering Company sent a piano for the apartment, allowing him to practice, teach, and compose at home. Edward reported to Templeton that they could see the Charles River from both sides of their apartment with red and green hills in the distance.[6] Within a few months, though, he began to do most of his practicing at the Chickering warehouse in the evenings, where Edward did not disturb his wife and neighbors, and where he enjoyed the solitude of the deserted building.[7]

As he had discovered in Frankfurt after his graduation from the Hoch Conservatory, teaching was the quickest and most reliable way to earn money. By 18 October he could report to Strong that he had three students who each paid five dollars per lesson. Additional students followed in the months after, allowing him to earn approximately $1,500 during his first winter in Boston. He confided to Strong, "I am working like a beaver and like it. Porterhouse Beef-steaks for breakfast and $5 an hour for lessons has always been my ideal."[8]

5. Letter, EAM to TS, 26 December 1888 [this portion written on 31 December], EMMC box 29/28.

6. These details are contained in letters from MacDowell to Strong, 13, 19, and 24 October 1888, EMMC box 29/27.

7. Letters, EAM to TS, 28 November 1888 and 3 January 1889, EMMC boxes 29/28 and 29/29.

8. Letter, EAM to TS, 19 October 1888, EMMC box 29/27.

Among his first students was Henry F. Gilbert, a twenty-year-old composition student whose lessons were financed by a wealthy Boston woman. Gilbert recalled the pains his young teacher took to establish his authority:

> At first my lessons were very ceremonious and I was treated in a very business-like manner. Did I arrive but three minutes before the appointed hour I was kept waiting in solitary state in the ante-room. Exactly as the hour struck I was ushered in to the presence by Mrs. MacDowell. And there we were. And didn't he put me through a course of sprouts! Well, I should say so. His exceeding strictness was undoubtedly left over from his recent German experiences. But he usually looked as if he'd just seen something funny (perhaps he had) and only kept himself from laughing by main strength of will. I was filled with admiration for the exact rectitude which was kept with regard to the lesson hour. It never began a minute beforehand nor ran a minute over. I supposed this was rendered necessary by the large number of his pupils, but I afterwards learned that at that time I was his only pupil.[9]

MacDowell's studio grew quickly, as curiosity over Boston's newest resident conspired with his growing reputation as a pianist and composer to attract students. He discovered to his disappointment that composition students were rare, but piano students were plentiful.[10] This sort of teaching was only marginally interesting to him, but financial need forced him to accept anyone who could pay during his first year.

Within a few weeks of his arrival, he reported to Strong that he had several students in counterpoint, several students in piano, the possibility of a women's class in music appreciation, and a "symphony" student who wanted to analyze orchestral works. The delay of the MacDowells' shipment from Germany put him in an awkward position:

> I am impatiently awaiting the boxes etc. etc. I haven't a single book of reference to lean on—so you can imagine how the three Counterpoint scholars worry me. As for the Symphony dissecting business it's maddening. You ought to hear me show off the B dur Symphony of Schumann,—"This Sir, is the great absquatulorum—can't live on land and dies in the water." I calmly picked out glaring "fifths" (of which Schumann was so intolerant in others) at a first glance, in the 1st movemt. Second Theme 7th bar between Klar[inett] & Fag[ott]. Ain't I clever!![11]

---

9. Henry F. Gilbert, "Personal Recollections of Edward MacDowell," *New Music Review* 2 (1912): 494.

10. T. P. Currier, "Edward MacDowell as I Knew Him," *MQ* I/1 (January 1915): 20–21.

11. Letter, EAM to TS, 24 October 1888, EMMC box 29/27.

T. P. Currier, another of these students from the Boston years, confirmed Gilbert's memory of their teacher's sense of humor. Both students recalled that he was always ready to see the humor in situations, and that when he thought of something truly funny, his eyelids would flutter rapidly before he broke into a wide smile or a deep laugh.[12]

The musicians of Boston were curious about this young man whose works had been published by Germany's most famous music publishers and played by the inimitable Teresa Carreño. The Boston papers ran articles on his arrival ranging from brief notices to longer biographical articles. MacDowell sent Strong a copy of the article that appeared in the Boston *Herald*, marveling at the response to his arrival.[13] Lang was the one musician who knew him personally, and it was his responsibility to introduce him to his colleagues. On 12 October Lang gave a reception "to over 200 people (all men, mostly musicians) to meet me. It was awfully kind of him—cigars and punch went around and altogether it was very interesting. Paine was there—also Foot[e]—Whiting—Gericke—Faelten—Maas—any amount of fellows whom it was very interesting to become acquainted with."[14] The composer and organist John Knowles Paine was the first professor of music at Harvard; Wilhelm Gericke was the conductor of the Boston Symphony Orchestra; Arthur Foote and Arthur Whiting were among the most prominent of Boston's younger composer-pianists; and Carl Faelten and Louis Maas were German immigrants who taught at the New England Conservatory of Music. After years of indifference from the German musical establishment, MacDowell felt as if he had stepped into a different world.

Despite the good-natured show of cordiality, MacDowell knew that what the musicians of Boston really wanted was to hear him play. During his last several years in Wiesbaden he had enjoyed the luxury of devoting his time to composition, with no public performances. Although he had kept a piano in his home and played it daily, he had not maintained his technique at the level of a concert artist. The early weeks in Boston were spent frantically drilling at the Chickering to regain the level of skill necessary to appear in public without embarrassing himself. Less than a month after his arrival in Boston, he informed Strong that "I play already very differently from what I did, and am, I think getting my old Virtuosität back."[15]

His debut took place on 19 November 1888 as assisting artist at a concert of the Kneisel Quartet. Franz Kneisel (1865–1926) was a Romanian violinist who

12. Currier, "Edward MacDowell as I Knew him," 17–18.

13. Letter, EAM to TS, 18 October 1888, EMMC box 29/27.

14. Letter, EAM to TS, 13 October 1888, EMMC box 29/27.

15. Letter, EAM to TS, 4 November 1888, EMMC box 29/28.

despite being five years MacDowell's junior was the concertmaster of the Boston Symphony Orchestra. Shortly after his arrival in Boston in 1885, he had formed a string quartet that gave concerts when the orchestra was not performing. This quartet eventually became so successful that the members resigned their orchestral positions in 1903 to devote themselves full time to chamber music concerts until they disbanded in 1917. Already in 1888 their concerts were central to Boston's concert life, giving MacDowell an auspicious showcase for his pianistic talents.

MacDowell's role in the concert consisted of playing the piano part in a quintet by Karl Goldmark, which he called a "rotten composition" and learned in three days. He also played three movements from his *Erste moderne Suite*, op. 10. After his performance he was recalled three times and told Strong that the reviews were all "fair to very good."[16] Performances at a pair of Apollo Club concerts conducted by Lang followed in early December, which MacDowell confided to Strong did not go as well as he would have liked. He also performed at private gatherings of the St. Botolph Club and the Harvard Musical Association, cementing his reputation for breathtakingly fast and yet unclear pianism.[17]

MacDowell was badly out of practice, but he was also a champion of the progressive wing of Romanticism that emulated Franz Liszt. Classical clarity and grace were less important to him than passion, fire, and color. For many of his musical colleagues in staid Boston, this was a new and unwelcome direction. If they had had their way, he would probably have settled into a routine of teaching with fewer and fewer performances. He had the exceptional good fortune, however, to win orchestral engagements from two prominent conductors that would lift his reputation as both pianist and composer.

In November, MacDowell reported that Wilhelm Gericke had offered him an engagement to play his unpublished Second Piano Concerto in March (later moved to April) with the Boston Symphony Orchestra. The Austrian Gericke (1845–1925) had been conductor of the orchestra since 1884, succeeding the short-lived George Henschel. Gericke had brought the ensemble to a high level of polish by importing European players and demanding strict discipline. For MacDowell's taste, however, the orchestra sounded too "glatt" [smooth]: "Whether it is owing to that big Music Hall or what—it is a fact that anything like real fire or a regular smashing chord never is heard in it."[18] MacDowell would not find out until January that tensions between the conductor and Henry Higginson, the orchestra's founder and guarantor, had caused Gericke to resign effective the following summer.[19]

16. Letter, EAM to TS, 21 November 1888, EMMC box 29/28.

17. Currier, "Edward MacDowell as I Knew Him," 21–22.

18. Letter, EAM to TS, 4 November 1888, EMMC box 29/28.

19. Letter, EAM to TS, 3 January 1889, EMMC box 29/29.

The other conductor who wanted to play the second concerto was Theodore Thomas (1835–1905), the most influential American orchestral conductor of the era. As leader of his own orchestra, he played a dominant role in New York while also introducing many smaller American cities to orchestral music through extensive tours. He added to his duties in 1877 the leadership of the New York Philharmonic, which he conducted until 1891 and shaped into one of the country's preeminent musical organizations. In the fall of 1888, he severed his long-standing agreement with the Steinway Company to conduct his concerts in their hall, committing himself instead to twelve concerts in New York's Chickering Hall.[20] He needed to schedule his season under these new conditions, and MacDowell was an artist who was associated with Chickering in Boston. Using Lang as an intermediary, Thomas offered MacDowell an engagement to play his concerto with the orchestra in March 1889.[21] The concerto had been written in Germany but never performed—in fact the orchestral parts were still not copied when he accepted the engagement. Thomas the confident and experienced conductor assured MacDowell that he would not need to see the score in advance of the first rehearsal, as long as the score and parts contained enough rehearsal cues to allow them to stop and start anywhere.[22]

As Strong learned of each new triumph through letters mailed weeks before, he congratulated his friend from a distance. At the same time, he warned him against too much piano playing:

> Well; good for the concert, good for you, good for Lang and good for the [Apollo] club! Bravo the whole lot of you,—lucky beggars! As for Gericke and your MS Concerto in March: I say play it, but also have him do your Lancelot or Hamlet & Ophelia: Propose it, man alive! You must now see that some of your "Orchesterwerke" are performed and you must not play too much: you must pose principally as Komponist. You must insist upon this, especially now that everybody sees that you can play.[23]

By the late nineteenth century, true composer-pianists like Rubinstein and Paderewski were increasingly rare, and in a highly specialized age, Strong recognized that his friend would be categorized as one or the other. Although it was easier to secure engagements as a pianist, the long-term goal was to be viewed primarily as a composer.

20. Letter, EAM to TS, 16 December 1888, EMMC box 29/28.

21. Letter, EAM to Theodore Thomas, 6 January 1889, Theodore Thomas Collection, Newberry Library, Chicago.

22. Letter, Theodore Thomas to EAM, 8 January 1889, EMMC box 31/37.

23. Letter, TS to EAM, 17 December 1888, EMMC box 31/30.

The other important avenue for establishing a reputation as a composer was publication, and here again MacDowell was surprised by his good fortune. In Germany he had been required to pay subventions to see most of his works in print. When he had not paid a subvention, he had signed away all rights and claims to future royalties. This had been a calculated risk on his part, for it had allowed him to make his works known through reliable editions printed by some of Germany's most reputable music publishers. The Breitkopf & Härtel name especially inspired respect among musicians. Only one of his works had been published by an American publisher, but this had not been a good experience. When he had published his songs *From an old Garden*, op. 26, with Schirmer, he gave up the right to royalties in exchange for a specially designed cover that was not delivered, causing him much frustration. He had no way of knowing whether these unfavorable conditions would be replicated in America or whether he might finally be able to earn some money from his compositions.

Shortly after his arrival in Boston, MacDowell was approached by Arthur P. Schmidt with a proposal to publish his works. MacDowell reported incredulously in a letter of 1 November that Schmidt had offered to invest $1,000 in his major works and to pay him in addition. On 4 November he elaborated on the offer as well as the response of Lang, who was still MacDowell's only confidant in Boston:

> Schmidt the publisher was here the other day and wants me to let him take entire charge of my compositions, that is, he wants to print every thing I have done and will do—both in Germany and in America. And pay me for them in the bargain and besides give me a Royalty on every copy sold.—I have talked it over to Lang and he thinks I ought still to keep with Hainauer for a year or two until my position is firmer here, and then commence with Schmidt. Schmidt is an honest fine fellow—but it seems his house is, comparatively speaking one of not much more than local fame. Schmidt of course is ambitious and would put out an enormous lot of capital on me and, try to pose as a "Welt firma"—but Mr. Lang thinks that, should he not succeed in forcing Schirmer, Ditson, and all the rest of them to knuckle under to him, that they would crush him. So I am afraid I'll have to trim for yet awhile, and stick to Hainauer. I did not let on all Hainauer's little jokes—but told him how H. complained about losing money on my things at which he shed tears of laughter.[24]

The offer seemed too good to be true after his German experiences. He had learned the hard way that publication was not remunerative and that publishers could not be expected to spend money or take pains to promote a young composer's work. Especially in light of Lang's reticence, MacDowell was leery of signing an agreement with a—to him—unknown local publisher.

24. Letter, EAM to TS, 4 November 1888, EMMC box 29/28.

Arthur Paul Schmidt (1846–1921) had emigrated from Germany in 1866, working first for other publishers before opening his own retail shop in 1876. He began publishing music the following year, and by 1890 he sold the retail business to concentrate exclusively on music publishing. A canny businessman, he had built his firm rapidly, and when MacDowell arrived, Schmidt aspired to more than local prominence. In 1889 he opened a branch of his publishing company in Leipzig and in 1894 added a branch in New York. In gratitude for the success he achieved in his adopted country, he made a practice of publishing American compositions, even large works with little chance of profit. His 1880 edition of Paine's Second Symphony was the first published score by an American in this genre, and he did similar honors for the orchestral works of Chadwick, Foote, Beach, and others. When Strong heard of Schmidt's generous offer and Lang's advice to reject it, he wisely suggested a middle path:

> Good for Schmidt! That sounds good indeed and is encouraging for you. If Schmidt has capital,—enough,—I don't think he need fear Schirmer or Ditson or any of 'em. Instead, as you say, of keeping on with Hainauer only, for a year or two hence, I should stick to Hainauer mostly, but should give Schmidt a trial and see how it works: you might give him one or two small things. As he seems well disposed to you, I should not ignore his offer entirely, for it might turn out well. It is only men like yourself who can help Schmidt fight competition, by giving him some of your compositions.[25]

MacDowell followed his friend's advice, giving Schmidt two songs on poems by Robert Burns, op. 34 ("Menie" and "My Jean"), the *Etude de Concert*, op. 36, that he had written for Carreño, and *Les Orientales*, op. 37, for piano solo. These works (with the exception of "Menie") had been written in Germany but were published by Schmidt in early 1889. Schmidt was determined to show his generosity to the young composer, as evidenced by a lavish dinner he hosted at his home for MacDowell, Chadwick, and Foote ("A gorgeous spread, about 18 courses, and splendid white wines [Johannisberger for one!], Champagne afterwards Cigars ad lib").[26] At the same time, MacDowell hedged his bets by publishing a set of three songs, op. 33 with Hainauer, under the same conditions as before.[27] This odd set of *Drei Lieder* contained one song with a text by Goethe and another with a sentimental text by his Wiesbaden realtor, J. Ch. Glücklich. The opus was dedicated to Mrs. B. L. [*sic*] Lang. In later years, "Menie" and "My Jean" were among MacDowell's best-selling songs, while the three songs published by Hainauer languished.

25. Letter, TS to EAM, 24 November 1888, EMMC box 31/30.
26. Letter, EAM to TS, 9 January 1889, EMMC box 29/29.
27. Letter, Julius Hainauer to EAM, 23 December 1888, EMMC box 30/52.

MacDowell also made inquiries about one other publication project for Schmidt. On 12 January, a few days after the meal at Schmidt's house, he wrote to Doris Raff, widow of his former teacher, to ask about the possibility of publishing his notes on counterpoint in the form of a textbook. Books on music theory and composition by the Leipzig professors Richter and Jadassohn had done very well in the German and US markets, and Schmidt no doubt wished to capitalize on Raff's fame with a similar book. Raff's daughter Helene replied on her mother's behalf on 20 February, initiating a correspondence that revealed that Raff had not preserved any usable notes but which eventually led to Schmidt's publication of two unpublished overtures on Shakespearian themes. Frau Raff was by this time in poor health, depressed about the meager inheritance her husband had left, and ill-equipped to handle business matters. MacDowell showed his loyalty to his former teacher by negotiating the financial arrangements, handling the details of shipping, and editing the works in order to obtain US copyright protection.[28]

MacDowell followed Strong's advice in regard to Schmidt, but he ignored his friend's earlier warning against playing piano too much. On the morning of 9 January he played a concert for a large audience of women at the Boston Art Club. The mixed program of standard repertoire, his own compositions, and works by Strong was enthusiastically received by the standing-room-only crowd. MacDowell found his technique returning and his confidence growing, which gave him a sense of boyish glee: "By the way what do you think of my Recitaling around in this swell manner? Do you understand it? I don't, I seem to be able to play à la Virtuos with no effort at all…What's coming over me any way? I'm not nervous a bit—and would, I think play after Rubinstein, such has my "cheek" become….The idea that I alone by myself can fill a hall dazzles me."[29] This was a feeling he had not experienced for many years, and the immediate gratification of performing was a thrill that surpassed the more private pleasure of composing and the drudgery of teaching. He was somewhat selective about the occasions on which he would play, however, refusing two offers to perform in private homes for wealthy Bostonians.[30]

28. MacDowell's letters to Doris Raff are in the Raffiana Collection of the Manuscript Division of the Bayerische Staatsbibliothek in Munich, while her letters to him are divided between the Manuscript Division and the Music Division of the Library of Congress. For a detailed discussion of this episode in MacDowell's life, see E. Douglas Bomberger, "Edward MacDowell, Arthur P. Schmidt, and the Shakespeare Overtures of Joachim Raff: A Case Study in Nineteenth-Century Music Publishing," *Notes* 54/1 (September 1997): 11–26.

29. Letter, EAM to TS, 9 January 1889, EMMC box 29/29.

30. Letter, EAM to TS, 19 January 1889, EMMC box 29/29.

Edward's first winter in Boston was filled with stimulating activities and new relationships, and his letters to his friend contain no references to the usual doldrums that beset him when the days were short. Even around the winter solstice, his letters are filled with puns and witty observations. One reason may have been that Boston was much farther south than Wiesbaden. At 42 degrees N latitude, the shortest day of the year in Boston had nine hours and seven minutes of sunlight, compared to Wiesbaden's eight hours and four minutes at 50 degrees N latitude.[31] A second reason was that the winter of 1888/89 was unusually mild in Boston, as he reported to Strong in March.[32] His busy schedule, the unseasonable warmth, and the unaccustomed light helped to avert his usual despondency. The only clue that his seasonal depression was still present may be found in his frequent references to food. He had a ravenous appetite all winter, and many of his letters contain specific references to foods he has enjoyed: "By the way maple syrup on hot cakes is not at all bad, specially toward the last when you 'sop up.'...A benison (not ven=) on you from yours of the (at last) satisfied appetite—(succotash and fried sweet potatoes!!)"[33] Though Edward's moods improved after his move to the United States, his cravings did not abate.[34]

During his first winter back in the United States, MacDowell took up photography as a new hobby. He had always been artistically inclined, and this new pursuit allowed him to create visually arresting images in a fascinating new way. For someone like MacDowell, with his seasonal depression, photography had an additional attraction, for it involves capturing and manipulating light. Edward became an avid student of darkroom techniques in order to improve his images. He wrote to Strong on one occasion about a trick he had learned to make the mountains more prominent in a landscape:

> My wife's uncle Prof. Perkins...gave me some good hints—for instance even when the mountains in your plate are very faint (they always are, d-n it) you can print them perfectly by passing your hand (holding a handkerchief) to and fro over the foreground while printing thus keeping the foreground comparatively in the shade while printing the mountains with the full force of the Sun. This keeps the foreground slower printing

31. J. Lammi, *Online-Photoperiod Calculator* http://www.sci.fi/~benefon/sol.html, accessed 6 February 2010.

32. Letter, EAM to TS, 10 March 1889, EMMC box 29/30.

33. Letter, TS to EAM, 16 November 1888, EMMC box 31/30.

34. Recent research has found that persons with SAD crave carbohydrates during the winter and consequently gain weight during the darker months. See Norman E. Rosenthal, "Diet and SAD," in *Winter Blues: Everything You Need to Know to Beat Seasonal Affective Disorder*, rev. ed. (New York and London: Guilford, 2006), 172–78.

and your mountains come out sharp and black. The handkerchief must be kept <u>moving</u> otherwise a shadow line would be seen.[35]

Because his finances were stretched, he did most of his own developing, in a darkroom he created by curtaining off a portion of a closet. His letters contain frequent references to the formulas he used to develop prints in his home darkroom, for instance: "Speaking of bromide paper the <u>middle quality</u> (smooth and thick) is the easiest to manage—Take care that the <u>Hypo</u> is not stronger than 3 parts H. to 16 p. Water and let them fix for 15 Min."[36] Whether because he had more disposable income or because he was squeamish about the chemicals, Strong sent most of his own plates to be developed by professionals.

MacDowell repeatedly urged Strong to move to the United States, referring often to a promise his friend seems to have made to join him in the spring. Instead, Strong relocated his family to the Swiss town of Vevey on Lake Geneva in spring 1889, where he felt the cost of living would be more affordable than in America. The letters of 1888–1889 also make it clear that Strong was not as ambitious as MacDowell. He was grateful when his friend played his music or convinced others to do so, but he was strangely unresponsive when he learned that his German publisher Jost & Sander was not making his scores available in the United States. MacDowell urged him in practically every letter to brush up on his keyboard skills in order to earn a living when he returned, to which Strong finally replied, "Don't, um Gotteswillen, ask me to practice pianoforte, for when I do I get disgusted with everything. With you practicing is like putting a fresh coat of paint on your house, while with me it is like building a house, which even when finished will be but a poor concern. You can hardly appreciate how discouraging it is for me."[37]

The voluminous correspondence between Strong and MacDowell affords an unparalleled opportunity to follow their professional triumphs and disappointments during the first year in America, along with the mundane details of their daily lives. By contrast, any correspondence between Edward and Marian and the New York branch of the family has been lost. They had made a habit of writing weekly letters since Edward and his mother left for Paris in 1876, but there is only one surviving letter from his parents during 1889. Edward confided to Strong on 26 January that his mother had accepted a position as secretary of Thurber's National Conservatory of Music at a salary of $2,000 per year, which Edward considered unwise. He wrote, "Of course it is none of my business whatsoever but it 'riles' me all the same for

35. Letter, EAM to TS, 2 April 1890, EMMC box 29/30.
36. Letter, EAM to TS, 12 March 1890, EMMC box 29/30.
37. Letter, TS to EAM, 24 November 1888, EMMC box 31/30.

reasons that you know of."[38] In the years ahead, Fanny's position would bring her into contact with many prominent musicians and allow her to advance her son's career through her uncanny ability to charm strangers.

The crucial event of MacDowell's first year in America was his debut with the Theodore Thomas Orchestra in New York on 5 March 1889, when he introduced himself to the New York public as pianist. Since *Hamlet* and *Ophelia* had been played in previous seasons, it was not his first appearance as composer, but still it was an auspicious event. Strong summarized its significance in a letter written after the performance but before he had received word on the outcome:

> I have thought much today about your concert with Thomas, and I feel pretty worried lest you should be nervous, or rather, should have been nervous,—for it is all over with by this time. After all, playing in N.Y. is a species of "crucial" test in that has a man a success there, it is at once known everywhere. If you were yourself and free from nervousness &c then the rest is assured,—no worry then. If you don't send me any of the papers, at any rate send me a copy of some of the better notices, by <u>better</u> I mean the longer and more detailed.[39]

Thomas was known as a kingmaker who seldom played American music. The record shows that he played many works by American composers over the course of his storied career but usually gave them only one hearing. Gossip among aspiring composers claimed that he was prejudiced against Americans, but he countered that he simply had very high standards for the works he would play.

As a pianist, MacDowell's lack of control under pressure had been a problem since his days in Marmontel's class. Currier noted that when he had played with the Kneisel Quartet in October, his fingers had run away with him, leading to slips and muddy playing. His first professional appearance in New York could have been an occasion when nervousness got the better of him, but as he had told Strong after the Boston Art Club concert, both his confidence and technique had grown surprisingly. By March, he was as well prepared as he could be, and he seems to have controlled his nerves at this very important concert.

The Second Piano Concerto had its origins in the abortive *Benedick and Beatrice* sketch that MacDowell had begun on his honeymoon to London in 1884.[40] Portions of this work eventually evolved into the second movement of the concerto, which

38. Letter, EAM to TS, 26 January 1889, EMMC box 29/29.

39. Letter, TS to EAM, 11 March 1889, EMMC box 31/31.

40. This sketch is reproduced in facsimile in Edward MacDowell, *Benedick: A Sketch for the Scherzo from the Second Concerto for Pianoforte*, intro. by John Erskine (New York: The Edward MacDowell Association, Inc., 1947).

gestated slowly during his Wiesbaden years. After his departure, Strong found a sketch for the concerto along with a scrap book containing scores of business letters on the floor of the Grubweg house and asked his friend what to do with them, to which MacDowell replied, "*Burn* the letter book [and] chuck the 2nd Concerto sketch to glory!!"[41] Strong indignantly refused: "I will not burn the letter-book but will wrap it up, seal it and deposit it in my box, labeled as your property, until I can hand it to you, then you can do what you 'darn please' with it. The 2nd Concerto sketch I shall not in the least 'chuck to glory'! Not much! I consider it mine forever more."[42] These two vital sources are now part of the Edward and Marian MacDowell Collection in the Library of Congress.

The rhapsodic first movement features three lengthy cadenzas for piano solo that serve as pillars of the structure. If the historical development of the concerto is heard as a competition between soloist and orchestra, the original Baroque form gave the first and last word to the orchestra, with short solo sections that served mainly as transitional passages between the crucial ritornello sections played by the orchestra. In the Classical era, the typical first movement of a concerto featured an orchestral exposition followed by a solo exposition, with an improvised cadenza for the soloist near the end of the recapitulation, bringing the forces more nearly into balance. Beethoven stretched the form further by starting his fourth and fifth piano concertos with short solo passages. Schumann and Grieg began their concertos with arresting flourishes for piano that set the tone for the movement. The achievement of Liszt, Tchaikovsky, and MacDowell was to give even more weight to the solo parts, tipping the balance in favor of the soloist. After a languid sixteen-measure orchestral introduction, MacDowell brings in the piano with a bold gesture to open the first of the three cadenzas. These cadenzas provide an expansive showpiece for the pianist and served as an ideal vehicle for Edward's introduction to the New York concert audience. The initial melodic ideas are developed throughout the first movement and reprised in the third movement. This extensive melodic development and the chromatic harmonies reflect MacDowell's stylistic loyalty to the New German aesthetic of Liszt and Wagner.

The second movement was MacDowell's favorite, employing his trademark breathtaking speed. Imagining the premiere from Germany, Strong wrote, "By this time you have shown Mr. Theodore Thomas that there is such a thing as good American music, and I hope that you had the splendid success you certainly deserve: tell me all about it. Did you take the second movement at the awful rate you did here? God bless me! My head spins and I see notes and sparks and stars

---

41. Letter, EAM to TS, 12 November 1888, EMMC box 29/28.
42. Letter, TS to EAM, 24 November 1888, EMMC box 31/30.

when I think of it! That and your Czardas were about the two <u>almightily fastest</u> things I ever heard. I'll bet you spiked the great Theodore's gun for him!"[43]

The reviewers assessed his playing favorably, but it was clear that they were more taken with the composition than with the pianist. The *Commercial Advertiser* attributed to MacDowell "a strong virile touch, not lacking in delicacy, and a very satisfactory command of the keyboard."[44] And W. J. Henderson of the *New York Times* added, "Mr. McDowell [*sic*] played the solo part well. He is not a virtuoso, but he has musical feeling, and that is what his composition needs for its proper interpretation."[45] MacDowell's extant correspondence to Strong contains just one brief mention of the concert: "The N.Y. Music papers, much to my astonishment were tremendously complimentary about my Concerto and piano playing."[46]

As Strong had noted, a success in New York soon echoed around the country. The late nineteenth century was a golden age in American music criticism: newspapers and arts journals gave large amounts of space to concert reviews, and groups of thoughtful and articulate critics vied with each other to analyze and describe important new works. James G. Huneker wrote an exceptionally complimentary review in the *Musical Courier*, a journal with a large national circulation; Henry E. Krehbiel, generally acknowledged as the dean of American music critics, showered praise on the young composer:

> His concerto afforded a delight of no mean order. It is a splendid composition, so full of poetry, so full of vigor, as to tempt the assertion that it must be placed at the head of all works of its kind produced by either a native or adopted citizen of America. But comparisons are not necessary to enable one to place an estimate upon it. It can stand by itself and challenge the heartiest admiration for its contents, its workmanship, its originality of thought and treatment.[47]

MacDowell scored a major triumph with this performance, which propelled him to national prominence in a way his Boston appearances had not.

The concert also brought him to the attention of Thomas, as verified by a famous one-liner. When Huneker told Thomas several weeks later that he thought the work was "very good for an 'American,'" Thomas interrupted him indignantly with the

---

43. Letter, TS to EAM, 11 March 1889, EMMC box 31/31.

44. "Music and the Drama: The Seventh Thomas Concert," *New York Commercial Advertiser* (6 March, 1889): 3.

45. [W. J. Henderson], "The Thomas Concerts," *NYT,* 6 March 1889, 4.

46. Letter, EAM to TS, [10 March 1889], EMMC box 29/30.

47. [Henry E. Krehbiel], "Music–The Drama: The Fifth Thomas Concert," *New York Tribune*, 6 March 1889, 6.

words "or for a German either."[48] In the coming years the conductor would return often to this work and others by MacDowell, helping to cement the reputation of his orchestral works. In honor of his former teacher and his mother's close friend, MacDowell had dedicated the work to Teresa Carreño. When she began performing it the following year in Germany, it proved to be the ideal vehicle for her fiery pianism, and she subsequently performed it more than forty times with orchestras around the world.

In the wake of his New York concert, MacDowell had a rude introduction to the ways of American publicity. After the successful premiere of his Second Concerto in New York, he received many compliments, including a letter from Huneker of the *Musical Courier*. This music journal was one of the country's most popular, and Huneker proposed to print an engraved portrait on the front cover of the 10 April issue along with a biographical article. This sort of publicity could be very helpful to an aspiring artist, and when Lang heard about it, he jokingly asked Edward what he had paid for it.

Much to Edward's surprise, on the day after the issue appeared he received a package from Marc Blumenberg, the journal's trade editor, containing fifty copies of his issue along with a bill for fifty dollars under separate cover. As the cover price of the journal was ten cents, he felt that this was extortion and returned the package unopened, stating that he could purchase all the copies he needed through local booksellers. Huneker wrote immediately to say that he thought MacDowell had *understood* that the thing needed to be paid for, and that usually the cost was somewhere between $75 and $100. He added that the engraving alone had cost twenty-five dollars and offered to pay for it himself because he had initiated the misunderstanding. Thereupon Edward's heart softened and he sent Huneker a check for twenty-five dollars, but in his next letter to Strong he warned him to be wary of anyone who approached him with such an offer.

From this point on, MacDowell became very cagey about supplying biographical information to authors. To F. H. Jules of the *Boston Transcript*, he wrote on 18 November 1889:

My dear Sir,

Your kind note of the 12th was received by me today, and while I beg to thank you heartily for it, I am sorry to have to refuse your request for data about myself. The fact is, I cannot help thinking that if my doings are not already known to you, that I certainly need not be mentioned in the article in question.—To put it plainer—if you know but little or nothing about me, how can I conscienciously [sic] allow you to write about me upon my own authority alone. If my biography is not known, why need it be—? I hope you will

48. Letter, James G. Huneker to EAM, 20 March 1889, EMMC box 30/61.

understand that my declining the honour you propose to pay me, is based entirely upon principle and that a wish to disoblige has no part in it.[49]

This attitude was exasperating to writers who wanted to make MacDowell's music known, especially when they were working under deadlines. The Chicago critic W. S. B. Mathews edited a book on American musicians for Granville L. Howe in 1889, one that is now known to historians as an important source of biographical information from the period. After a failed attempt to secure information from MacDowell, the editor vented his spleen in this letter of 28 October 1889:

Dear Mr. McDowell;

Your modesty is all poppy cock (pardon) and out of place. It has never prevented you from allowing your name to appear upon the title page of a good many beautiful pieces of music. It has permitted you to fill a prominent place as teacher of piano in European conservatories. It did not hinder you from appearing as a concert pianist at Paris with a concerto of your own. I do not ask you to puff yourself, but I do think you can give me the date of your <u>birth, place,</u> name of your teacher, and the names of your compositions, and much other matter necessary to complete the story without any impropriety. To spare your blushes; you might dictate the information to Mrs. McDowell in the dark. I think you owe it to Mme. Carreño and to your excellent mother to do this very soon. I must have a photograph. <u>You are the best American composer of piano music that we have and we</u> <u>cannot</u> <u>leave you out of the book.</u> Hoping you will reconsider your ill-timed decision. I remain

Very truly yours,
W. S. B. Mathews.

Don't fail, please, my dear sir. This is to be a beautiful book, and while it will have some in it who never would have been missed, it will carry information to many thousands.[50]

MacDowell evidently did not respond to this attempt to shame him into compliance, because the brief notice in the book is full of errors and is not accompanied by a photograph.[51]

On 13 April 1889, MacDowell made his debut with the Boston Symphony Orchestra (BSO), again playing his Second Piano Concerto. At the public rehearsal on the 12th, the 4,000-seat auditorium was filled to overflowing, with audience members crowding onto the sides of the stage, and he was recalled three times.[52]

49. Letter, EAM to J. H. Jules, 18 November 1889, Irving and Margery Lowens Collection.
50. Letter, W. S. B. Mathews to EAM, 28 October 1889, EMMC box 30/79.
51. *A Hundred Years of Music in America*, ed. W. S. B. Mathews (Chicago, 1889; repr. New York: AMS Press, 1970), 697.
52. Letter, Templeton Strong to EAM, 12 April 1889, EMMC box 31/31.

The curiosity was intense, and MacDowell did not disappoint the citizens of his adopted home. The Boston critics praised his performance at the concert on the 13th, noting that the orchestra members were especially supportive of the pianist who had made such an impact during his first half year in Boston.[53]

The BSO held an important place in American culture at this time. Whereas the New York Philharmonic was a cooperative in which members voted for their conductor, shared profits equally, and made administrative decisions democratically, the BSO was the pet project of one exceptional individual. Henry Lee Higginson (1834–1919) was a wealthy banker who established the orchestra in 1881 with the goal of creating a world-class instrumental ensemble in his hometown. He personally guaranteed all deficits, and in return for his investment exercised an unusual level of personal control. Higginson wanted his players to dedicate their best energies to his organization and consequently forbade them from playing dances or other outside engagements on days when his orchestra rehearsed or performed. He gave the conductors of the BSO artistic freedom, but he exercised his prerogative to replace them if he did not agree with their artistic direction. As noted earlier, Gericke had already resigned by the time he led the orchestra in MacDowell's concerto, soon to be replaced by another European conductor, Arthur Nikisch. The rumor that reached MacDowell's ears was that Higginson's wife believed that Gericke played too much Wagner, leading to his dismissal. In the coming years, Nikisch would introduce even more music by Wagner and similar composers, leading to more discord in conservative Boston. For MacDowell, the opportunity to play with Theodore Thomas in New York and Wilhelm Gericke in Boston in the space of five weeks brought him to the attention of the leading musicians of the country.

His run of good luck was not over, as he learned in a letter from his father written 23 May 1889. Thomas McDowell's extant letters are normally brief and businesslike, but in this case he was writing on behalf of Fanny, who was too exhausted from her work at the National Conservatory to pick up a pen herself. The long letter related that Fanny had received a visit that day from Frank Van der Stucken, who had asked her to approach her son with a proposal for a concert in Paris. The Exposition Universelle, which took place every eleven years, was to include a series of concerts featuring the national music of different countries, and Van der Stucken had been asked to conduct a concert of American composers. Among other works, he wanted to present MacDowell's Second Piano Concerto with the composer as soloist. He offered to pay travel expenses and hotel expenses for a week, along with

53. See for instance "Boston Symphony Orchestra, 22nd Concert, Music Hall," *Boston Home Journal*, 20 April 1889.

a share of the profits in the unlikely event that the concert yielded any. Thomas urged his son to respond quickly, as the conductor urgently needed to finalize his plans. He closed by saying, "he said there were many who wanted their own composition presented in this Concert, but he wanted the <u>best</u> only & so he wanted you."[54]

MacDowell was none too fond of American Composers' Concerts, and he had turned down several invitations to participate in similar events in Cincinnati since moving to Boston. But this opportunity was too good to miss, and he immediately agreed to participate. In a letter to Strong he shared the good news:

> My dear Old Boy,
>
> Why oh why is there no letter from you? I hope you are not under the weather at all—It seems ages since I have gotten a sight of your fist.—Now I am going to spring something on you which fills <u>me</u> with extasy [*sic*] and I hope will make you also rejoice. What do you say to my making a trip to <u>Vevey</u> this Summer? hey!! You see there is going to be an American Concert at the Trocadéro in Paris (part of the Exposition of course) and I am to play my 2nd Concerto—my expenses there and back are to be paid—but I don't see why I cannot afford to look you up in Vevey and having the <u>devil</u> of a good time with you. Why couldn't you run up to Paris and hear the Concert—we could return together—there you could see the Exposition and also see Van der Stucken who will lead—He seemed to admire you and Bergen Symphony enormously when I last saw him (which was when I first landed) and surely only <u>waits for the</u> <u>chance</u> to play something of yours....I shall stay in Paris no longer than is necessary on account of expense, and make straight for <u>Schweitz</u>. How I look forward to telling you all the news etc. etc....I have <u>so</u> much to tell you old boy that I am afraid I'll <u>bust</u> before I get there—My wife will come along too Oh Lord! Won't it be a lark.[55]

Edward and Marian sailed from New York on the *Bretagne* bound for Le Havre on 15 June 1889. They wanted to limit the expense of staying in Paris during the Exposition and so made directly for Vevey, Switzerland, where Strong had moved several months earlier. His friend and his family were spending the summer in the mountains, allowing Edward and Marian to have use of their home in Vevey to rest and practice for the upcoming performance.[56] Strong did not follow MacDowell's advice to accompany them to Paris to meet Van der Stucken, proving once again that his professional ambitions did not match those of his friend.

54. Letter, Thomas F. McDowell to Eddie MacDowell, 23 May 1889, EMMC box 30/74.

55. Letter, EAM to TS, 27 May 1889, EMMC box 29/30.

56. Templeton Strong, "Edward MacDowell as I Knew Him, ninth paper," *Music Student* 8/8 (April 1916): 223.

The organizers of the Exposition Universelle of 1889 wanted to bring the world to Paris. They created an event that highlighted both French technology—the Eiffel Tower was erected for this event—and exotic cultures from around the world. It was here that Claude Debussy was famously exposed to the Javanese gamelan that exercised such a profound impact on his compositional style. The Annamite theater from Southeast Asia was another exotic performance that garnered much attention from Europeans. Capitalizing on the taste for exotic cultures, Buffalo Bill Cody brought his show to Paris simultaneously with the Exposition, even though he was not a part of the official program. The series of concerts in the Trocadéro, across the Seine from the Exposition grounds, was designed to showcase art music from countries outside the normal sphere of French concert life. In addition to Van der Stucken's American concert were afternoons of Russian, Norwegian, Italian, and Spanish art music.

Orchestral music comprised the majority of the long program, as Van der Stucken sought to introduce the best of recent American works to the international audience. In addition to MacDowell's Concerto, the long program included Foote's overture *In the Mountains*, op. 14, Van der Stucken's suite *The Tempest*, op. 8, Chadwick's dramatic overture *Melpomene*, Huss's *Romanze et Polonaise* for violin and orchestra, Paine's Prelude to *Oedipus Tyrannus*, op. 35, Arthur Bird's *Carnival Scene*, op. 5, and Dudley Buck's rousing Festival Overture on *The Star-Spangled Banner*. Paine and Buck were the senior statesmen of the group, while Foote, Chadwick, Huss, MacDowell, Bird, Lang, and Van der Stucken represented the younger generation. The one thing that they all had in common was an international aesthetic that eschewed any hint of folklorism and made no claims to be distinctively American.

But this was not what the French critics expected. By presenting an entire program of American works, Van der Stucken created the expectation that these compositions would evince a unified school of composition with uniquely American—in other words exotic to French ears—stylistic characteristics. With this expectation, the critics were bound to be disappointed. The most typical comment was that the American compositions drew on influences from European composers, a fact that should not have been surprising but was nonetheless cause for derision from many of the critics. Julien Torchet summed up the overall impact of the concert thus: "The performance was relatively cold, despite the exuberant efforts of the expatriate colony to provoke enthusiasm. It seems to me that the public did not prove to be completely fair in these manifestations; they were wrong to demand an original school from composers who do not boast of having one, and they should have listened without preoccupations of this sort."[57] The critics had very little context on

57. Julien Torchet, "Concert de musique américaine au Trocadéro," *Le Monde artiste* 29/29 (21 July 1889): 449. For a more extensive discussion of this concert and the critical reaction it inspired, see

which to critique American music, for as Victor Wilder admitted, "The program of this concert...carried ten names; they are all practically unknown to us, because—it is necessary to repeat unceasingly—our vainglorious indifference leaves us in the most crass ignorance of what is produced beyond our borders."[58] MacDowell was arguably the most famous of the composers on the program but was unknown to most of the critics. None of the reviewers mentioned MacDowell's student years in Paris, and there is no reason to think that any of them knew he had been a student of Marmontel. For MacDowell, his performance at the Exposition must have had a sort of poetic symmetry, since his last public appearance in Paris had taken place during the previous Exposition in 1878. For the critics, he was as much a stranger as the other Americans on the program.

After the Paris concert, the MacDowells returned to Switzerland for a month with Strong. In his recollections about the summer, Strong wrote in great detail about the hikes they took together and Edward's passion for his new hobby of photography. Marian was in good health, allowing them to undertake mountain hikes of many miles. They took pictures of the scenery, including a log cabin that Strong believed was the inspiration for the MacDowells' famous cabin in Peterborough, New Hampshire, years later. Strong recalled that "Edward inoculated me with the virus of the photographic mania, which he had contracted in America, and which he retained during the remainder of his life; photography becoming a very great source of delight to him."[59] There is not a word in his reminiscences of any musical discussions or the things that Edward had been so eager to tell him. By the time Edward and Marian left in mid-August, though, they must have covered everything, for Edward's note from Lausanne was uncharacteristically brief: "Dear old boy. Will you sometime when you go to town tell them at the post that any letters that may come for me can find me at 13 W. Cedar St. Boston. Please don't chew up my base ball bat, but bring it with you when you come, and may it be soon—E."[60]

For Edward MacDowell, 1888/89 was a year of returns, both literal and figurative. His return to the United States meant both a commitment to his native land and a repudiation of the German home that he had found artistically attractive but professionally disappointing. His concerto performance with Theodore Thomas in New York was a culmination of this return, when he achieved a symbolic victory both as composer and performer in his hometown. The performance of his

E. Douglas Bomberger, "The Exposition Universelle of 1889: American Music on a World Stage," chap. 5 of *"A Tidal Wave of Encouragement,"* 45–64.

58. Victor Wilder, "La Musique américaine au Trocadéro," *Gil Blas* (16 July 1889): 3.

59. Strong, "Edward MacDowell as I Knew Him, ninth paper," 223.

60. Undated postcard, EAM to TS, postmarked Lausanne, 13 August 1889, EMMC box 29/31.

concerto at the Exposition Universelle in Paris was also a return, as he revisited the city he had left abruptly before completing his studies. Finally, the return to the United States also necessitated a return to piano performance, forcing him to play in public dozens of times during his first year to supplement his income. This brought him back to the career path that his parents had envisioned for him, and it would force him to reconsider his own professional goals in the years ahead.

CHAPTER TEN

The Politics of Musical Boston

E DWARD MACDOWELL'S FIRST YEAR IN BOSTON HAD BROUGHT THE KIND OF success that most musicians can only imagine. His Boston colleagues had welcomed him cordially, but it was clear that his success would eventually alter the pecking order in this city of rich musical traditions. MacDowell now faced a political landscape that was complicated and potentially treacherous for him. As the novelty of his presence in Boston wore off, it became obvious that among his many gifts was little evidence of tact and diplomacy.

Boston was a city that valued culture and learning. The Boston Symphony Orchestra, founded by Henry Lee Higginson in 1881, had already become one of the world's premiere orchestras under the leadership of Henschel and Gericke. Arthur Nikisch, who took the helm in 1889, improved the ensemble further and provided numerous opportunities for Boston composers and soloists, including MacDowell. Boston's churches hired organists and singers to provide high-quality music for their services. The wealthy citizens of Boston ("Brahmins") supported the arts lavishly, creating a rich climate for musical performance and generous support for local composers. Boston's publishers—Oliver Ditson, A. P. Schmidt, Boston Music Company and others—competed for the privilege of publishing the best works of the Boston composers.

When MacDowell arrived in this climate of artistic ferment, he was thrilled at the opportunities, especially in contrast to his lean years in Germany. But Strong warned him to be wary of the established Boston musicians, who might not welcome him with open arms if his activities threatened their income in any way.

In his first letter from Boston on 7 October 1888, Edward had already sensed the animosity:

> Don't write to anyone—the musical people here (I mean America) are all enemies to each other, and the amount of lies, gossip and "hearsay" that goes about is simply bewildering. We are as yet Friends to everybody, as everybody wants us on their side—therefore don't let a word be heard from you to anyone till you can profit by my experience....Remain the (personally) "great unknown" till you can see by my experience what strange wire-pulling goes on all the time here.

The two made a pact that they would be completely frank in their comments but would burn each other's letters after reading them, a promise that neither man kept. More than one hundred letters eventually made their way to the Library of Congress, providing not just a startling exposé of Boston's musical politics during this era but also an insight into Edward's weaknesses in interpersonal relations.

In many instances it is clear that MacDowell knew the politically expedient thing to do but bridled at doing it. He justified this by claiming that he was maintaining his independence or upholding his artistic standards. In the fall of 1888 he was offered a generous commission of $100 to write an anthem for the Ruggles Street Baptist Church. He worked on it for months but in the end gave up and forfeited the commission. Marian remembered years later that the church leaders "must have thought him mighty stupid—But once for all he made up his mind that he could never do his best work to order."[1] This was the only instance when he attempted a sacred composition, which may have been another factor in his inability to complete the commission. His ambivalent childhood relationship to the Quaker Meeting, along with the Quaker interdiction against music in worship services, must have compounded his discomfort. MacDowell also refused to play for private events at the homes of Boston's wealthy citizens. He wrote to Strong on 19 January 1889 that he had refused $100 to play a recital for the Beethoven Club because "'Private parlor hired musician' is not my line."[2]

MacDowell's main point of contact in Boston was B. J. Lang, the conductor who had convinced him during a visit to Wiesbaden that he should return to the United States. This man was extremely well connected in all areas of Boston's musical life in his multiple roles as organist, conductor, and teacher. Lang hosted a large gathering of musicians in MacDowell's honor shortly after his arrival in October 1888, and he conducted his works regularly on choral concerts of his Cecilia and Apollo Clubs. He took MacDowell to baseball games and introduced him to persons who could be helpful to the newcomer. As MacDowell noted to Strong, however, he did not do

1. "Marian MacDowell's Personal Records," 73–74, EMMC.
2. EAM to TS, 19 January 1889, EMMC box 29/29.

the one thing that would have been most useful—send him students. This as much as anything led MacDowell to resent Lang.

Within a few months of his arrival, MacDowell began to lose respect for the older man and had the temerity to disagree with him publicly. On 21 February 1889, he wrote to Strong:

> You know old boy, the great trouble with Lang is, that he wants to be the Lord God in Boston and cannot imagine any one differing from his opinion in the slightest manner. I most certainly do in very, <u>very</u> many things and have the courage to say so. For instance when Rosenthal the pianist came here, Lang went and <u>sniffed</u> all through it, <u>I</u> applauded like <u>thunder</u> for he certainly plays tremendously. Lang afterwards said <u>he</u> nor any of <u>his</u> scholars never would want to play in that "wretched firework Liszt style" and appealed to me for corroberation [*sic*]; I simply said, I though [*sic*] Rosenthal a very splendid pianist— and changed the subject—I don't think he ever can forgive me that and now my getting some of his own scholars (old ones too, Mrs. Smith for instance had lessons of him for 7 years and seems only now to be "waking up") makes him inwardly furious.[3]

Two days later, MacDowell reported on Lang's performance of Strong's choral work *Die verlassene Mühle*. The reviews in all the papers had been excellent, but after the concert Lang asked MacDowell what he thought of the tempi. As he reported to Strong, he was not about to give him an undeserved compliment simply to be nice, and so he told him that the tempi were too slow. To this MacDowell reported that "He said jokingly, but I fancy inwardly seriously, that he was going to write you that <u>I</u> was the only one who could find fault with the performance!! I told him to just blaze away without regard to politeness if he felt like it!"[4] On 11 March, the more diplomatic Strong urged his friend to be more politic, and he made it clear that he wanted no part in a dispute with this influential man. On 4 April Strong described at length his efforts to patch things up with Lang, giving his friend a lesson in diplomacy that Edward sorely needed:

> I said in my letter of thanks to Mr. Lang—"MacDowell wrote me as you did, viz: that there was an occasional flatness at the first concert, but that the second concert went finely." I know that Lang thinks you write to me, & I don't wish him to think that you damned everything right and left that had anything to do with the concert, and from selfish motives also, I wrote as above, for it would have been hard lines had I to write to him thus: "I understand that the concert went like Hell, notwithstanding what you say, and I thank you for taking so much trouble and regret the abominable performance." &c &c Did I write so, Mr. Lang would say your report was accountable but I am not going

---

3. Letter, EAM to TS, 21 February 1889, EMMC box 29/29.
4. EAM to TS, 23 February 1889, EMMC box 29/29.

to be the cause of any trouble between you and Mr. Lang,—not if I know it, so that I preferred telling this damned lie, which after all does nobody any harm,—a lie in the cause of peace and goodwill.[5]

Things seem to have gone better with Lang during the summer and fall of 1889, but in the winter of 1890 their relationship again grew strained. On 8 April 1890 MacDowell wrote Strong a long litany of complaints against Lang, most of which revolved around their competition for students. During his second year in Boston (1889–1890), MacDowell's studio grew substantially, as he curtailed his public performances in favor of more lucrative teaching opportunities and more time for composing. He had earned $1,500 during his first year in Boston (mostly through performances), but he earned $2,500 during his second year (primarily through teaching). This evidently began to take a toll on Lang's income, or at least his reputation as Boston's leading teacher. MacDowell reported on gossip that he had heard about Lang's attempts to keep students away from MacDowell. He cited as an example a piano student of Lang's who had requested harmony lessons from MacDowell but never followed through with setting up a time and ended up studying harmony with Lang. He told Strong:

> Lang came to see me, and came out with the astonishing remark, that "should it happen (naming "for instance" the lady spoken of above) that one of his pupils came to me for lessons, no matter how untalented she or he were, that it would make him feel very badly"—thus you see trying to warn me off—I simply laughed and said I was here to make my living and if any one wanted lessons of me I could not afford to refuse them for any nonsensical ideas like that. Well, he said he only wanted me to know how he thought about such matters, so we dropped the question....He is a charming man personally and I am sorry he is not more reliable. I think he got me to Boston to play off against Baermann (the pianist) but never reckoned that it would work both ways, and now is regretting it bitterly.[6]

Unlike Strong, MacDowell felt compelled to tell Lang exactly what he thought, no matter the consequences. Because of his audacity, Lang and the other Boston musicians gradually distanced themselves from him. In the succeeding years, Lang conducted many of MacDowell's choral works as they were written, but he conducted Strong's works even more often.

MacDowell did not fare much better with the other Boston composers. The letters allude frequently to his distrust of Arthur Foote and Arthur Whiting, who like him earned their living teaching and performing on piano while also establishing

5. TS to EAM, 4 April 1889, EMMC box 31/31.
6. EAM to TS, 8 April 1890, EMMC box 29/30.

modest reputations as composers. He viewed any overtures at friendliness with suspicion, and he particularly resented their habit of gossiping about other musicians in his presence. On 1 March 1890 he described an evening spent with Foote and Chadwick:

> My dear boy, they are all the same. I had good proof of it the other night—There was some question of forming a "Composers' Club" and Chadwick Foote & myself met to see what could be done to start such a one—and the abuse I heard indulged in about almost every body was immense. I got kind of mad at all that back biting and at last when Chadwick said the object of the proposed club ought to be the "exchange of ideas" I saw the chance I had been waiting for and got up and I fear rather drily said "I don't think I care to swap" and cleared out. Of course it broke up in a laugh but when you are not there you can be sure they talk about you as they do about everybody else, at least that's the way I feel and consequently don't take much stock in them—[7]

MacDowell prided himself on being "straight" with everyone he met, but this frequently led him to insult other musicians in public. It seems that his own extreme sensitivity to criticism did not transfer to a corresponding empathy for the feelings of others, and within a few years the Boston musicians began to steer clear of him.

Compounding the interpersonal problems with other composers was a fundamental difference in their aesthetic views. MacDowell and Strong viewed themselves as modern composers who were building on the experiments of Liszt and Wagner to create new and challenging music for the future. In their view, the Boston composers were too conservative, basing their music on European styles that had long been passé. After hearing a performance of Foote's String Suite No. 2, op. 21, he reported to Strong in a letter of 25 November 1889: "Foote's String Suite—which he trotted out to us in Wiesbaden—was done by Nikisch (and the Boston Symphony), had lots of success (applause), but it is 'rot de la rot.' By gum, I don't mind its being prehistoric but it is bad prehistoric."[8] His highest disdain was reserved for Otto Dresel, a German immigrant whose reactionary views were legendary but who was well connected with Boston's elite. On 3 January 1889 he reported to Strong that Dresel's dislike of Wagner had been the reason behind Higginson's decision to remove Gericke as conductor of the Boston Symphony Orchestra, calling him "a rabid old rotten egg" in one sentence, "this old antediluvian camel" in the next, and "Herr Esel" [ass] in the next. Small wonder that he repeatedly urged Strong to burn his letters after reading them.[9]

---

7. EAM to TS, 1 March 1890, EMMC box 29/30.
8. EAM to TS, 25 November 1889, EMMC box 29/31.
9. EAM to TS, 3 January 1889, EMMC box 29/29.

On 29 March 1890, Edward reported that he had been "'striking' on the Symphony Concerts" because they interfered with his musical ideas. Unfortunately, he was not using the extra time for composition but was putting it all into photography. In the same letter he excitedly reported that mixing his own developing solution saved him 75 percent of the cost, allowing him to spend more time in his darkroom developing bromide prints.[10] Many of his letters contain advice for Strong on chemical formulas and developing techniques, and the two men exchanged photographs regularly.

The musician whom he respected most in the Boston group was George Whitefield Chadwick, whose personality was diametrically opposed to his own. Chadwick was six years older than MacDowell, and he too remembered his European years with fondness. In a memoir written for his children thirty years after MacDowell's arrival in Boston, Chadwick recalled the curious impression he made:

> With me, MacD was very frank + companionable for a time. He and Mrs often came to our house and we had many long walks, rides and talks together. Of others he was suspicious and shy. It was difficult to get him to commit himself on any subject except publishers and royalties. From these he was absolutely convinced that we were all getting a raw deal. He disliked some of our friends, especially Arthur Whiting who was a bit too witty for him. He had a subtle vein of irony of his own, but he was very careful of its use among strangers. He would not go out among people if he could help it and was very ill at ease when he did so.[11]

Chadwick had the skills that MacDowell lacked when it came to relationships. He enjoyed socializing and often planned "Kneippe" (German-style beer parties) with the local musicians. He maintained ties with musicians in other cities and leveraged these connections into performance opportunities for his compositions. He became close with the conductors of the BSO and benefited from their patronage. He enjoyed being part of organizations and clubs, both socially and professionally, something the introverted MacDowell avoided whenever possible.

If Chadwick's strengths were in areas where MacDowell was weak, his weaknesses were in areas where MacDowell excelled. Chadwick's letters and memoirs show an atrocious lack of concern for spelling and grammar, and MacDowell noted with horror that his friend did not proofread his scores when they were being prepared for publication. He and Strong were fastidious with publishers' proofs, and

10. Letter, EAM to TS, 29 March 1890, EMMC box 29/33.

11. George Whitefield Chadwick, Memoir, Spaulding Library, New England Conservatory, Boston.

they frequently proofread each other's scores because they could be more precise with scores they had not composed themselves. MacDowell was difficult with publishers, in one case requiring A. P. Schmidt to make corrections in pen on scores that had been inadvertently printed with uncorrected errors. Chadwick, on the other hand, was blithely unconcerned about such niceties.[12]

Their respective personalities and attitudes toward their music are reflected in the events surrounding two concerts organized by Frank Van der Stucken. MacDowell had been thrilled to accept the invitation to perform his Second Piano Concerto at the Paris Exposition of 1889 under Van der Stucken's direction. The concert also included Chadwick's *Melpomene*, a "dramatic overture" based on the Greek muse of tragedy. Whereas much of Chadwick's output is light-hearted and "Irish" (as MacDowell disparagingly described his Symphony No. 1 to Strong), this serious work begins with an overt allusion to Wagner's Overture to *Tristan und Isolde*, developing this and other themes in an expansive and intensely Romantic piece of orchestral tone-painting. MacDowell had heard the work previously in Boston, so he recognized that Van der Stucken made some significant changes to the score for the Paris performance, most notably having the percussion play the tam-tam with snare drum sticks rather than a soft mallet (an effect that the milk dealer's son described as a "cow micturating in a tin pail").[13] MacDowell was by this time disenchanted with Van der Stucken, and he delighted in reporting this injustice to Chadwick upon his return to Boston. Chadwick's anger was increased when he received the score back from Van der Stucken with numerous changes marked into the parts.

Later that winter, Van der Stucken was invited to repeat the Paris concert in Washington, DC, on a gala occasion that Jeannette Thurber organized to promote her National Conservatory of Music with legislators on 26 March 1890. Van der Stucken invited both MacDowell and Chadwick to reprise their performances, but MacDowell flatly refused. Chadwick pointedly asked Van der Stucken whether he intended to play his work the way he wrote it or with the changes. In the end, Chadwick made up with Van der Stucken and participated in a very important professional opportunity. MacDowell stayed away and refused to loan the score of the as-yet-unpublished Concerto, but ironically Van der Stucken was so eager to include his name on the program that he obtained a copy of *Ophelia* and performed it without the composer's permission.

12. Letter, EAM to TS, 31 March 1890, EMMC box 29/33, reported that he forced Schmidt to correct two errors by pen in each copy of *Les Orientales*, op. 37; he reported in the same letter that Schmidt told him Chadwick "<u>will not</u> correct proofs (!!!)."

13. Letter, EAM to TS, 13 November 1889, EMMC box 29/31.

It is not insignificant that all of the conflicts cited above took place in late winter. Even though Boston was slightly farther south than Wiesbaden, MacDowell's seasonal depression continued to flare up each year as winter dragged toward spring. Again and again, the correspondence shows that MacDowell's frustrations most often swelled to the point of public confrontations between February and early April. When he broke off a relationship or complained about ill treatment at the hands of others, he does not seem to have made the connection that these events nearly always occurred when he was weary of winter and longing for spring. During this time of year especially, he was unwilling to "go along to get along," instead breaking off relationships or refusing professional opportunities on principle.

Occasionally, his spirits were buoyed by positive events at this time of year. On 13 February 1890, Teresa Carreño played perhaps the most important performance of his music to date. She had taken a year off to refine her technique before venturing onto the concert stage again. In the fall of 1889 she had traveled to Germany, where the concert agent Hermann Wolff introduced her to the Berlin public and scheduled performances in other German cities. The German public was conquered by her dazzling technique and fiery temperament. For her third performance of the Berlin concert season, she proposed to play MacDowell's First Piano Concerto, which had never been heard in Berlin. Wolff told her that the German public was too conservative to accept an unknown modern work, to which she reportedly replied, "No MacDowell, no Carreño!" The manager acquiesced, and she scored a brilliant success for herself and her young protégé. She wrote to MacDowell the following day congratulating him on the success of his work. In the same letter, she gave him a bit of "grandmotherly advice." She told him that Hans von Bülow would soon be visiting Boston, and she urged him to pay a visit to the famous German pianist and to be nice to him. Like Chadwick, she understood the importance of connections and did not want to see MacDowell waste the hard-won reputation she had earned for him through her performances in Germany. Like Strong, she did not want to see her young friend lose supporters by speaking too frankly.

Edward, however, took pride in his independence and preferred to make his own way without asking for help from others. This kept him from realizing how crucial his friends were to his success. In another passage from the memoir cited above, Chadwick wrote:

> B.J. Lang found him very "difficile" although I am sure his efforts were meant in all kindness....[MacDowell] would not go out among people if he could help it and was very ill at ease when he did so. It was for this reason that he resented Lang's good offices. He tried to "arrange" functions for him and Mac thought he wanted to pose as his discoverer.

MacD really had B.J to thank for his start for he produced his Suite (his first work) and his first P.F. concerto at his concerto concerts and did a lot of talking.[14]

Genius alone is not enough to make a career, and Edward had the good fortune to find persons like Carreño, Strong, Chadwick, and Lang who believed in him enough to help him advance despite his lack of political tact. During his early years in Boston, their support allowed him to establish himself and prepare for his greatest triumphs.

14. Chadwick, Memoir.

CHAPTER ELEVEN

MacDowell the Pianist

ACDOWELL'S TEACHER MARMONTEL SUMMED UP HIS PLAYING SUCCINCTLY
in January 1877: "Has excellent pianistic qualities but lacks self-control."
MacDowell had refined those qualities under Heymann, and he had begun his
career in Germany by filling engagements as a piano performer and teacher. But
after his marriage in 1884, piano took a back seat to composition. His last years in
Germany had seen no performing and only a little piano teaching. Upon arrival in
Boston, necessity forced him to rely on his piano skills immediately to earn a living,
and during the next several years he made his reputation as much by performing
and teaching as by composing. This change of direction had a profound impact on
his composition, as his intense engagement with the piano influenced not only
the genres in which he composed but also the ways he wrote for the instrument. It
was during the Boston years that MacDowell refined the pianism that would be his
greatest legacy to American music.

MacDowell immediately set to work to regain his facility when he arrived in
his new home in October 1888, but there was not enough time to become completely comfortable before his first appearance at the Kneisel Quartet concert of 19
November 1888, when he was still a bit rusty. This debut set the tone for his reputation as a pianist in the years ahead. His student T. P. Currier, who had the advantage
of working closely with MacDowell but also hearing the gossip after the concert,
summarized the reaction in this way:

> Few pianists have encountered more opposition in Boston than that which Edward
> MacDowell met when he made his first appearance there as a pianist in the autumn of
> 1888. His was a style of piano playing which to many of his hearers was not only unfa-
> miliar, but totally inexplicable. Amazement and feeble applause greeted him at a Kneisel

Concert early in the season. Such astonishing velocity, such lack of clean-cut finger work, such vague, inarticulate melodic delivery,—playing which went by so rapidly that one did not have time to realize what it was all about; it could not be classified. The average concert-goer's opinion was probably voiced by a prominent piano teacher, who remarked to another, "That's too much for me. When a pianist plays a scale I want to hear every note of it."[1]

MacDowell's technique emphasized speed at the expense of clarity. As Currier quipped, "He took to prestissimo like a duck to water." Throughout his performing career he worried that his fingers would run away from him, causing him anxiety and stage fright before his concerts. Marian recalled, though, that once Edward sat down at the instrument and began to play, his fears vanished, and he was able to focus on the sounds he produced. By the new year, his confidence was growing, and on 26 January he reported that he had played twenty-one times in public in Boston so far. MacDowell relished the immediate response to his performances, and he and Marian needed the money his playing generated, but Strong was not so enthusiastic. In the previously cited letter of 17 December 1888 he had advised his friend: "You must not play too much: you must pose principally as Komponist. You must insist upon this, especially now that everybody sees that you can play."[2]

Striking a satisfactory balance among teaching, performing, and composing remained a challenge for the rest of MacDowell's career. Amid the flurry of performances and the scramble to find students, he composed virtually nothing during his first year in Boston. Though he received many engagements and captivated his audiences, the critics of both the solo and the concerto performances agreed that he was a better composer than a pianist. He consequently reduced his performances significantly after the first year in favor of composition and teaching.

MacDowell's playing was indeed unconventional. As noted by Currier, he played rapid passagework with breathtaking velocity, aiming for an impressionistic wash of sound rather than the pearly clarity then in vogue. He also used an immense dynamic range from almost inaudible pianissimos to fortissimos so loud that chords were harsh and percussive. The harshness of his chord playing was frequently criticized, especially in the standard repertoire. Curiously, when he played his own works, these defects were minimized by passages that call for bell-like semi-detached chords and melodies, for instance in this passage from "Shadow Dance" [Schattentanz], op. 39, no. 8. Measures 25–28 establish a whispery right-hand accompaniment, under

1. T. P. Currier, "MacDowell's Technic as Related to his Piano Music," *Musician* 13/3 (March 1908): 113.
2. Letter, TS to EAM, 17 December 1888, EMMC box 31/30.

which the marcato chordal melody enters in m. 29. The passage benefits from both indistinctness in the right-hand passagework and percussiveness in the melody:

11.1 "Shadow Dance," op. 39, no. 8, mm. 25–32

This piece is one of the Twelve Etudes, op. 39, the first set of works that MacDowell wrote after returning to composition in the fall of 1889. The year of piano performances and teaching affected his compositions dramatically, and he now embarked on a series of works for piano that reflected his new awareness of the expressive subtleties and technical possibilities of the instrument.

Written during the fall and winter of 1889/90, the set of twelve etudes filled a need for lower-advanced repertoire in his teaching. The pieces are more challenging than the simpler etudes of Heller and Burgmüller, but they are not as difficult as the etudes of Chopin and Liszt. Like the twenty-seven Chopin Etudes and the Transcendental Etudes of Liszt, each of the pieces explores a single technical problem or characteristic touch, allowing the student to focus on the development of specific pianistic skills. At the same time, they are evocative character pieces that are effective in performance. Several of the pieces, most notably the "Shadow Dance," op. 39, no. 8 and the "Hungarian," op. 39, no. 12, became very popular as recital pieces. MacDowell follows the example of Liszt in assigning each study a title that reflects the intended mood. They are not overly specific, however, as titles like "Romanze," "Arabesque," "Idyll," "Intermezzo," "Melody," and "Scherzino" are more suggestive than programmatic. Three of the etudes carry dance titles: "Alla Tarantella," "Dance of the Gnomes," and "Shadow Dance."

"Scherzino," op. 39, no. 11, is among the most difficult technically, being almost entirely devoted to double notes in the right hand. The majority of the piece is in double thirds, as in the opening four measures:

11.2 "Scherzino," op. 39, no. 11, mm. 1–4

Likewise, the "Dance of the Gnomes," op. 39, no. 6, is unrelenting in exploring mordents, and "Arabesque," op. 39, no. 4, is a wrist study in rapid repeated chords. "Alla Tarantella" is a rapid study in leggiero fingerwork and dynamic contrasts in the characteristic 6/8 meter of the tarantella.

MacDowell was clearly interested in more than technique, however, as the pieces explore sonority and touch to an even greater degree than speed. As a pianist, MacDowell was often cited for his imaginative use of both the soft pedal and the damper pedal. In the excerpt from "Shadow Dance," the triple-pianissimo dynamic begs for the soft pedal, while the bass notes are most effectively sustained through half-pedaling (see ex. 11.1). The result is a texture with three clearly differentiated sonorities that interact and complement each other. The composer identified the "Romanze" as an etude in singing touch. In it he explores a variety of melodic and accompanimental patterns that challenge the student to make the melodies sing as they move through different pianistic textures.

The tour de force is the final etude, "Hungarian," op. 39, no. 12. This piece is clearly heir to the Hungarian dances of Brahms and the Hungarian Rhapsodies of Liszt, but its technical difficulties are within reach of the lower-advanced student. It provides an introduction to virtuoso playing through whirling scales, large leaps, blind octaves, and martellato chords while also reinforcing basic techniques in forearm rotation and two-against-three rhythmic patterns. Most importantly, the etude is a showpiece, which is fun to play and dramatic in performance.

The Twelve Etudes, op. 39, were published by A. P. Schmidt in spring 1890 and immediately found an audience. Royalty records show that the "Shadow Dance" outsold all the other etudes as a single sheet, but the set of twelve etudes as well as the compilations of the first and second halves of the set enjoyed strong sales for decades. MacDowell had found the right combination of technical accessibility and musical integrity, no doubt a direct result of his immersion in piano teaching and performance during the previous year.

Schmidt was eager for more music from MacDowell, and he floated ideas to the composer for choral works, organ voluntaries, and orchestral compositions with piano. The publisher had recently opened a branch office in Leipzig and hoped to make his venture distinctive by selling high-quality American music in Europe.[3] MacDowell was not willing to commit himself exclusively to Schmidt, but the publisher made it very attractive for the struggling composer. Among the more curious collaborations was a set of *Sechs kleine Stücke nach Skizzen von J. S. Bach* [Six short pieces after sketches by J. S. Bach], published in October 1890.

MacDowell wrote to Strong, "You will probably be horrified to learn that I have made 6 piano pieces from 'Sketches' by – – – – – – J. S. <u>Bach</u>!!!! I am <u>not</u> getting bald but it <u>did</u> make me feel slightly <u>antique</u>. However I console myself with the thought that I <u>did</u> put just a <u>little</u> cayenne in them and feel kind of secure in the thought that J. S. B. is dead."[4] The result is a MacDowellian reworking of Bach rather than an edition of Bach's original. Using six pieces from Bach's Notebooks for Wilhelm Friedemann Bach and Anna Magdelena Bach as starting points, he expanded them by adding chromatic inner voices, octave doublings, extensive articulation, tempo, and expression markings, and some added trios in minor keys. In the words of John F. Porte, "They are charmingly and cleverly written, although not always satisfying, it is to be feared, to the strict purist."[5] The opening of MacDowell's arrangement of the familiar Minuet in G illustrates his approach:

11.3 J. S. Bach "Minuet in G," arranged by MacDowell, mm. 1–16

3. "An American Music House in Europe," *Boston Musical Herald* 11/7 (July 1890): 152–53.

4. Letter, EAM to TS, 26 February 1892, EMMC box 29/32.

5. John F. Porte, *Edward MacDowell: A Great American Tone Poet, His Life and Music* (London: K. Paul, Trench, Trubner, 1922), 155.

MacDowell's reworkings of Bach show the influence of Liszt. Like that Romantic pianist, MacDowell did not hold the works of past composers to be inviolable texts. Rather he viewed them as frameworks from one time and place that could be updated to reflect contemporary tastes and techniques. The sprinkles of "cayenne" add a tongue-in-cheek flair and also give insights into MacDowell's aesthetics and his preferred techniques as a pianist.

After two seasons of reduced performing, MacDowell returned to the concert stage in earnest during the winter of 1891/92, when he performed a series of three solo recitals in Boston on 6 November, 15 January, and 18 March. Currier took credit for convincing his teacher to limit the number of works by other composers in favor of his own compositions. This format showed him to best advantage, as his quirky performances of standard repertoire by well-known composers baffled the critics, but his performances of his own works were revelatory. This series of recitals did as much as anything to warm the Boston critics to MacDowell's music. Most importantly, his solo recitals during the next decade allowed him to stimulate interest in his more difficult compositions that might have appeared too daunting in the score, notably the first two of his four piano sonatas, the *Sonata Tragica*, op. 45, and the *Sonata Eroica*, op. 50.

In the piano sonatas, MacDowell created large works in traditional Classical forms. Each of them has a descriptive title, but like the two concertos, any programmatic connotations are evocative rather than explicitly descriptive, and the composer gave few clues to their extra-musical content. Here he disciplined the Lisztian techniques of thematic development, motivic connections among the movements, heroic virtuosity, colorful chromaticism, and intense emotion into more-or-less conventional multimovement sonatas. This combination created the most successful and enduring American piano sonatas before World War I.[6]

The third movement of the *Sonata Tragica*, op. 45, was introduced by the composer on his solo recital of 18 March 1892. The complete score was published a year later by Breitkopf & Härtel, continuing MacDowell's practice of giving his most important compositions to European publishers. The sonata was inspired by the memory of the grief he experienced at Raff's death, which may seem odd since it had occurred nearly a decade earlier. But because of negotiations with the composer's widow, Doris, he was intensely involved with Raff's manuscripts at about the time he was writing his *Sonata Tragica*, which explains the connection.[7] Marian summed up her husband's views on musical programs in this way: "I am anxious not to convey the impression that there was ever a specific 'story' embodied in the piece

---

6. On the reception history of the sonatas, see William S. Newman, *The Sonata Since Beethoven,* vol. 3 of *The History of the Sonata Idea* (Chapel Hill: University of North Carolina Press, 1969): 758–68.

7. E. Douglas Bomberger, "Edward MacDowell, Arthur P. Schmidt, and the Shakespeare Overtures of Joachim Raff: A Case Study in Nineteenth-Century Music Publishing," *Notes* 54/1 (September 1997): 11–26.

itself. Nothing could be farther from my intention or the facts. MacDowell held that a poetic name given a piece helped a performer in his interpretation, without limiting his imagination. Furthermore his writing was never descriptive in a realistic sense; it was the expression of a mood which might be awakened by a scene, a poem, an idea or an experience."[8]

The four movements of the *Sonata Tragica*, op. 45, are in the keys of G minor, B-flat major, C minor, and G major. The first movement begins with a Largo maestoso introduction characterized by Scotch snap rhythms, which recur throughout the work:

11.4 *Sonata Tragica*, op. 45, mm. 1–4

This dramatic theme is embellished with scales, arpeggios, and octave scales before settling on a unison D in measure 17. The movement proper then begins in Allegro risoluto tempo (see ex. 11.5).

This theme permeates the entire movement and recurs in the other movements as well, reflecting MacDowell's idea that "if the composer's ideas do not imperatively demand treatment in that [the sonata] form, that is, if his first theme is not actually dependent upon his second and side themes for its poetic fulfillment—he has not composed a sonata movement, but a potpourri, which the form only aggravates."[9] Though it does not reflect the extensive thematic development of the Liszt sonata or the tight melodic construction of his own Piano Concerto No. 1, the first movement of MacDowell's *Sonata Tragica* is built around interdependent thematic relationships arising from this first theme.

---

8. MM, *Random Notes on Edward MacDowell and his Music* (Boston: A. P. Schmidt, 1950), v.

9. Quoted in Lawrence Gilman, *Edward MacDowell: A Study* (New York: John Lane, 1908), 147.

11.5 *Sonata Tragica*, op. 45, mm. 18–25

The second movement is a rapid scherzo in 6/8 that features too many octaves and low sonorities to achieve the lightness of MacDowell's better works in this genre. The third movement is an expansive largo featuring dotted rhythms characteristic of the *marche funebre*. The melodic and textural variations as well as the dramatic sweep of the movement help to explain MacDowell's choice to play it as a separate piece before introducing the entire sonata. The fourth movement is based on a triumphant theme in G major that is abruptly interrupted in its final appearance. Marian explained the significance of this passage in terms of the program: "He wished to heighten the darkness of tragedy by making it follow closely on the heels of triumph. Therefore, he attempted to make the last movement a steadily progressive triumph, which at its climax, is utterly broken and shattered…thinking that the most poignant tragedy is that of catastrophe in the hour of triumph."[10] It is tempting to read into this comment an analogy to Raff's death at the moment of MacDowell's first major triumph, but neither the composer nor his wife was that explicit.

The sonata was soon taken up by other pianists who had the necessary virtuosity and were looking for large-scale American works. Most important among these was William Mason, who had been a student of Liszt and a friend of Raff during the early 1850s in Weimar. He wrote a letter introducing himself to MacDowell on 10 January 1894, and the two became close in subsequent years. A formidable virtuoso himself, the older pianist introduced the *Sonata Tragica* by playing it daily at the resort of Appledore on the Isle of Shoals, convincing himself and the other guests of the artistic value and popular appeal of this difficult work.[11] Not long afterwards, he received another major work from his young friend.

The *Zwölf Virtuosen-Etüden* [Twelve Virtuoso Etudes], op. 46, had appeared in March 1894, a year after the first sonata. With this set, MacDowell expanded

10. Quoted in Rupert Hughes, *Contemporary American Composers* (Boston: L. C. Page, 1900), 53–54.

11. William Mason, *Memories of a Musical Life* (New York: Century, 1902), 255–56.

the concept of his earlier collection of etudes by creating a set of much more demanding technical studies with similarly evocative titles. Again, dance titles figure prominently, as in No. 5 "Elfentanz," No. 6 "Valse triste," and No. 12 "Polonaise." Even the most programmatic of the set, No. 3 "Wilde Jagd" and No. 10 "Märzwind," are evocative without being strictly descriptive. Most of the etudes explore one or two virtuoso techniques in depth, as for instance right-hand passagework in No. 2 "Moto Perpetuo" and No. 5 "Elfentanz," repeated chords in No. 10 "Märzwind," and blind octaves and leaps in No. 12 "Polonaise." In these etudes, MacDowell placed more emphasis on technique than he had in the earlier etudes, which were concerned primarily with sonority. His student Currier recalled the composer's comment when he gave him the autograph: "You won't like them, and probably no one will....They are too strange, too dissonant."[12] Indeed these did not enjoy the widespread popularity of the earlier set, although several of them were much played by concert pianists.

Several of MacDowell's works from the later Boston years were clearly influenced by his teaching. Breitkopf & Härtel published two books of Technical Studies in 1894 and 1895. In the preface to the first book, MacDowell clarifies his intentions and also gives clues about his own piano teaching:

> In my opinion physical development and music are two different things, and, although musical talent is a *sine qua non* in pianoforte playing, it cannot reach its full expression without a thorough command of the muscles of the hand, wrist, and arm. I have found it advisable to keep the purely physical part of piano playing entirely separate from its musical side, as this allows a concentration of the mind not otherwise practical. I therefore beg the student who may use these exercises, to consider them from a purely "athletic" standpoint.[13]

The exercises in Book I all require the pianist to hold down one or more fingers while playing patterns in accelerating rhythms with the remaining fingers. Like the similar exercises published by Ernö Dohnanyi in 1929, MacDowell's studies have no musical interest whatsoever but allow the pianist to develop strength and finger independence through repetition of difficult and awkward patterns. MacDowell warns against "over-fatigue" when practicing this encyclopedic compendium of finger patterns. He also advises pianists to use a dumb keyboard if possible.

Between 1894 and 1900, MacDowell was engaged in another lucrative publishing venture that was an offshoot of his teaching. He edited a series of about

---

12. T. P. Currier, "Edward MacDowell as I Knew Him," *MQ* 1/1 (January 1915): 38.

13. Edward MacDowell, *Technical Exercises*, pt. 1 (Leipzig: Breitkopf & Härtel, 1894), 2.

forty piano compositions by European and American composers published first by Breitkopf & Härtel, then by Breitkopf's New York agent P. L. Jung, and finally by A. P. Schmidt.[14] The first series of twenty-two works consisted exclusively of contemporary European composers, while the later series expanded this core repertoire with works from the Baroque era. Unlike the Bach publications of 1890, these were not recompositions but faithful editions enhanced with fingering, articulation marks, and dynamics.

MacDowell's *Air et Rigaudon*, op. 49, consisted of two short pieces composed for the series *Half Hours with the Best Composers*, edited by Karl Klauser.[15] According to Marian, this was the only piece he ever composed "to order," despite his earnest attempt to fulfill the commission from the Ruggles Street Baptist Church in 1888/89.[16] Both the slow "Rigaudon" and the faster "Air" emulate French Baroque style but with extended harmonies of the seventh and ninth. This combination of old and new elements would later be explored extensively by MacDowell's former classmate Debussy in his *Suite Bergamasque* and especially in *Pour le Piano*, begun in the year that MacDowell's *Air et Rigaudon* appeared in print but not published until 1901.

The last of MacDowell's major piano works from the Boston period, the *Sonata Eroica*, op. 50, was published in late 1895 and dedicated to William Mason, whom he had learned to know while beginning the composition in 1894. The dedication was no doubt a gesture of gratitude for his new friend's advocacy of the *Sonata Tragica*, but Mason later admitted that the *Eroica* was not as successful in his performances as the *Tragica* had been. This sonata is the most overtly programmatic of MacDowell's abstract works, bearing the subtitle "Flos regum Arthurus," a reference to the knights of the Round Table. Lawrence Gilman quotes MacDowell's elaboration on the theme: "While not exactly programme music, I had in mind the Arthurian legend when writing this work. The first movement typifies the coming of Arthur. The Scherzo was suggested by a picture of Doré showing a knight in the woods surrounded by elves. The third movement was suggested by my idea of Guinevere. That following represents the passing of Arthur."[17] These

---

14. The complicated publication history of this series is traced in O. G. Sonneck, *Catalogue of First Editions of Edward MacDowell* (Washington: Government Printing Office, 1917), 61–66. Sonneck states, "Bibliographically the matter is so complicated that without an analysis, as is attempted below, no collector can possibly verify real first editions."

15. The pieces, along with a biographical sketch, appeared in *Half Hours with the Best Composers*, ed. Karl Klauser (Boston: J. B. Millet, 1894), 834–44.

16. MM, *Random Notes*, 10.

17. Gilman, *Edward MacDowell: A Study*, 151.

tantalizing hints have inspired repeated attempts at exegesis, from a 1916 article "What inspired the Scherzo of MacDowell's 'Eroica'? A Dispute Ended" to a 2010 paper "A Newly Revealed Program in the Autograph of Edward MacDowell's *Sonata Eroica*."[18]

More important than the precise correlation of the music to the legend, however, is MacDowell's masterly manipulation of musical materials. With or without the program, it is clear that the composer created a piece of dramatic sweep in which thematic interconnections tie the four movements into a satisfying whole. The opening gesture demonstrates the range of his rhetorical ambitions:

11.6 *Sonata Eroica*, op. 50, mm. 1–9

The gravity of this somber introduction is contrasted by a restless principal theme that rises from triple *pianissimo* to triple *fortissimo* in fifteen measures. The second theme employs extended harmonies and sighing appoggiaturas to support a characteristic MacDowellian melody that is almost sentimental in its emotional intensity:

18. "What inspired the Scherzo of MacDowell's 'Eroica'? A Dispute Ended," *Music Student* 8/6 (February 1916): 153. Paul Bertagnolli, "A Newly Revealed Program in the Autograph of Edward MacDowell's *Sonata Eroica*," paper delivered at the Elizabethtown College MacDowell Festival and Symposium, 4 December 2010.

Simply, yet with pathos. ♩. = 44
Mit volksthümlichem Ausdruck.

11.7 *Sonata Eroica*, op. 50, mm. 55–60

In the first movement's virtuosic coda, left-hand melodies are accompanied with mysteriously whispering right-hand arpeggios, culminating in a furious scale passage using minor scales with raised fourth and seventh degrees, a favorite of MacDowell's.

The second movement is a scherzo that succeeds more fully than that of the *Sonata Tragica* because of its lighter textures and greater variety, while the third movement is a haunting adagio. In the "Fiercely, very fast" final movement, MacDowell creates a whirlwind of dramatic motion and intense emotion, culminating in a coda that reprises the theme of the first movement's opening adagio. In the first two sonatas, much more so than in the symphonic poems or the concertos, MacDowell showed himself to be a master of large-scale architectural design, pacing the dramatic tension and thematic contrasts effectively to create a logical and satisfying whole. For those familiar only with his most unassuming short piano pieces, this aspect of his creative output is a surprising discovery.

From this time to the end of his career, he adopted the pattern of limiting his performances to a month or two during the winter in order to segregate the two aspects of his creative life. He discovered the benefits of hiring a concert agent to arrange his tours with income guaranteed in advance. From 1888 to 1891, he was associated with the Boston piano firm of Chickering & Sons, who placed a piano at his disposal and helped with concert arrangements. In December 1891, as he prepared to expand his touring performances, he switched to Steinway & Sons in New York. His agent at Steinway was Charles F. Tretbar, with whom he became increasingly disenchanted. Starting in 1894/95, he worked exclusively with Kurt

Moebius, who represented Breitkopf & Härtel in New York.[19] In this way he was able to develop a loyal following outside of Boston and New York. Currier opined that he actually played better and more often outside of the major metropolitan centers, allowing his western audiences to hear him in a way that his eastern colleagues never did.[20]

As MacDowell's popularity grew during the 1890s, the piano recitals and concerto appearances enhanced the sale of his publications. This sort of strategic cross-platform promotion was beneficial for his reputation, but it revived the old conflict that had plagued him since his student days. As we have seen, the skills and personality traits of a successful concert artist are dramatically different from those of a composer. By segregating his two careers, he attempted to balance their demands, but like his Austrian counterpart Gustav Mahler, he discovered that the stress of pursuing two careers exacted a toll on his mental and physical health, which was only intensified by his heavy teaching schedule. There can be no doubt, though, that the subtlety of his mature piano works was the direct result of his intimate involvement with piano playing and teaching. In the words of Marian MacDowell: "He did, what now is not common, he put his best work into the piano music—this reached thousands when the finest orchestral work is heard by hundreds—He himself quickened the knowledge of it by playing it."[21]

19. Margery M. Lowens, "The New York Years of Edward MacDowell" (PhD diss., University of Michigan, 1971), 114–15. A letter from Moebius to MacDowell of 18 October 1894 shows that Tretbar did little on his client's behalf and that Moebius felt he could do a better job for MacDowell [EMMC box 30/15]. If the 4 March 1895 accounting from Moebius for concerts in Madison Square Garden in New York on 28 February and 2 March is an indication, the concert tours were not highly profitable [EMMC box 30/15]. Their benefit for MacDowell was to introduce his music to a broader public.

20. Currier, "Edward MacDowell as I Knew Him," 29.

21. Letter, MM to TS, 4 June 1914, EMMC box 51/3.

CHAPTER TWELVE

The Darkest Winter

F OR THE FIRST EIGHT YEARS OF THEIR MARRIAGE, EDWARD AND MARIAN MacDowell were together almost constantly. He had no reason to write to her, and his letters to Strong seldom mention her, making it difficult to get a sense of their relationship. During the winter of 1892–93, a life-threatening illness forced Marian to seek treatment in Philadelphia while Edward stayed in Boston. Most of his daily letters to her have been preserved in the Library of Congress, providing an unparalleled opportunity to understand the depth of his feelings for her, to follow the ups and downs of his developing career, and to observe the impact of his often-debilitating seasonal depression through a winter made darker by anxiety over Marian's health.

The summer of 1892 was spent in Peterborough, New Hampshire, a small town in the southern part of the state where the MacDowells had previously vacationed in the summer of 1890. After spending the summer of 1891 in Maine, they returned to New Hampshire, where the climate was not so damp and foggy. At some point during the summer, Marian suffered heat stroke, as related by Edward in a letter to Currier: "My poor wife has had a very bad time of it. The heat brought on heart failure and she came as near the edge as I ever want to see any body. For two weeks it was touch and go at any moment....There is a capital doctor here, but my sister-in-law really saved her life."[1] Her recovery was slow, and early in the fall they decided to send her to a specialist in Philadelphia, who treated her until the following April. Edward stayed in Boston to teach, visiting occasionally on weekends and writing regularly. Though she urged him in one of her early letters not to be "dependent" on her or to write every day, she saved nearly one hundred letters

---

1. Quoted in T. P. Currier, "Edward MacDowell as I Knew Him," *MQ* 1/1 (January 1915): 36–37.

written between October 1892 and April 1893. Most of these are undated, but evidence from the contents shows that during many weeks he did indeed write daily. These letters are now preserved in the MacDowell Collection in the Library of Congress Music Division; unless otherwise noted, all letters cited in this chapter are from that group.[2]

The early letters after her relocation reveal his loneliness and his concern about her health. On a Monday night shortly after she arrived in Philadelphia, he confessed:

> I've been having a private little snivel all to myself and though it isn't the first by any means, I can't help writing just a word to you and hoping and praying that you are get-ting some sleep and doing better. I am so anxious to "see land" and have you back again. When I think of you with the light turned up wandering about those rooms at midnight it simply makes me crazy.—if at least you had Anna in the next room—I suppose I am a blazing fool but it seems to me as if I <u>ought</u> to be there.

He had seriously considered the possibility of moving with her to Philadelphia, but he knew that his income would be better in Boston, where he was already well established. Hundreds of miles away, he was unable to care for her, but he worried constantly and urged her to relax, sleep, and follow the doctor's orders.

Early in the year, the issue of finances arose frequently. He was uncertain how much money to send her, and as his lessons were just starting to get underway, he did not have as much cash on hand as he would later in the year. In one letter he suggested that she "let a week run over" in the hotel bill to give him time to send her more money. Later in the year he reassured her constantly that they had plenty of money for her expenses (while also complaining about the meager state of his bank account). He urged her not to borrow money from his mother, who was eager to help, but rather to be patient for money he would send. As he got busier with his activities in the winter, he took to sending her the checks he received from his students when his schedule did not permit him to cash them himself. The costs of the treatment were steep, as she needed to pay the specialist, rent a hotel room, and for much of the year support her sister who accompanied her. Eventually they seem to have settled on the sum of $100 per week for her expenses, which was half of his normal weekly income of $200.

The need for so much money kept Edward extremely busy throughout the win-ter. His reputation as a teacher continued to grow, allowing him to be selective in accepting students. He reported in a letter from early March, "Two more applications

2. EMMC, box 31, folders 54–55, 56–57, and 59.

<u>refused</u> today. Two people are coming to play for me on Saturday who I will take if they are good enough." At five dollars per lesson, he needed to teach forty per week in order to earn $200. Compounding the challenge of making his living from private teaching was the fact that he did not charge his students in advance. Instead, he waited until they had taken ten or fifteen lessons and then sent them a bill for the cost of those lessons. When students did not respond promptly to his bills, he sent them again, causing a delay of months between the first lesson he had given and the receipt of payment for that lesson.[3] Although his fee was among the highest in Boston, it was still a difficult and at times demeaning way to earn a living.

Practicing piano and responding to correspondence took up most of his evening hours, leaving no time for composition and little for social engagements or concert attendance. He was never fond of exercising, but his dog Charlie needed regular walks, which gave him an excuse to circle the Boston Common regularly. On Election Day in November, he and Charlie had to dodge the drunks who were out celebrating, and on 23 February he reported on a fight between Charlie and a bulldog that attacked him on Charles Street. MacDowell was surprised that his pet did not cower but turned and "licked that dog out of his boots." He told Marian that he wanted to reward him with a beefsteak but the stores were closed for Washington's Birthday.

His performance engagements were relatively sparse that winter. On 18 and 19 November 1892 he played his First Piano Concerto with the Boston Symphony under the baton of Arthur Nikisch. On 27 and 28 January 1893, Nikisch and the BSO played his *Hamlet and Ophelia* for the first time in Boston. On 3 March 1893, Lang's Apollo Club sang a recent composition for male chorus, *Dance of Gnomes*, and on 27 March, he played in a recital by the Kneisel Quartet that featured the premiere of his *Sonata Tragica*, op. 45. In contrast to his first year in Boston, when he had played dozens of small engagements, he limited his performances in the winter of 1892/93 to high-profile concerts that would enhance his reputation without taking too much time away from his grueling teaching schedule. Outside of Boston, MacDowell's music continued to grow in popularity. In late February, he learned that his *Dance of Gnomes* had been performed by David Loring's chorus in San Francisco, while the Suite, op. 42, had been performed three times by Georg Riemenschneider in Breslau. This conductor, who led an orchestra in the same eastern German city where his publisher Hainauer was located, was a consistent supporter of MacDowell, writing articles on his works in German papers and regularly performing his orchestral works. The suite was also performed in Cologne that winter.

3. Examples of his bills may be found in the Harvard University Special Collections (Miss Dunbar) and EMMC 29/11 (Miss Morrison).

Edward complained frequently of being too busy, as his days were occupied with teaching and his evenings with business correspondence, practicing piano, and writing to Marian, leaving virtually no time for composition. Nonetheless, he found time to pursue his photographic passion when his evenings permitted. In the fall he sent a question to the journal *Photographic Times*, but he reported to Marian that he was dissatisfied with the answer he received. He experimented with a new developing technique—platinum prints—which required him to order special paper from New York. He described the disappointing results in a December letter: "I tried some platinum prints today with the usual result—back ache & headache and a lot of spoiled paper." After turning to other subjects, he added a postscript to his letter: "<u>Damn</u> photography." Another December letter alluded to the challenges of pursuing this hobby during the winter: "I went to the Photograph place and gave them the negative today. The <u>enlargements</u> will be in time they say—but the <u>prints</u> need sunlight and as that is so very uncertain this season they cannot promise them before Xmas. I am awfully sorry but how can it be helped? The large ones I am going to try to do myself in platinum prints in the evening."

Without Marian by his side, Edward was forced to cope with social situations that she would normally have handled. Early in the year, he was confronted by Mrs. Deland about his friend Templeton Strong, who had moved to Boston at Edward's urging in the fall of 1891. After less than a year, Strong returned to Switzerland in the summer of 1892. Though he later claimed that his departure was for health reasons, there were rumors in Boston that an affair had ruined his marriage. Edward reported on the prodding he received from a Miss Derby and Mrs. Deland in a letter to Marian:

> Miss Derby asked me what kind of a woman Lizzie was. I told her it needed someone cleverer than I to tell "what kind" <u>any</u> woman was without a better acquaintance than I had with Strong's household. If Mrs. Strong wants to she can raise Hallelujah with Strong and Lizzie which would be real pleasant for the family pride all around.—specially as <u>that</u> little bit of scandal would antedate <u>anything</u> Strong could bring up. Mrs. Deland asked whether I didn't think Strong a very "peculiar" person. I said all musicians were supposed to be peculiar. Well, she said, I think its degrading to the art to think that musicians are tolerated when they act like scamps—which was pretty strong, but I of course would not talk Strong over to her in any way and simply ignored it and let her see that just that I wouldn't do.

MacDowell was torn between his loyalty to his old friend and his distaste for the man's actions. In the margin, he predicted to Marian that Strong would lose the divorce case and that his wife would receive alimony with custody of their children.

Like many shy persons, Edward found that he could not produce quick responses to prying questions, but later he ruminated over the situation, regretting his stammered answers or rehearsing the response he wished he had made. His letter to Marian about a dinner party in January 1893 makes his discomfort palpable:

> Among other things the other night Mrs. Deland (before them all) said she hoped Bishop [Phillips] Brooks' death had not had a bad influence on your health. I said I thought not. She said she had not written to you about it as she did not like to break it to you! I said that you always saw the Transcript and as you did not know Bishop Brooks personally that I did not think you—etc—etc. These people are crazy. After dinner it was Brooks again until I thought I would jump. Ms. D. asked me at dinner if I had seen the Merington's play. I said yes and she asked me how I liked it. Well, I said I thought the second act had quite a dramatic moment in it.—So what has this idiot of a woman to do but to call over to Mrs. Whitman that she was so glad that Mr. MacD. liked the play—then went on to say that they all thought it very poor!!!—I tell you it is just as bad or worse in "litterature" as it is in music....Then this old fool of a Mrs. Elliot turned to me and said she thought it must be so delightful to have one's compositions tried in the symphony concerts!!!!—Then she got off the old joke about "how unlovely" the German peasant was! Hell on earth—can anyone wonder that it is hard to sleep after going through such maddening trials.

The most upsetting occurrences of this type were those that involved other musicians. He continued to be on poor terms with Arthur Foote, reporting in January 1893: "I think I shall have nothing to do with Foote. I was talking with old Rogers when Foote came up. I held out my hand and instead of acting like a gentleman he ignored it and said 'is your wife back?' I simply said you were too ill to risk the bad weather here yet and went on talking to Rogers. It wouldn't take much to make me mash that ugly snout of his in." He continued to feel anxious about his position in the musical hierarchy of Boston, expressing his frustration about local musicians who seemed to be doing better than he despite modest abilities. He also expressed to Marian his jealousy of European musicians like Dvořák, Paderewski, and Busoni who were lionized by the American public out of all proportion—in MacDowell's private opinion—to their actual attainments.

MacDowell's anxiety and frustration were intensified by the two appearances with the BSO. On 18 and 19 November he played his First Piano Concerto under the baton of Arthur Nikisch. His letters from the weeks before the concerts vacillated between devil-may-care nonchalance and complaining about minor details like the fit of his dress suit. He reported with relief that the first performance came off well despite uncomfortable heat in the auditorium and several slips in the orchestra. He wrote to Marian, "I was not nervous only when the first violins jumped a measure I had to jump too though for the millionth part of a second I was scared out of my senses." The following night he was recalled three times and enthusiastically congratulated by musicians who came backstage to greet him. He admitted, though, that his mood was low after the concert, causing him to question the value of the performance. A bouquet of flowers sent by Marian awaited him when he returned home, unleashing a flood of emotion:

> The pansies came & I found them when I got back and feeling upset any way and "kinder blue" they nearly upset me entirely, you dear old piggy. Well I am glad it's over and done with and I feel that I had but keep out of it in future and give that time to composition. With my present income it is not worth the terrible anxiety. I really don't think if I had practiced half as hard, (and I really have done my level best,) it would have made it any worse in fact perhaps I might have play'd better. Nikisch is not a first rate conductor for concertos and any way concertos are an abomination and a desolation. I am really all over the "horror" of it now and have only a feeling of regret that I didn't do more. Still its over and I don't think I will be easily tempted again.

The reviews were very good, and after reading them he admitted to Marian, "I feel just as if I had escaped from the Indians with even my scalp almost intact." The excitement and anxiety of the event caused him to commit a husband's ultimate faux pas—he forgot her birthday on 22 November and did not remember to apologize until the 24th.

On 27 and 28 January 1893, Nikisch and the BSO played MacDowell's *Hamlet and Ophelia* for the first time in Boston. What should have been a triumph turned into the composer's greatest frustration of the winter. The guest soloist on the same concert was the Polish pianist Ignace Paderewski, who was then enjoying immense popularity with American audiences, despite what MacDowell described to Marian as sloppy playing and stiff technique. Edward loaned his copy of the score and parts of his tone poems for the performance, but curiously, the author of the program notes did not contact him for information. Eager to hear the orchestra's interpretation, he canceled his Thursday afternoon lessons to attend the public rehearsal. The tickets for the rehearsal and the concerts had sold out within thirty minutes on Monday, but he assumed that as composer he would be allowed to hear the rehearsal. Instead, he was barred from entering the auditorium without a ticket.

He was so livid after this experience that he could not sleep at all and was a wreck the following day. By chance, he had been invited to dinner with B. J. Lang and his wife, who innocently asked about the rehearsal. When the truth spilled out, they were indignant, but Lang wisely talked MacDowell out of boycotting the Saturday performance, pointing out that since the public did not know what had happened behind the scenes, it would seem churlish to stay away. To add insult to injury, they told him that their daughter Margaret had to be out of town for the weekend and had requested permission to attend a closed rehearsal in order to hear MacDowell's work. Nikisch had graciously granted her wish.

Reviews of the concert were mixed, with most reviewers complaining about the lack of information on the composer's intentions in the program booklet. One paper, the *Journal*, listed MacDowell before Paderewski and praised his work while expressing reservations about the Polish pianist. Most other reviewers succumbed to the reputation of "The Lion Tamer," devoting first attention to the guest soloist and discussing MacDowell's work after. An added distraction was the last-minute disappearance of the first horn player, who chose the day of the premiere to leave his wife and took a train to New York too late to be replaced.

William F. Apthorp wrote in the *Boston Transcript*, "Mr. MacDowell's 'Hamlet' and 'Ophelia' do not throw much more light upon what this immensely talented, but enigmatic, young musician strives after in his compositions—unless his aim be to combine beauty of tone-color with emotional expressiveness, and nothing else. In the 'Ophelia' there are some moments of approach to recognizable musical form and coherence; but for the most part these two poems sound very much like rambling preluding."[4] The work is indeed one of MacDowell's most challenging scores, inspired by the free form of Liszt's tone poems and the chromatic harmonies of Wagner. Without adequate guidance from the program notes, the critics were at a loss to assess the work at first hearing, and Apthorp in particular was puzzled by the apparent formlessness of the work. The loneliness that plagued Edward during the winter of 1892/93 was made tangible in the alienation of being barred from the rehearsal of his own work and reading the uncomprehending reviews afterward.

Perhaps in response to his loneliness, Edward made an uncharacteristic decision in January. Never a joiner, he was leery of clubs and other organizations, maintaining his distance from professional associations and social clubs. But in late January he was voted into the St. Botolph Club, a men's club whose members included many of the most prominent musicians, artists, and writers of Boston along with the patrons who supported them. Apparently embarrassed about this move, he justified it to Marian by saying, "That Botolph is 30 a year and an entry fee of 30 more. I'll have to take it out in stationery. If I can only get in [with] the painter set or the doctor set it may repay me." Elsewhere he said that he had joined because of the food, but clearly he longed for companionship with Marian gone at this dismal time of year. That winter he became accustomed to sharing meals with Currier and other members at the club, and he valued his membership for the rest of his years in Boston.

4. [W. F. Apthorp], "Theatres and Concerts," *Boston Evening Transcript*, 30 January 1893.

The two performances in March were much more successful, and each in its own way was an omen of the acclaim that awaited MacDowell in the years ahead. On 3 March 1893, the Apollo Club sang his *Dance of Gnomes*, a spritely piece for men's chorus that features an infectious bouncing pattern for the second basses. Dedicated to the Loring Club of San Francisco, it was performed there just a few weeks before the Boston premiere. The text, written by the composer himself, paints a bizarre picture of ugly gnomes dancing by moonlight in a forest. These "ugly, hairy imps" are contrasted with "flower fairies, proud frail mockers," who flaunt their beauty and scorn the gnomes. The staccato articulation and rapid tempo create a work that seems more instrumental than vocal.

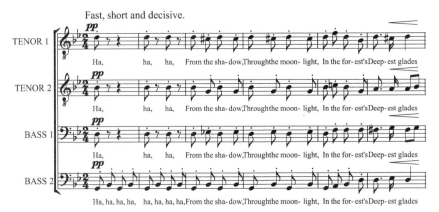

12.1 "Dance of Gnomes," op. 41, no. 2, mm. 1–6

Arthur P. Schmidt had published the work late in 1890, but this was the first time it had been performed in Boston.[5] The composer did not attend, but he regretted this decision when he was told repeatedly of its "enormous success." The reports were confirmed in an unusual way, as he told Marian, "I saw Chadwick and he looked so glum that it must have been true (he had a chorus right after mine)." The Cecilia Society, Lang's other choral group, immediately invited him to write a piece for one of their upcoming concerts.

5. According to O. G. Sonneck, *Catalogue of First Editions of Edward MacDowell* (Washington: Government Printing Office, 1917), 33, it was deposited for copyright on 10 January 1891 but bore the copyright date of 1890.

For the rest of the month of March, he spent every spare moment practicing for the Kneisel concert. He wrote to Marian on 14 March, "It seems impossible for me to get a decent practise at that Sonata and it scares me blue to think of playing it in two weeks—I wish I could back out of it." He did not visit her in Philadelphia the weekend before the concert, writing, "Oh Lord haven't I just got to hump on that Sonata." Not long after, he reported, "My fingers go like the devil and I play like Hell—but no matter I'm desperate." He memorized the sonata, but two days before the concert he still reported, "guess it will be alright Monday though I shudder when I think of how little I actually know the thing." He urged her not to send flowers this time, saying that "if it goes badly it makes me so ill and kind of sick at heart to know you were so confidently counting on success."

In fact she did send a bouquet of daffodils, which arrived in the afternoon before the concert and made him "awfully afraid I would bust up entirely." The performance was a resounding success with the public and critics, as he was recalled repeatedly and congratulated backstage by friends and critics alike. He reported on a brief encounter that in retrospect he would see as a turning point in his career. William F. Apthorp, the influential music critic of the *Boston Transcript*, had been lukewarm in his assessments of MacDowell's previous works. On the night of the Sonata performance in the Kneisel Quartet concert, however, he joined the crowd of well-wishers, as Edward described to Marian: "The funniest of all was—Apthorp who came back and held out both hands and said '<u>Now</u> I understand you I have learned my lesson—it is a splendid work'!!! just then the door to the stage opened and the public must have seen him holding my hand (!) which must have made him feel queer." Apthorp's review in the *Transcript* acknowledged a new understanding of MacDowell's intentions, and his future assessments of the composer's works were much more favorable.

The first two weeks of April, immediately after MacDowell's performance with the Kneisel Quartet, were eventful ones in Boston's musical life. On 1 April he reported that Chadwick had been fired from his church job and that his young protégé Horatio Parker had been hired as organist at Trinity Church at the highest salary ever paid in Boston. On 7 and 8 April the BSO played Margaret Ruthven Lang's overture, which he described as "rotten—poorly orchestrated, no sign of a climax—and no 'form.'" The program notes by Apthorp incorrectly stated that she had studied composition with MacDowell, a piece of misinformation that he tried in vain to correct. On 13 April, Foote played a new suite for piano that MacDowell disliked. He was affronted when the papers were supportive of the new work, claiming that Bacon of the *Herald* was always polite and that Apthorp was forced to write a positive review of the Foote piece after having praised Lang's overture. After expressing his exasperation with these politics he added, "I <u>aint</u> 'patient', and I <u>aint</u> 'good' but I do love you like thunder."

As the winter drew to a close, Marian finally improved, and they made plans for her return in April. On Saturday, 8 April, he wrote, "Good night my darling— you are getting well and strong and I more decrepit every day—Sometimes I feel a hundred—so you must have pity on your poor old husband and get back before he dies of old age!!" We have no reports of their reunion—his letter of 16 April full of detailed instructions for the trip home on 19 April was his last—but we can be sure that it was a relief to both. In a letter written more than thirty years later, Marian's friend Helen Ranney recalled Edward's mood during that long winter:

> I never shall forget that poor despairing boy of yours, the winter you were in Philadelphia. I longed to pack him up and bring him home to care for, with my brother. He was so frightened about you, the treatment seemed so unusual and he was so lonely and desolate. Such love as his for you was a beautiful thing! I always thought of the Brownings, you two together. Such unions are the ones we should cling to, in spite of the dramas and separations.[6]

The letters of the winter of 1892/93 are strikingly similar to those written after Marian's departure from Frankfurt in 1883. In both cases, her absence made him anxious about her health, and the normally busy and self-centered composer lavished his wife with attention and love in his letters. She surely would not have wished him to suffer, but there must have been at least a subconscious gratification in being able to hold his attention so thoroughly. An irony of their relationship is that her illnesses evoked his most compassionate attention. In both cases, the winter blues exacerbated his vulnerability, deepened his loneliness, and intensified his need for her. In March, Edward expressed the despondency that so often gripped him at this time of year:

> I talk rather wild dear—but don't get mad—I do feel so miserable and despondent and tired it seems sometimes as if I couldn't stand it being away from you much longer and yet of course it would be folly to come back (even if you could) until everything goes well. I would go down to you tonight but it might upset us both to have to go through the pain of parting and I know it would upset me anyway. I am perfectly well, really, but as the winter comes to an end it seems as if the separation from everything I have to love in this world was too hard to bear.

What we now term "Seasonal Affective Disorder" or SAD, causes its victims to become despondent and unproductive when the days are shortest. Though primarily the result of limited light exposure, its effects can be exacerbated by stress and

6. Letter, Helen Ranney to MM, December 1929, EMMC box 48/47.

anxiety arising from external conditions. MacDowell's normal pattern was to put up a brave front during the fall and early winter but to give in to despair in the late winter as he waited impatiently for spring. During this winter, more than any other since 1883/84, external circumstances exacerbated his normal seasonal patterns. The uncertainty over Marian's health shook him profoundly just as the weight of the winter blues took away his ability to cope. When he finally returned to composition after a long hiatus during this anxious winter, his works would have a new-found air of melancholy. The depth of emotion in these late works, enhanced by a compositional technique that continued to gain polish and sophistication, would result in his most important and lasting works.

CHAPTER THIRTEEN

International Tastes vs. American Opportunities

MACDOWELL'S RETURN TO THE UNITED STATES COINCIDED WITH A SHIFT IN public attitudes toward American music. After decades of musical advances that went largely unnoticed in the face of prevailing tastes for European music, Americans finally awoke in the mid-1880s to the need to support American composers. In a flood of patriotic protectionism, concert organizers banded together with conductors and soloists to produce hundreds of concerts featuring exclusively American music. The resulting flood of "American Composers' Concerts," characterized by Wilson G. Smith as "a tidal wave of encouragement," created an unprecedented window of opportunity for American composers during the late 1880s and early 1890s.[1]

MacDowell returned home at the ideal time to capitalize on this newfound interest in music by American composers. His works were eagerly sought by publishers and performers, and American audiences were more receptive to music composed by their countrymen than ever before. But his aesthetic ideals had been formed in Europe, and his natural reticence made him leery of throwing in his lot with other composers. He struggled during the early Boston years to reconcile his need for performance opportunities with his distrust of the American Composers' Concert movement. His outspoken opposition to such concerts after he became famous would brand him as a maverick (and an ingrate, in the eyes of some).

---

1. Wilson G. Smith, "American Compositions in the Class and Concert Room," *Etude* 6/8 (August 1888): 129. The movement has been chronicled in depth in E. Douglas Bomberger, *"A Tidal Wave of Encouragement": American Composers' Concerts in the Gilded Age* (Westport, CT and London: Praeger, 2002).

At the heart of MacDowell's attitude was his firmly held belief in an international musical style. As articulated in the December 1887 letter to Lachmund (see chapter 8), he believed that music had evolved beyond the particularism of national styles to a higher state of universal artistic composition that transcended simple nationalism. The context of MacDowell's letter was a series of five concerts presented by the conductor Frank Van der Stucken in New York during November 1887. The highly anticipated event—which included performances of MacDowell's *Hamlet* and Strong's Symphony No. 1—had been covered extensively in the press. Some of the reviews raised MacDowell's hackles by their attempts to characterize American style, in effect telling composers how they should compose rather than making an honest effort to understand each composer's intentions and assess what they heard. He told Lachmund, "I am afraid it will <u>hurt</u> American Composers more than help them. A set of American Concerts suggest [*sic*] that there ought to be an <u>American</u> style or <u>School</u> of composing which is utter <u>nonsense</u>." He admitted, however, that Van der Stucken had been "kindness itself," and that it was "an unthankful act" to criticize his project.[2]

The American Composers' Concert movement continued to provide windfalls for MacDowell in the years ahead. On 9 May 1888, the Detroit Conservatory of Music presented an entire concert of MacDowell's works as part of its American Composers' Series. At the 1888 Music Teachers' National Association (MTNA) convention in Chicago, Teresa Carreño played his First Piano Concerto with the Theodore Thomas Orchestra on 5 July before a crowd estimated at ten thousand. MacDowell's twelve years in Europe and his impressive list of German publications made his music particularly attractive to concert promoters hoping to add credibility to their efforts on behalf of American music. Here was what they all hoped for—a genuine American composer with bona fide European endorsements.

No struggling young composer can afford to turn down performance opportunities, but with each American Composers' Concert, MacDowell's ambivalence toward the notion grew. On 29 March 1889 he wrote to Strong:

> I have been twice asked to go out to Cincinnati to play or to lead some of my compositions, all expenses paid by the College of Music, but as the concerts were to be <u>American</u>—(Chadwick, Foote, Whiting, Van der Stucken, Huss, Gleason, Pratt, Foerster, Kelley are all going)—I flatly refused. If somebody does not help me make this stand, American Composers will be called the "Mutual Admiration Society," or perhaps, which would be worse, the "<u>un</u>happy family."[3]

---

2. Letter, EAM to Carl V. Lachmund, 22 December 1887, NYPL.

3. Letter, EAM to TS, 29 March 1889, EMMC box 29/30.

The tipping point seems to have come at the Paris Exposition of 1889, when he played his Second Piano Concerto in an American concert organized by Van der Stucken. This event provided Edward and Marian the opportunity to revisit Europe a year after their departure, spending a month with Strong in addition to performing at the Exposition. His work with Van der Stucken on that occasion soured him on the conductor, however, as he lost respect for his organizational ability and for his integrity as a musician.

If MacDowell had high hopes for the artistic success of the concert, he was sorely disappointed. The French press wrote patronizingly of the performances and used the occasion to rehash stereotypes of the New World. Most reviewers spent more space generalizing about America and Americans than they did commenting about specific works, as in this statement by Alphonse Duvernoy: "The Americans are a people too young and formed of elements too diverse to possess a well-defined musical school at this time. Originality in art, or more precisely, artistic nationality, is only found in older nations where the races have long been blended into a homogeneous whole."[4] Victor Wilder stated that "The musical art of Americans is like their nationality, an amalgam of races in which the fusion is not sufficiently complete to constitute an irreducible type," adding that the primary influence on all the composers was Mendelssohn.[5] Even some of the American critics present in the audience succumbed to this line of reasoning. According to an anonymous reviewer in the *New York Times*, "What we still lack almost entirely is abandonment to any sense of spontaneous coloration or originality. We are neither German nor French, and, unfortunately, not American. However, there are science of composition and a certain cleanness of cut and method that will bring out other qualities in time and finally make a musical school to add to our art department."[6]

Perhaps because of its disadvantageous position as the second number in the concert, MacDowell's concerto did not receive a sympathetic hearing. Most reviewers felt it was pleasant but not remarkable, preferring instead the works of Van der Stucken and Chadwick. In contradiction of the reviews that had accompanied the work's performances in New York and Boston a few months earlier, most critics found MacDowell the pianist superior to MacDowell the composer. Knowing what we know of the composer's independent spirit, the faint praise of Alfred Bruneau must have been particularly galling: "I consider it necessary to encourage highly this significant manifestation, and I cite with great pleasure the names of Arthur Foote, MacDowell, Chadwick, Dudley Buck, Huss, John K. Paine, Arthur Bird, and

4. Alphonse Duvernoy, "Revue musicale," *La République française*, July 29, 1889, 3.

5. Victor Wilder "La Musique américaine," *Gil Blas*, 16 July 1889, 3.

6. L.K., "American Music in Paris," *NYT*, 28 July 1889, 9.

Margaret Ruthven Lang, whose works I would consider as so many promises for the future."[7] MacDowell had no desire to be viewed as a promise of future greatness, nor did he wish to be lumped together with composers he did not respect. Above all he wanted to be judged as an individual rather than as a representative of his nation. Every musician is eventually confronted with bad reviews, but on the occasion of his return to Paris, MacDowell was greeted with unfair reviews, which did not take his work seriously. Anyone who attributed his intensely chromatic Second Concerto with its unconventional formal structure to the influence of Mendelssohn simply was not paying attention. No wonder he blamed the format of the American Composers' Concert for this disappointing failure.

Back home, the consensus was that the event had been a *succès d'estime* constituting a milestone for American music. It served as a validation of the American Composers' Concert movement, which grew exponentially during the next several years. For MacDowell, who had witnessed the concert and the critical response firsthand, it bolstered his feeling that these sorts of concerts should be avoided at all costs.

Upon his return to the United States after the summer, he adopted a cautious attitude toward American Composers' Concerts. Van der Stucken invited him to reprise his concerto performance in a concert in Washington, DC in March 1890. The program was essentially the same as the Paris Exposition concert, but this time it was sponsored by Jeannette Meyer Thurber, his old acquaintance from his days at the Paris Conservatory. She was lobbying for a congressional charter for her National Conservatory of Music, and invitations to this gala event went to an impressive list of rich and powerful men in American politics. MacDowell's antipathy toward Thurber, for whom his mother now worked as personal secretary (overworked, in Edward's opinion), was matched by his growing distrust of Van der Stucken. As noted in chap. 10, he refused to play his concerto on the concert, but Van der Stucken obtained the published score of his *Ophelia*, which he played without MacDowell's permission on the concert in Lincoln Hall on 26 March 1890.[8]

MacDowell's ambivalence toward American Composers' Concerts did not prevent him from accepting engagements that he believed would be professionally advantageous. At about the time he was refusing to participate in the Washington concert, he agreed to perform at the MTNA convention in Detroit the following July. The association offered him $100 plus expenses to play his Second Concerto

7. Alfred Bruneau, "Musique," *La Revue indépendente* 12/34 (August 1889): 209.

8. "Inaugural Concert American Compositions at Lincoln Music Hall, Washington, D.C., Wednesday Evening, March 26th, 1890, at 8:15," found in Margaret Ruthven Lang Scrapbook, Boston Public Library Rare Book Room.

on one of three gala American Composers' Concerts. He agreed when he learned that Theodore Thomas would conduct the orchestra. The event offered him a high-profile showcase for his work and an opportunity to renew his acquaintance with America's premiere conductor while also being paid for his trouble, which evidently was enough incentive to set aside his scruples.

The performance of MacDowell's Second Concerto on the evening of 2 July 1890 was a rousing success. To the members of the MTNA, who had devoted their best energies during the past decade to proving the value of American music, the appearance of MacDowell was a vindication of their efforts. The review in the *Musical Courier* attested to the warm welcome he received before playing a note: "Mr. E. A. MacDowell was greeted with an amount of applause on his appearance that must have made him feel that he had a warm place in the affections of his fellow workers in the vineyard of art. And he deserves it, for he certainly ranks very high as a composer, independent of any nationality whatsoever."[9] The performance went very well, with *Freund's Music and Drama* calling the concerto "the popular hit of the evening." MacDowell was recalled three times, and the man who just two years earlier had languished in obscurity in Wiesbaden was treated like a celebrity. According to the *Detroit Free Press*, "E. A. MacDowell, the celebrated composer, is an extremely modest man. In fact his personality illustrates the truism that genius is never offensively assertive. When, after the performance of his concerto Tuesday night at the rink, Mr. MacDowell returned to the hotel and donned a white tennis suit his appearance was decidedly picturesque, as he strolled among his friends, receiving their congratulations."[10]

The warm welcome he received from the MTNA did not thaw his opposition to American concerts, however. The association's leaders had made an exception to their normally rigorous selection process by inviting MacDowell to perform and also paying his expenses. At the end of the convention, MacDowell was elected chair of the examining committee that would screen submissions of American compositions for the next convention, despite the fact that he was not a member of the organization. He declined to accept this position, to the embarrassment of the MTNA executive committee.

During the 1890/91 concert season, American composers benefited from two new organizations founded on their behalf. Both the Manuscript Society of New York (MSNY) and the American Composers' Choral Association (ACCA) were created for the purpose of hearing new works by American composers. The MSNY limited its performances to premieres of unpublished American works, which was

---

9. "M.T.N.A.: The Fourteenth Annual Meeting in Detroit," *MC* 21/2 (9 July 1890): 52.

10. "Notes Picked up at Random and Set Down," *Detroit Free Press*, 4 July 1890, 2.

a windfall for composers but created a limited pool of truly high-quality works. These organizations each gave three large public concerts in New York between November 1890 and April 1891, generating much discussion in the musical press. Soon composers in other cities followed suit by founding similar organizations.

In Chicago, the composer Frederick Grant Gleason met with other local composers to consider the possibility of such a group. When he wrote to MacDowell for advice in April 1891, his Boston colleague expressed cautious support but waxed eloquent on the subject of American concerts:

> I fear the M. S. club in New York cannot be called a startling success from the accounts I have had of it.—On the other hand a broad minded, liberal <u>non</u> "mutual admiration" society which might replace the M.T.N.A. (in case of its demise) would be a splendid thing and of lasting benefit. The M.S. club handicapped itself by the M.S. side of it, and by its uniform American programmes.—A society which would give foreign unheard <u>novelties</u> (Rimsky-Korsakov, Glazunoff, Benoit, D'Indy, Heidingsfeld, Weingartner) side by side with <u>American</u> unheard novelties would not only encourage <u>reciprocity</u> abroad but would in my estimation show the public that Americans can hold their own in modern music. As it is now, whenever an exclusively American concert is given, the players, public and press seem to feel obliged to adopt an entirely different standard of criticism from the one accepted for miscellaneous concerts—Some people would run down an American concert <u>before</u> hearing the music—and others would praise it (also <u>before</u> hearing it.)[11]

From this point on, MacDowell became increasingly vocal in his opposition to American Composers' Concerts, even as the manuscript societies in New York, Philadelphia, and Chicago flourished. His contention that American composers could not get a fair hearing when their works were segregated by nationality was a valid point that needed to be aired. But his attitude could also be seen as self-serving, since his own works were doing very well without any advocacy from nationalist organizations.

MacDowell's aesthetic views are reflected in his next major orchestral composition, the *Suite für grosses Orchester* [Suite for large orchestra], op. 42, written in 1890–91 and published in June 1891. Schmidt had told MacDowell when he arrived in Boston that he would publish his orchestral works without charge and pay him royalties as well. MacDowell had given Schmidt a number of piano and vocal works during his first two years in his adopted home, but the *Suite*, op. 42, was the first orchestral work that he wrote in Boston. The publisher's desire for new American works was intensified by the opening of a branch office in Leipzig, where he hoped

---

11. Letter, EAM to Frederick Grant Gleason, 10 April 1891, Gleason Collection, Newberry Library.

to break into the competitive German market by selling high-quality music by American composers. MacDowell's suite was ideal for this venture.

The work consists of four movements whose titles were published in German with English translations. Like so many of MacDowell's works, the movements of the suite are suggestive of scenes from nature without being explicitly programmatic:

I. In einem verwünschten Walde [In a haunted forest]
II. Sommer-Idylle [Summer Idyll]
III. Gesang der Hirtin [The Shepherdess' Song]
IV. Waldgeister [Forest Spirits]

A supplemental movement, "Im Oktober [In October]," was published in June 1893 to be inserted between movements 2 and 3 of the original. As might be surmised from the titles, the work is not nationalistic but is instead universal in its aesthetic. The haunted forest could as easily be found in New England as in Germany, and the warmth of the summer sun is equally soothing to Americans and Germans. Even though the harmonic palette is strongly influenced by Wagnerian chromaticism, there is nothing inherently German about the musical or programmatic content. With this work, MacDowell put his aesthetic ideals on display for his American colleagues while hoping to attract a German audience as well.

Compared with his previous orchestral works, this suite shows a new mastery of orchestration. Despite its title, the orchestra is not unusually large, with pairs of woodwinds, four horns, two trumpets, three trombones, two percussionists, and strings. MacDowell uses this palette of colors masterfully to create a scintillating score full of ingenious effects. The first and last movements in particular have a lightness not found in his earlier orchestral works written in Germany. There is much more "white space" in the score as melodies and melodic fragments are tossed from section to section, and accompaniments are generally lighter and more transparent. The opening movement begins slowly and mysteriously before launching into an energetic allegro furioso. The score is thick with accidentals as MacDowell repeatedly uses chromatic scales for color. Both the second and third movements are based on lyrical themes that contrast with the vigorous outer movements. The final movement brings back the opening of the first movement as a brief reminiscence, makes prominent use of the large brass section, and introduces a syncopated theme of infectious energy (ex. 13.1):

13.1 "Waldgeister" from *Suite for grosses Orchester*, op. 42, rehearsal C

The final appearance of this jaunty motive is paired with a walking bass line in the bassoons and low strings that gives it the punch of cakewalk rhythms (ex. 13.2). In his recording of the Suite, the conductor Howard Hanson gives this passage a raucous reading that seems perfectly natural among the parade of other forest spirits that flit through the lively movement.[12]

13.2 "Waldgeister" from *Suite for grosses Orchester*, op. 42, 8 measures before rehearsal O

During the next several years, this suite was performed frequently on both sides of the Atlantic, enjoying what Marian called "a queer popularity in Germany for two or three years."[13] The reasons for this popularity may be attributed to the colorful orchestration, the tuneful melodies, and the suggestive nature imagery without an explicit program. But this work in particular benefited from the fad for American concerts, and the circumstances surrounding its premiere show MacDowell's obstinate position on this issue.

The *Suite für grosses Orchester*, op. 42, was deposited for copyright on 20 June 1891. Within a short time of its appearance, MacDowell learned of an impending performance. The Boston conductor Carl Zerrahn had purchased the score and parts with the intention to play them during the Worcester Festival in September. This important festival was an annual event that took place in central Massachusetts, attracting large audiences from Boston and garnering extensive coverage from the Boston papers. It was an auspicious place for a premiere of Edward's new work, but as plans developed, he learned that the proposed concert was to be an American Composers' Concert, in which his suite would be programmed with other American orchestral compositions. Furious at this turn of events, he wrote to A. C.

12. Eastman-Rochester Philharmonic Orchestra, cond. Howard Hanson (New York: Polygram, 1994) [originally recorded in 1961].

13. Marian MacDowell, Typescript autobiography vol. 3, p. 97, EMMC box 39/13; quoted in Alan Howard Levy, *Edward MacDowell: An American Master* (Lanham, MD: Scarecrow Press, 1998), 72.

Munroe, secretary of the Worcester association, to demand the removal of the suite from the program. Upon receiving an insulting reply from Munroe, he wrote to the president of the association to no avail. In early September he received a letter from Zerrahn inviting him to attend the concert and conduct his own work, which was the custom for Boston composers whose works were played at the Worcester Festival. When MacDowell refused, Zerrahn told him that he was proceeding with the concert despite the composer's protests.

On the same program were two other premiere performances, including one by the respected composer Victor Herbert. MacDowell wrote to Herbert to assure him that he did not mind being associated with him on the same program, but that he objected to the all-American concert in principle. He admitted, though, that once a work was in print, the composer lost control over its performances. MacDowell boycotted the festival, but Marian traveled to Worcester to hear this important premiere. In the end, he fared very well. The piece was praised as the best work on the program, and his principles were intact. Chadwick wrote to him afterward to confirm the good impressions:

> I have been trying to get around to telling you how much I enjoyed and admired your suite at Worcester....it made everything else on the program sound sick! ...What I particularly like about the whole thing is its conciseness and delicate touch—the purity of its color and freedom from stiff periods and cadences. All this is not modern German style and the Lord be praised if somebody can get away from that. The little phrase for muted horns at the end of the A maj movement is lovely—entirely successful. The work is full of striking effects of delicate color—and all so simple too![14]

The year 1891 had been remarkably productive for MacDowell, as he also completed two movements from a projected symphony on the "Song of Roland" that he had begun in Germany. This publication he entrusted to Breitkopf & Härtel, and he deposited it with the United States Copyright Office himself less than two months after op. 42 was deposited by Schmidt. *Die Sarazenen & Die schöne Aldâ*, op. 30, received several performances but then fell quickly into obscurity while the suite remained popular. It is not clear whether this was because the German publisher did not promote it successfully or whether its strong flavor of "modern German style" decried by Chadwick doomed it with American audiences.

In August 1891, as he was protesting the performance of his suite at Worcester, he received a letter from Franz Xavier Arens. This German-American conductor and composer had been an orchestral leader in Cleveland and had presented his compositions at the MTNA conventions. In fall 1889 he went

---

14. Letter, G. W. Chadwick to EAM, EMMC box 30/24.

abroad to study vocal technique in Berlin, where he also decided to present a series of American Composers' Concerts to German audiences. His first tour in 1891 had seen concerts in Berlin, Dresden, and Hamburg in April, followed by a concert in Sondershausen in July. Now he wrote to MacDowell and other American composers to ask for the loan of scores for the second season as well as for financial support. MacDowell later claimed that he counseled Arens not to pursue the plan, but that letter has not survived, and in fact the conductor played excerpts from MacDowell's Suite, op. 42, on every concert of the 1892 season. In an apparent inconsistency, the composer who had protested violently against his inclusion on all-American concerts in Washington and Worcester sat silently as his works were featured on similar concerts in Berlin on 30 January, Dresden on 19 March, Weimar on 23 March, Leipzig on 9 April, and at the prestigious Vienna Exposition on 5 July.[15]

The tour received significant attention from German reviewers, who devoted much more thoughtful consideration to the concerts than had their Parisian counterparts in 1889. MacDowell's suite was invariably singled out for high praise, not because of any inherently "American" qualities but because of its craftsmanship and inspiration. This review from Hans Paumgartner must have been precisely the sort of reception that MacDowell yearned for:

> A quality—and it is not one of the smallest—is possessed by MacDowell: he is interesting. Further, one can hear so much Wagner in the MacDowell suite without being allowed to blame him for plagiarism because of it. A composer who wishes to depict and illustrate like MacDowell and announces his work to be a picturesque, characteristic piece of music through the prescribed representations of the individual movements of the suite will not immediately find new colors in the [paint] can....If we observe only his inherent talent and command of artistic resources (and MacDowell possesses both), we can still be satisfied. Poetic feeling, which happily and colorfully gives expression to the music, is present throughout.[16]

Here was a respected European critic who heard MacDowell's music as creative and well crafted without being either derivative or exotic. MacDowell's international aesthetic had found an understanding audience, ironically in the midst of the all-American programming that he so deplored.

---

15. For a more detailed discussion of the tour and its relation to the American Composers' Concert movement, see "The Arens Tour of 1891–1892: Propaganda, Parochialism, and All-American Concerts" in Bomberger, "*A Tidal Wave of Encouragement*," 87–120.

16. dr. h. p. [Hans Paumgartner], "Aufführung von Werken amerikanischer Componisten," *Wiener Zeitung* 154 (7 July 1892): 2–3.

When Arens returned to the United States in August, he was greeted by controversy. The critic George H. Wilson had used the columns of his *Boston Musical Herald* to question the motives and competence of Arens before the season began in January. In response to the positive reviews that greeted the concerts, Wilson opined in July, "of course Mr. Arens can secure bushels of good notices commending his scheme; press notices in the majority of cases are at the call of any good-mannered fellow the world over." This attracted the ire of rival American journals, most notably the *Musical Courier* and the *American Art Journal*, which had supported the Arens tour from the beginning. A 24 July editorial by Henry E. Krehbiel in the *New York Tribune* further decried the tour by quoting the negative opinions of some European reviewers.

This very public debate put MacDowell in a difficult position. His opposition to American Composers' Concerts was already well known, but his music had fared very well in the Arens tour. He was urged to make a public statement by both Wilson and the *Musical Courier*, and he chose to accept James Huneker's invitation to publish his views in the latter journal, condemning Wilson's tactics while also distancing himself from Arens's tour. On the subject of the negative European reviews quoted by Wilson and the *New York Tribune*, he wrote: "Do our own critics (of whom I personally have always been rather proud) confess that they are inferior to the foreign 'authorities' quoted? If they do not, why then reprint a set of obviously incorrect and worthless criticisms, and by calling their authors 'authorities,' or agreeing with them, thus directly contradict what they themselves have said of the same works?"[17] MacDowell walked a very fine line by criticizing the tour but at the same time accepting the benefits that it accorded him as a composer. In a letter from his new home in Indianapolis later in the year, Arens reminded MacDowell of those benefits:

> Now whatever views you may hold in regard to the influence on a young composer to have his works performed in a country where up to date such a thing as a musical score written by an American had been considered an impossibility, you for one did not suffer through these performances, for at every concert your suite was enthusiastically recd and just as enthusiastically criticised....You are now known in Europe as one of the composers of the day, American or otherwise, while in some of the cities visited, your name had never been mentioned, and in others only as a piano composer. Of course, you ultimately would have found your way, but not until someone else had taken you up (as Mdme Carreño had done with your piano works) Vide Wagner's friends.[18]

17. "A Letter from E. A. M'Dowell," *MC* 25/6 (10 August 1892): 6.
18. Undated letter, Arens to "My dear sir," EMMC box 30/5.

Arens could hardly be blamed for feeling that MacDowell was ungrateful for his advocacy in Europe, where the suite was soon embraced by German orchestras. Not one to hold a grudge, Arens played the work again during the Indianapolis May Festival on 23 May 1893, borrowing a copy of the score from MacDowell to refresh his memory.

One of the challenges faced by a successful man is the transition from obscurity to fame. After years of needing to shout just to be heard, he suddenly finds that people pay unexpected attention to everything he says. Almost over night, he needs to adjust his modes of communication to take advantage of this newfound respect without sounding shrill. In December 1892, shortly after the Arens debate, the *Musical Courier* mentioned his name in its year-end retrospective, showing just how far MacDowell had come in capturing the ears of the public:

> [T]he unhappy American composer, who from being contemptuously pilloried, gorged with praise, and lately stupefied with indifference, is at last coming to a realizing sense of his position. He now knows that he must stand on his own legs, metaphorically, and must throw away those adventitious crutches, "American composers' concerts," "Yankee Doodle programs," &c. E. A. MacDowell's (he is certainly an American and certainly a composer to be proud of) views on the subject were sound from the outset—a composer of music first and foremost, then an American.[19]

Curiously, MacDowell does not seem to have realized that his views were heard and respected, for in the years ahead he became increasingly strident in his opposition to concerts devoted to American works, attacking organizers of such concerts with a vehemence out of all proportion to this frankly tangential aspect of the American concert scene.

After figuring prominently in the public debate over American Composers' Concerts in the early 1890s, MacDowell was drawn into the debate over compositional Americanism in the mid-1890s. The catalyst for this discussion, ironically, was a Czech composer, Antonín Dvořák, who lived in the United States only from 1892 to 1895 but managed during those three years to alter the entire musical landscape in the country.

In her efforts to promote her National Conservatory of Music, MacDowell's old friend Jeannette Meyer Thurber had invited him to join the faculty in 1888, which he refused to do. He had also declined the invitation to participate in the gala concert in Washington in March 1890 in support of her lobbying for a congressional charter for the school. In her boldest move, she convinced Dvořák to accept the directorship of her conservatory in fall 1892 at a salary of $15,000, approximately six times

19. "1892. A Retrospective Glance," *MC* 25/25 (28 December 1892): 8.

MacDowell's annual salary. This was cause enough for him to be jealous, but he was also piqued at the Czech composer's aggressive efforts to reshape the discussion on American music. During the 1892/93 year, Dvořák instituted a nationwide composition competition to identify promising American works. Among the winners was Henry Schoenefeld's "Rural" Symphony, a genre of picturesque composition that MacDowell found distasteful.

With only limited familiarity with the people and culture of his adopted home, Dvořák made a number of bold pronouncements on the future of American music. A *New York Herald* article of 21 May 1893 quoted his views on American music, among which was the statement, "I am now satisfied that the future music of this country must be founded upon what are called the negro melodies. This must be the real foundation of any serious and original school of composition to be developed in the United States."[20] This notion flew in the face of the international musical style espoused by MacDowell and many of his Boston colleagues, and the negative reaction was swift. Although MacDowell did not participate, a long list of musicians responded to Dvořák's pronouncements in a 28 May article in the *Boston Herald*. The consensus of Paine, Beach, Chadwick, Lang, and others was that the Czech composer was insufficiently familiar with American conditions to make such pronouncements, and that his exclusive favoring of one type of ethnic music did not take into account the breadth of American culture.[21] Dvořák later broadened his ideas to include Native American music and even the music of European immigrants, but it was his initial pronouncement that garnered the most attention.

Since his earliest compositional efforts, MacDowell had avoided any hints of American folk or popular styles in his music. As he had explained to Lachmund, his goal was to compose in an international style that transcended particularism. MacDowell was not drawn to folkloristic nationalism of the sort that Schoenefeld employed in his "Rural" Symphony or his briefly popular "Marcio fantastico" from the *Suite caractéristique*, which depicted an African American celebration with syncopated rhythms inspired by minstrel shows. This latter work drew much comment from German critics on the Arens tour, who were fascinated by what they heard as bizarre vulgarity. Strong surely spoke for MacDowell when he wrote in an 1888 letter about another American composer known for references to folk style: "Chadwick seems to want to do fine things and, judging from the sinfonie, to avoid ear tickling; for this I respect him. Somebody ought, (in kindness to him,) to 'gently' tell him that there are portions of his sinfonie and others of his works that are touched with

20. Quoted in Adrienne Fried Block, "Boston Talks Back to Dvořák," *I.S.A.M Newsletter* 18/2 (May 1989): 10.
21. Reprinted in ibid.

vulgarity: as this is a trait <u>that foreigners expect and look for in American work</u>, every American ought to do his utmost to avoid even the ghost of it."[22]

On 16 December 1893, Dvořák premiered his first major work written on American soil, the Symphony in E Minor ("From the New World"). This work, which is one of the nineteenth-century's most beloved symphonies, did more than any of his ideological pronouncements to reshape the debate over Americanism in music. Any connections to American folk music in the work were well disguised, but he repeatedly emphasized their importance in interviews about his compositional process. Thus the work became emblematic of his attempts to create a new American style. In advance of the Boston premiere two weeks later, MacDowell expressed his disdain in a letter to his mother:

> Dvorak's new Symphony is to be played here Saturday, an American Symphony with such a Kefloozlum Bohemian title as he puts to it will be a novelty. Now if he will only give lessons in his kind of American language (to match the symphony) the thing will be complete. I suppose he calls his carbuncle "a gin blossom"—There only remains for him to go into politics now—He might compose music to the "Tammany Ring" just as Wagner did for the "Nibelungen Ring." I suppose he calls his bank account "From the new world" too. If I ever meet him I am going to practice my "Czech" on him. This would be less painful to me than his "American."[23]

MacDowell's resentment was more than personal jealousy in this case, for he must have felt that Dvořák had co-opted something that did not belong to him. As MacDowell reflected on Dvořák's achievement in the years ahead, he eventually reconciled himself to the notion of writing an overtly American work that quoted folk music. He came to believe, however, that African American musical materials lacked the gravity and integrity necessary for serious musical composition. He turned instead to the music of Native Americans, whose "manly and free rudeness" he found compatible to his own artistic aims.[24] The "Indian" Suite, op. 48, would be MacDowell's most successful orchestral work, a composition that would cement his fame and in a curious way label him forever as an American composer.[25]

22. Letter, TS to EAM, New Year's Eve, 1888, EMMC box 31/30.

23. Letter, EAM to Fanny MacDowell, 27 December 1893, NYPL.

24. Quoted in Lawrence Gilman, *Edward MacDowell: A Study* (New York: John Lane, 1908), 84.

25. This work has been the subject of more commentary than any of MacDowell's works and continues to elicit scholarly analyses in the twenty-first century. For more extensive discussions, see: Richard Crawford, "Edward MacDowell: Musical Nationalism and an American Tone Poet" *Journal of the American Musicological Society* 49/3 (Autumn 1996): 528–60; and Michael V. Pisani, *Imagining Native America in Music* (New Haven: Yale University Press, 2005).

Seldom in his compositions does MacDowell quote directly from other musical sources. His melodic ideas are nearly always original, and it could be argued that most similarities to previously existing music are coincidental. When he does quote from another source, he prefers to leave the reference hidden, like a puzzle. The "Indian" Suite, op. 48, provides a striking exception to this rule, as many of its melodies are based on a specific source that MacDowell made no attempt to hide. According to his student Henry Gilbert, MacDowell expressed an interest in seeing some native music and asked Gilbert to look some up. Gilbert brought him a copy of Theodore Baker's *Über die Musik der nordamerikanischen Wilden* [On the Music of North American Indians], which had been submitted as a dissertation to the University of Leipzig in 1882.[26] MacDowell used several of Baker's transcribed melodies as the basis of his thematic material for the "Indian" Suite.

More than a century after the fact, it is easy to chastise MacDowell for relying on printed sources rather than going directly to the oral sources of the music. In her 1995 dissertation, Tara C. Browner takes him to task for relying on Baker's book rather than on personal contact with Baker or his subjects. She also decries his use of melodic fragments from the tunes rather than entire melodies as would be the practice of Arthur Farwell and other "Indianist" composers in future decades. Most significantly, she associates his ideas with those of Social Darwinism, impugning his view of native music as an "exotic other" rather than a living culture.[27] As a resident of Boston and New York, he had little opportunity to encounter authentic performances, and it is true that MacDowell did not go out of his way to correct this deficiency. On one occasion in the mid-1890s he received a visit from the author Hamlin Garland and asked him what he thought of Alice Fletcher's transcriptions of Omaha songs. Garland sang them in the way he remembered hearing them in the West, whereupon MacDowell commented, "you make these things of mine seem like milk and water."[28] As Richard Crawford notes, however, MacDowell was less interested in the particulars of Indian culture than in its universal implications, just as he had earlier been fascinated with the ideal of medieval chivalry but unimpressed by the ruins of medieval castles.[29] This is a reflection of his lifelong interest in reading as stimulation to the imagination, and it is also another example of the

26. Henry F. Gilbert, "Personal Recollections of Edward MacDowell," *New Music Review* 2 (1912): 496–97.

27. Tara C. Browner, "Baker and Edward MacDowell," in "Transposing Cultures: The Appropriation of Native North American Musics, 1890–1990" (PhD diss., University of Michigan, 1995), 45–52.

28. Hamlin Garland, "Roadside Meetings of a Literary Nomad," *Bookman* 71 (March 1930): 46; quoted in Francis Brancaleone, "Edward MacDowell and Indian Motives," *American Music* 7/4 (Winter 1989): 360.

29. Crawford, "Edward MacDowell," 559–60.

introvert's desire to keep the world at arm's length. Direct contact—whether with exotic music, overgrown ruins, or the politics of a musical career—was distasteful to him.

The five movements are: 1. Legend; 2. Love Song; 3. In War-time; 4. Dirge; and 5. Village Festival. The compositional history of the suite is not completely clear, but it seems likely that the "Dirge" was begun in 1891, significantly before the other movements, which were completed in the fall of 1895 not long before the New York premiere on 26 January 1896. This movement is the only one that does not have an obvious connection to the tunes in Baker's dissertation, showing only a passing similarity to one of the songs. MacDowell discussed its relation to the other numbers of the suite in a 1903 interview: "Of all my music the dirge in the 'Indian Suite' pleases me most. It affects me deeply, and did when I was writing it. To me it seems to tell a world sorrow. In it an Indian woman laments the death of her son. The 'Indian suite' is the result of my studies of the Indians, their dances, and their songs. With the exception of the dirge the suite is the development of the themes which came to me from these people. The dirge is my own."[30]

The "Indian" Suite stands apart from MacDowell's other works in its use of folkloristic nationalism. Ironically, when subsequent generations of critics claimed that MacDowell's music was derivative of European models, they pointed to this work as the exception in his oeuvre. In actual fact, this was the piece that can most clearly be heard as derivative of a European model, since it follows Dvořák's prescription for how American music should be written. Edward MacDowell's goal was to create a universal aesthetic that expressed his own individuality regardless of national affiliation. The "Indian" Suite was an exception to this rule, and one that he would seldom follow again. His reasons for eschewing folkloristic nationalism in music were grounded in his views on internal motivations versus external manifestations, as he explained in a lecture delivered some years later:

> A man is generally something different from the clothes he wears or the business he is occupied with; but when we do see a man identified with his clothes we think but little of him. And so it is with music. So-called Russian, Bohemian, or any other purely national music has no place in art, for its characteristics may be duplicated by anyone who takes the fancy to do so. On the other hand, the vital element of music—personality—stands alone....Music that can be made by "recipe" is not music, but "tailoring."...Before a people can find a musical writer to echo its genius it must first possess men who truly

30. "America's Leading Composer," *San Francisco Chronicle*, 3 January 1903, 14; quoted in Margery M. Lowens, "The New York Years of Edward MacDowell" (PhD diss., University of Michigan, 1971), 278.

represent it—that is to say, men who, being part of the people, love the country for itself: men who put into their music what the nation has put into its life; and in the case of America it needs above all, both on the part of the public and on the part of the writer, absolute freedom from the restraint that an almost unlimited deference to European thought and prejudice has imposed upon us. Masquerading in the so-called nationalism of Negro clothes cut in Bohemia will not help us. What we must arrive at is the youthful optimistic vitality and the undaunted tenacity of spirit that characterizes the American man. This is what I hope to see echoed in American music.[31]

Here finally is the manifesto that reconciles MacDowell's views on American concerts and folkloristic nationalism in music. He opposed both on the grounds that they inhibited the individualism and true creativity that would provide the only real basis for lasting artistic contributions. Just as he refused to be merely "one of the gang" of American composers, he challenged his fellow composers not to allow American music to be "one of the gang" of national styles based on exotic folk music. His aspiration was to be truly worthy of the pantheon of great composers by transcending the expectations of both his overenthusiastic countrymen and the skeptical European critics.

The premiere performance of the *Indian Suite*, op. 48, took place in New York on 26 January 1896, on a program that also included the First Piano Concerto with the composer as soloist. This evening was one of the great triumphs of MacDowell's career, and one that would ultimately determine his fate. Unknown to MacDowell, a committee of trustees and faculty members from Columbia University was present in the audience that evening to assess his fitness for a recently endowed position as chair of a new department of music at that prestigious institution. Fanny had been conspiring with Marian behind Edward's back to find a way to bring the couple to New York, and she had had several meetings with Columbia officials about the possibility of an appointment for her son. Knowing the importance of reputations and connections, she arranged for a delegation to attend the high-profile event. Edward succeeded so brilliantly that, in the words of Professor John Burgess, "we went away from that concert pretty well convinced that MacDowell was our man."[32] The goal of the committee was lofty—they wanted nothing less than to appoint America's greatest composer as first professor of music at the university. The man

31. Quoted in Gilman, *Edward MacDowell: A Study*, 83–85.

32. John W. Burgess, *Reminiscences of an American Scholar: The Beginnings of Columbia University* (New York: Columbia University Press, 1934), 284. This book gives a detailed account of the selection process, including Burgess's heroic efforts to obtain a reference letter from Paderewski when another candidate appeared ready to move ahead of MacDowell.

who had resisted the moniker "American composer" for so many years won the position by being in the right place at the right time.

When MacDowell was contacted by Columbia's president Seth Low later that spring, he was presented with a difficult decision. He was well established in Boston, he earned a comfortable though unpredictable income as a composer and teacher, and he enjoyed complete independence. A Columbia professorship would give him less independence but more financial stability, along with even more esteem than he presently enjoyed. The offer tendered by Low in a letter of 13 April 1896 included an annual salary of $5,000 and a promise of significant autonomy in shaping the new program. MacDowell accepted promptly.

Over the next several months, Edward and Marian wrapped up their affairs in Boston while he laid the plans for a completely new curriculum in music at Columbia. Their lives were made even more hectic by the impending relocation of Templeton Strong and his family to New England for the second time. The Strongs reunited with the MacDowells in their favorite summer destination of Peterborough, New Hampshire, where they now had a home purchased during the winter. This property would become an important refuge for Edward and Marian in the years ahead, and it would also inspire some of his most important compositions.

CHAPTER FOURTEEN

A Cabin in the Woods

S INCE CHILDHOOD, EDWARD HAD LIVED IN CITIES AND VACATIONED IN THE
country. His memories of summer days at his grandparents' farm in Orange
County, with his conservatory friends at Émancé, and with Strong in Switzerland
were among his most pleasant. When the days were long and the weather was
warm, he felt drawn to escape the hot and crowded city into nature, preferably to
the north, where the days were even longer.

Edward and Marian had experimented with different summer getaways since
moving to Boston in 1888. The summer of 1889 had been spent in Vevey, Switzerland,
and the summer of 1890 was spent in Peterborough, New Hampshire, where they
returned in 1892 and 1893. They tried York, Maine, in 1891 and Cumberland, Maine,
in 1894. In 1895 they spent another summer with Strong in Switzerland. But their
favorite retreat was the small town of Peterborough, a few hours outside Boston.
As MacDowell's professional reputation grew and his income increased accordingly,
they finally took the opportunity to fulfill their dream of owning a country home,
when they purchased an eighty-acre farm there in 1896.[1]

The property had a Cape Cod cottage named Hillcrest by the previous own-
ers, a name the MacDowells retained. Marian found the home on her own and
agreed to purchase it for $1,500—$500 down and $1,000 in a mortgage. When
she telegraphed the news to Edward, he replied, "All right, in your name, your
responsibility." Having the papers drawn up in her name turned out to be a wise
decision, as it made the transfer of property easier during his final illness. Over

---

1. The details of the purchase and renovations are detailed in Marian's memoirs, EMMC box 39,
II-78–86.

the years the couple enlarged the house and added acreage to ensure their privacy. The first summer was spent moving the barns, but during the following summer of 1897 they added a music room to the cottage, their first major renovation. This isolated wing provided Edward more privacy, but he still longed for more separation when he worked, and they began investigating the possibility of another building. Edward consulted the architect George Edward Barton, who sent him detailed plans for building a log cabin in October 1898.[2] Marian had the log cabin built in the thick forest at a distance from Hillcrest, completing most of the work in secret before they returned for the summer of 1899. Edward enthusiastically joined in the work of completing the cabin, inscribing the words "Edward and Marian/August 1899" in the wet cement of the hearth.[3] This secluded refuge allowed Edward even more solitude for his creative work in the remaining years of his life.

MacDowell explained the importance of a summer retreat in an April 1896 interview, after they had purchased Hillcrest but before they had moved in. His comments show that even during the Boston years his compositional activities were mostly confined to the summer months, and they also demonstrate how dependent he was on inspiration to compose:

> I never attempt composition in the winter, but give all my time to routine work. In the summer I hire a house somewhere out in the country, go out there and fish, shoot, ride,—in fact live like a human being once more. Then when I have sufficiently worn off the effect of living in town I begin to think seriously of work. Some fine day I feel just in the mood for it and sit down to it. I almost never make any notes beforehand, but when I get an idea go to work and finish it up at once. It's of no use to say before I begin what I am going to do. I can only work as I feel, and sometimes accomplish nothing at all when I have felt that I was beautifully primed up....I have been out of town recently, selecting and engaging my house for the summer. It is near P—, in southern New Hampshire. I drove out from town, breaking through snowdrifts eight feet deep in places. Nothing at all spring-like as yet, but it will be lovely in summer, and I shall work finely there.[4]

The first of the works composed at the Peterborough farm was a set of ten piano pieces titled *Woodland Sketches*, op. 51, written during the summer of 1896. Like so many of MacDowell's short character pieces, they are suggestive of extramusical ideas without telling a specific story. In this sense the composer found a middle ground

2. Letter, George Edward Barton to EAM, October 1898, MacDowell Collection, Library of Congress Manuscript Division, box 6.

3. The construction of the cabin is described in Margery M. Lowens, "The New York Years of Edward MacDowell" (PhD diss., University of Michigan, 1971), 235–37.

4. John Lathrop Mathews, "Mr. E. A. MacDowell," *Music* 10 (May 1896): 34.

between the abstract character pieces of Brahms and the explicitly programmatic works of Richard Strauss. Structurally, most employ the ABA form typical of the genre, while harmonically they contain a remarkable and well-disguised array of contemporary techniques. Technically, there are only a few virtuosic passages, and most of the pieces feature simple melodies over chordal accompaniments. The chords contain such large and awkward stretches, however, that few of the pieces are appropriate for beginning pianists. The open intervals and chord voicings are essential stylistic elements of these deceptively simple pieces.

The prevailing mood of the set is nostalgic melancholy reflective of the pastoral setting in which they were composed. Edward and Marian often walked or drove in the woods, and his experiences on these outings served as the inspiration for No. 3 "At an Old Trysting-place," No. 5 "From an Indian Lodge," and No. 8 "A Deserted Farm." MacDowell was struck by the atmosphere of decline in this part of rural New England that had been a thriving agricultural region until a generation before, when many residents had left for richer farmland in the Midwest. "At an Old Trysting-place," with the expression marking "Somewhat quaintly; not too sentimentally," portrays the return of a former resident to the place where he had met his lover in his youth. "A Deserted Farm," inspired by an abandoned property where he and Marian ate their lunch one day, begins and ends with a melancholy depiction of the decaying farmstead in F-sharp minor, contrasted with a middle section in the parallel key of F-sharp major. This middle strain, marked "pianissimo as heard from afar," represents echoes of the barn dances held there in bygone times. "From an Indian Lodge" evokes a now-extinct Native American tribe, which was only a distant memory by the time of MacDowell's arrival. He mourned the passing of these people and their quiet dignity in the same way he had yearned for days of medieval chivalry as a child. For thematic material he returned to Baker's dissertation on Indian music, selecting two songs from the Walla-Walla tribe and one from the Brotherton Indians. Another kind of nostalgia is reflected in No. 7 "From Uncle Remus," inspired by his reading of the Joel Chandler Harris stories. Like Stephen Foster, MacDowell had no direct experience with the American South, but he evoked elements of the culture in this charmingly nostalgic piece that imitates the banjo (ex. 14.1).

MacDowell was also inspired by nature, as the most significant pieces in the set depict images of the wildlife surrounding his farm. "To a Wild Rose," "Will o' the Wisp," "To a Water Lily," and "By a Meadow Brook" are among the most iconic of MacDowell's works, forming a point of entry into his oeuvre for generations of piano students.

In the opening number of the set, "To a Wild Rose," MacDowell struck a balance between simplicity and sophistication that continues to captivate listeners.

14.1 "From Uncle Remus" from *Woodland Sketches*, op. 51, no. 7, final 10 measures

The composer credited the work's popularity with the fact that the publisher spread it generously over two pages rather than squeezing it into one as he did with "At an Old Trysting-place." The phenomenal popularity of the work goes beyond its layout, however. In contrast to "At an Old Trysting-Place," which develops a long-breathed melody of sixteen beats, "To a Wild Rose" relies on short melodic fragments (ex. 14.2):

14.2 "To a Wild Rose" from *Woodland Sketches*, op. 51, no. 1, mm. 1–8

Closer examination reveals that the spare melody is supported by a chordal accompaniment thick with non-chord tones and extended harmonies. The A in the second measure is a pedal point retained from the first measure, creating a barely noticed dissonance, while the fifth and seventh measures use a ninth chord whose dissonance is minimized by its spacing. The climax of the piece also features dissonant non-chord tones and extended harmonies in an intensification that prepares the return of the main theme (ex. 14.3):

14.3 "To a Wild Rose" from *Woodland Sketches*, op. 51, no. 1, mm. 21–28

The chord that is reiterated high in the keyboard and made lush with the pedal may be heard as an E dominant ninth, but the fact that the E is sounded only once and dies out so quickly makes it sound more like a G-sharp half-diminished seventh chord, a favorite of MacDowell's former classmate Debussy and also a version of Wagner's so-called Tristan chord. The simple melody ends its final phrase with a folksy Scotch snap rhythm that belies the underlying harmonic complexity.

No. 2 "Will o' the Wisp" is the most virtuosic of the set, with a fleet lightness that calls to mind Currier's comments about his love of extreme speed. The chromatic moving right-hand figure that enters in m. 7 is a distinctive MacDowell texture that the composer first tried in the "Shadow Dance" from Twelve Etudes. Here it is treated with more subtlety but in service of a similar image of ghostly night spirits. Its charm relies on a hemiola effect that creates fleeting dissonances with the left-hand melody (ex. 14.4):

14.4 "Will o' the Wisp" from *Woodland Sketches*, op. 51, no. 2, mm. 5–12

No. 6 "To a Water Lily" is the piece most closely allied to the impressionistic style. Marian MacDowell recalled that she introduced her husband to this plant on one of their walks in the woods. Fascinated by the showy flowers floating on the surface of a murky pond, he saw in them a metaphor for the slums of Manhattan's Lower East Side. He told her that out of this foul atmosphere would spring some of America's future leaders. His tone picture portrays the floating blossoms in the ethereal key of F-sharp major, using triple pianissimo, pedal effects, and harmonic parallelism to reflect the weightless appearance of the flowers. The opening passage (ex. 14.5) is scored on three staves to facilitate reading the widely spaced texture:

14.5 "To a Water-Lily" from *Woodland Sketches*, op. 51, no. 6, mm. 1–8

This is also one of his earliest pieces that changes meter—the middle section is in 3/2. The piece rivaled "To a Wild Rose" in popularity and presaged the trend a decade later among American composers for impressionistic textures.

The first nine pieces of the set are distinctive character pieces with little indication of a cyclic arrangement. The final number, "Told at Sunset," draws thematically on earlier pieces in the set, most notably "A Deserted Farm," "From an Indian Lodge," and "At an Old Trysting-Place." The Scotch snap, or reverse dotted rhythm, is used extensively in this piece, which could have been called "The Apotheosis of the Scotch Snap." This distinctive rhythmic pattern, also known as Lombardic rhythm, figured prominently in the music of Vivaldi and in the Scotch Strathspey dance, but it has a special affinity for speakers of American English. The sound of this rhythmic figure mimics the characteristic accentuation of two-syllable words in that language.[5]

5. This idea is explored in Victor Fell Yellin, "Prosodic Syncopation," in *A Celebration of American Music: Words and Music in Honor of H. Wiley Hitchcock*, ed. Richard Crawford, R. Allen Lott, and Carol J. Oja (Ann Arbor: University of Michigan Press, 1990), 449–59.

With this set of ten pieces, MacDowell's fame reached a new level. His appointment at Columbia University had reflected his solid reputation as a composer of art music, but the *Woodland Sketches* represented a bold foray into new territory. Like Schumann and Mendelssohn before him, MacDowell succeeded in elevating the genre of *Hausmusik*, or accessible piano compositions for the middle-class parlor, to the highest artistic level. The combination of integrity and popularity that he strikes so effortlessly in this set is the most elusive quality in musical composition, and one that many great composers never manage to find. Published by P. L. Jung in the fall of 1896, it became an instant hit. Upon his death, it was reported that the set had sold more than one hundred thousand copies. Perhaps most ironically, MacDowell was contacted by Breitkopf & Härtel in July 1898 with a cordial request to take over the European distribution of the set in order to bring the full weight of their reputation to bear in spreading his fame. He responded diplomatically that he would not interfere with the business arrangements of his American publisher, but he took the opportunity to point out that the royalty numbers they had given him for recent sales of his earlier works did not correspond to his reputation, calling into question either the integrity of their bookkeeping or their ability to market his works effectively. This letter was the opening salvo in a battle that would drag on for years.

The Peterborough property became a welcome retreat as Edward settled into his work at Columbia University. The new job was overwhelming in its demands, and he and Marian used their Peterborough home as an escape from their busy urban lifestyle in New York. Edward quickly found that he had no time for composing during the academic year. The amount of music that he managed to complete during these summers was remarkable, calling to mind the similar working methods of his Austrian colleague Gustav Mahler, who restricted his compositional activities to the summers when he was not conducting.

In the summer of 1896, MacDowell sketched a piano piece titled "Calm," depicting the ocean. During the following two years the idea gestated and evolved until he returned to it in earnest during the summer of 1898. The result was eight *Sea Pieces*, op. 55, the composer's most ambitious set of character pieces. For MacDowell, ocean crossings had played an important part in the major transitions of his life, as he had traveled to and from Europe to study, to get married, to begin his career in Boston, to perform at the Paris Exposition, and to visit his friend Strong. He had also lived in close proximity to the ocean during his childhood in New York and during his years in Boston.

Dolores Pesce notes that MacDowell's contemplation of the ocean is a departure from the traditions of Europe and America.[6] Whereas previous poets and composers

6. Dolores Pesce, "The Other Sea in MacDowell's Sea Pieces," *American Music* 10/4 (Winter 1992): 411–40.

had viewed the ocean as a powerful and dangerous force that inspired fear, MacDowell views it as a representation of the sublime. He focuses on the grandeur and infinity of the ocean rather than on its menace, opening possibilities for philosophical contemplation of nature. This is clearly reflected in the wide range of the keyboard textures (ex. 14.6), as in the closing measures of the first piece, "To the Sea":

14.6 "To the Sea" from *Sea Pieces*, op. 55, no. 1, mm. 27–32

Using several ingenious melodic references to Weber's *Oberon* and Wagner's *Flying Dutchman*, the composer creates a set that is unified thematically. Dotted rhythms and recurring melodic fragments are used consistently throughout the work to connect the separate movements. He signals his intentions for each of the eight pieces with an epigraph of his own composition or drawn from another writer. The epigraph to the final number, "In Mid-Ocean," summarizes the sublimity of the sea and its ability to dwarf our human concerns:

Inexorable!
Thou straight line of eternal fate
That ring'st the world,
Whil'st on thy moaning breast
We play our puny parts
And reckon us immortal!

With *Sea Pieces*, MacDowell again moved into new artistic territory. Combining the formal structure of the *Woodland Sketches* with the sweep and grandeur of the sonatas, he aspired to create a cyclical composition that was unified in theme and yet diverse in its expressive elements. The result was his favorite of the sets of character pieces.

During the same summer, MacDowell also completed his *War Song*, op. 6, for men's chorus; *Six Fancies for the Piano*, op. 7; and *Four Songs*, op. 56. The reason for the broken sequence of opus numbers was that opp. 6 and 7 were among a series of pieces published under the pseudonym "Edgar Thorn(e)," written and published between 1896 and 1898. Marian later gave two explanations for his decision to publish under this name. During his early years in New York, MacDowell directed the Mendelssohn Glee Club, an amateur men's chorus. He wrote a significant amount of music for this group, but it was said that his modesty prevented him from forcing them to sing his works. By publishing them under another name, he allowed the chorus to choose to sing them on their own merits rather than because they were composed by the director. The rest of the Thorn pieces were for solo piano, written in a popular style that the composer hoped would ensure robust sales. Marian's childhood nurse Sister Kathleen was now married with several children to support and a husband who could not adequately provide for their needs. Marian later recalled that Edward assigned the royalties from the Thorn pieces to Sister Kathleen in hopes that this would ease her hardships. The pieces did not sell well, however, until the composer's true identity was revealed years later.[7]

MacDowell was not a natural songwriter, and many of his early solo songs had been plagued by predictability in melody and phrase structure. With the *Four Songs*, op. 56, he achieved a new maturity in some of his best songs. Three of the four use the composer's own poems, a trend that would be continued in the *Three Songs*, op. 58. The melody of the first number, "Long ago, sweetheart mine," has a sentimental grace in keeping with the *Woodland Sketches*, along with the characteristic Scotch snap rhythm (ex. 14.7) that had figured so prominently in that set.

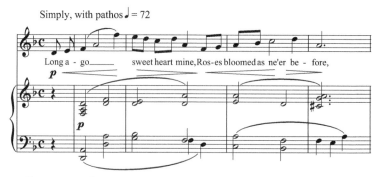

14.7 "Long Ago," op. 56, no. 1, mm. 1–4

The middle section of the song modulates to the relative major before returning to the opening tonality in the third verse. Of the four songs, No. 2 "The Swan bent low to the Lily" and No. 3 "A Maid Sings Light" became especially popular.

7. Letter to Allan Robinson, 30 April 1908, EMMC box 51/2.

The latter song has a singable melody and dramatic flair that are often missing in MacDowell's songs. His childhood lack of experience with church music and his adult absence of interest in opera were certainly responsible for the relative weakness of many of his songs. The final song in the set, "As the Gloaming Shadows Creep," uses his own translation of a text by the thirteenth-century minnesinger Frauenlob. He had previously set this text for men's chorus, the only text he set twice. The song is slow and somber, with an expansive tessitura and dynamic range reminiscent of the *Sea Pieces*.

Although the Peterborough property served as a haven for Edward and Marian during their New York years, the renovations and expansions they undertook added a financial burden that his Columbia salary could not fully cover. Hillcrest was both a blessing and a responsibility for the couple, and its mystique would be central to the rest of their lives together.

Plate 1: Edward MacDowell at age 3 and a half (Library of Congress)

Plate 2: Self-portrait at age fourteen (Library of Congress)

Plate 3: Autographed photo of Teresa Carreño, December 1874 (Library of Congress)

Plate 4: MacDowell in Germany at age eighteen (Library of Congress)

Plate 5: Café Milani an der Zeil in Frankfurt, where MacDowell lived, 1883–84 (Stadtarchiv Frankfurt)

Plate 6: MacDowell and Strong in Wiesbaden, 1888 (Library of Congress)

Plate 7: Palais du Trocadéro, where MacDowell played his concerto on 12 July 1889, shown beyond the Eiffel Tower (Douglas Bomberger)

Plate 8: Edward and Marian in Switzerland, Summer 1903 (Library and Archives of Canada)

Plate 9: Photo signed by MacDowell after his breakdown (Margery Lowens)

Plate 10: Edward and Marian during his final illness (Library of Congress)

Plate 11: Anna Baetz with Marian (Library of Congress)

Plate 12: Marian on the porch of the log cabin in Peterborough (MacDowell Colony)

BOOK THREE

Edward MacDowell in New York

CHAPTER FIFTEEN

Columbia University, 1896–1901

THE SELECTION OF EDWARD MACDOWELL TO PLAN AND LEAD A NEW department of music at Columbia University reflected the trustees' view of his stature as "the greatest musical genius this country has ever produced." From an educational and administrative standpoint, it was a risky choice. MacDowell had attended five schools, but he had not completed the prescribed course of study in any of them. Furthermore, he had never studied or taught in a university. This did not prevent him from holding strong opinions, though, as noted in Seth Low's nomination letter to the trustees of 4 May 1896:

> He is modest in bearing but has, withal, the confidence in himself that is born of power. He is prepared to accept the appointment, if tendered to him, upon the general condition that the University will give to him its full confidence and complete support. This naturally does not mean that the Trustees are expected to waive their right to shape the policy of the University as to music any more than they would consent to waive it as to any subject included in the curriculum of the University. It means simply that Mr. MacDowell, in accepting the responsibility for the results to follow the creation of the new chair in music, wishes to be assured that the conditions exist which would justify him in accepting such responsibility, for he very frankly says that a failure on his part to produce good results as professor of music in this University would be more disastrous to him than to the University.[1]

This basic question of who would set the policies, procedures, and overall philosophy of the department was of paramount importance in a new department to be

1. "Report of the Special Committee on the Chair of Music," Columbia University Trustees' minutes, 4 May 1896, 154.

built from the ground up. Whether America's "greatest musical genius" was the best man for this job remained to be seen.

Among those who commented publicly on MacDowell's appointment was the *New York Tribune* critic Henry E. Krehbiel, who began his 10 May editorial with a blunt statement: "Personal considerations being removed from the case, it is possible to express disappointment at the purpose of the trustees with relation to the foundation as implied in the appointment of Mr. MacDowell. It would seem as if nothing is to be done to place music on a proper footing in Columbia."[2] Krehbiel went on to speculate that the position at Columbia had been created for MacDowell and to say that the choice of a composer and pianist was unfortunate, since it signaled the university's intention to establish a program in practical music rather than one on broad humanistic lines. Thanks to his first clause, though, readers assumed that Krehbiel's article expressed sour grapes at not having been chosen himself. MacDowell's friend Henry T. Finck, a rival New York critic, sarcastically urged him three days later to reconsider his acceptance so as not "to stand in the way of a great critic and lecturer."[3] After much merriment in the press over the critic's audacity in thinking himself the equal of the great composer, a chastened Krehbiel wrote MacDowell a private letter on 18 June assuring him that he had not been a candidate for the position and wishing him well.[4]

Amid the hubbub over this supposed rivalry, the ideas in Krehbiel's editorial did not receive the consideration they deserved. His main point was that the practical side of music—performance and composition—was best taught in a conservatory. He reprinted a lengthy letter from "an amateur musician, who is a regular graduate of Harvard University, and who was an attendant on the musical courses." In this letter the alumnus decried the curriculum there as well as the teaching of Professor John Knowles Paine. His exposé described the historical lectures as too superficial and the classes on theory and composition as too technical. He noted that the advanced courses in canon, fugue, and free composition generally attracted only two or three students. By contrast, he held up the fine arts courses of Charles Eliot Norton as ideally suited for the undergraduate in search of broad exposure to culture. Krehbiel endorsed this model, concluding his editorial by stating:

> Columbia should not teach piano playing. There are much better facilities offered for that in this city than Columbia could offer. Nor should she try to turn out composers.

---

2. Henry E. Krehbiel, "Music in Columbia College: What the New Department ought to be," *New York Tribune*, 10 May 1896; repr. in *Music* 10 (June 1896): 205–9.

3. Letter, Henry T. Finck to E. A. MacDowell, 13 May 1896, EMMC box 30/37.

4. Letter, Henry E. Krehbiel to E. A. MacDowell, 18 June 1896, MacDowell Collection, Library of Congress Manuscript Division, box 6.

On the other hand, she has the opportunity of doing in the right way what no other American university has done, but what continental universities have shown the value of—putting the study of music on a plane with the study of literature, history and philosophy, as one of the materials of broad and generous culture.[5]

This view was echoed by the *Columbia Literary Monthly*, which argued in a May editorial that the department's goal should be "to make good listeners," leaving the training of professional musicians to conservatories.[6]

But MacDowell disagreed, as he had stated to Low in a letter written before his nomination:

> In America we sadly lack composers. On the other hand our audiences throughout America compare favorably to those of any country in the world when it comes to musical appreciation, knowledge and culture. This is a fact and a very simple one to prove. If the aim of a university should be, not to train musicians' minds and encourage productive talent, but simply to increase the general understanding and appreciation of music by the amateur, then it seems to me that a chair of music is unnecessary, as a series of lectures given by outsiders would serve the purpose equally well.[7]

This fundamental disagreement over what music could and should do at Columbia would be at the heart of MacDowell's work for the next eight years. He had studied at the Paris Conservatory and the Hoch Conservatory, where the goal was to train musicians at the highest level of technical skill. His reputation in Boston had allowed him to teach many students at a high level of development while refusing students whose prior training did not meet his standards. He had no desire to return to the drudgery of Darmstadt and Michelstadt.

This debate was not merely an internal question for Columbia University but a broader one for American culture. As Joseph Horowitz has demonstrated, the trajectory of musical development was at a critical juncture in the 1890s. Orchestras, opera companies, musical criticism, music publishing, and virtually every other aspect of classical music infrastructure had expanded since the Civil War and were now on a par with European institutions. This was the heyday of art music consumption and appreciation in the United States with one important exception. Horowitz argues that the country built a classical music culture around performance

5. Krehbiel, "Music in Columbia College," 208–9.

6. "Editorial," *Columbia Literary Monthly* 4/8 (May 1896): 342; quoted in Margery M. Lowens, "The New York Years of Edward MacDowell" (PhD diss., University of Michigan, 1971), 126.

7. Letter, Edward MacDowell to Seth Low, 27 April 1896, quoted in Douglas Moore, "The Department of Music," in *A History of the Faculty of Philosophy, Columbia University*, ed. Jacques Barzun (New York: Columbia University Press, 1957), 271.

rather than composition, paying top dollar and lavishing attention on performers, conductors, and ensembles to the virtual exclusion of American composers. In this way the development of classical music culture was very different than in Europe, where composition took precedence.[8] MacDowell's ideas for musical instruction at Columbia were designed to address weaknesses in American composition; Krehbiel's proposal would instead bolster America's strength by creating knowledgeable consumers of classical music as literature.

On 1 June 1896, at the start of a very busy summer moving into his new home in Peterborough, hosting the Strongs, and making plans to relocate to New York (not to mention composing the *Woodland Sketches*), MacDowell sent his curricular proposals to President Low. His goals, which were adopted and expanded in the years ahead, were twofold. On the one hand, he created a technical curriculum that would prepare students to teach and to compose. On the other hand, he would "treat music historically and aesthetically as an element of liberal culture."[9] The classes to achieve these ends would be separate, but it was assumed that some students would choose to enroll in both courses of study. With this curriculum, the new professor agreed to balance what he really wanted to do (train professionals) with what others expected him to do (teach music appreciation). The questions of how the two courses would differ, how best to balance their conflicting demands, and how to adapt his expectations to two very different student populations remained open.

In thinking about his goals for the curriculum of Columbia University, MacDowell floated another, much more radical proposal to Low. Despite MacDowell's lack of academic credentials, he had always been a man of broad culture. From childhood he had been intensely interested in literature of all types, reading extensively in poetry, philosophy, and other topics. He had also developed his artistic skill to a very high level, first in drawing and painting, and later in photography. His musical compositions reflect these interdisciplinary connections to the sister arts, and he rightly believed that his broad background was essential to his artistic individuality. He therefore proposed that the administrative structure of the university be changed to better facilitate interactions among the arts: "In my humble opinion, a great step in advance would be made if Literature, Sculpture, Painting, and Music could form an independent faculty thus making it possible to associate a major course of music with a minor course of one of the kindred arts or vice versa."[10] Low supported the spirit of this idea, and in fact he recommended that architecture would also be a natural addition to such a department. Administratively, though, he was not ready

8. Joseph Horowitz, *Classical Music in America: A History* (New York: Norton, 2007).
9. Announcement reproduced in "Things Here and There: Music at Columbia," *Music* 11 (November 1896): 90.
10. Letter, EAM to Seth Low, 1 June 1896; quoted in Moore, "The Department of Music," 272.

to move ahead with this new structure. He consoled MacDowell with the assertion that the administrative structure—his bailiwick—would not inhibit MacDowell's ideals:

> Some day, as I think I told you, I hope that music and art and architecture may be united in a Faculty of Fine Arts. In the meanwhile, in the system which prevails here, there is no difficulty in making just such a combination of courses as you propose, so far as the subjects are taught at Columbia. In other words, with us the Faculties are simply administrative divisions of our work. Speaking generally, a student in any school may combine courses under different Faculties without let or hindrance.[11]

MacDowell experienced for the first time a phenomenon that would become all too familiar in the years ahead: a creative innovation that seemed simple and logical in his idealistic view died when confronted with the administrative complexities of a large organization like Columbia. He had not yet discovered how difficult it is to fight administrative inertia, though, and he nourished the hope that his idea would one day be implemented.

Immediate concerns were more pressing. Within months the university would break ground for the new campus at Morningside Heights on the Upper West Side, but at the time MacDowell joined the faculty, classes were still being held in cramped quarters on Forty-ninth Street. He was given an office there, but since the university had no classroom space to spare, arrangements were made for him to teach his classes in Carnegie Music Hall, a new building just south of Central Park. Andrew Carnegie had built the structure in 1891 as a business venture and as a home for the New York Oratorio Society and New York Symphony Society (both conducted by his friend Walter Damrosch). Two towers of artists' studios were added between 1893 and 1896, where the university rented a classroom for MacDowell to teach in. The location of MacDowell's teaching may seem inconsequential, but psychologically it must have affected his thinking on music at Columbia. During his first year at the university he was not teaching in a regular university classroom where he would rub shoulders with other professors on a regular basis. Instead, he was many blocks away in a building that was designed for and used by professional musicians. He was more likely to encounter a violinist of the New York Symphony than a professor of British literature. Compounding this disconnection was the schedule that he selected. In order to rent the space in Carnegie Hall, Low pressed MacDowell for his teaching schedule early in the summer of 1896. He chose a schedule that many professors would find grueling by teaching his four classes back-to-back on Wednesdays and Saturdays. He must have appreciated the flexibility it gave him in scheduling the rest of his week, though, because he retained

11. Letter, Seth Low to EAM, 4 June 1896; quoted in ibid., 273.

a similar schedule throughout his years at Columbia. It also allowed him to accept a small number of advanced piano students who came to his apartment for lessons.

In building a program from scratch, MacDowell needed to order materials for his teaching and for the library. He did not believe in using textbooks but instead preferred to use musical scores as reference material, storing them in the classroom for ready access. He set about using the budget allotment that was given him to purchase scores for the library and also for departmental use. His first priority was to assemble the complete works of major composers, many of which were available from Breitkopf & Härtel. These he ordered every year in installments as his budget allowed, supplementing them with donations from his own collection. As a consequence, the Columbia University library today has one of the most complete collections of MacDowell first editions in the world.

When the semester began, MacDowell quickly learned how demanding the new position would be. From this time forward, many of his letters begin with a complaint about being busy or overworked, as in this letter to his Boston friend T. P. Currier in fall 1896:

> If you only knew how wildly busy I am you would forgive my not writing—probably you do, any way. I wish you would write oftener. Boston seems far, far away, but the friends in it somehow grow dearer....I am delighted with my work in many ways, though composition is as far off as ever, and I haven't touched the piano for many months. If I live until spring I will give up complaining about my health and look down with a pitying smile on malt-fed Sandows and the rest....I have received many offers of engagements, the last being to deliver a course in New Orleans. I will do three weeks piano playing in January and February....Oh! the hustle and bustle of this city![12]

Although President Low had advised him to come to Columbia free of any "entanglements," MacDowell could not resist the invitations that came flooding in after his appointment. Added to his teaching, curriculum planning, administrative concerns, and other duties, these activities left no time for composition.

Shortly after beginning his first semester at Columbia, MacDowell traveled to Princeton, New Jersey, to receive an honorary doctorate. The ceremony on 22 October 1896 not only commemorated the 150th anniversary of the College of New Jersey but also celebrated its transformation into Princeton University. President Grover Cleveland attended the ceremony and delivered an address. MacDowell was the only musician to be honored with the degree of Doctor of

---

12. Quoted in T. P. Currier, "Edward MacDowell as I Knew Him" *MQ* 1/1 (January 1915): 46–47. Eugen Sandow (1867–1925), the father of modern bodybuilding, was popular during the mid-1890s, particularly after the Edison Studios captured his posing on a short film released in 1894.

Music on that occasion.[13] From this point on, many press reports referred to him as "Dr. MacDowell," a useful title for a university professor.

The curriculum devised by MacDowell consisted of two series of courses that each embraced multiple topics. Courses 1 and 2 were the general music-appreciation classes, tracing Western music historically from the ancient Greeks to the present. The approach was primarily historical and aesthetic, with a necessarily limited amount of theoretical discussion because of the diverse backgrounds of the students. The other courses were technical in nature: Course 3 covered theory, aural skills, and introductory composition; Course 4 covered counterpoint and fugue; and Course 5 offered free composition, analysis, instrumentation, and symphonic forms. During the first year, 1896/97, Course 2 was not offered.

In the letter to Currier, MacDowell added, "The lecturing is intensely interesting and I think it has been fairly successful." This was the aspect of the position that was most unfamiliar for the composer, and it took some adjustment. In later years, the question of whether MacDowell was a "good teacher" came up frequently, and in fact Marian herself seems to have contacted a large number of his former students in 1908 in order to answer that question to her satisfaction. The Marian MacDowell Collection in the Library of Congress contains some of the glowing tributes that students sent her in the form of letters. Obviously, the dissatisfied students did not respond.

There were two eyewitnesses whose opinions are more valuable, as both possessed powers of observation that later made them successful writers, and both recognized that the question of MacDowell's teaching effectiveness was too complex for a yes-or-no answer. John Erskine (1879–1941) took courses in general music, theory, and composition during his freshman and sophomore years. He went on earn his master's and doctoral degrees from Columbia and served as professor of English at the university from 1909 to 1937. The prolific novelist Upton Sinclair (1878–1968) studied at Columbia University briefly after studying at City College in New York. Financial exigencies forced him to leave before earning a degree, but he achieved fame with his 1906 novel *The Jungle*, the eleven novels of the Lanny Budd series, and numerous other works of fiction. He recalled in 1925: "Edward MacDowell was the first man of genius I had ever met. I was going in for that business myself, or thought I was, so I lost nothing about him; I watched his appearance, his mannerisms, his every gesture. I listened to every word he said and thought it over and

13. *Memorial Book of the Sesquicentennial Celebration of the Founding of the College of New Jersey and of the Ceremonies inaugurating Princeton University* (New York: Charles Scribner's Sons, 1898), 161. In his autobiography, John Burgess recounts arranging for Seth Low to receive an honorary doctorate from Amherst College when he took over the presidency of Columbia. It is possible that he or another university official made similar arrangements for MacDowell to become credentialed.

pondered it."[14] Both men were in MacDowell's classes during the early years, and both wrote probing memoirs about his teaching.

MacDowell came to Columbia with no experience as a lecturer, which as both Eskine and Sinclair pointed out is a specialized skill. Sinclair noted cynically, "I would not say that Edward MacDowell was a successful teacher after the university pattern. He was lacking in that pedagogic technique which can now be acquired through correspondence courses."[15] Erskine noted also that he was at a disadvantage compared to some of the other Columbia lecturers:

> Lecturing is a branch of literature, not of music; it is a vestige of minstrelsy with the harp-playing left out. Musicians lecture well only if they possess an extra talent, not necessarily related to their art. For prolonged discourse their special medium is not words, and when they use words for musical interpretation their comments, even when helpful, are likely to be disjointed, a series of lightning flashes, bound together by the structure of the music they illuminate.[16]

MacDowell's introverted nature and discomfort with public speaking kept him from developing into a traditional lecturer, but he soon discovered that he could communicate his ideas better in other ways. Sinclair recalled that it was he who steered his new teacher in a different direction, although other students also claimed to have had a hand in the transformation:

> I had developed a habit of staying after the class, and talking with him, and I said, "You are not a man of words, why do you try to lecture in words? You ought to play us the music and talk about it before and afterwards." Being a really great man, he was willing to take good advice, even from a boy. He began hesitatingly to try it, and in a very short time his class in general musical culture had come to consist of listening to MacDowell play some music, and then asking him questions about it.[17]

After he abandoned pure lectures in favor of a method combining demonstration, analysis, and questions, he became a more effective teacher. This method allowed him to minimize the verbal aspect of teaching but also to respond spontaneously to issues as they arose rather than planning everything in advance. This suited his personality much better.

Compensating for his weakness as a lecturer, MacDowell brought his prodigious talents as a musician to the classroom. He had a broad knowledge of musical

14. Upton Sinclair, "Memories of Edward MacDowell," *Sackbut* (London), 6 (December 1925), 128.
15. Ibid., 128.
16. John Erskine, *The Memory of Certain Persons* (Philadelphia, New York: Lippincott, 1947), 75.
17. Sinclair, "Memories," 128.

repertoire that grew as he ordered scores for the department library and digested them in preparation for class. This knowledge gave him the ability to make connections between unrelated works in response to questions that arose in class. He also had the ability to demonstrate passages at the piano, an essential skill before the era of recording technology in the classroom. He would often apologize in advance when he sat down to play, but the students were invariably impressed, especially in the general music courses where most students were not musicians. A final skill that was noted by nearly all his former students was his prowess at the chalkboard. He had requested boards with musical staff lines before he started teaching, and he proved adept at writing musical notes quickly and clearly on the board. Sometimes when the class was stuck, he would ask a student to come to the board and write the passage under discussion, after which they would discuss and modify it.

Erskine noted that his teaching "was most effective with students who were already well grounded."[18] In his view, MacDowell's brilliance compensated for a lack of organization in the early years. He also noted that the disparity of student backgrounds in these years was a handicap. Erskine recalled that William Henry Humiston was already an experienced musician who soon embarked on a successful career. There was also a sizable group of "serious and fairly competent youngsters," including Angela Diller, George Matthew, and Hugh Martin, all of whom went on to careers in music. These students were supplemented by amateurs and auditors who "should have been spending their time elsewhere." He humorously recalled one society lady who came to class in a black satin dress and white gloves: "We learned to watch for the moment when he would imperil the costume by sending her to the blackboard, himself in a gesture of chivalry handing her the chalk and the powder-scattering eraser."[19] But numerous students recalled his compassion for his students, as expressed by Humiston: "His kindliness toward serious students, even when they made stupid mistakes, was one of his most remarkable qualities. On the other hand, toward a superficial student he was often sarcastic, but even his sarcasm was so gentle that the victim never felt its sting."[20]

Both Erskine and Sinclair recalled MacDowell as a man of genius who was out of place in the regimented and tradition-bound halls of academe. Their contact with him was valuable precisely because it was so different from typical university teaching. He was not a smooth or well-organized lecturer, but his brilliant observations allowed students to make unexpected connections and to see the world in a different light. His unorthodox approach was like manna in the desert to those students

18. Erskine, *Memory of Certain Persons*, 75.

19. Ibid., 76.

20. W. H. Humiston, "Personal Recollections of Edward MacDowell," *Musician* 13/4 (April 1908): 160.

who craved transformational aesthetic and intellectual experiences. For them, his teaching was superior to that of the polished lecturers and famous authors who populated the other departments on campus. Sinclair compared his teaching to that of George Woodberry (1855–1930), a professor of comparative literature who had joined the faculty in 1891. Like MacDowell, he challenged the students with connections between the arts and with an unconventional teaching style. Sinclair recalled: "These were the two men in the place who did most for me. They helped me to understand the true spirit of beauty, and to assert and defend through my whole life the free creative attitude."[21] Erskine recalled that even his physical appearance stood out from the staid atmosphere of the university campus: "He seemed an out of door man, full of energy and health. When he strode across the campus in his tweed suit, with his cane hooked over his arm, even the least musical passer-by looked at him twice. Yet in spite of this wholesome impression, the deep-seated nervous trouble which eventually destroyed him, already began to show itself, on occasions."[22]

MacDowell's responsibilities on campus precluded virtually all composition during the academic year, but he did write several pieces of occasional music for Columbia, which met with differing responses. MacDowell had noticed that during commencement ceremonies the band filled time while each candidate walked to the platform to receive his diploma. For the 1900 ceremony, he wrote a series of short fanfares to be used at this point in the ceremony. Erskine recalled, "I was present at their first and only performance. They dwarfed other items in the ceremony, and the Faculty and Trustees, as I recall, looked startled at so much trumpeting as though Gabriel were putting on a rehearsal."[23] The following year, he was told that the president did not want them.

A more successful commission came from an unusual source. As MacDowell reported to his friend Hamlin Garland on 1 January 1901:

> I wrote three college songs these last two or three days—words and all—Talk about your blue jay swooping across the abyss!!—College songs are not in my line but as I was requested to write them by our centre rush football player I did so at once. Now if the footballers get everlastingly licked next Autumn (under the spell of these songs) I shall have to go into retirement for a while. There's more to the "Chair of music" in a college than appears on the surface.[24]

21. Sinclair, "Memories," 129.

22. Erskine, *Memory of Certain Persons*, 78.

23. John Erskine, *My Life in Music* (New York: Morrow, 1950), 11–12.

24. Letter, EAM to Hamlin Garland, 1 January 1901, Doheny Memorial Library, University of Southern California.

He added several more songs over the next half year, six of which were published by Schmidt in May 1901. Written for male chorus, the songs were popular with the students, and subsequent editions were published in a lower transposition (1902) and for women's voices (*Two College Songs*, 1907).

During the first year at Columbia, MacDowell was a one-man department, teaching all of the music courses and handling all the administrative duties without a secretary or any other teachers. In the second year, Low approved the hiring of one of his students, Leonard B. McWhood, to assist with grading and other duties. MacDowell had plans to expand the offerings, however, and during his third and fourth years he had the opportunity to do so. The university promoted McWhood to the rank of tutor, taking over some of the basic theory and aural skills courses. In 1899/1900, the university hired the conductor Gustav Hinrichs to establish a university chorus (Course 8) and a university orchestra (Course 9), while MacDowell added a composition seminar (Course 7). By the fall of 1900, Columbia University offered eleven courses in music: MacDowell taught the two general courses for undergraduates along with counterpoint and three composition classes at different levels, McWhood taught three courses in theory and dictation, and Hinrichs directed the two ensembles. In just four years, MacDowell had more than doubled the number of courses and had created a program that served not only the general undergraduate but also aspiring composers.

The department also benefited from the move to Morningside Heights in 1897, where their facilities were integrated into the new university campus. Initially the department was housed in West Hall, one of the old buildings formerly part of the Bloomingdale asylum, but as the program expanded they also used rooms in some of the new buildings. Leaving Carnegie Music Hall gave the music faculty more flexibility in scheduling classes, but it did not eliminate the frustrations of shared facilities. In a letter of 6 February 1901, MacDowell complained that the elocution students who used Schermerhorn 509—where many of the music classes met— had been pounding on the piano, which belonged to the Music Department. He demanded that the university registrar tell any other departments who used the room that the instruments were not to be used without permission.[25] As the university expanded, facilities continued to be crowded, leading to inevitable conflicts that irritated the department chair.

The demands of university teaching and administration forced MacDowell to acquire a new set of skills. He proved himself remarkably adaptable not only to the demands of teaching but also to those of administration, as demonstrated in an absurdly comical exchange of letters in spring 1901. At this time, MacDowell was

25. Draft letter to Geo. B. Germann, Edward MacDowell Letter Book, EMMC box 33.

still expanding the department library of scores, committing most of his annual budget of $680 to this goal. In May, after it was clear how much money remained in his budget, he placed an order with Breitkopf & Härtel for bound scores of seven Wagner operas and Mozart's complete works in seventy volumes, for a total of $468.63. When the publisher sent the bill on 20 May to the university library instead of to the music department, S. E. Wallace of the library's ordering department received it and wrote to McWhood. She learned that he was out of town, at which point she contacted MacDowell in Peterborough for instructions. He had already learned of the mixup from McWhood, and he asked her to send the bill and the Wagner scores to him, holding the Mozart scores until he returned. Complicating the matter was a new university rule that all book purchases by departments needed to be approved by the president, a rule that MacDowell skirted by calling the bound scores "music" rather than books. Knowing that he would lose any unspent money on 1 July, he forwarded the bill to the Bureau of Purchases for payment. Thomas Little, chief of the Bureau of Purchases, wrote on 11 June that paying the bill would overdraw his department account by $21.99, recommending that he wait until after the start of the new budget year. MacDowell responded on 19 June that he had forgotten about a credit of $20, asking Little to pay the bill for musical scores. Little wrote back on 20 June with a detailed list of expenditures totaling $233.36, demonstrating that the department did not have sufficient funds to cover the bill. MacDowell responded with his own itemized list of expenditures, promising to ask the publisher to charge the music to this year's budget but the binding and shipping to next year's budget. He then wrote to Breitkopf & Härtel to request a revised bill, to which they acceded. On the same day, he wrote to Hinrichs to say that he had $18 left in the account (because the revised bill shifted $40 from this fiscal year to next) and asked him to find a way to spend it before 1 July. The conductor responded on 22 June that he had purchased "some standard things for the orchestra which we did not yet have," allowing MacDowell to close the fiscal year with exactly one penny in the account.

This mundane sequence of events illustrates the existential trap in which MacDowell found himself. Chosen to lead the department because the search committee believed him to be America's greatest composer, MacDowell devoted ever more time and mental energy to petty bureaucratic tasks. In the words of Rollo Walter Brown, "he was wholly unblessed with the labor-saving instinct,"[26] and he invested the same intellectual energy to outmaneuvering the purchasing officer as he had previously invested in his creative work. In five years he

26. Rollo Walter Brown, *Lonely Americans* (New York: Coward-McCann, 1929), 113.

had built a department from nothing, expanded the faculty and course offerings, and attracted a loyal cohort of students. His work was a testimony to his ability to master a complex new task and perform it satisfactorily. But as this new task became routine, he came to suspect that he had neglected something much more valuable.

CHAPTER SIXTEEN

Outside the University

MACDOWELL'S ENTIRE CAREER TO DATE HAD BEEN THAT OF A FREELANCE musician. As such, he had grown accustomed to dividing his energies among a variety of pursuits. And despite his protestations of being free to choose his students, performance opportunities, and composition projects, he surely had learned the cardinal rule of the freelance musician: never refuse an opportunity to make money. Even before his relocation to New York, he began receiving offers, and Seth Low's advice to limit his outside activities in order to assess the artistic situation before making commitments fell on deaf ears.

The first such offer came from the Mendelssohn Glee Club, an exclusive men's chorus consisting largely of Manhattan businessmen. The organization had been founded in 1866 and had been directed since 1867 by Joseph Mosenthal, a German immigrant who played violin in the New York Philharmonic for forty years. Under Mosenthal's leadership, the club achieved a high level of musicianship while maintaining its exclusive social cachet. It was said that becoming a member of the Glee Club was harder than entering the elite "Four Hundred" of New York society. A wealthy benefactor had built a clubhouse with a 1,100-seat auditorium in 1892, giving the Glee Club a permanent home and allowing it to earn rent from bachelor apartments on the upper floors. Among the tenants of these apartments was the impecunious Winslow Homer, whose offer to draw the members of the club "with their mouths open or shut" in payment of back rent was refused.[1]

---

1. Joe Flynn and Bob Pierce, "The Five Jubilees," Mendelssohn Glee Club website, www.mgcnyc. org/history.htm (accessed 15 October 2011).

· 224 ·

The venerable Mosenthal died in January 1896, leaving the club without a qualified leader. When the press reported MacDowell's acceptance of the Columbia University position a few months later, the club offered him the directorship. MacDowell asked the opinion of Seth Low, who initially counseled him to refuse the appointment so as to keep his options open when he arrived in New York. The club leaders were persistent, however, and after further consultation with the trustees (some of whom no doubt knew of the wealth and prestige of its members), Low reversed his opinion. MacDowell agreed to become the club's new director in the fall of 1896.[2]

MacDowell had admired the sound of male choral singing since his years in Frankfurt, and he had written several compositions for Lang's Apollo Club in Boston (whose founding had been inspired by a Mendelssohn Glee Club concert in 1871), but he had no experience as a conductor. Marian later recalled, "I have always been amazed at the way he seemed to be able to take up with no real experience a new form of work as for instance what he did at Columbia." According to her memoirs, he told them frankly that he had no experience, but they insisted on his appointment.[3] The weekly rehearsals provided a welcome break from his university work, and with a chorus that was accustomed to the disciplined taskmaster Mosenthal, he was able to achieve excellent results.

He conducted three concerts in the 1896/97 season and three more in the 1897/98 season. The programs for these concerts featured a varied selection of works by recent European and American composers. He contributed a number of his own compositions, under both his own name and his pseudonym Edgar Thorn. On several of the concerts, he played groups of his solo piano works. The concerts were not reviewed in the press, but his work was reputed to have been successful. At the end of the second season in spring 1898, he abruptly resigned his position. To members who had hoped for thirty years of stability like Mosenthal had given, this was disappointing, but the new conductor Arthur Mees evidently did not hold a grudge. On his first concert on 29 November 1898, he programmed the premiere of Edgar Thorn's *War Song*, op. 6, and MacDowell's *A Ballad of Charles the Bold*, op. 54. The works of the erstwhile conductor were heard often in subsequent years.

In 1898, friends of Joseph Mosenthal presented $7,500 to Columbia University to endow a music fellowship in his name. Given every other year to a promising composition student, the first Mosenthal Fellowship was awarded in 1899 to Angela Diller, who studied harmony, orchestration, composition, and

2. Three letters from Low in EMMC box 30/72 deal with this issue: 20 May 1896, 29 May 1896, and 1 June 1896.

3. MM Notebook I-49, EMMC box 39/5.

piano with MacDowell from 1896 to 1903.[4] Diller became an influential teacher of piano, founded the Diller-Quaile piano school, and published numerous books, articles, and piano methods. Later recipients of the fellowship included Allen Brings, Harold Brown, Chou Wen-Chung, Rachel Eubanks, and Edward Kilenyi.

Though he changed his stance on MacDowell's involvement with the Mendelssohn Glee Club, Seth Low was more adamant on the issue of his new professor's piano teaching. He communicated the views of the Trustees in a letter of 1 June 1896: "There would be [no] objection, as I told you, to your taking part in public performances, as we discussed at our first meeting. I do discover, however, a little feeling on the part of some of the Trustees that it might be somewhat infra dig. [beneath your dignity] if you were to become a teacher of the pianoforte in New York while holding the position of Professor of Music in the University."[5]

The notion that piano teaching was beneath the dignity of a university professor was part of the discussion over the role of music instruction at Columbia. The administration did not want its new professor to sully his hands with such menial labor, but it is no surprise that MacDowell ignored their advice. For him, the practical and the theoretical could not be separated, and thus piano teaching continued to play an important part in his life after the move to New York. He initially limited his piano studio to advanced pupils from Boston who wished to continue their studies, but he eventually added new students, especially after resigning the directorship of the Mendelssohn Glee Club. Even at the rate of six dollars for a half-hour lesson, he had to turn away eager applicants. Among the grateful students in New York was Aimée Gottschalk, who later described his aversion to mechanical exercises and the intense engagement that he brought to the biweekly group lessons. She summarized his personality and appearance in this way:

> Unlike many fellow musicians of his day, MacDowell was the polished gentleman, well-groomed, pleasant-voiced and exceedingly courteous. He seemed to possess extraordinary vitality and an unusual resilience. In those beautiful brilliant blue eyes shone a mischievously keen sense of humor. Though rather shy, deliciously trenchant sarcasm could be his weapon to counter an infrequent cocksureness in a student. But reversely, he met timidity more than half way, with a gentle, big-brotherly understanding....MacDowell possessed a rare combination of never seeming to take himself too seriously, and an

4. "First Award of the Mosenthal Fellowship in Music," *Columbia Spectator* 42/21 (2 May 1899): 2. This brief article quotes MacDowell's laudatory assessment of the pieces Diller submitted with her application.

5. Letter, Seth Low to EAM, 1 June 1896, EMMC box 30/72.

intense earnestness in offering his best to his students. His uncompromisingly high ideals were to cause him more suffering than the world may ever realize.[6]

MacDowell insisted as part of his Columbia contract negotiations on a month's leave each winter for concert tours. He did not perform during his first winter in New York, but he resumed touring in 1898, continuing the practice throughout his Columbia years. He generally left in late January or early February, performing a series of concerts outside the East Coast metropolitan areas. These allowed him to enhance his national reputation and boost sales of his compositions. They also added to his workload, however, as the weeks before his annual tour always required a heroic effort to get his hands back into shape and learn enough repertoire while teaching full-time.[7]

To accommodate Edward's piano teaching and practicing needs, the MacDowells needed a spacious apartment where the piano would not bother the neighbors. They continued the pattern they had established in Germany and Boston by moving every year or so in search of a better situation. The high price of rent in Manhattan meant that they could not afford as much space as they had enjoyed in Boston, and their proximity to other residents created additional headaches. In April 1901, when the resident of the apartment below the MacDowells contracted smallpox, MacDowell's students stopped coming to their lessons, resulting in a loss of income. In a blistering letter to the landlord, he demanded that they seal the floor to keep germs from migrating into his apartment after the man returned from the hospital.[8]

Among the many organizations that approached MacDowell after his arrival in the city, there was one that he was able to deflect without regret. Years earlier, MacDowell had expressed his reservations about the Manuscript Society of New York in a letter to his Chicago colleague Frederick Grant Gleason (see chap. 13). The group had been founded in 1889 with the lofty goal of providing American composers with opportunities to hear their unpublished works in professional-quality performances. In the intervening years, it had degenerated into a mutual admiration society of local composers. Though there were still good musicians associated with the group, its reputation had declined as the influence of less-talented members grew. MacDowell was invited to join upon his arrival in New York, but he politely declined. Like the Mendelssohn Glee Club, the Manuscript Society was persistent, and within a few years, he would play a crucial role in its history.

6. [Clara] Aimée Gottschalk, "A Memory of MacDowell," *Bulletin of the Stojowski Students' Association* (May 1940): 3–4.

7. For an intimate view of the challenges and rewards of these tours, see T. P. Currier, "Edward MacDowell as I Knew Him," *MQ* 1/1 (January 1915): 28–30.

8. Letters to and from E. F. Dodson of McVickar and Company in EMMC indicate that the landlord wanted $1,600 per year for the apartment, but that Edward was willing to pay only $1,400.

MacDowell also declined membership in the Century Club, a social club that counted President Low and other Columbia faculty among its members. When his friend Robert Underwood Johnson proposed his nomination in March 1898, the composer responded that he was "such a stay at home" that his election would deprive another more deserving candidate of the benefits of the prestigious club.[9]

A social obligation that he could not dodge, however, was meals with his parents. Fanny was happy that the younger couple was finally close at hand, and she also liked to show off her famous son to her friends. Marian realized that his mother's expectations could easily become burdensome, so she devised a solution to control their contact. She hired a cook to prepare a weekly meal with good wine at their apartment, which both couples enjoyed. This created a relaxed, predictable social setting and helped to smooth the sometimes-rocky relations between mother and son.[10] Marian later recalled that Edward gave his parents $50 per month during their first five years in New York and $300 per year thereafter as repayment of the costs of his European education.[11]

In the fall of 1896, MacDowell began placing his works with a new publisher. Kurt Moebius had learned the publishing trade with Breitkopf & Härtel in Leipzig, and in 1891 he relocated to New York as the firm's American representative. While working in this capacity, he also began publishing music under his own imprint with the pseudonym P. L. Jung. MacDowell had grown to trust Moebius during his Boston years, when the New York agent served as an intermediary in the sometimes-contentious dealings with Breitkopf & Härtel. Thus between 1896 and 1898 MacDowell gave opp. 51 to 56 inclusive to P. L. Jung, along with a number of edited volumes of other composers and all of the Edgar Thorn compositions. Moebius now had the enviable opportunity to publish two of MacDowell's most profitable sets of piano works, *Woodland Sketches*, op. 51 and *Sea Pieces*, op. 55, along with the popular *Four Songs*, op. 56. The publisher ran into financial difficulties in 1899, at which point he sold his entire catalogue to Schmidt in Boston. A letter in the summer of 1899 indicates that Moebius owed MacDowell back royalties of $749.48, but that other creditors were ahead of him in line.[12]

New York opened doors to new friendships and spelled changes in his old ones. Among the persons with whom Edward became close was Hamlin Garland, an author whose works he had admired for some years. Garland was born in the

9. M. M. Lowens, "The New York Years," 177.

10. Ibid., 174–75.

11. Letter, MM to William H. Humiston, undated but within a year of MacDowell's death in January 1908, EMMC box 52/9.

12. Letter, Kurt Moebius to EAM, 11 July 1899, EMMC box 30. See also M. M. Lowens, "The New York Years," 194–95.

same year as MacDowell, but he recalled being in awe of Edward when the musician moved to Boston in 1888 and he paid fifty cents for standing room at one of his concerts. In 1894, during a visit to Chicago, MacDowell expressed an interest in meeting Garland, whose recently published book *Crumbling Idols* he had read and admired. The two of them met in MacDowell's hotel room, where they discussed Garland's views on American dependence on European models in the arts and literature. Garland's manifesto urged American writers to take radical action: "Rise, O young man and woman of America! Stand erect! Face the future with a song on your lips and the light of a broader day in your eyes. Turn your back on the past, not in scorn, but in justice to the future. Cease trying to be correct, and become creative. This is our day. The past is not vital. It is a highway of dust, and Homer, Aeschylus, Sophocles, Dante, Shakespeare are milestones."[13] Though he was not ready to invest his works with the level of local color that Garland advocated, MacDowell told him, "My problems as a composer are precisely those you have delineated in your essays. I am working toward a music which shall be American in the creative sense. Our music thus far is mainly a scholarly re-statement of Old World themes. In other words, it is derived from Germany, as all my earlier pieces were."[14] The two parted with the promise to spend more time together in the future, and Edward's relocation to New York made that promise a reality.

Always a shy person, MacDowell preferred to initiate new relationships by letter. On 10 October 1899, he wrote to Edvard Grieg, the famous Norwegian composer, with the request to dedicate his third piano sonata to him. In this letter he recalled a review in the *Musikalisches Wochenblatt* that had said his music itself was a dedication to Grieg. He added, "your music lies closer to my heart than I can well say. I have dedicated much to you in my thoughts, and this will be my excuse for sending you some of my music. If I do not receive your permission for the dedication I will at least have at last told you of my love for and loyalty to Ed. Grieg."[15] The composer replied affirmatively on 26 October, and the two initiated a correspondence that lasted several years. Their music had much in common, and each respected the other highly, although they never met in person.[16]

13. Hamlin Garland, *Crumbling Idols* (Chicago and Cambridge: Stone and Kimball, 1894), 190.

14. Hamlin Garland, *Roadside Meetings* (New York: Macmillan, 1930), 320.

15. Letter, EAM to Edvard Grieg, 10 October 1899, Griegsamlingen, Bergen Off. Bibliotek, Bergen, Norway.

16. Their relationship and the similarities between their respective concertos in A minor were examined in Ohran Noh "Edvard Grieg's Influence on American Music: The Case of the Piano Concertos in A-Minor from the Pen of Edvard Grieg and Edward MacDowell," paper presented at The International Edvard Grieg Society Conference in Bergen, Norway, 30 May 2007. The

In his Third "Norse" Sonata, op. 57, and Fourth "Keltic" Sonata, op. 59, MacDowell accomplished his major artistic achievements of the Columbia years. He did not complete any orchestral works during this period; instead he poured his broadest, most heroic inspirations into the sonatas. Both reflect his reading of ancient sagas from Scandinavia and the British Isles; both reflect a fascination with his own Celtic heritage; and both reflect the "antimodernism" that T. J. Jackson Lears identifies as an important part of urban American culture in the late nineteenth century.[17] Both works are dedicated to Grieg, the first by design and the second by default. A year after writing to Grieg about the dedication of the Third Sonata, MacDowell wrote to the Irish author William Sharp (whom he knew only by his pseudonym, Fiona Macleod) with a similar request. Sharp received the letter while in Italy, but his enthusiastic letter of acceptance—entrusted to an Italian urchin for delivery to the post office—never reached the composer, forcing him to dedicate the sonata to Grieg.[18] His Norwegian colleague was pleased to accept another dedication, noting the family connections between the Irish legends that inspired the work and the Norse Volsunga Legend.

At the head of the "Norse" Sonata, MacDowell included a short verse of his own:

Night had fallen on a day of deeds.
The great rafters in the red-ribbed hall
Flashed crimson in the fitful flame
Of smouldering logs.
And from the stealthy shadows
That crept 'round Harald's throne,
Rang out a Skald's strong voice,
With tales of battles won;
Of Gudrun's love
And Sigurd, Siegmund's son.

The solemn images in this poem are reflected in the slow, somber tempos of the first two movements, ranging from 46 to 69 beats per minute for the half note in

paper is available for download on the society's website: http://www.griegsociety.org/default.asp?kat=1009&id=4530&sp=1.

17. The connection between Lears's work and the compositions of MacDowell is explored in Kara Anne Gardner, "Edward MacDowell, Antimodernism, and 'Playing Indian' in the Indian Suite," *MQ* 87/3 (Fall 2004): 370–422.

18. MM, *Random Notes*, 20.

the first movement, and 50 beats for the quarter note in the second movement. The third movement begins "Allegro con fuoco (With much character and fire)" at 138 beats per minute but concludes in a "Dirge-like" 40 beats per minute.

The shadowy images of heroic legends related by glimmering firelight inspired some of MacDowell's most innovative writing for the piano. Tonality is intentionally obscured through non-chord tones, delayed resolutions, pervasive chromaticism, and modulations to distant keys. Rhythms are likewise shifting and unpredictable. These characteristics are especially evident in the opening of the first movement, marked "vague, with somber coloring." Neither the key nor the meter is clear until m. 10, setting a tone of ambiguity for the entire piece. The non-traditional textures offended the critic W. S. B. Mathews of Chicago, who wrote, "That any person still retaining a ghost of a love for the music of Beethoven, Bach, Brahms, Liszt, Wagner, Schumann (to mention only the most original of all composers), can still have a love for this sonata, and an enjoyment in playing it, is in the last degree unlikely." He went on to call it a pity that MacDowell was capable of writing respectable salon music but chose instead to indulge in "the quest for the profound and the intensely new and deep."[19]

The Fourth "Keltic" Sonata, op. 59, was MacDowell's favorite. Like the Third, it is prefaced by a poetic epigraph:

Who minds now Keltic tales of yore,
Dark Druid rhymes that thrall,
Deirdre's song and wizard lore
Of great Cuchullin's fall.

The reference harks back to a time when the composer's ancestors fought epic battles against ruthless enemies instead of squabbling with university purchasing officers. He portrayed Deirdre's legendary beauty in the tender second movement, and he immortalized Cuchullin [Cúchulainn]'s heroic death in the final movement. The Celtic warrior's superhuman strength and stamina, along with his uncertain origin, spawned the legend that he was half god and half human. He fought numerous battles against Ireland's enemies, and when mortally wounded in his last battle he chained himself to a stone monolith so that he could die standing up. His enemies did not realize that he was dead until a bird came and sat on his shoulder. MacDowell creates a furiously virtuosic octave study of tremendous speed, range, and dynamic variation. In an explicit piece of tone painting, the dead hero is portrayed by a slow, somber chordal passage with bird calls in the upper register. His enemies exult in a final triple-fortissimo flourish of octaves. The sonata is a

19. [W. S. B. Mathews], "Editorial Bric-a-Brac," *Music* 19/4 (February 1901): 412.

232 · EDWARD MACDOWELL IN NEW YORK

culmination of MacDowell's interest in Celtic prehistory as well as his expanding expressive range. Not only is it his most technically demanding piano work, but its dynamic range spans from *pppp* to *ffff*.

In his three-volume *History of the Sonata Idea*, William S. Newman compares MacDowell favorably to Grieg by acknowledging that the American handled the larger forms more naturally and flexibly, and that his piano textures are more interesting. He concludes the comparison by stating: "performers are likely to return to one or another of his sonatas again and again, perhaps more than to Grieg's Op. 7, for several compelling reasons. The sonatas abound in frank songful melody, in opportunities to emote with judicious abandon, and in piano writing that makes good sounds and pleasurable technical challenges. Furthermore, the forms are invariably timed right and last only long enough to state their messages and achieve their goals."[20] In these four works, MacDowell had found the ideal vehicle for his large-scale ideas, combining his intimate knowledge of the piano with his symphonic aspirations.

Grieg was not the only composer to whom MacDowell was favorably compared. The German conductor Anton Seidl famously stated in 1892 that he found the works of MacDowell preferable to those of Brahms.[21] The famous French composer Jules Massenet was widely quoted as saying: "How I love the works of this young American composer, MacDowell! What a musician! He is sincere and individual—what a poet! What exquisite harmonies!"[22] In his 1900 survey of American composers, Rupert Hughes stated that MacDowell was nearly unanimously regarded as the country's greatest composer, going on to say that not a few persons would vote him the best living composer in the world.[23] MacDowell had achieved his goal of artistic parity with the European masters, and he had achieved it on his own terms, without appealing to jingoistic nationalism. At the age of thirty-nine, he was at the top of his profession.

20. William S. Newman, *The Sonata Since Beethoven*, vol. 3 of *The History of the Sonata Idea* (Chapel Hill: University of North Carolina Press, 1969), 767.

21. Anton Seidl, "The Development of Music in America," *Forum* 13 (May 1892): 386–93. This article may have been ghost-written by Henry T. Finck; nonetheless it was often cited in assessments of MacDowell's position.

22. Quoted in Henry T. Finck, "Edward MacDowell: Musician and Composer," *Outlook* 84 (22 December 1906): 987.

23. Rupert Hughes, *Famous American Composers* (Boston: L. C. Page, 1900): 34–35.

CHAPTER SEVENTEEN

The Price of Fame

B Y THE TIME HE SETTLED IN NEW YORK, MACDOWELL HAD ACHIEVED fame beyond his wildest dreams. He was the first American composer of art music to be well known and widely performed on both sides of the Atlantic. His publications were sold in large numbers around the world. He was admired by prominent European musicians like Grieg, Massenet, and Paderewski. And he was regarded as an authority on contemporary music and an inspiration for American musicians. This newfound fame came at a price, however, as he learned the meaning of Voltaire's aphorism, "What a heavy burden is a name that has become too famous."

Marian recognized the stress that he carried, and she did her best to keep his home life stable. She later recalled that since he was so easily upset, she let him have his own way in all the small decisions of life. In the larger decisions, though—like the purchase of their Peterborough home—she became adept at engineering what she wanted, even leaving him with the impression that she was following his wishes.

With his new status came a heavy load of correspondence. His administrative work at the university involved numerous memos and official letters to persons on and off campus. There was frequent correspondence with his publishers and professional colleagues regarding new editions, upcoming concerts, and other matters. His private piano teaching involved countless notes about scheduling and payment. In addition to these routine tasks, MacDowell's fame brought him numerous unsolicited letters from persons seeking advice or favors. He was unfailingly generous in answering such inquiries, particularly if they piqued his curiosity. In July 1900, for instance, he received a letter from a dentist in Nebraska who had played for Paderewski and was encouraged by the great pianist's response to consider giving up dentistry and becoming a musician. MacDowell wrote back promptly with the advice to stick to dentistry.[1] Even in the Boston years, though, he began to lose patience with questions that wasted his time, as in an April 1895 letter to the young composer Arthur Farwell:

> My dear Sir: I really cannot advise you as to a proper title. You must stand a little on your own feet. An Italian-English Dictionary would be a good thing to consult as to translation of terms. I think in my songs, I retained the usual p & f, but have forgotten. As for where your dedication should be placed—do think it over yourself and decide. How on earth can I tell?…All these questions of yours have to do with more or less mechanical details which I think you ought to be able to solve by this time—something like the sharps and flats, etc. etc. in the pieces. "Ritard" is retard in English, "crescendo" is "increase",—for Heaven's sake man use your thinker; and I am not an "intelligence Bureau." Working hard all day makes me savage you see. All of which is meant in a kindly spirit by Yours truly E. MacDowell[2]

Marian helped with the correspondence, but he still handled much of it himself. Curiously, he kept up the torrid pace of correspondence during the summers in Peterborough, perhaps out of fear of falling behind on his responsibilities.

One of the casualties of Edward's move to Columbia University was his correspondence with Templeton Strong. His old friend had sold his belongings and relocated with his family to New England in the summer of 1896, only to learn that the MacDowells were moving to New York. Edward did his best to convince him to come to New York, offering him the Mendelssohn Glee Club directorship and the possibility of a future position at Columbia, but Strong returned to Switzerland, where he remained for the rest of his life. The two had no contact during MacDowell's first three years at Columbia, and it was only in the fall of 1899, when Edward wrote to Strong, that the two reestablished contact. In his letter of 9 October 1899, Strong confided that his timidity and lack of confidence in his skills had prevented him from accepting Edward's invitation three years earlier. He described his comfortable life as a painter in Switzerland, with a standard of living he could never have achieved as a musician in America. He also chided his old friend for his own career choices:

> It did me good a few days ago to see Currier, who loudly sang your praises and told me of the splendid work you have been doing at Columbia, none of which surprised

---

1. Both the letter from C. Sitzer on 10 July 1900 and MacDowell's draft response of 21 July are found in MacDowell's letter book, EMMC box 33.

2. Letter, EAM to Arthur Farwell, 5 April 1895, Arthur Farwell Collection. Sibley Library of the Eastman School of Music.

me in the least. My one regret at hearing it all (just as it was when you first went to Boston and I begged of you to confine your lesson giving to the mornings or afternoons exclusively),—well, my one regret was, hearing that your duties probably prevented your composing during the winter. This I honestly and most <u>heartily regret</u>. Your teaching is valuable, we all know: but your composition is about <u>ten thousand times more valuable</u> and I don't think you quite realize it.[3]

By this time in his life, MacDowell's compositions had pecuniary as well as artistic value, and this aspect of composition caused him no end of headaches. As a young man in Germany, he had given away the rights to his early compositions in order to see them published. When he became famous, he was able to negotiate much better terms with Schmidt and Jung, allowing him to supplement his teaching income with substantial royalties from his later publications. But the sacrifices he had made in his early career still rankled. Rather than forget those early decisions and move on to enjoy the fruits of his fame, MacDowell became increasingly obsessed with settling the old scores with his German publishers.

The primary issue at stake was that of the US copyrights. Before the copyright revision of 1891, the United States did not participate in international copyright treaties. Therefore, the law did not recognize foreign copyrights and did not allow foreign authors or publishers to register works for copyright in the United States. Only US citizens could register works for copyright, and therefore MacDowell believed that the right to sell in the United States the works that he had published in Germany belonged to him rather than to Breitkopf & Härtel, Hainauer, and the other German publishers. The contracts he had signed, however, granted them exclusive publication rights "in any editions and for all countries and [all] times."[4] They believed that he had signed away his rights in accordance with the laws of the country in which they were published; he believed that US copyright law made the contracts invalid in the United States.

Everything changed with the wholesale revision of the US copyright statutes effective on 1 July 1891. From that point on, foreign publishers were entitled to copyright protection in the United States so long as they followed the registration and deposit requirements of the new law. MacDowell was furious when he learned in 1901 that Hainauer was registering his works from the 1880s. Several of these had already been reissued in American editions by Schmidt, but now Hainauer asserted that his claim took precedence. Because of his friendship with MacDowell and also because of his own financial stake, Schmidt hired a lawyer to contest the claims.

---

3. Letter, TS to EAM, 9 October 1899, EMMC box 31/33.

4. Contract with Julius Hainauer for the publication of piano pieces, opp. 17 and 18, dated 9 October 1883, "Business Letters," 160–61, EMMC box 32.

MacDowell's fight with Breitkopf & Härtel was even more bitter. The reputation of Germany's leading music publisher was so valuable to him that he was still willing to pay half the production costs for his Sonata, op. 50, in 1895. He continued to feel, though, that he was not getting the respect he deserved from the firm. He also suspected that they were not giving him a fair percentage of the profits as his works became more popular. On the one hand, he suspected that they were under-reporting the number of copies sold, and on the other he found out that the percentage they were giving him was not correct. MacDowell challenged the publisher for offering wholesale discounts [*Rabatt*] to distributors that were higher than the agreed-upon rate in his contracts. They were largely unresponsive to his complaints until he hit the jackpot with *Woodland Sketches*, published by the P. L. Jung imprint of their New York agent Kurt Moebius in 1896. At this point the German firm took notice of the commercial potential of their American composer and angled for the opportunity to publish an equally remunerative title.

As MacDowell's fame grew, he was able to exercise more control over the appearance of his published scores. Since the earliest publications in Germany, virtually all his scores had borne the name "E. A. MacDowell" on the cover. In early 1897, during his first year at Columbia, he decided that he preferred "Edward MacDowell." In August he wrote to all his publishers, asking them to change the title pages for future publications as well as for works already in print. Schmidt's representative recommended the compromise "Edw. MacDowell" for works already in print, which would have allowed them to modify the existing plates rather than engraving entirely new plates, but the composer insisted on this change. Despite the expense, his publishers agreed to the modification in order to placate one of their most successful composers.[5]

MacDowell was furious to learn in January 1903 that G. Schirmer had gathered copies of his earlier works and bound them into a collection that they were selling separately. Because the music had already been purchased, MacDowell did not receive royalties on this compilation. Schmidt wrote to him on 31 January to reassure him about the publication and tell him that there was nothing that could be done to stop it. Schmidt added: "I fully realize the reciprocity of loyalty; and I think that you will never have just cause to complain of me on that score, or of any lack of appreciation on my part."[6]

This obsession with protecting his name also caused MacDowell to refuse dedications and to attempt to block the performance of his works when he did not approve of the setting. In November 1899 he learned that the young Lithuanian

5. The history of this transition is traced in Margery M. Lowens, "The New York Years of Edward MacDowell" (PhD diss., University of Michigan, 1971), 164–65.

6. General Letter Book, 1901–1904, Schmidt Collection, Library of Congress Music Division.

pianist Leopold Godowsky had dedicated one of his recently published etudes to MacDowell without his permission. MacDowell was aware of the composer's fanciful paraphrases of the Chopin Etudes, and he objected strenuously to the publisher, G. Schirmer, about having his name attached to something that he considered disrespectful to Chopin. He soon learned that it was William Mason who had suggested the dedication to MacDowell of Godowsky's Concert Study, op. 11, no. 3. Mason explained that in his view the paraphrases were not objectionable: "The various voices so polyphonically treated, especially as regards the progression of the inner parts, that the idea of any disrespect to Chopin never occurred to me. To re-arrange a piece,—thus taking undue liberty with a composer's work is <u>one</u> thing, while to paraphrase it is quite another. Please observe the somewhat subtle distinction."[7] Op. 11, no. 3, was not one of these paraphrases but was instead an original work by Godowsky. Nonetheless, MacDowell was deeply affronted by the unexpected dedication. MacDowell explained in a curmudgeonly letter to his old friend and champion Mason, "I am afraid—indeed I am certain the present generation is sadly inferior."[8] Godowsky confided to his wife in a letter of April 1901 that Schirmer had turned lukewarm toward him and that he believed MacDowell was the cause.[9]

MacDowell could be equally curmudgeonly with his oldest friends. He nursed a grudge against Teresa Carreño, who during her marriage to Eugen d'Albert had discontinued playing MacDowell's music at her jealous husband's request. Her third marriage lasted only from 1892 to 1895, but this period coincided with MacDowell's growing fame. When Carreño returned to playing his music, she needed to apologize to both Fanny and Edward, the second of whom was not so quick to forgive as the first. When he learned of her plans to play several of his pieces on a 24 April 1897 concert in Louisville, he telegraphed her: "Would consider personal favor if you left me out this being only occasion you play MacDowell this season would prefer not having my weakest piano work beside Brahms best."[10]

As America's best-known composer, MacDowell found ready ears for his views on all aspects of music. The subject on which he was most outspoken was that of American Composers' Concerts. The fad of the late 1880s had died down, but such

7. Letter, William Mason to EAM, 30 November 1899, EMMC box 30/78.

8. Draft letter, EAM to William Mason, 2 December 1899, EMMC, box 33.

9. Letter, Leopold Godowsky to his wife Freda, 24 April 1901, edited by Gregor Benko, International Piano Archives at the University of Maryland. www.lib.umd.edu/PAL/IPAM/godowskyletter.doc (accessed 12 November 2011).

10. Quoted in Marta Milinowski, *Teresa Carreño "by the grace of God"* (New Haven: Yale University Press, 1940; repr. New York: Da Capo, 1977), 261.

concerts were still a regular part of the American music scene. Time and again MacDowell refused to allow his pieces to be performed on such concerts, even if this made enemies for him. When the MTNA presented eight concerts of exclusively American music at its annual convention in Cincinnati on 21–23 June 1899, MacDowell saw to it that none of his pieces was heard. This attitude made him seem aloof and unwilling to associate with his American colleagues, but he saw it as a matter of principle. He elaborated on his views in a widely published letter to the Federated Music Clubs:

> An "American" concert is, in my eyes, an abomination, for the simple reason that it is unfair to the American. Such a concert offers no standard of judgment, owing to our want of familiarity with the works presented. Then, if our work is preferred to another, it only does harm to the weaker work, without helping the stronger one to any fixed value. Added to this, an American concert is a direct bid for leniency on the part of the public, which, I need hardly say, is immediately recognized by it. American music must and will take its position in the world of art by comparison with the only standard we know—that of the work of the world's great masters, and not by that of other works equally unknown to the world. In other words, we crave comparison with the best in art, not only the best in America. If our musical societies would agree never to give concerts composed exclusively of American works, but, on the other hand, would make it a rule never to give a concert without at least one American composition on the programme, I am sure that the result would justify my position in the matter.[11]

MacDowell had the opportunity to effect significant change in one such musical society, the Manuscript Society of New York. He had been opposed to the goals of the organization from its foundation, and he had repeatedly spurned their overtures after moving to New York. In early 1898 three officers of the society paid him a call to renew their invitation to join the organization. In May they offered him the presidency of their group, but again he turned them down. The society had been in decline for years, as it became increasingly difficult to obtain high-quality manuscript compositions for public concerts. The group had not been able to attract and retain members of MacDowell's stature, but MacDowell opposed the manuscript stipulation as well as the restriction to American composers only.

In May 1899, after a full year of negotiations, MacDowell finally agreed to accept the presidency but on his own terms. He demanded that the organization be renamed the Society of American Musicians and Composers and that it be

---

11. "MacDowell on 'American' Concerts," *Musical America* 2/20 (May 20, 1899): 5.

reorganized along the lines of the Allgemeiner Deutscher Musikverein (ADMV). Just as he had benefited from the liberality of the ADMV in 1882, he wished to make the Manuscript Society more inclusive: "The widest liberality will also be used in the selection of works for production by the Society and musicians will be afforded an opportunity of hearing their compositions performed in other lands. It will not be an essential condition hereafter that a composition submitted for performance shall be in manuscript, and the Society will be at perfect liberty to present any composition which will add to the value of the programmes, or which it will profit American musicians to hear."[12]

The constitution and bylaws were rewritten over strenuous objections from many longtime members, and MacDowell set about instituting his new regime the following fall. With each of the monthly private meetings in November and December 1899 and January 1900, he increased the number of European composers on the programs, until by the third program there were no American works among the eleven performed. At the board meeting on 4 January, the day after this performance, MacDowell submitted a letter saying that he would resign unless the entire board resigned. He explained that he was dissatisfied with the current board and needed the power to reorganize it according to his own goals. After much discussion, the board agreed to resign en masse and called a special meeting of the membership on 2 February. At this meeting, the membership refused to allow their elected board to be replaced by presidential appointments. MacDowell refused to budge, and on 21 May his resignation was accepted and the Society reverted to its original name and structure.[13]

More than just a principled stand against musical segregation, MacDowell's break with the Manuscript Society in early January was another example of his reaction to the winter blues. It cannot be a coincidence that his resignation was submitted when he was suffering from light deprivation. This time of year was always difficult for him, and as he had done so often before, he severed his ties at the darkest time of year. His opinions on American concerts were so well known that the Manuscript Society should never have invited him to join their organization. They hoped that his prestige would revive their flagging fortunes, but they did not anticipate his stubborn insistence on reshaping the society, and neither he nor they could anticipate his emotional volatility in the dead of winter.

12. Quoted in Sumner Salter, "Early Encouragements to American Composers," *MQ* 18/1 (January 1932): 103.

13. For a more detailed discussion of MacDowell's presidency of the Manuscript Society of New York, see "Manuscript Societies and the Ghettoization of New Music" in Bomberger, *"A Tidal Wave of Encouragement,"* 145–64.

A famous person like MacDowell made an easy target for critics. Despite widespread acclaim for his playing and compositions, there were a few detractors, most notably W. S. B. Mathews. This Chicago critic and piano teacher had first encountered MacDowell's obduracy (see chap. 9) when he compiled his landmark book *A Hundred Years of Music in America* in 1889. MacDowell's refusal to cooperate angered the author. Mathews subsequently rose to a position of influence in Chicago music circles, and with the founding of his journal *Music*, published monthly from 1892 to 1902, he gained a national audience. The journal was less newsy than the *Musical Courier*, featuring instead long articles by good writers on topics of current and historical interest. Each issue contained an editorial column by Mathews titled "Things Here and There" or "Editorial Bric-a-Brac," which he used as a bully pulpit to comment on music and musicians in America. Over the course of the next decade, Mathews steadily escalated his attacks on MacDowell, criticizing his playing, his teaching, his compositions, his professional relations, and anything else that occurred to him. The critic's April 1900 column listed his grievances against MacDowell, starting with his Columbia appointment and continuing through his opposition to American Composers' Concerts and his refusal of the Godowsky dedication before ending with the sentence: "Meanwhile, when things quiet down a little, perhaps some one will state what particular use to Columbia University or to the world at large this extremely bumptuous [*sic*] young American composer is?"[14] In February 1901 he stated unequivocally that MacDowell was not the great American composer, and in November 1901 he slammed his easier works as barren and his larger works as "bombastic, laborious, and empty."[15] By the time *Music* ceased publication in early 1903, Mathews's feud with MacDowell was infamous.[16]

On the other side were enthusiastic defenders who appeared from nowhere. Newton J. Corey of Detroit was so upset by Mathews's negative comments on MacDowell's *Sonata Eroica* in his book *The Masters and Their Music* that he sent MacDowell a letter expressing his outrage at this unfair attack. He followed this with a lengthy article in the *Musical Courier* of 6 March 1901 rebutting Mathews's attacks

14. W.S.B.M., "Editorial Bric-a-Brac," *Music* 17/6 (April 1900): 638–39.

15. W.S.B.M., "Editorial Bric-a-Brac," *Music* 20/1 (November 1901): 432.

16. The *Salt Lake Herald* reported in its 15 February 1903 issue: "The Musical Leader of Chicago announces the demise, or absorption, of Music, Mr. W. S. B. Mathews' magazine. Mr. Mathews is a gentleman who, not long ago, wrote two articles on American song writers in which Edward MacDowell, whose songs are worth more than all other American songs put together, was not even mentioned. This, of course, had nothing to do with MacDowell's giving Mathews a piece of his mind, some time ago, about the way he sneered at Paderewski. Mathews was evidently bound to be up to date. That may be the reason why his magazine has proved such a great success."

and calling into question his qualifications as a critic.[17] Even though MacDowell did not know Corey, he was grateful that someone took his side against the unprovoked attacks by the Chicago gadfly.

Even more significantly, in the spring of 1900 MacDowell received a letter from a young writer by the name of Lawrence Gilman, who asked for information for an upcoming article. When the article appeared in the 1 August issue of Boston's *Musical Record*, the composer was taken aback by the author's high praise and perceptive analysis. MacDowell wrote a grateful letter of thanks on 12 August, and four days later he confided to the Boston critic Philip Hale, "I have written prettily to Edward [*sic*] Gilman. I wonder who he is."[18] In the coming years, Gilman would become MacDowell's foremost champion, publishing numerous articles and two books on the composer, who cooperated by providing access to primary documents and sharing his opinions with the author. Gilman's views on MacDowell have colored the perception of the composer ever since. Gilman's 1908 biography effusively praised the composer's originality at the expense of all other American composers, which Marian and Strong believed contributed to a backlash of resentment. Indeed, the canny Schmidt told Marian later that year, "There are still people in existence to whom the very name of MacDowell acts like a red rag on a bull."[19]

The intensity of feelings both for and against MacDowell is the surest sign of the composer's stature in American music. His unique musical individuality, his meteoric rise to the top of American musical life, and his curmudgeonly relations with so many contemporaries conspired to make him a marked man. In hindsight we can recognize that both the praise and the criticism were overblown, but for the man himself, the swirling vortex of critical opinion only compounded his stress. His Boston friend Currier noted in an 1899 visit that he seemed older and weighed down with responsibility. MacDowell did his best to keep up a jolly front, but he confided, "The only thing is to be as useful as we can." To Currier, this confession had an ominous sound.[20]

17. N[ewton] J. Corey, "Mr. Mathews on MacDowell," *MC* 42/10 (6 March 1901): 9–10.
18. Draft letter, EAM to Philip Hale, 16 August 1900, EMMC box 33.
19. General Letter Book, 1906–1909, 29 October 1908, Schmidt Collection, Library of Congress Music Division.
20. T. P. Currier, "Edward MacDowell as I Knew Him," *MQ* 1/1 (January 1915): 48.

CHAPTER EIGHTEEN

Columbia University, 1901–1904

HEN FRESHMAN JOHN ERSKINE REGISTERED FOR CLASSES IN THE FALL OF 1896, Dean John Howard Van Amringe discouraged him from taking any classes in music with the newly appointed MacDowell, saying, "It's against my judgment. You're here to get an education!" Erskine responded, "if MacDowell's instruction were not good for me, the Trustees had erred in providing it." His music classes turned out to be among the most inspiring of Erskine's college career, laying the foundation for his future work as a university professor. But the attitude of the dean convinced him that the university wanted the famous MacDowell on its faculty roster rather than music in its curriculum.[1]

During his first five years on campus, MacDowell had established the Music Department on a solid footing. He had built the curriculum from the ground up, and he had expanded the course offerings to encompass not only general music but also theory and aural skills, chorus and orchestra, and advanced composition. From its beginnings as a one-man department, his program had grown to a staff of three. The library now included complete works of many of the major composers, along with a representative collection of recent music. The one goal that MacDowell had not achieved by the turn of the century was the one he had shared with President Low during their initial conversations: a department that would integrate music with the sister arts of painting, sculpture, and comparative literature. Low had pointed out that there were no impediments to a student who wished to take courses in several of these areas, but MacDowell continued to dream of a unified Department of Fine Arts.

1. John Erskine, *The Memory of Certain Persons* (Philadelphia: Lippincott, 1947), 73.

In the fall of 1901, Seth Low was elected mayor of New York on the strength of his accomplishments at Columbia. He had been responsible for the move from Forty-ninth Street to Morningside Heights and had worked to transform Columbia College into a university during his eleven-year tenure. Rather than take a leave of absence, he resigned his position as president of Columbia, allowing the university to move in a new direction. Low's strong connections to the city of New York had served the university well and had made it a vital part of the city; his successor would have the opportunity to make the university into a national leader in higher education.

Nicholas Murray Butler (1862–1947) was dubbed "Nicholas Miraculous" by Theodore Roosevelt, reflecting both the importance of his accomplishments and the size of his ego. He earned his PhD in philosophy from Columbia in 1884, and after further studies in Paris and Berlin, he was appointed professor of philosophy at his alma mater in 1885. He was instrumental in the founding of the New York School for the Training of Teachers, which later became Columbia University Teachers College. He served as president of the university from Low's resignation through 1945, longer than any other president of Columbia. His focus was always national and global, as he supplemented his leadership of Columbia with service on a variety of outside boards and other organizations. His work for international peace earned him the Nobel Peace Prize in 1931. A man of enormous political influence as well as strong literary opinions, Butler used his position on the Pulitzer Advisory Council to overturn the jury's selections of Sinclair Lewis's *Main Street* in 1921, Maxwell Anderson's *Mary of Scotland* in 1934, and Ernest Hemingway's *For Whom the Bell Tolls* in 1941.[2] But for all his administrative skill and influential connections, Butler was not a friend of the arts. In the words of his biographer Michael Rosenthal, "Painting and music played no part in Butler's life; his taste in fiction ran to the sentimental effusions of Charlotte Yonge, and the poem he most esteemed was John Greenleaf Whittier's maudlin 'In School-Days.'"[3]

Butler was named interim president when Low resigned in October 1901, and he was formally elected as Low's successor in January 1902. Within weeks of the announcement, MacDowell presented his ideas on the future direction of the arts at Columbia to Butler, including a combined Department of Fine Arts that would encompass music, sculpture, painting, and comparative literature as well as the requirement that all Columbia undergraduates take two courses in the fine

---

2. Michael Rosenthal, *Nicholas Miraculous: The Amazing Career of the Redoubtable Dr. Nicholas Murray Butler* (New York: Farrar, Strauss & Giroux, 2006), 266–67; Edwin McDowell, "Publishing: Pulitzer Controversies," *NYT*, 11 May 1984, sec. C, 26.

3. Ibid., 265–66.

arts in order to graduate.[4] What MacDowell did not realize was that this was the worst time to make his case for significant change. A new administrator is typically besieged by faculty members who have been unable to win approval for their pet projects from the predecessor. The prudent administrator—particularly if he is in an interim position—withholds definitive judgment until after things have settled down and he has had a chance to review all the competing proposals. This is exactly what Butler did when contacted by MacDowell in February. We do not know precisely what Butler said in person to MacDowell, but over the next several months it became clear that what MacDowell thought he had heard was not what the president-elect actually intended to communicate. From this time on, the two men worked under different assumptions, with the head of the music department assuming that it was only a matter of time until the new organizational structure was implemented, and the university president leaving all options on the table.

In February and March 1902, MacDowell contacted numerous persons about his plan. He told faculty members and artists that the university had endorsed his proposal, and he approached potential donors for financial support. He arranged dinners and other events to meet with wealthy New Yorkers who might be interested in his scheme, led by Howard and Helen Mansfield.[5] On 11 March he wrote to wealthy art collector Henry Osborne Havemeyer urging him to endow a chair in painting and sculpture, explaining: "The authorities have given their sanction to the scheme and Mr. Butler tells me that if a chair of Painting and Sculpture can be founded (it would need as a minimum $100,000) the matter would be taken in hand immediately. Our plans for the creation of this faculty have been thoroughly worked out and President Butler will be glad to give details to anyone interested."[6] He closed the letter by apologizing for his lack of experience in asking for endowments and saying that any level of support would be appreciated. This sort of fundraising must have irritated the new president if he heard what MacDowell was doing. Presumably Butler had suggested the $100,000 endowment knowing full well that it would be impossible to raise; MacDowell took the suggestion as his marching orders.

MacDowell also contacted artists and faculty members with whom he hoped to work. A long letter dated 28 February from William R. Ware, chair of architecture, expressed cautious support for the general notion of allied arts while articulating

---

4. Letter from Butler to EAM, 8 February 1902; cited in William Bell Dinsmoor, "The Department of Fine Arts and Archaeology," in *A History of the Faculty of Philosophy, Columbia University*, ed. Jacques Barzun (New York: Columbia University Press, 1957), 254.

5. Margery M. Lowens, "The New York Years of Edward MacDowell" (PhD diss., University of Michigan, 1971), 251–52.

6. Letter draft, EAM to [Henry Osborne] Havermeyer, 11 March 1902, EMMC box 33.

concerns about the logistics of such a combination at Columbia. A letter from the sculptor Frederick William MacMonnies—whose *Bacchante and Infant Faun* had been rejected by the Boston Public Library after it was condemned by the Women's Temperance Union for "drunken indecency"—congratulated MacDowell on the scheme in March. Helen Mansfield recalled in 1906 that MacMonnies was an artist that MacDowell hoped to add to the new faculty.[7]

The burst of energy to garner support for the proposed Department of Fine Arts coincided with unusual energy in several other endeavors at the same time. MacDowell's appointment book shows that he taught more than twenty half-hour piano lessons per week at his apartment in the winter of 1901/02, perhaps to compensate for missing his usual recital tour that February. Throughout the winter, the battle with German publishers intensified. He granted Schmidt power of attorney to deal with Hainauer and Breitkopf & Härtel, but he still needed to scour his old letter books (including the one that Strong had fortuitously saved from destruction in 1888) for contracts and royalty statements. At the same time, he completed three new works: *Three Songs*, op. 60, *Fireside Tales*, op. 61, and *New England Idyls*, op. 62. This compositional activity was the most unusual aspect of the frantic winter of 1901/02.

Since his earliest days in Germany, virtually all of MacDowell's creative activities were accomplished during the second and third quarters of the year, between April and September. This was when he completed new compositions and took positive steps toward improving his professional life (e.g., enrolling at the Hoch Conservatory in 1879, moving from Frankfurt to Wiesbaden in 1884, moving to Boston in 1888, accepting the appointment at Columbia in 1896). Between October and March, on the other hand, he was less productive, seldom completed new works, and his professional decisions were often destructive rather than positive (e.g., leaving Paris in 1878, resigning his position at Darmstadt in 1882, attacking Breitkopf & Härtel in 1885, declining the commission from the World's Columbian Exposition in 1892, resigning the presidency of the Manuscript Society in 1900). We have seen repeatedly that the late winter months of February and March were especially trying for MacDowell, as he lacked the energy to compose or the patience to deal with petty annoyances. He ran the risk of making rash professional decisions while so despondent.

The winter of 1901/02 was different, though, and a large part of the motivation seems to have been financial. During the summer of 1901, Marian had again become dangerously ill. She required two operations, causing Edward much anxiety and forcing the couple to go into debt. She spent much of the summer in a Boston

7. Letter, Frederick William MacMonnies to EAM, 18 March 1902, MacDowell Collection, Library of Congress Manuscript Division, box 6; M. M. Lowens, "The New York Years," 252.

hospital, where Edward was forced to live in a hotel. He confessed to his parents that he was very depressed and that the experience had taken a heavy toll not just financially but also emotionally. On 13 January 1902 Marian confided to Schmidt that they had spent nearly all of Edward's half-year royalty check in repaying the last of Marian's medical bills ($450). She wrote, "It made me sick again, almost, to have it go for that but thankful it was there to go. I don't really feel worth it all."[8] Looking forward, Edward had been granted a sabbatical leave for the 1902/03 academic year, but his salary would be at half pay. It is not hard to understand why in the winter of 1901/02 MacDowell embarked on a heroic effort to get as many new things into print as possible, all under the imprint of Schmidt, his most loyal and remunerative publisher. The fall of 1901 saw the publication of extensively revised editions of *Six Idyls after Goethe*, op. 28; *Six Poems after Heine*, op. 31; and *Marionettes*, op. 38, which he expanded from six to eight movements. He also completed *Three Songs*, op. 60, in December; *Fireside Tales*, op. 61, in January or February; and *New England Idyls*, op. 62, in May.

As a group, these works represent a new direction for the composer. On 20 August 1901, with Marian still in the hospital, he had written to his mother, "Musically, I have at present neither the freshness of the beginner nor the anything of anybody else—just a soggy blank; and I have acquired an imbecile feeling for everything."[9] This cryptic comment is reflected in the revisions and the original pieces from this period, which are pervaded by a melancholy mood and a new-found harmonic ambiguity.

Oscar Sonneck, the first head of the music division of the Library of Congress, characterized MacDowell's revisions in this way: "MacDowell was one of those composers who retain a fatherly interest in their works even after publication. Eminently of a self-critical turn of mind, he would detect flaws in his published compositions and found no rest until he had given them that finish of detail which is so characteristic of his art at its best."[10] A comparison of the European editions of opp. 28, 31, and 38 from the late 1880s with the revised editions published by Schmidt in November and December 1901 shows how much the composer's aesthetic had evolved. In addition to the "finish of detail" noted by Sonneck, the later works contain less virtuosity and more harmonic complexity. MacDowell's harmonic palette in 1901 was much more varied and subtle than it had been fifteen

---

8. Letter, MM to APS, 13 January 1902, Irving and Margery Lowens Collection.

9. Letter, EAM to Fanny MacDowell, 20 August 1901, NYPL.

10. Oscar George Theodore Sonneck, "MacDowell Versus MacDowell: A Study in First Editions and Revisions," originally published in the Proceedings of the Music Teachers' National Association for 1911; repr. in *Suum Cuique: Essays in Music* (New York: Schirmer, 1916), 90.

years earlier, greatly enhancing the expressive range of *Marionettes*, op. 38, in partic-ular. Both versions remain worthy of performance, and the revisions offer tangible evidence of his changing aesthetic views.[11]

The six piano pieces of *Fireside Tales*, op. 61, were intended to have a popular appeal. The first and last numbers, "An Old Love Story" and "By Smouldering Embers," are frankly sentimental, continuing in the vein of the *Woodland Sketches* of 1896. By contrast, the four middle pieces are among the most technically difficult of MacDowell's short piano works, using the entire keyboard and presenting a variety of difficulties from extreme speed in "Of Br'er Rabbit" to mercurial changes in "Of Salamanders." The individual pieces are also among MacDowell's most descriptive: "From a German Forest," for example, evokes a variety of textures, including folk-song, birdsong, and male chorus (which he names specifically in his performance instructions). There are also sudden unprepared key shifts that call to mind the magical superstitions of German folklore. Francis Brancaleone has identified sev-eral quotations of Wagnerian leitmotivs in this piece, which further emphasize the connections to MacDowell's youth in Germany.[12] "A Haunted House" was inspired by one of the deserted structures that he and Marian visited during their walks through the New Hampshire countryside. She later recalled that they thought they heard footsteps and the rustling of long skirts in a neighboring room, but upon entering found only branches tapping on windows and strips of wallpaper moving in the breeze.[13] These images are vividly portrayed in rapidly changing textures.

New England Idyls, op. 62, represent the culmination of this new direction. There are sudden shifts to distant keys and large areas of harmonic instability, as for instance in "In Deep Woods," op. 62, no. 5, which opens with a page of harmonic instability before finally reaching the first tonic chord in m. 11. There is more chromatic col-oration than ever, as in the languid, shimmering tones of "Mid-Summer," op. 62, no. 2, and the pungent fragrances of "With Sweet Lavender," op. 62, no. 4. MacDowell employs shifting meters so often in "From a Log Cabin," op. 62, no. 9, that he does not bother to notate each new time signature. This set of ten pieces inhabits the same musical world as those of his contemporaries Mahler, Strauss, and Hugo Wolf, but it has an individual stamp that is unmistakably MacDowell.

11. In addition to Sonneck, Edward Burlingame Hill analyzed these revisions: "MacDowell's Marionettes," *Musician* 15/10 (October 1910): 653, 703. He argued that the revisions were designed to increase sales by making the works accessible to less-advanced pianists, an assertion with which Sonneck strenuously disagreed.

12. Francis Brancaleone, "Wagnerian Influence and Motives in the Works of Edward MacDowell," paper delivered at the Edward MacDowell Symposium and Festival, Elizabethtown, Pennsylvania, December 2010.

13. MM, *Random Notes on Edward MacDowell and his Music* (Boston: Schmidt, 1950), 23–24.

Most characteristic of MacDowell's aesthetic is his depiction of extramusical images. Each piece is preceded by a short poem by the composer that sets the mood for the piece but does not tell a precise story. Marian explained: "MacDowell held that a poetic name given a piece helped a performer in his interpretation, without limiting his imagination. Furthermore his writing was never descriptive in a realistic sense; it was the expression of a mood which might be awakened by a scene, a poem, an idea or an experience."[14] In devoting ten pieces to scenes in New England, MacDowell came as close as ever to an autobiographical account, laying bare some of his own deepest feelings and also his impressions of the adopted home where he spent his happiest summers.

MacDowell was struck by the sense of decline and abandonment that characterized the part of rural New Hampshire where he lived. Marian writes of his fascination with abandoned farms, Indian relics, old-growth forest, and other symbols of the vibrancy of previous generations. The *New England Idyls* are permeated with nostalgia and melancholy for the old ways. "To an Old White Pine," op. 62, no. 7, evokes the image of a centuries-old remnant of the virgin forest that was spared by the early settlers who had cleared his land. The lone tree towered above the surrounding trees of more recent vintage. The composer depicted it with rising series of chords supported by long crescendos similar to the closing measures of "To the Sea," op. 55, no. 1. There are several numbers devoted to garden images, pervaded by an air of tranquility. "Indian Idyl," op. 62, no. 6, uses two melodies from Theodore Baker's dissertation *"On the Music of North American Indians,"* one of which was also used in the *Indian Suite,* op. 48 (see chap. 13). As in "From an Indian Lodge" from *Woodland Sketches,* op. 51, no. 5, MacDowell recalls the Indian as a tragic figure of the nostalgic past—understandable in a region of the country where Native Americans had been absent for generations.

The set also contains three pieces on specific seasons that in conjunction with earlier seasonal depictions give us insights into his changing moods. The chromatic inflections of "Mid-Summer" reflect his impression of the bold colors of summer flowers but in a slow tempo marked "Dreamily." The poem heading the piece sets a mood of tranquility:

Droning Summer slumbers on
Midst drowsy murmurs sweet.
Above, the lazy cloudlets drift,
Below, the swaying wheat.

14. Ibid., v.

In describing the piece, Marian recalled his love of the bright flowers and his bewilderment at "the sudden lavish approach of summer." "The Joy of Autumn," op. 62, no. 10, in E major shares many characteristics with "In Autumn" from *Woodland Sketches*, op. 51, no. 4, in F-sharp minor. The colorful keys reflect MacDowell's love of the improbably bright foliage of autumn in New Hampshire, while the rapid tempi reflect the energy he found in the crisp air after a languid summer. The tempo markings are nearly identical, with the earlier piece labeled "Buoyantly, almost exuberantly ($♪$. = 132)" and the later one removing the qualifier "almost." The earlier piece is in 6/8 meter with nearly constant eighth-note motion throughout. The later work is more varied, alternating between 3/4 and 9/8. The middle section of this work is in D minor, providing a more somber counterpoise to the exuberant opening and setting up brilliantly the dazzling splash of color and virtuosity that closes the piece and the set.

The significance of the D-minor middle section of "The Joy of Autumn" becomes clear when compared with MacDowell's two depictions of winter: both "Winter," from *Vier kleine Poesien*, op. 32, no. 4, and "Mid-Winter" from *New England Idyls*, op. 62, no. 3, share the key of D minor, foretold in the middle section of "The Joy of Autumn." These two pieces are among MacDowell's bleakest compositions, opening in pianissimo and triple pianissimo respectively. The later work is further qualified with the instruction "with muffled, somewhat thick tone" (ex. 18.1).

18.1 "Mid-Winter" from *New England Idyls*, op. 62, no. 3, mm. 1–8

The earlier of the two pieces, written in 1887 during his final year in Wiesbaden, rises above the dynamic of piano only twice, for a brief measure of mezzo forte in each case. It contains the marking "tristamente" [sadly] in m. 27, and over the fourth measure from the end, the word "cold" is written in his student W. H. Humiston's copy.[15] The later work, by contrast, begins with a similar air of frigid somberness but rises to a thunderous climax of rushing scales and triple-fortissimo chords before sinking back into frozen melancholy.

MacDowell's winter key of D minor also appears in "From Puritan Days," op. 62, no. 8, subtitled "In Nomine Domini." The striking similarity of this piece to the mood and tempo of the winter pieces (ex. 18.2) reveals the composer's feelings about the experience of the earliest European settlers of New England and—presumably—their faith. The score is amply peppered with picturesque markings portraying their somber existence: "pleadingly," "with pathos," "despairingly," and "steadily resolute and firm." Permeating the piece is an oppressive air of resignation closely related to the two winter pieces. MacDowell reveals much in the piece about his own views and feelings, as he does in the other pieces of this highly autobiographical set.

Brancaleone provides a fitting summary of *New England Idyls* when he states, "the composer calls on all of his experience and skill to write fragile pieces without pose, light-hearted pieces without formula, emotional pieces without excess, and complex pieces without obscurity."[16]

18.2 "From Puritan Days" from New England Idyls, op. 62, no. 8, mm. 1–4

Having succeeded in writing so much music of this quality during the busy winter of 1901/02, MacDowell had high hopes for his sabbatical leave in 1902/03, writing to Schmidt in January 1902: "I hope at last the time has come when I may do something unhampered by piano lessons and College lectures. It makes me feel young to think of it and even the poverty of half pay for the year does not

15. Personal collection of Irving and Margery Lowens.

16. Francis Brancaleone, "The Short Piano Works of Edward MacDowell" (PhD diss., CUNY, 1982), 250.

daunt me. I hope I will <u>do something</u>."[17] The university would need to offer fewer courses than usual, but he hoped to minimize the disruption by arranging for a promotion and salary increase for McWhood. His request on McWhood's behalf in early March was denied by the university administration, but his assistant agreed to teach an overload anyway while also holding another part-time position at Vassar College.

In April, the month of Butler's inauguration, the president-elect submitted his report on the Fine Arts to the Trustees' committee on education. While his report acknowledged that Columbia's current offerings in the arts were "cursory and inadequate," he went on to outline what he saw as the proper role of the arts in a university:

> [I]t is no part of the plan which is here proposed, to enter upon giving that instruction which, in the Middle Ages, was known as the "art, mystery, and manual occupation" of either music, painting, sculpture, or indeed architecture. It is my belief that it is the part of wisdom for the University to refrain from offering this instruction, but to recognize it when adequately given in existing ateliers, conservatories, and private or incorporated schools. In this way the University would give the historical, philosophical, and theoretical instruction, while other teachers and organizations would provide the practical training and apprenticeship which is part of all art education. In this way the University would become the ally rather than the rival of existing art schools and teachers ...I regard this division of labor between the University on one hand and special educational instrumentalities on the other, as fundamental to the development of a sound plan for instruction in the fine arts.[18]

MacDowell was stunned when he read this report. He had been circulating his proposal and Butler's initial letter of response to artists and potential donors under the assumption that they were in agreement, but he now realized that this was not the case. In a letter of 22 May he expressed his disappointment to Butler. He argued that the omission of applied instruction in sculpture and painting was an injustice to the visual arts, since literature classes teach writers, architecture classes train architects, and music classes train composers. He also renewed his request that all students at Columbia be required to take courses in the arts (reducing his demand from two to one). Meanwhile the trustees accepted Butler's report, and on 2 June, they removed the Department of Architecture from the Faculty of Applied Science

17. Letter, EAM to APS, 21 January 1901 [*recte* 1902], Columbia University, Special Collections; quoted in M. M. Lowens, "The New York Years," 249.
18. "Report of the Committee on Education and Instruction in the Fine Arts and Resolutions Adopted May 5, 1902," 6–7; quoted in Dinsmoor, "The Department of Fine Arts and Archaeology," 254–55.

and the Department of Music from the Faculty of Philosophy, making them independent departments under the president's jurisdiction until such time as a new
administrative unit combining the arts could be established.[19]

By the time MacDowell left New York in late May, the accumulated stress of
Marian's illness, their financial worries, the conflict surrounding his Fine Arts proposal, the extra piano teaching, and the work on revised and new compositions had
exhausted him. His mother wrote in a letter to her grandson (Walter's son Frank)
on 30 May: "Uncle Edward and Aunty Marian go to Peterboro on Tuesday, and
have already sent away their things. Now begins his year's vacation. Aunt Marian
is pretty well, but Uncle Edward is very tired, and I shall be glad if this lovely
weather continues until they leave town."[20] An honorary doctorate presented by
the University of Pennsylvania on 18 June must have lifted his spirits even if it did
not relieve his exhaustion. As he sat in Philadelphia that summer morning, one
wonders whether the events of the past winter gave irony to the words of the citation read in his honor:

> There is no art the possession and cultivation of which more distinguishes a high from
> a low degree of civilization than music. There is no influence that appeals to our senses
> more refining, more pervasive, more elevating, more comforting....Music receives by
> universal approbation the entire devotion of those unusual minds that have been gifted by
> nature with peculiar aptitude for its study, and for their benefit the great universities have
> set apart special departments and as a reward reserve special honors.[21]

After seven years of devotion to his "special department," MacDowell had earned
the opportunity to rest and return to his creative pursuits.

A sabbatical leave is the most revered benefit of university teaching, but one of
the most misunderstood by those outside of academe. When MacDowell's mother
spoke of "his year's vacation," she misunderstood the purpose of this tradition.
Institutions of higher education do not merely train students for careers; their purpose is to cultivate the life of the mind and to create new knowledge. The great
university professors are those whose research and creative work is at the forefront
of exploration, but who are also able to inspire their students to a similar devotion
to intellectual advancement. Sabbatical leaves had been introduced by Seth Low as
one of the linchpins in his transformation of Columbia College to a university. The

19. Douglas Moore, "The Department of Music," in Barzun, *A History of the Faculty of Philosophy*, 273–74.

20. Letter, Fanny MacDowell to "My dear boy," 30 May 1902, NYPL.

21. Presentation citation, University of Pennsylvania Proceedings of Commencement, 18 June 1902, quoted in Letter, Janet Andrews to Margery L. Morgan, 29 July 1968.

sabbatical allows a professor the time and freedom to choose how best to further his intellectual goals, returning to campus with renewed insight and vigor for his teaching. The challenge for the sabbatical recipient is to organize this large block of time into activities that will yield tangible results.

Edward and Marian seem to have taken a well-deserved rest in Peterborough during the summer and fall of 1902. He completed his *New England Idyls* and spent a great deal of time on preparations for a concert tour scheduled for the winter. This tour was the solution to his reduced income and limited opportunities for piano teaching during his sabbatical year. With his normal fee for a recital set at $250, MacDowell stood to gain a great deal if he could schedule enough performances. It came at a price, though, as recitals had their own demands. Upton Sinclair recalled: "He spoke of these concert tours, which he had to take. One spent all one earned in New York City. They were very wearing; few people realized the nervous and physical strain involved in giving a pianoforte concert—it was a giant's labor, and one was bathed with perspiration at the end."[22] Knowing full well the demands, MacDowell scheduled the longest tour of his career in the winter of 1902/03, committing a third of his sabbatical year to the endeavor.

In early December he and Marian took the train to Toronto, where he opened his tour with a recital at the conservatory on 6 December. They worked their way across the country for the rest of the month, arriving in California around Christmas. During the next month, he played recitals in Los Angeles, Sacramento, San Francisco, Oakland, and Berkeley, including a performance of his Second Piano Concerto with Paul Steindorff's orchestra in San Francisco on 8 January. The warmth of California at the darkest time of year was enchanting; as Marian recalled a year later, "we lost our hearts out there, and never expect to regain them until we go again."[23] By late January they were back in the Midwest, where he performed in Indianapolis, Oberlin, and Chicago. This segment of the tour involved more traveling, as he interspersed concerts in Washington, Brooklyn, Pittsburgh, and Wells College with the midwestern dates. The tour concluded with a series of concerts in Buffalo in late March. By this time, he was exhausted, writing to Marian, "Arrived at last in this rotten hole and found an ancient upright in the room....I froze half the way up and boiled the rest and shall doctor up tonight hard....Otherwise all goes well but it's like going to a funeral to me."[24]

22. Upton Sinclair, "Memories of Edward MacDowell," *Sackbut* 6 (December 1925): 131.

23. Letter, MM to Isabelle Moore, 8 April 1904, New England Conservatory Library.

24. Letter, EAM to MM, 18 March 1903, EMMC box 31/58.

The tour took MacDowell to places he had never performed before, and consequently the crowds were large and enthusiastic. Reviewers agreed with their colleagues in the East that his renditions of his own works were revelatory. By this time, MacDowell's compositions were well known throughout the country, but the composer had a unique way of interpreting them that shed new light on his intentions. Some reviewers were critical of his technique in the difficult Keltic Sonata, and others were puzzled by the differences between what they saw in the scores and what they heard from the composer's playing, but in most cases they agreed that the composer brought them alive in ways that other interpreters did not. By contrast, his playing of standard repertoire was not acclaimed. The *Washington Times* called his performances of other composers disappointing in comparison to Paderewski, Gabrilowitsch, and Mark Hambourg, who had recently performed there.[25] He included Beethoven's "Moonlight" Sonata, op. 27, no. 2, on nearly every program, despite a growing chorus of discontent about his quirky interpretation of the well-known work. After criticizing his technique and disregard for dynamic markings in his own compositions, Professor Edward Dickinson wrote of the Beethoven sonata performance at Oberlin: "Equally surprising was it to hear from such a musical scholar as Mr. MacDowell a conception of the 'Moonlight' sonata so unsatisfactory....Such things are more than bad taste, they are positively immoral. It is not ungracious to say this. *Noblesse oblige* is always a good motto, and the greatest artist is but the servant of the art which is greater than he."[26] MacDowell responded to Dickinson with a lengthy letter defending his interpretation, evoking an even longer letter from Dickinson arguing his original point.[27] The reviews find MacDowell caught in the dilemma he had struggled with since his youth. Was he a performer who owed his public faultless technique? Was he a scholar who owed the Classical composers fidelity? Or was he a composer whose only mandate was originality?

He returned from his travels in late March 1903, still recovering from an attack of influenza that had forced him to perform in Chicago with a high fever. The couple did not rest for long, though; they embarked on 11 April for England. In preparation for this trip, he and Marian devoted some of their precious hours in Peterborough to burning musical manuscripts, thinking that if their ship went down, his posthumous reputation would suffer from knowledge of incomplete or

25. "Edward MacDowell is Greeted Warmly," *Washington Times*, 7 March 1903, 7.

26. [Edward Dickinson], "Edward MacDowell," *Oberlin Review* 30 (12 February 1903), 297–98; quoted in M. M. Lowens, "The New York Years," 282–83.

27. This exchange of letters between two college professors shows MacDowell could hold his own in a discussion of arcane matters of music history and interpretation. Draft letter, EAM to Edward Dickinson, EMMC; Letter, Dickinson to EAM, 6 April 1903, MacDowell Collection, Library of Congress Manuscript Division, box 6.

immature works.[28] In England he made his long-awaited debut as piano soloist with the Philharmonic Society of London. The concert on 14 May introduced America's most famous composer to the British public. Except for the London *Times*, the press was enthusiastic.[29] The pleasure he took in this event was dampened by another bout of illness, this time bronchitis. He and Marian chose to leave England early in search of a more favorable climate in Switzerland, but not without a brief visit to Paris in late May.

When he arrived in Switzerland, he was greeted by his old friend Templeton Strong, who had last seen the couple in Peterborough in the summer of 1896. Strong later recalled:

> I was at once struck with the great change wrought in my friend. This was no longer the Edward of days gone by, ever sprightly, ever laughing, ever jocular, and apparently tireless. If he was gentle in the past, he had now become even more so—far more subdued, and occasionally wearing the expression of a man who had in some way been very cruelly deceived, and who strove to conceal it. He seemed ill, without apparently being so, was somewhat self-deprecating and seemed also in a certain measure to have lost his ambition. Something at times in his expression made me fearful, but I dismissed my thought as being impossible. He still occasionally joked in his amusing way, but the old "verve" was missing, and he laughed yet more gently and more rarely than in the past. His movements had become slower, a fact that was not alone attributable to his having become rather stouter; he appeared a tired man, disposed to be somewhat apathetic, which it was not at all his nature to be. I was in a better position to notice the change in him than those who constantly saw him. To them the change was unnoticeably gradual; to me it was a shock.[30]

MacDowell was physically and mentally tired, in need of the rest he had not found during the winter. Strong found the couple a hotel room in Villars-sur-Ollon, not far from Strong's chalet, and urged him to rest. To encourage his friend to compose, he arranged for a separate studio for Edward, supplied with a piano and staff paper.

The correspondence between the two men that summer shows that MacDowell did everything but compose. He spent a great deal of time on his photographic

28. This event was described as a "holocaust" in W. H. Humiston, "Personal Recollections of Edward MacDowell," *Musician* 13/4 (April 1908): 161. Among the works consigned to the flames was a projected music-drama on the subject of the Holy Grail, which would not have been an opera per se, but rather "a combination of pantomime and tableaux" predominated by the orchestra with minimal singing. Lawrence Gilman, *Edward MacDowell: A Study* (New York: John Lane, 1908), 92–93.

29. M. M. Lowens, "The New York Years," 287.

30. TS, "Edward MacDowell as I Knew Him: Tenth Paper," *Music Student* 8/9 (May 1916): 275.

hobby, he worked on lectures for the upcoming year at Columbia, and he attended to his always-heavy load of correspondence. He took daily walks, he seemed in reasonably good health, and many of his letters contain the sort of puns and jokes the two friends had shared since their youth. The summer was an unusual one, as Europe was in the grip of unseasonably cold and rainy weather. MacDowell joked in one letter that he had found a way to save the Fr. 1.50 charged for a bath: he stepped onto his balcony in the buff and let the thick fog do the work, with no fear of being seen by anyone else.[31] The precious sunshine that renewed him every summer was scarce in 1903. On one of the rare sunny days of the summer, the MacDowells joined Strong on a hike, during which he snapped several candid photos of the couple (plate 8).

For at least the third time that year, he came down with another respiratory illness in Switzerland. He joked in a letter to Strong that Marian slathered his chest with pungent herbs and shut the doors to give him the benefit of the fumes. He went on, "I forgot to say she kept me spooning into myself all the afternoon the following chemicals—Gelseminum—Belladonna (Homeopathio) and a glorious black medicine we got in Chicago—I still live in spite of it all and I wanted her to have at least one <u>complete</u> '<u>own way</u>'....My wife has just forced two 'bryonia' tablets on me (internally) to clamp down the cure. I emit a distinctly chemical atmosphere and fear to smoke lest something in my stock should blow up."[32]

Though in many ways Edward seemed normal, something was clearly wrong. He reported in a letter to his mother that he kept mixing up French and German, though Marian did just fine.[33] He became despondent and easily frustrated, not only about his teaching preparations and the awful weather but even about photography. That summer he sent some of his films to Strong's developing man rather than process them himself, with disappointing results. He experimented with the new lightweight Kodak camera, also with disappointing results. Most importantly, he produced no creative work in music. The subject is not mentioned in any of the extant letters, and there is no evidence that he composed at all, except for one passing reference to "<u>rotten</u> musical ideas."[34]

As in the past, the one subject sure to evoke strong emotions was royalties. When he received his July royalty check from Schmidt, he wrote a peevish letter

31. TS, "Edward MacDowell: Eleventh Paper," *Music Student* 8/10 (June 1916): 298.

32. Letter, EAM to TS, Monday [n.d.], EMMC, box 29/35.

33. Letter, EAM to Frances MacDowell, 3 July 1903, NYPL.

34. Letter, EAM to TS, 7 July 1903, EMMC, box 29/35: "I can't help my letters are imbecile—The high air, fog, pyrotechnics and damp,—rich food and gigantic indigestions and <u>rotten</u> musical ideas."

bemoaning the low sales. He had hoped that his concert tour of the previous winter would result in a dramatic increase in sales, but this was not the case: "Successful public performance is the most powerful advertisement a publisher can have and if it did not accomplish anything for my works it certainly is not my fault and what the remedy may be I do not know."[35] On his way home from Switzerland, he took the opportunity to visit Breitkopf & Härtel in Leipzig on 6 or 7 September. There he had a cordial visit with a representative of the firm, reaching a verbal agreement that was a satisfactory resolution of their long-standing dispute. When he received their letter of 7 September summarizing the agreement in writing, however, he went ballistic. From England he wrote a strong letter on 17 September demanding the terms that he recalled from their meeting and refusing to accept those outlined in their letter of 7 September.[36] The firm replied that his recollection was different from theirs, but promptly capitulated to his request for 10 percent royalties, with a warning: "In a strictly businesslike sense, you have obtained what you wanted. But it is only on the condition that your unfriendly correspondence will cease in the future that we have resumed our relations with you. We are, however, convinced that you will stop writing unpleasant letters, now that we have had the opportunity to discuss together the matter in a thorough and precise way, and to lay down the conditions according to your wishes."[37]

Within weeks he was back in the classroom at Columbia. During his absence, McWhood had taught one of his courses in advanced harmony, but the others that he typically taught had been suspended for the year. A student, Mary Crocker, reported that "Prof. MacWhood himself could only 'properly introduce' us to 'Music' on her good behavior, chaperoned by Rule and Precedent. So the following fall it was decided advisable for us to repeat advanced harmony with Prof. MacDowell (just returned from Europe) and then take Practical Composition, both of which studies came under the head of 'Course 7' (1903–1904)."[38] As a consequence, MacDowell had a heavy load that included some courses arranged differently than in the past. He and Marian lived in the Westminster Hotel, an older hotel on Sixteenth Street, a great distance from campus, which added time to his commute.

The transition back to the classroom after sabbatical is challenging for any professor; after his exhausting concert tour and the dismal summer in Switzerland,

35. Letter, EAM to APS, 6 July 1903, Irving and Margery Lowens Collection.

36. Letter, EAM to B&H, 17 September 1903, Sächsisches Staatsarchiv, Leipzig, Verlag Breitkopf & Härtel Nr. 2633.

37. Letter, B&H to EAM, 21 September 1903, EMMC box 30/18; trans. M. M. Lowens, "The New York Years," 293.

38. Letter, Mary Crocker to MM, EMMC, box 43/34.

MacDowell found it especially trying. He confided to Strong on 31 October: "I haven't a joke left in me. I get more sinister minded every day. Am in a continuous state of grinding my teeth and controlling my profane vocabulary."[39] Hamlin Garland was shocked at his friend's "strangely sad, almost vacant, expression" when he saw him at a dinner in late November: "He was like a man utterly tired out and in danger of collapse....To him I said, 'You are overworking.' He admitted this but added, 'I see no help for it. I must teach to earn a living.'"[40] At the root of his despondency was the feeling that his work at Columbia had been a failure. He wrote to Strong in November about his teaching, "I often feel like a dog standing on his hind legs—I do it—but not gracefully."[41]

Throughout his career, MacDowell had been tortured by self-doubt. Marian saw this most poignantly when he performed. She recalled that after the first performance of the *Sonata Eroica* in Boston, she and her friends felt that he had played beautifully, but that when she found him backstage he was "white, and as if he were guilty of some crime." After much discussion he admitted that three movements had gone well but he "had been a d—fool in one." She tellingly summed up the incident with the words, "I grew to be very used to this as the years went on, for he could not help emphasizing to himself what he did badly, and ignoring the good."[42] This habit of ruminating over imperfections must have made the previous winter's concert tour a living hell, as he performed more concerts than ever before, but without his usual mastery. The return to Columbia in fall 1903 reminded him of another area where he felt he had fallen short of his ideals.

During his absence, the music offerings at Columbia had again been subjected to a change of administrative structure. President Butler was pursuing a reorganization of the university into divisions of related departments, including one that would combine architecture, comparative literature, fine arts, and music. But rather than create a new Fine Arts Department in the university as MacDowell had proposed, his intention was to incorporate the fine arts offerings of Teachers College into the university structure. The music offerings at Teachers College had also been expanded significantly, with three faculty and nearly as many courses as in MacDowell's department. Strangely, the *Fine Arts Announcement, 1903–04* listed the music and art courses from Teachers College alongside those of the university.[43]

39. Letter, EAM to TS, 31 October 1903, EMMC box 29/36.

40. Hamlin Garland, *Companions on the Trail: A Literary Chronicle* (New York: Macmillan, 1931), 213; quoted in M. M. Lowens, "The New York Years," 303.

41. Letter, EAM to TS, 20 November 1903, EMMC, box 31/33.

42. The entire incident is recounted in Gilman, *Edward MacDowell: A Study,* 91–92.

43. *The Fine Arts Announcement, 1903–04,* 17–22; cited in M. M. Lowens, "The New York Years," 301–2.

To MacDowell, this was an affront of the first order, which in his mind equated the department he had worked so hard to build with courses for kindergarten teachers.

Shortly after the new year, MacDowell learned that his request for a promotion for McWhood and a budget increase for the music department had been denied. He drafted two letters to Butler expressing his disappointment,[44] and he went to see the one man at the university whom he considered a true ally: John Burgess, who had arranged for his hiring and was now a dean. He shared his discouragement with Burgess, who had already noticed that upon returning from sabbatical he seemed "more restless and depressed than ever." He told Burgess that he considered his work at Columbia a great failure, to which his friend replied, "I told him that nobody else thought so and that his feeling was only an apprehension of his sensitive nature." Burgess urged him not to resign, but to ask for a change of duties if he was too discouraged to continue his teaching. When MacDowell left his home that Sunday afternoon in January, Burgess had the impression that the music professor would follow his advice.[45]

We do not know precisely how MacDowell arrived at his decision, but by now we know very well how his mind worked in such situations. If he felt that a small part of his accomplishment had fallen short, he could not help ignoring all the positives and focusing on that one negative. Even minor shortcomings were amplified as he ruminated over them incessantly. For him it was very difficult to distinguish petty inconveniences from serious problems, a trait that Marian enabled by giving him his way in all the small things of their life together. His strong principles kept him from compromising, but he lacked the perspective to know which principles were worth fighting for. When he did take a stand, his shyness made it difficult for him to talk face-to-face with those who disagreed, preferring instead to state his case in a letter. Most importantly, when the days were short and the meager sunlight was only a thin shaft through the icy air, Edward could not wait patiently for gradual change. Time and again, he had found it preferable to lash out in desperation to make major changes. On 18 January 1904, MacDowell wrote to President Butler:

My dear Sir:—

I beg to tender my resignation as head of the Department of Music at Columbia, to take effect at the end of the College year. I wish to assure you that the matter of Mr. MacWhood's advancement has absolutely no connection with my resignation. If I can in

44. Bound letterbook, MacDowell Collection box 1, Butler Rare Book and Manuscript Library, Columbia University.

45. John W. Burgess, *Reminiscences of an American Scholar* (New York: Columbia University Press, 1934), 286–87.

any way be of service in the matter of arrangements for the coming year, I beg you will call upon me.

Respectfully yours,

Edward MacDowell[46]

Butler later told the trustees that this letter came as a complete surprise, and it gave no hint as to the reasons behind it. Not knowing MacDowell well, he did not know how seriously to take the resignation letter. As a seasoned administrator, he no doubt recognized that it could have been a ploy to negotiate for something that MacDowell wanted. He scheduled a meeting for 21 January, at which time he learned that MacDowell found it difficult to divide his time between composition and university teaching, and that he wished to devote more time to the pursuit on which his future reputation would rest. A week later they met again, and Butler presented the possibility that MacDowell could remain at Columbia in a "research professorship, but freed from the duties which he found onerous, another professor being appointed to carry the burden of teaching in the department."[47] He also invited MacDowell to write up his suggestions for improvement of the music instruction at Columbia University.

As had happened a number of times in recent years, MacDowell's recollections of these conversations differed from Butler's. The president told the board that MacDowell left his office promising to think it over, and for that reason he did not present the resignation to the trustees at their meeting on 1 February. MacDowell later claimed, "The research professorship offered me by the president consisted of my lending to Columbia the use of my name, with no duties, and no salary. I immediately refused it as I was unwilling to associate my name with a policy I could not approve of."[48] We cannot know for sure what transpired when the reticent MacDowell and the politically astute Butler met behind closed doors, but within days their differences became public.

On 3 February, a delegation of three students came to see MacDowell, having heard a rumor that he intended to resign his position. He confirmed that he had submitted his resignation and offered to send them a copy of his report on music at Columbia when it was completed, but he forbade them to communicate anything to the press except the fact of his resignation. Again, we cannot be entirely sure what he said when goaded by the students, but he evidently trusted them to keep their mouths shut. Recognizing a scoop of major importance, the students

46. Minutes of the Board of Trustees, 110.

47. Ibid., 108.

48. Quoted in "The Case of Prof. MacDowell," *Evening Post*, 10 February 1904, 9.

immediately spilled their story to a reporter for the *Evening Post*. The reporter called MacDowell, who confirmed that he had resigned, and made the unfortunate mistake of confiding that he would soon be submitting a report to the trustees criticizing the handling of music and the other arts at Columbia. The reporter's subsequent call to Butler received a "no comment."

That evening's edition of the *Post* trumpeted "MacDowell to Resign" from the top of page 1. The story quoted MacDowell extensively, blaming his resignation on the university's failure to adopt his plan for the fine arts. He was also quoted as decrying the lack of knowledge of the fine arts among Columbia's students. He was further quoted as saying that after the recent resignation of Professor Woodberry of the comparative literature department, whom he considered "the only spark of ideality in the university," he could not remain there any longer. The article ended, "Professor MacDowell's declarations were laid before President Butler this afternoon by a reporter for the *Evening Post*. The President declared that he did not consider them important, and had nothing to say."[49] The next day the story spun out of control, as the *Times, Sun, World, Herald,* and *Tribune* each printed increasingly vivid versions of the story. The *World* quoted him as calling the Department of Fine Arts "inefficient and practically useless," and college graduates as "the merest barbarians."[50] Less than twenty-four hours after his chance encounter with the three students, New York's newspapers had quoted him as insulting the university, the president, the entire faculty, and the entire student body.

A horrified MacDowell wrote to Butler on 4 February, "I was shocked to read the newspaper accounts of my resignation. The reported interviews are very incorrect and were unauthorized by me." He explained how the students had approached him for a statement and how he had forbidden them to communicate anything to the press except the fact of his resignation. He also denied any knowledge of Woodberry's resignation.[51] The next day Butler wrote a cordial letter to MacDowell offering his condolences that he and the university "have been made to suffer from the 'yellow' journalism which, unfortunately, rules in this city." He noted that the *Globe* had printed MacDowell's denial of the *Post* interview and suggested that he send a similar denial to the other papers that had expanded on the *Post* interview but had not printed the retraction. He closed his letter by saying, "I look

49. "MacDowell to Resign: Head of Music Department at Columbia," *Evening Post*, 3 February 1904, 1.

50. "College Men Boors, says Professor," *World*, 4 February 1904.

51. Letter, EAM to Nicholas Murray Butler, 4 February 1904, reprinted in Minutes of the Board of Trustees, 110–11.

forward with pleasure to the receipt of your suggestions as to the place of music in a university, for I am very sure that they will be both important and helpful."[52]

At this point MacDowell could have salvaged the situation by publishing a retraction, but he did not do so. When a retraction was not forthcoming, Butler wrote to the *New York Times* himself on 8 February, knowing that this paper would be happy to print a criticism of the rival *Post*. He began his letter,

> It is not my habit to notice inaccurate or unjust statements concerning Columbia University or its work which may from time to time find their way into print, but the widely circulated falsehoods concerning the contemplated resignation of Professor MacDowell of the department of music require that an exception be made. This exception is demanded by the fact that the statements which have been printed are in effect a wholly false and unjustifiable attack upon Columbia University, its influence, and its teaching staff. Every professor in the university feels outraged by them.[53]

Butler went on to defend his decision not to comment on the initial *Post* article, criticizing the unfair journalistic tactics of the reporter who called him. He quoted MacDowell's letter of 4 February in full to show that the original story had been false, and he issued a stern reprimand to the paper, stating that by printing these falsehoods "that paper sinned against the light and became sponsor for an attack upon Columbia University which on the following morning was copied by the newspapers in this and other cities." But the president was not content simply to denounce yellow journalism. He continued, "While it is not possible or desirable to administer Columbia University in or through the newspapers, it now seems proper that a brief statement of the actual facts in this case should be made." He proceeded to state that MacDowell's resignation had come with no warning, that he had given his desire to compose as his only reason for resigning, and that he had not mentioned any plan for the fine arts since the one that had resulted in the Division of Fine Arts two years earlier. He went on to state that only the lack of resources had prevented the university from giving the arts the attention they deserved.

Butler was attempting to justify his own actions and to rescue the university from charges that it had treated MacDowell unfairly. In the words of the committee convened by the trustees to investigate the incident later that spring, "If [MacDowell's] communications to the press had stopped here, your Committee would not have thought it necessary to pay further attention to the incident, and would have considered Professor MacDowell guilty of nothing worse than very

52. Letter, Nicholas Murray Butler to EAM, 5 February 1904, EMMC box 30/21.

53. "Columbia and the Department of Music: Statement by President Butler," *NYT*, 8 February 1904, p. 8.

great imprudence."[54] But MacDowell, like Butler, was not willing to leave an inaccuracy uncorrected. He objected to the statement that his resignation was occasioned only by his desire to compose more, an assertion that he felt bound to correct. The next day, when MacDowell sent his report with recommendations for music at Columbia to the trustees, he also took the liberty of sending a copy to the *Evening Post*, as he had promised he would. Whether intentionally or inadvertently, the 10 February issue of the *Post* printed his cover letter from 9 February along with the undated report, giving the impression that it had been in the hands of the trustees for some time when in fact they had not yet seen it. In the report, MacDowell outlined his unsuccessful efforts to create a combined Department of Fine Arts, he bemoaned the lack of undergraduate preparation in the arts, and he criticized the coupling of his program with that of Teachers College, stating that "the Division of Fine Arts thus acquires somewhat the nature of a co-educational department store, and tends towards materialism rather than idealism."[55]

MacDowell's views were widely reported in the press, touching off a lively debate over the aims and limitations of higher education. President Jacob Gould Schurman of Cornell University used this speech at his university's annual alumni dinner on 11 February to take issue with MacDowell's statements. He questioned the composer's definitions of idealism and materialism, arguing that MacDowell was actually describing a contrast between emotion and intellectualism. He further stated that the university was no place for training in the arts: "No university can train poets, musicians, painters, or other artists, in the absence of natural endowments, and these are much rarer than the aptitude for intellectual pursuits. But given the requisite artistic capacity, it is to be developed and trained by doing rather than by knowing, so that the studio or conservatory, and not the university classroom or laboratory, seems the proper place for its cultivation. The college and the university cannot create composers like Dr. MacDowell or sculptors like Mr. St. Gaudens."[56] On 14 February an editorial in the *New York Times* supported Schurman's views, stating in essence that MacDowell was overqualified for the position at Columbia, which needed instead "a man of keen sensibility and wide cultivation, with the outfit, as to music, of a gifted amateur and dilettante."[57] An article in the *Literary Digest* on 20 February decried the "Transit of Idealism" from Columbia University, equating MacDowell's resignation

54. Minutes of the Board of Trustees, 109.

55. *Evening Post*, 10 February 1904.

56. "Schurman on MacDowell: Disagrees with Professor's Views on Art in Colleges—New Coach for Cornell Football Team," *NYT*, 12 February 1904, 3.

57. "Music in Colleges," *NYT*, 14 February 1904, 6.

with those of two other professors: William R. Ware of the School of Architecture and George E. Woodberry of the Division of Comparative Literature.[58]

But in the eyes of the university administration, MacDowell's greatest transgression was contradicting the university president. By publicly refuting Butler's version of the story of his resignation, MacDowell sealed his fate. The secretary of the Board of Trustees wrote to him on 29 February to confirm the genuineness of the published letter and report of 10 February, which MacDowell did on 2 March, stating in part, "My reason for sending a copy of this paper to the *Evening Post* was to correct President Butler's published statement of the day before, in which he gives my personal work as being the sole reason for my resignation from Columbia University." At their meeting on 7 March, the trustees accepted his resignation and added the following:

> RESOLVED that the Trustees, in accepting Professor MacDowell's resignation to take effect on the date named by him, express their serious disapprobation of his action, in sending to the newspaper a letter enclosing for publication a copy of a report addressed by him to the Trustees, and simultaneously forwarded by him to the President, for submission to the Board. The report in question was consequently published on February 10, 1904, not only without the consent of the Trustees, but before they had any opportunity to peruse it. The Trustees regard Professor MacDowell's act in making public an official report, as an offence against propriety, a discourtesy to the Board, and a breach of that confidence which the Board always seeks to repose in every officer of the University.[59]

The incident shows two proud men who each insisted on stating his version of the story to the public. MacDowell had misjudged the workings of university politics by thinking that he could challenge the word of the president.

The trustees, meanwhile, had moved on. A press release of the following day noted the acceptance of MacDowell's resignation with no mention of his censure. It announced the appointment of Cornelius Rübner, described as "one of the greatest living musicians and teachers of music, as a pianist he is perhaps only excelled by Paderewski." The press release went on to note that McWhood had been promoted from tutor to adjunct professor (as MacDowell had unsuccessfully proposed) and to state that "he has borne the burden of the teaching work," implying that he had done more in previous years than MacDowell. The statement ended with the words: "It is felt by the University authorities that with the coming of Mr. Rübner and the advancement of Mr. McWhood, the Department of Music will be so greatly strengthened as

58. "A 'Transit of Idealism' at Columbia University," *Literary Digest* 28/8 (20 February 1904): 253–54.

59. Minutes of the Board of Trustees, 114–15.

to make a much stronger appeal than heretofore both to the students of the University and to the city of New York as a whole."[60]

MacDowell was again faced with a public inaccuracy. According to Marian, he asked McWhood to issue a correction, but his longtime associate refused on the grounds that it would hurt him with the president. He wrote to each trustee individually to ask for a retraction of the statement that McWhood had "borne the burden of the teaching work," but to no avail. Finally he himself wrote to the *Evening Post* on 23 April refuting the notion that McWhood had done the majority of the teaching. By this time it was old news and must have seemed peevish to those who noticed it at all.[61]

In just a few months, MacDowell's place in the world had been transformed. From his position as America's most famous composer and most respected university music professor, he had fallen disgracefully. He felt that he had been stabbed in the back by Butler, by the Board of Trustees, and by McWhood. The unkindest cut of all came from Dean John Burgess, who wrote on 8 April:

> My dear Prof MacDowell:
>
> The time has arrived when I deem it due to Pres Butler to inform you that I am responsible for his statements in regard to Prof Rübner, and that any further attacks which it may please anybody to make upon those statements should be aimed at me instead of at him. You are at liberty to make this fact known as widely as you may desire.[62]

Burgess was the man who had first been approached by MacDowell's mother about her son. He had arranged for President Low to hear MacDowell's triumphant 1896 concert in New York, and to seal the appointment he had obtained a letter from Paderewski stating that MacDowell was the best man for the job. He recalled in his memoirs that when MacDowell resigned, he was asked for his opinion on a successor. He immediately recommended Rübner, a Danish pianist who served as court pianist to the grand duke of Baden. Burgess had heard him play in a hotel salon in the resort of Wilhelmshöhe, near Kassel, the previous summer, and though he was not musical himself, he was charmed by the man's personality and trusted the opinion of the American women who were present in the hotel. When he cabled Rübner about the Columbia opening, the reply was "Wegen Unkenntniss der Sprache unmöglich" [impossible because I don't know the language], to which

60. Unidentified newspaper article quoted in M. M. Lowens, "The New York Years," 312.

61. More than twenty years later, the misunderstanding still rankled. McWhood sought to clarify his position in an address before the MTNA. After his speech in December 1923, Marian strongly urged McWhood in a letter of 20 January 1924 not to publish his version, but to no avail: Leonard B. McWhood, "Edward MacDowell at Columbia University," *Papers and Proceedings of the Music Teachers' National Association*, 18th series (1924): 71–77.

62. Letter, John Burgess to EAM, 8 April 1904, MacDowell Collection, Library of Congress Manuscript Division, box 6.

Burgess replied, "We are not asking you to teach philology, but music." Rübner was brought over for an interview at the expense of one of Burgess's wealthy friends and hired to begin in fall 1904. Burgess felt it was a change for the better: "His geniality and generosity were a great contrast to his predecessor's reticence and too self-centered nature, and he soon won his way into the affection of his colleagues and pupils."[63]

For MacDowell it was a slap in the face not only to him personally but to American music. He wrote to Oscar Sonneck, "There are many talented men here who are a thousand times more fitted for the position. The situation for American Art is extremely discouraging."[64] Eight years after their quest to find America's greatest musical genius to lead their music department, Columbia University had replaced him with an obscure European who did not speak English. What is more, they believed they had made an improvement. During the next fifty years, American institutions would prove time and again that German professors, conductors, and instrumentalists were more respected than native sons. MacDowell saw the future but no longer had the power to change it.

63. Burgess, *Reminiscences*, 288–89.
64. Letter, EAM to O. G. Sonneck, 31 March 1904, EMMC box 30.

CHAPTER NINETEEN

A Living Death

THE REMAINDER OF THE 1903/1904 ACADEMIC YEAR PASSED IN A PERFUNCTORY manner, as MacDowell met his classes but avoided contact with McWhood and the university administration. His futile efforts to secure a retraction of the statement regarding McWhood's role in the department took much of his attention, as he drafted and redrafted statements for the press and the trustees.[1] Marian later recalled that he did not sleep for weeks after the scandal, as he ruminated over the events without resolution. During the last week of classes in May, a group of thirty-six students presented him with a silver loving cup crafted by Tiffany & Co. and inscribed, "To Prof. E. A. MacDowell with the high esteem and affection of his classes at Columbia University, May 14, 1904."[2]

On 14 June he and Marian left for Peterborough, where they stayed through November. In letters written that summer, MacDowell repeatedly refused new commitments on the grounds that he was overworked, but there is little evidence of any creative work from this time. A minor revision of the "Praeludium" of the *Erste moderne Suite*, op. 10, seems to have been his sole musical accomplishment of the summer. A detailed letter of 7 October to "Messrs Manning Maxwell & Moore, Machinists" with questions about assembly and maintenance of a circular saw he had purchased shows that his mind was actively engaged in problem solving, but not of a musical

1. A notebook with numerous drafts is found in the Special Collections of the University of New Hampshire–Durham; additional drafts are in the Butler Rare Book and Manuscript Library, Columbia University.

2. The cup is described in [Richard S. Angell], *Catalogue of an Exhibition Illustrating the Life and Work of Edward MacDowell, 1861–1908* (New York, Columbia University Library, 1938), 18, and is in the Butler Rare Book and Manuscript Library, Columbia University.

nature.[3] When the weather finally turned cold they returned to New York and took up residence at 911 Seventh Avenue, two blocks south of Central Park.

Without Edward's university salary, the MacDowells relied on his royalties and piano teaching for their support. His fee was $6.00 per half-hour lesson, with an additional charge of $15.00 for a season's worth of biweekly artist's classes on Saturday mornings. He quickly assembled a group of students made up of those who had studied with him previously and some new students. Though MacDowell no longer held an official position, he was in great demand, as the biweekly class of regular students was often supplemented by artists from Boston or Washington. Like Liszt before him, MacDowell avoided technical issues in these master classes, concentrating instead on larger questions of style and interpretation.

MacDowell's reputation as one of America's great artists was confirmed by his election as a founding member of the American Academy of Arts and Letters, an offshoot of the National Institute of Arts and Letters (NIAL). This latter group of 150 distinguished leaders in art, music, and literature had been established in 1898 with MacDowell as one of its members. By early 1904, the members wished to reorganize, and MacDowell was appointed to a committee that proposed creating an elite academy of thirty members within the larger body of the NIAL, which would be expanded to 250 members. On 2 December 1904, the members of the Institute selected the first seven members of the elite group by secret ballot: authors Samuel L. Clemens, John Hay, William Dean Howells, and Edmund Clarence Stedman; painter John LaFarge; sculptor Augustus Saint-Gaudens, and MacDowell. Each of these men represented the highest level of accomplishment in his field, and as the only musician in the group, Edward received the validation of his peers in the other arts.[4] Later that winter, he was instrumental in supporting Charles Follen McKim's proposal for a music prize at the American Academy in Rome, serving on the Board of Trustees of this organization.

MacDowell's state of mind during the crucial winter of 1904/5 is described by several eyewitness accounts, but none is so detailed as the diary of John Pierce Langs (1883–1967). A native of Niagara Falls, New York, Langs had studied piano since the age of five and had spent a year in Berlin. He studied piano and composition with MacDowell at Columbia and then secured a position at the University of Colorado at Boulder in 1902. In the fall of 1904 he returned to New York in order to renew his studies with MacDowell. On 21 November he wrote in his diary: "I walked down to McDowell's after my late breakfast, and made definite arrangements for

---

3. Draft letter, EAM to Messrs Manning Maxwell & Moore, 7 October 1904, EMMC box 33.
4. For a detailed discussion of the selection process, see Margery M. Lowens, "The New York Years of Edward MacDowell" (PhD diss., University of Michigan, 1971), 318–23.

piano lessons. He won't take composition-pupils, but he'll let me show my things to him occasionally, in an informal way."[5] For the next six months, each week contains one or more diary entries mentioning his lessons with MacDowell.

Langs was gratified by his teacher's encouragement, and he felt that he received more praise than during his previous studies. Often their lessons were unconventional, as on 30 November, when he noted, "instead of a formal lesson, we had a long talk on divers subjects." True to his promise, MacDowell occasionally looked at his student's compositions: "December 18 Sunday. At ten this morning I went down to MacDowell's, and spent nearly two hours with him showing him my songs. He wasn't wildly enthusiastic over them, but he seemed to think some of them possible if not probable, and moreover he gave me some good advice both about composing and publishing. He is very kind indeed—as I've always known him to be." After his weekly private lesson on 21 December, he noted that MacDowell's generosity with his time caused the schedule to back up and keep students waiting, an occurrence he called "invariable." On Christmas Eve, Langs noted: "The class is much more fun than it used to be: the new maidens are awfully agreeable." On 28 December, Marian hosted the class members and friends for tea in their apartment.

With the beginning of the new year, MacDowell was unusually complimentary to his student, even when Langs was unprepared for his lessons. Before long, though, he began to notice a change in his teacher's demeanor:

15 February: I walked down to MacDowell's and played my Mendelssohn Prelude and Fugue—not much to his satisfaction; he was in a reminiscent mood, however, and I heard stories of Saint Saëns, Heimann, Raff, and Nicolaus Rubinstein.

22 February: I walked down to MacDowell's this cold, raw day, and played rather poorly, but enjoyed even more than the usual amount of talk—which really begins to attain tremendous proportions.

8 March: I had a rather unsatisfactory lesson, inasmuch as I didn't manage to play more than the first movement of my Fantasy although I very much desired help on the others. Mac was in a very talkative mood and it was quite impossible to head him off politely. (At the same time I'm of course proud to be the recipient of his confidences.) ...I shouldn't be surprised if MacDowell's occasional indifference to the business of my lesson-hour were due to the fact that after a forenoon of teaching he's tired and disposed sub-consciously to follow the pleasure of gossiping [rather] than the duty of instruction. He quite forgets himself in his colloquys.

---

5. John Pierce Langs diary, uncatalogued collection, Library of Congress Music Division.

16 March: Again we talked much, this time, however, about my affairs, rather than his; he has promised to consider my prospects for next year and to give me advice.

22 March: I walked down to Mr. MacDowell's between eleven and twelve, and had for lesson another of our interminable talks on all possible subjects.

The 8 March entry goes on to say that the subject of much of the conversation was his bitterness about the Columbia situation. On that day he expressed himself freely on the shortcomings of Butler, McWhood, and Rübner. During a visit of his old friend T. P. Currier from Boston in mid-April, he was still obsessed with this topic:

> His looks and response to my eager greeting struck a chill to my heart. Pale, and thin, all his old brightness and energetic bearing gone, he seemed like one just up from a serious sickness. With no show of interest he replied feebly and almost inaudibly, "I'm not very well. Where is Mrs. Mac Dowell?" Already he had begun to cling helplessly to her. At dinner he brightened somewhat. Yet he found little to talk about except the one thing that still, after a year, was constantly going around in his mind: his break with Columbia. All its details he rehearsed with painful elaboration, in the manner of one utterly weary of the struggle. No other subject excited any interest on his part.[6]

Marian's sister Nina alluded to verbal problems in a letter of about the same time: "If only that curious trouble with his tongue would improve—this nervousness is a great deal but I don't think it is all. Everything is going well I think. He is made a good deal of and he has one or two splendid pupils....Their finances are in a good state too so that if only rest does E. good everything will be all one could wish."[7] Langs played a recital of MacDowell's works for a group of distinguished guests at the home of Charles McKim on 4 April, receiving high praise from the guests and deep gratitude from the MacDowells. When Langs took his last lesson on 29 April, he was invited to visit them in Peterborough, and they were actively planning a trip to the western United States and to Europe in the fall.

    None of the winter's unusual behavior prepared Langs for the letter he received on 10 August: "I got a letter from Mrs. MacDowell bearing the shocking news that Mr. MacDowell is so ill (with some complicated spinal-nervous trouble) that he has a constant medical attendant and a weekly physician from Boston. Sorrowful enough, and withal a bit mysterious! I still hope it's only a specious [sic] of serious overwork, and much as I believe in Mrs. MacDowell's devotion to her husband I fear she urged him too much last Spring." By this time, Langs had bowed to pressure from his

6. T. P. Currier, "Edward MacDowell as I Knew Him," *MQ* 1/1 (January 1915): 49.

7. Undated letter, Nina Nevins to Anna Nevins, February to April 1905, EMMC.

mother to abandon his musical aspirations, and instead of returning to New York to study music in the fall, he enrolled in law school.

During the summer and fall of 1905, MacDowell continued to decline with no apparent cause. He was not teaching and he was not writing, but nonetheless his condition did not improve. Old friends rallied around Marian, but they were baffled by his inexplicable breakdown and failure to recuperate even in the idyllic setting of his beloved Peterborough. In retrospect, Henry T. Finck could recognize the signs of impending tragedy:

> He began, early in 1905, to show signs of decline. He complained to his wife and to me that he had lost his spontaneity in composing. I complained to my wife that I didn't like to talk to him any more—he seemed "so queer." This queerness was so exaggerated during our next visit to him at Peterboro, N.H. [summer 1905] that we wondered if he was addicted to the use of some drug. But soon the terrible truth dawned on us. He was losing his mind! All efforts to arrest the brain disease were useless, although the leading specialists were consulted. It was not actual insanity, characterized by delusions, melancholy leading to maniacal outbursts, and homicidal or suicidal attacks. These things he was spared. It was simply a gradual, premature decay of the mind. At forty-six he was like a man of ninety-six, a man in his second childhood.[8]

As a precaution, Marian had Edward sign a power of attorney on 22 July, after which she took full control of his affairs.[9] The MacDowells returned to New York in late October and settled at the Westminster Hotel, since the apartment building at 911 Seventh Avenue was being demolished to make way for new construction. This hotel would be their winter home until his death.

Who were the "leading specialists" who were consulted? The primary physician in charge of MacDowell's case was Dr. Loomis L. Danforth, a friend who had sung in the Mendelssohn Glee Club under MacDowell's direction. Though he was undoubtedly sympathetic and discreet, Danforth was not a specialist in neurological disorders. He served on the gynecological staff of the New York Homeopathic Medical College, where he was a colleague of MacDowell's cousin Dr. Charles McDowell. The essential principle of homeopathic medicine is "let like be cured by like." Patients are given diluted solutions of toxins, which are thought to stimulate the body's protective responses to those toxins. Introduced in Germany in the late eighteenth century, homeopathic remedies were not regulated in the United States

8. Henry T. Finck, "Musical Genius and Insanity," *Etude* 33/5 (May 1915): 340; repr. as "MacDowell's Last Days," *Music Student* 7/12 (August 1915): 257.

9. This document was signed on 22 July 1905 and notarized by Carl Hansmann, the attorney who had represented Edward in his suit against Breitkopf & Härtel. It was not recorded in the County of New York until 3 January 1906. EMMC Box 57/12.

until the 1930s. Among the experts Danforth consulted was M. Allen Starr, one of the country's leading neurologists. He examined MacDowell during the summer of 1905, but he evidently was not actively involved in his subsequent treatment.[10]

Edward's illness—whatever it was—ebbed and flowed in fall 1905. When Hamlin Garland came to visit for the first time on 7 November, he was surprised to find his old friend so well: "I was instantly relieved. He greeted me with a cheery word and his familiar shy smile, and began at once to ask after my wife and my little daughter. He was dressed in a beautiful suit of light gray and looked very handsome. I could not share Marian's anxiety. On the contrary I thought her overwrought and needlessly alarmed, but as we chatted I noticed an alarming change in him. He grew tired and the brightness went out of his face."[11] During the next few days he came to realize that Edward's occasional moments of clarity were balanced by lethargy, sadness, and confusion.

Garland finally confirmed MacDowell's condition publicly with a press release that appeared on 28 November 1905. His eloquent description of his friend's condition was reprinted throughout the country:

> In view of the many inquiries concerning Edward MacDowell's health, his friends ask you to permit me to make report of his present condition. Mr. MacDowell is suffering from profound nervous prostration brought on by insomnia and overwork. The crash came suddenly last March [sic] at the close of a very busy winter and his physicians advised immediate return to the country, and above all absolute rest, believing that he would soon be restored to his usual good health. In this they and all his friends have been disappointed. He has grown steadily worse and his medical advisors now take a very serious view of his case. They say that he may possibly recover some part of his physical vigor but that he will never compose again. As one eminent specialist said, "It is a case of an oversensitive, highly wrought brain burning itself away in overwork." Absolutely temperate in all other ways, MacDowell has been too prodigal in labor. As a teacher he gave the best of himself. As a professor of music he delved deep and the very intensity of his genius as a composer has caused him to run his brilliant courses swiftly....His spotless purity of life and the lofty standards which he always upheld have been an inspiration to all who knew him intimately. It is a tragic thing to speak of him as though his active life were done, but so it seems we must now do unless some miraculous and unexpected change takes place.

---

10. His letter of condolence to Marian after Edward's death indicated that he learned of Edward's death through the newspapers rather than firsthand: Letter, M. Allen Starr to MM, MacDowell Collection, Library of Congress Manuscript Division, box 2.

11. Hamlin Garland, *Companions on the Trail: A Literary Chronicle* (New York: Macmillan, 1931), 376–77.

There is this small measure of consolation to those who love him; he is entirely free from mental or physical pain and quite cheerful.[12]

The tragedy of his situation captured the imagination of the public, and the vagueness of the diagnosis—"profound nervous prostration"—led reporters to dig for further information. Naturally, the events surrounding MacDowell's resignation from Columbia appeared alongside announcements of his condition. In an effort to manage the publicity, Marian vigorously denied the rumor that she blamed the Columbia scandal for his breakdown, telling the *Evening Post*, "This is no time for any bitterness over the past."[13] Privately, though, she did not deny her suspicions. She wrote to Strong: "He really has not overworked this past year, but the worries and heart-burnings at Columbia, and the bad accident, seem to have pushed him over the edge,—possibly this might have come anyway."[14] In her opinion, Edward's condition had resulted from his anxiety and disappointment over the Columbia scandal exacerbated by an accident in which he had been struck by a hansom cab on a New York street.

As the news spread, letters of sympathy and offers of help poured in—from Grieg and Strong in Europe, from colleagues and former students now scattered around the country, and from total strangers who admired his music. Seth Low sent Marian a generous check, Schmidt gave her advances on Edward's royalties, and friends made arrangements to visit while there was still a chance Edward would recognize them.

By November 1905, it was clear that Marian and her housekeeper Elizabeth could not care for Edward without additional help. Because of his extreme insomnia, he needed round-the-clock care, prompting Marian to hire a nurse by the name of Anna Baetz, who helped care for him from 14 November until the end of his life. Her "diary," containing reminiscences of her initial time with MacDowell and weekly entries as he neared death, provides valuable clues about the progression of his illness, the treatments, and Marian's state of mind. Even though it is not detailed or extensive, she had a trained nurse's ability to describe the symptoms of her patient's mysterious illness.[15]

---

12. "E. A. MacDowell a Wreck: His Days of Work Over," *New York Tribune*, 28 November 1905, 1.

13. "Edward MacDowell: End of a Great Composer's Career," *New York Evening Post*, 28 November 1905. In a move that must have seemed eerily reminiscent of February 1904, Marian wrote to the *Evening Sun* to correct a report in one of the morning papers that she had connected his collapse with the Columbia scandal: "MacDowell's Breakdown: Composer Doesn't Realize Condition and is Happy," *Evening Sun*, 28 November 1905.

14. Letter, MM to TS, 31 October 1905, EMMC box 51/2.

15. A typed transcript of the diary is found in EMMC box 1.

Nurse Baetz arrived every evening after MacDowell was put to bed. She reported that he did not sleep much that first winter, rising at 3:00 a.m. or earlier. She tried to keep him quiet, talking to him for hours on end to prevent him from getting up and wandering around the house. Marian told her the insomnia had been even worse during the summer of 1905. He also lost muscular control of his legs, and by December 1905 he could no longer walk. At times he became very "cross" [irritable], but he was never physically violent. Though usually sweet-tempered, he occasionally flared up: "He never made a mistake about the people he liked and never confused them with the people he did not like. I once mentioned the name Damrosch; at once he flared up and looked wild, so I knew he did not like him for some reason."[16] They played cards together when he was able, but since he became upset if he lost, she had to rig the game in his favor.

On 30 December 1905, John Pierce Langs returned to New York for a short visit. He wrote in his diary: "Budget of old let me into the MacDowells' rooms, and I talked with Mr. MacDowell for about twenty minutes. Mrs. MacDowell, who was sleeping, I didn't see." Four days later, on 3 January 1906, he paid a more extended visit, which allowed him to speak at length with Edward, Marian, and the servant Budget. The latter told him it was one of Edward's good days, in contrast to the previous day when he had been crying and gnawing his teeth. Of his interactions with his teacher, Langs wrote, "It was not so awful to be with Edward as I had feared it would be. He knew me and talked about my playing, urging me to go concert-touring. All of his talk was rational—only a little childish—but he could not seem to remember names and he recurred again and again to the same topics. He spoke distinctly, slowly and softly, much as last year." In retrospect, Langs wished he had recognized that Edward had been repeating himself and speaking in an unusual manner during his lessons the previous winter.

Marian spoke with Langs about the doctors' prognosis for her husband: "He was so much better than I expected to find him. Yet Mrs. MacDowell says the doctors hold out no hope. They say the brain-tissue has really broken-down. They have been searching for the underlying physical cause that is present in nearly all such cases and have found none. They have had—she says—to lay it all to overwork and worry. Thus his case is from another standpoint remarkable." It is unclear how the doctors knew his case was hopeless; without a surgical examination, they would have no way to confirm that the brain tissue was disintegrating. Likewise their assertion that his illness resulted from overwork and worry is far from conclusive. Their admission that they had not identified the underlying cause is significant and tragic.

16. Baetz diary (EMMC box 1), 5.

Hidden in this diary entry, though, is a clue that is more important than all the speculations of his doctors. In addition to speaking with Marian and Edward, Langs spoke with their servant and used the observational skills that would later serve him in his work as a lawyer:

> He looks fairly fleshy and has some color. Budget said he eats well *but doesn't sleep without dope*, but I couldn't see a sign of morphine except in certain nervous motions of the hands: his eyes were as clear and steady as might be. His legs are very weak: he walks unsteadily. But his arms are marvelously strong, and he delights to flourish them and show his muscular wrists and hands: his grip is very powerful. This looks like spinal trouble. After receiving the whole impression I found it difficult to think that his case was hopeless.

Here, quite possibly, is the underlying cause that the doctors had missed. MacDowell's primary symptom from the beginning of his illness had been insomnia. In fact, he had long suffered from this affliction, and never more so than after the Columbia scandal. He had no pain, and the doctors could not identify a physical ailment of any kind. Therefore the only logical drug for MacDowell to take was sleeping medicine. Morphine, although it could induce sleep, was used for pain, and Langs could see that MacDowell did not have the characteristic constricted pupils of the morphine user. In 1905, the drug of choice for a patient who needed sleep was bromide.

The effectiveness of potassium bromide as a sedative was discovered in 1857, and in short order it and its close relative sodium bromide were widely used to treat insomnia and epilepsy. The compounds formed the basis of both prescription medicines and over-the-counter (OTC) remedies such as Bromo-Seltzer and Dr. Miles's Nervine, both of which were extremely popular in MacDowell's day. Bromides were part of so many drugs that it was possible for patients to inadvertently receive an overdose through the interaction of prescription medicines with over-the-counter remedies. Bromism, or bromide poisoning, has been called a "clinical chameleon" because its symptoms vary so widely from patient to patient.[17] The extensive literature on the illness contains case studies of patients who exhibited such diverse symptoms as "restlessness, irritability, ataxia, confusion, hallucinations, psychosis, weakness, stupor, and coma."[18] Before the banning of bromide compounds from sleeping medicines in 1975, bromism was reported to have been responsible for 5–10 percent of psychiatric hospital admissions. Compounding this problem was that chronic bromide poisoning could be self-perpetuating, as the

17. M.W.P. Carney, "Bromism—A Clinical Chameleon," *Nursing Times* (5 July 1973): 859–60.
18. Delia A. Dempsey, "Bromides," *Poisoning & Drug Overdose*, Kent R. Olson, ed., 5th ed. (New York: Lange Medical Books/McGraw-Hill, 2007), 140.

drug itself exacerbated the insomnia and irritability, causing patients to take increasingly large doses in a misguided attempt to address the symptoms.[19]

Since the late 1880s, MacDowell had come into contact with another source of bromides. Both silver bromide and potassium bromide were essential ingredients in photography at this time. MacDowell used plates coated with silver bromide in his camera. When exposed to light, the compound changed color, thus creating the image on the plate. The development process consisted of applying chemicals to the plate to fix the image and remove the extra silver bromide. One popular technique among photographers was to add potassium bromide to the developing solution in order to achieve sharper images and better contrast. In fall 1892, MacDowell had sent a question to the "Queries and Answers" column of the *Photographic Times* for advice on a problem he was having with reversal of images on his plates. The editors responded with advice on how to solve the problem, stating that it occurred most commonly "when larger quantities of a bromide are added to the developer."[20]

It is very possible, then, that MacDowell had suffered from chronic bromism for years. His initial exposure to low levels of bromide in his home darkroom (described as a seven-foot closet) was probably compounded when he discovered OTC sleeping medicine with bromides. After he collapsed, his well-meaning doctors likely prescribed additional sleeping medicine to combat the only obvious symptom of his puzzling disease. The net result was that they slowly poisoned him to death.

In February 1906 he developed an infection and ran a fever over 103°; the following month he improved noticeably, playing piano and walking as he had not done all winter. In April his improvement was announced in the press, holding out hope for a complete recovery.[21] Because bromides can be eliminated by the body in a matter of weeks, it is not uncommon for bromism to wax and wane depending on the blood levels at any given time. Edward's brief recovery was a false hope,

19. Among the extensive literature on bromism, these articles provide a good introduction: Peter C. Whybrow and John A. Ewing, "Self-Perpetuation of Bromide Poisoning," *British Medical Journal* (8 October 1966): 886–87; John E. Morgan and Edgar N. Weaver, "Chronic Bromism Simulating Neurological Diseases," *Virginia Medical Monthly* 96 (May 1969): 262–64; R. H. Gerner, "Bromism from over-the-counter medications," *The American Journal of Psychiatry* 135/11 (November 1978): 1428; Beatrice Alexandra Golomb, "Bromism," Chapter 10 in *A Review of the Scientific Literature as it Pertains to Gulf War Illnesses* (Rand, 1999), http://www.gulflink.osd.mil/library/randrep/pb_paper/mr1018.2.chap10.html, accessed 28 January 2012.

20. MacDowell told Marian in a letter to Philadelphia about this response, which appeared in "Queries and Answers," *Photographic Times* 22/581 (4 November 1892): 568.

21. "Edward Mac Dowell Greatly Improved: Eminent Composer Rallies in an Astonishing Manner and May Recover," *Musical America* 3/22 (14 April 1906): 1.

though, as he soon had a relapse. The MacDowells left for Peterborough on 21 May, stopping in Boston for two nights to see Schmidt and arriving at Hillcrest on 23 May. That summer he was happy and loved to spend his days outside. He improved significantly in August and September, and he was able to recognize his parents when they came for a visit. Marian shared her feelings with Strong on 31 August:

> Were he unhappy I would try to hope the time would be short for him, but he [is] far from that most of the time, and now that I have grown to endure calmly the sight of such a terrible change I can take comfort in having him as he is. It is not Edward, it is merely a beautiful exquisite creature, but not one of the revolting characteristics we are in the habit of associating with people in his condition. Very irritable at moments when made to do almost anything requiring effort, but with me always gentle and lovely with moments of keen realization of his connection with me, but never thank God, of his condition.[22]

Often Nurse Baetz was charged with making him do the things he did not want to do. The servant James reported to her that MacDowell said, "don't take me back to that old lady, she gives me medicine that I don't like and tells me that Dr. Danforth wants me to take it, but I don't believe it."[23] She did get to see his gentle side during his long sleepless nights, when he told her about the cabin he had built and recounted incidents from their previous visits to Peterborough and from his years in Germany. MacDowell's condition took an alarming turn as the days grew short: "The patient was very noisy the fall of 1906. Mrs. MacDowell hardly knew what we would do with him in New York, as he made such a loud noise when being undressed or put to bed; She wrote to the Westminster, and they put up an extra door which made a little private hall to deaden the sound."[24] Reluctantly, they returned to New York on 29 November.

While Marian struggled to cope with her private tragedy, the country's music lovers were curious for news of the famous composer's condition. Both Henry Finck and James G. Huneker, eminent critics who were also friends, published articles in 1906 that gave glimpses into the composer's private life. Finck's long article for the *Outlook* gave an overview of his career with many comments from Marian. The author addressed his illness only in passing, but he clearly blamed much of his subsequent trouble on the stress of working at Columbia. He recalled MacDowell's tendency to headaches and insomnia, noting that at the time of his resignation, "there was some acrimonious discussion, which aggravated MacDowell's insomnia and hastened his breakdown. But the germs of his mental disease were busy long

22. Letter, MM to TS, 31 August 1906, EMMC box 51/2.
23. Baetz diary, 13.
24. Ibid., 9.

before that. More than a decade previously he would say and do strange things when in the throes of composition....MacDowell was intemperate in one thing only—his passion for work."[25]

Huneker took a very different approach in his 24 June article for the *New York Herald*. He described his visit to the composer in heart-wrenching detail, painting a poignant picture of the composer's condition:

> Despite occasional days brightened by a flitting hope, the passing of Edward MacDowell has begun. He is no longer an earth-dweller. His body is here, but his brain is elsewhere. Not mad, not melancholy, not sunken in the stupor of indifference, his mind is translated to a region where serenity, even happiness, dwells....Never a dissipated man, without a touch of the improvidence we ascribe to genius, a practical moralist—rare in any social condition—moderate in his tastes, though not a Puritan, he nevertheless has been mowed down by the ruthless reaper of souls as if his were negligible clay. But he was reckless of the most precious part of him, his brain. He killed that organ by overwork....He burned away the delicate neurons of the cortical cells, and to-day he can't even say "pianoforte" without a trial. He suffers from aphasia and locomotor ataxia has begun to manifest itself.[26] It would be tragedy in the household of any man; it is doubly so in the case of Edward MacDowell....With his mental disintegration sunny youth has returned to the composer. In snowy white, he looks not more than twenty-five years old, until you note the grey in his thick, rebellious locks. There is still gold in his moustache and his eyes are luminously blue. His expression suggests a spirit purged of all grossness waiting for the summons. He smiles, but not as a madman; he talks hesitatingly, but never babbles....His wife, of whose devotion, almost poignant in its earnestness, it would be too sad to dwell upon, is his faithful interpreter.[27]

He sent a clipping of the article to Marian with the words: "I shant apologize for the crudities of the enclosed article. If it wounds by the frankness as regards Edward's condition please remember that here in New York, I have been forced to listen to the shameful assertion that the poor dear old boy was 'shamming.' I hate to write this; but it's the truth; such is human malignity."[28]

25. Henry T. Finck, "Edward MacDowell: Musician and Composer," *Outlook* 84 (22 December 1906): 987.

26. Aphasia is the inability to speak clearly. Locomotor ataxia is a degeneration of the spinal column resulting in an unsteady, stamping gait. Huneker is hinting at the possibility that MacDowell is suffering from syphilis.

27. James G. Huneker, "The Passing of Edward MacDowell," *New York Herald*, 24 June 1906, magazine sec., 2; repr. in James G. Huneker, *Unicorns* (New York: Charles Scribner's Sons, 1924): 6–17.

28. Letter, James G. Huneker to MM, 25 June 1906, EMMC box 45/51.

Huneker compared MacDowell's illness to those of Schumann, Donizetti, Smetana, Hugo Wolf, and most notably Nietzsche, all of whom were known or reputed to have died of syphilis. The critic was not alone in seeking a parallel for MacDowell's curious decline. An anonymous article in the September issue of the *Metronome* compared his condition to that of Schumann, drawing additional parallels between the wives of these two musicians. A month later, W. Francis Gates wrote of the parallel between MacDowell and Robert Franz, calling attention to the quality of their songs and the belated admiration each composer earned after he became ill.[29]

The poignancy of these reports of the debilitated composer and his brave wife inspired numerous offers of support. As mentioned earlier, Seth Low sent a generous check combining his own donation with those of wealthy friends. According to Finck, who administered the donation, it amounted to more than $10,000.[30] In October 1906, Marian learned that the Carnegie Foundation for the Advancement of Teaching had voted to award Edward a pension of $1,500 per year, equivalent to that reserved for professors who had taught for twenty-five years.[31] The most generous support, however, came from the Mendelssohn Glee Club. Members of MacDowell's old chorus launched a fund-raising campaign in spring 1906 under the name of "The MacDowell Fund." In addition to nationwide press coverage, the group made personal contacts with more than four thousand persons in an effort to establish an endowment that would support the composer and his wife in the event of a long illness. Thanks to savvy publicity, the fund eventually raised nearly $40,000 on behalf of Edward and Marian.[32] Living in a hotel with two nurses and a manservant to do the heavy lifting required a lot of money, but the donations meant that Marian was in no immediate danger of poverty.

The most difficult aspect of Edward's illness was the uncertainty. The doctors could not find a cause, and they held out no hope for recovery, but they had no way of knowing how long he could live. In January 1907 he became weaker, and Dr. Danforth told Marian it was heart failure. That winter Nurse Baetz recorded good days and bad, but in general he slept better and was very quiet. He became

29. "The Fate of Robert Schumann and Edward McDowell [*sic*]," *Metronome* 22/9 (September 1906): 15; W. Francis Gates, "Robert Franz and Edward MacDowell–A Parallel," *Musical Review* 9/6 (October 1906): 28–29.

30. Letter, Henry T. Finck to MM, 1 April 1908, EMMC box 44/8. Further details of Finck's role in the fund-raising process may be found in Henry T. Finck, *My Adventures in the Golden Age of Music* (New York: Funk & Wagnalls, 1926), 398–99.

31. Letter, Henry S. Pritchett to MM, EMMC.

32. M. M. Lowens, "The New York Years," 350–53, gives a detailed account of the Mendelssohn Glee Club's efforts.

increasingly childlike, taking pleasure in reading the same books over and over again, staring out the window, and listening to a pocket watch that he had owned since childhood. When he was a boy, someone told him that the ticking watch was saying, "Ed-die, Ed-die," and this sound reassured him as his mind slipped away.

On 3 May 1907 they again traveled by train to Peterborough for the summer. The strain was wearing on his caretakers, as each in turn became ill that summer. Nurse Baetz reported: "One Sunday in July he was sitting very quietly; all at once he screamed and said, 'he had lost his fortune.' He cried so loud that you could hear him all over the house. He seemed to realize there was something missing; the same evening he had another such time, saying, 'I am worried about my work.' We were all so surprised as he had been very quiet and talked so little."[33] Such outbursts were rare, as he became increasingly uncommunicative, grinding his teeth and weeping quietly. He was put on a liquid diet early in the summer because of stomach problems, but this caused him to lose weight rapidly. She reported on 14 October that he still took his medicine well. By the fall he was nearly comatose, but as before, fragments of his past life surfaced. Nurse Baetz took notes in late October 1907:

> One morning last week Doctor [MacDowell] said, "I am going to Rome;" "I have put it off too long;" another day he said, "Beethoven is quite right about some things." He saw his shoes on a chair and said "I want my shoes." Two months ago he could not have said that and "Marian in the Garden," and often when she comes in he cries. Today, he said to her, "I love you;" another time, "you are pretty." One day he said "Liszt is here and I feel that I am going to die." Another time, "it is time to die." I think he knows that he is sick.[34]

Shortly before they left for New York, Marian discovered the letters that he had written her during her convalescence in Philadelphia during the winter of 1892/93. The love expressed in those old relics made her happy for what they had shared, but it also reminded her of the parallel to their present situation. During the summer her illness had flared up again, and she needed treatment herself. As much as she might have wanted to stay in Peterborough to allow him to die in his beloved Hillcrest, she was forced to return to New York on 7 November to preserve her own health.

The last two months of MacDowell's life took him through the darkest days of the year one final time. For Marian, these months would always be clouded by the memory of that winter. She wrote to a friend in December 1930: "these long nights, short sunless days bring back too vividly twenty-three years ago, when I was

---

33. Baetz diary, 18.
34. Ibid,. 21.

just waiting for the end, and sort of running a race, as to whether I would not go first….How MacDowell would hate to have me, every December & January, go over and over those days—he would be so angry at me—and probably is—for I do honestly think he knows what I am doing."[35] Even as Marian sought treatment for her lameness and Edward sank closer to death, he continued to recognize her. On the morning of 23 January 1908, as he appeared unconscious and was clearly failing, she said, "won't you give me a kiss," and was surprised when he lifted his lips. Throughout the day she sat with him and read from a prayer book. He passed away at 8:00 p.m., surrounded by his parents, his wife, Marian's sisters and nephew, and his caretakers. Nurse Baetz said, "Such a death as his I have never witnessed." There was no struggle, no filling of the lungs; he just went to sleep peacefully.[36]

On his certificate of death, Dr. Loomis L. Danforth listed the cause of death as "Paresis (dementia paralytica)," a diagnosis commonly associated with third-stage syphilis.[37] Understandably, Marian kept this diagnosis from the press, and syphilis was not mentioned in any of the obituaries. For the rest of her life, she vigilantly guarded her husband's reputation, and when she went to her own grave in 1956, the association of MacDowell's death with syphilis was nothing more than a whispered rumor.[38] Ironically, the May 1906 issue of the *Monthly Cyclopaedia of Practical Medicine* contained a brief article titled "Bromide Poisoning Mistaken for Paresis." In this article, M. Allen Starr—who had seen MacDowell in 1905 but was not actively involved in his treatment—described two separate patients who appeared to have paresis but who were in fact suffering from bromism resulting from self-medication with sleeping aids. In both cases, the simple elimination of bromides led to complete recovery. The symptoms described are remarkably similar to those of MacDowell:

> In both patients there developed, in the course of four months, a gradually increasing hebetude of mind, a progressive failure of memory, and an imperfect power of attention, so that business transactions were imperfectly carried out and in several cases neglected without reason, important letters being written only in part, and telegrams were begun and left unfinished. An unusual irritability of temper developed during this time, so that any remonstrance at neglect of work was resented, and any opposition produced

---

35. Letter, MM to Nina Maud Richardson, 8 December 1930, MacDowell Collection, Library of Congress Manuscript Division, box 9.

36. Baetz diary, 25–26.

37. Curiously, the death certificate also gives the date of death as 22 January; Nurse Baetz's diary and all the obituaries state that he died on 23 January.

38. The case for this diagnosis is presented in an article by Huneker's biographer: Arnold T. Schwab, "Edward MacDowell's Mysterious Malady," *MQ* 89/1 (Spring 2006): 136–51.

outbursts of rage. The patients both showed unsteadiness in gait, a general weakness of the muscles, imperfect tremulous handwriting, inability to walk far without undue fatigue. Examination revealed thickness of speech, tremulousness of the eyelids, facial muscles and hands, diminution but no loss of knee-jerks, and a maudlin facial expression, a lack of mental acuteness, and an indifference to their actual condition. It had been noticed that both patients were liable to fall asleep in the daytime, but were restless and wakeful at night. At night both patients had, at times, seemed bewildered as to their surroundings; one had frequently dressed and walked about the streets in the night."[39]

Had Nurse Baetz seen this description, she would have recognized her patient's symptoms. Without a blood test, it is impossible to prove conclusively that Edward died of bromism, but the circumstantial evidence could hardly be stronger.

The death of Edward MacDowell touched off a flood of public accolades, accompanied by the very private mourning of his friends. The funeral service took place at 10:00 a.m. on Saturday, 25 January at St. George's Church, just steps from the Fifteenth Street Quaker Meeting where he and his family had worshipped in childhood. The service was a simple one, but the guests and honorary pallbearers included many of the country's artistic luminaries. MacDowell's pupil William H. Humiston played the third movement of MacDowell's *Sonata Tragica* on the organ as the casket entered the church; the Mendelssohn Glee Club sang during the service; and Sam Franko led the American Symphony Orchestra in MacDowell's "Dirge" from the *Indian Suite*, op. 48, as the casket left the church. This much was reported in the press, but Nurse Baetz's account is more personal: "Poor Mrs. MacDowell, how did she ever stand it. She did not keep her eyes from the casket one moment, but looking straight ahead of her, without a veil over her face so that nothing was between her and the casket that held her precious one; her all upon earth. The expression of her face was like one that did not know her surroundings, only thinking of the one who had gone and it was so hard for her to walk. Mr. Harry Nevins walked with her and at one time she almost fell from him."[40]

After the service, the family accompanied the casket to the train station, where they boarded the same car that he had used as an invalid. Marian rode alone in sight of the casket on his final trip to Peterborough. On Sunday afternoon, 26 January, Edward MacDowell was laid to rest not in a cemetery but in a private gravesite on his property in Peterborough, facing his beloved Mount Monadnock. The casket was opened for those in attendance to see before being lowered into the grave. Nurse Baetz reported that Marian and Fanny stood hand in hand, and that as the

39. M. Allen Starr, "Bromide Poisoning Mistaken for Paresis," *Monthly Cyclopaedia of Practical Medicine* 9/5 (May 1906): 193–95.
40. Baetz diary, 28.

casket was opened, the sun came from behind a cloud and shone on Edward's face.

The *Boston Journal* noted on 24 January:"With the death of Edward A. MacDowell closes the first great chapter in the history of American music. Wherever the beauty and the power that mark true musical art are appreciated, there his works have made a lasting impression. He was the soul of honor and of poetry."[41] Such eulogies echoed around the world, and European papers showered him with praise never before accorded an American musician. Defenders and detractors alike acknowledged that MacDowell's works had achieved a level of artistic and commercial success unheard of in American art music. His romantic struggle and death enhanced his unique stature in the musical world, one that would only grow in the years ahead.

41. "MacDowell," *Boston Journal*, 24 January 1908, obituary file, EMMC box 1.

CHAPTER TWENTY

MacDowell's Legacy

D URING THE SUMMER OF 1907, MARIAN INVITED EDWARD'S FORMER STUDENT
William H. Humiston to Peterborough to sift through the composer's manuscripts in search of anything publishable. He did not find much, because Edward
had burned many early and incomplete works in the spring of 1903 before leaving
for Europe. Humiston did not make any major discoveries, but he confirmed his
impression that "MacDowell was one of the severest critics of his own work that
ever lived. He was continually revising."[1] The world was curious about MacDowell's
work and eager for anything more from the composer who had been stricken
before his work was complete.

MacDowell was not a man of words, but nonetheless his work as a teacher
made his writings of interest. In September 1908, Schmidt issued a slim volume
of MacDowell's verses drawn from his song texts and the epigraphs of some of his
instrumental compositions. The first five hundred copies of the book sold so well
that Schmidt ordered a second print run of five hundred in October.[2] Schmidt also
pursued the publication of a compilation of Edward's Columbia lectures, but this
took longer to come to fruition. Schmidt approached Philip Hale about editing the

1. William H[enry] Humiston, "Personal Recollections of Edward MacDowell," *Musician* 13/3
(March 1908): 161.

2. Letters, APS to F. H. Gilson Company, 22 September 1908 and 29 October 1908, General Letter
Book, Schmidt Collection, Library of Congress Music Division. This was the first commercial
publication of a collection that had been privately printed in 1903.

lectures, but the critic declined because of insufficient time to do the work properly. They were eventually published in 1912, edited by W. J. Baltzell.[3]

One major musical work remained unpublished at MacDowell's death. The symphonic poem *Lamia*, based on Keats's poem of the same name, had been written in Wiesbaden right before he returned to the United States. Marian recalled that at the time they could not afford the subvention that would have been required to publish it with Hainauer or Breitkopf & Härtel. He also was not able to arrange an informal run-through in America to check the parts, as he had always done with his orchestral works in Germany. For this reason, he allowed the youthful work to be included on lists of his compositions as op. 29, but he never published it. Some years later, he gave the score to his friend Henry T. Finck, to whom it was dedicated.

In the fall of 1907, Schmidt tried to convince Finck to allow him to publish the score, but Finck did not wish to relinquish the only existing holograph score. Eventually he relented, and Schmidt published it in the summer of 1908. Marian was torn about the publication and eventual performance of the work, but she was grateful for the possibility of royalties. She explained to Hale, who wrote the program notes for the first performance, that she relented for three reasons. First, he had always intended eventually to revise and publish it. Second, it seemed best to do this while she was still alive to vouch for its authenticity. Third, if it were to be published, it was best to do so as early as possible.[4]

The first performance was given by the Boston Symphony Orchestra on 23 October 1908 under the direction of the recently appointed conductor Max Fiedler. Most reviewers recognized it as a youthful work and evaluated it accordingly. The critic H. T. Parker of the *Transcript* was a bit less forgiving, however, as Hale had warned Marian that he would be.[5] Like *Hamlet and Ophelia* and *Lancelot and Elaine*, *Lamia* is steeped in the aesthetic of Liszt and Wagner, and in fact Edward had confided to Finck that he considered it "Wagnerisch." The programmatic content is not as explicit as in many of the works of Richard Strauss, who had developed the genre of the symphonic poem in the intervening decades. MacDowell's work was clearly of another era, and Parker's response contributed to the growing impression that MacDowell was a master of piano miniatures but was not adept at the larger forms.

---

3. Edward MacDowell, *Critical and Historical Essays*, ed. W. J. Baltzell (Boston and New York: Schmidt, 1912; repr. New York: Da Capo, 1969, with introduction by Irving Lowens). The whereabouts of the original manuscripts of these intriguing essays on a range of musical topics are unknown.

4. Undated letter [early October?], MM to Philip Hale, EMMC box 52/11.

5. The review is reprinted in "Boston's Discovery of 'Lamia,'" *Literary Digest* (7 November 1908): 670.

Marian MacDowell's greatest fear had been that she would precede Edward in death. Ever since her childhood accident, she had suffered from back problems, and the strain of lifting Edward aggravated her old injuries, forcing her again to use crutches. Her serious illnesses in 1892 and 1902 had left her weakened and susceptible to colitis and other intestinal diseases. When he finally died, she was exhausted and grief-stricken, with little will to live. Adding insult to injury, she became estranged from Fanny McDowell shortly after the funeral and was unable to repair the rift before Fanny's death on 12 July 1909. That she survived at all is surprising; that she lived on for nearly fifty years and found a way to leave an indelible mark on American culture is remarkable. The accomplishments of the remainder of her life reflect both her indomitable spirit and her devotion to her husband's memory.

The Mendelssohn Glee Club's efforts to raise money for Edward's support had been successful. The final accounting revealed that the club had raised $39,712.18, of which $10,780 had been disbursed during the final two years of Edward's illness and to cover burial expenses.[6] The leadership of the club proposed placing the remaining $28,932.18 into a fund that would provide a modest pension for Marian's support for the rest of her life. To their surprise, she rejected this offer in favor of another plan. Her idea was to use the money to support an artists' colony on the couple's Peterborough property where composers, authors, and visual artists could create their works in solitude as Edward had done. When the financier J. P. Morgan heard of this plan, he withdrew his support, stating that he would give money to support MacDowell's widow but would not sink money into the sort of bohemian venture she had in mind.[7]

The genesis of this plan dated to the early stages of Edward's illness. According to Marian, he became concerned about the future of their property, and he suggested the idea of opening it to other artists who could benefit from the seclusion he had treasured. She assured him that she would take care of it, and he never mentioned it again. On 29 October 1905, she presented the idea of preserving their Peterborough home as an artists' colony to the recently formed MacDowell Club of New York.[8] This group, comprised largely of Edward's former students, would become a significant cultural force in the city in years ahead. She mentioned the idea again in a letter

6. Allan Robinson, "The MacDowell Fund," *MC* 56 (25 March 1908): 11.

7. Two versions of this story are recounted in Bridget Falconer-Salkeld, *The MacDowell Colony: A Musical History of America's Premier Artists' Community* (Lanham, MD: Scarecrow Press, 2005), 39.

8. Minutes of the MacDowell Club of New York, cited in Robin Rausch, "The MacDowells and their Legacy," in *A Place for the Arts: The MacDowell Colony, 1907–2007*, ed. Carter Wiseman (Hanover, NH: The MacDowell Colony, 2006), 59.

to Henry Krehbiel on 18 December 1905, stating that the model for this colony was the American Academy in Rome, which Edward had helped to plan during the year before his breakdown.

The MacDowell Club and the Mendelssohn Glee Club came together to form the Edward MacDowell Memorial Association in March 1907. As Edward lay dying, Marian signed a deed of gift granting to the newly formed association the original property they had purchased in 1896 along with several parcels of land acquired in the intervening years. In a remarkable document she laid out the conditions of the gift and with it her own task for the decades ahead. The property would be devoted to the purpose of bringing artists from different fields into contact with one another, "who being there brought into contact may learn to appreciate fully the fundamental unity of the separated arts." She relinquished legal ownership of the land and buildings on condition that the association assume two mortgages totaling $2,350 and allow her "occupancy, use, enjoyment, and management" of the property for the rest of her life.[9]

That summer, she put her plan into action by inviting the sculptor Helen Farnsworth Mears and her sister, the author Mary Mears, to be the first "colonists" on the Peterborough property.[10] While workmen constructed a studio for them to live and work in, the sisters lived in a run-down tenement adjoining the original Hillcrest property that Marian had purchased the year before. In the years ahead, more studios were built, the tenement and several other old buildings were remodeled, and additional parcels of land were purchased. Marian lived in Hillcrest and managed a growing colony of artists who were selected purely on the basis of talent, without regard for race or social standing. She played the roles of office manager, spokesperson, and mother hen to a growing family of artists from all fields. She was forced to use tact and diplomacy not only in corralling the bohemian lifestyles of her guests but also in convincing the outside world of the value of her unconventional scheme.

To bring attention to her project, she mounted a series of outdoor pageants starting in 1910. With shrewd insight, she enlisted the help of Peterborough residents to perform the history of their town set to the music of her late husband. Staged annually from 1910 to 1914, the pageants brought national attention to the colony, won Marian the goodwill of Peterborough's citizens, and started a craze for pageants in the United States. Characteristically, she planned and exe-

9. Deed of gift, EMMC box 69.

10. For further information, see Mary Mears, "The Work and Home of Edward MacDowell, Musician," *Craftsman* 16/4 (July 1909): 416–27.

cuted the pageants on her own initiative, without the approval of the MacDowell Association board.[11]

When the first pageant closed its season $2,000 in the red, Marian took to the road to raise funds. As her husband had done when he returned from Germany in 1888, she polished her rusty piano skills and began giving lecture recitals of his music. These recitals proved to be so popular that she continued them for the next twenty-five years, crisscrossing the country to play concerts and spread the word about the MacDowell Colony. Despite ongoing illness and advancing age, she found these concert tours personally invigorating and beneficial to her Peterborough endeavor. By the time she died in 1956 at the age of ninety-eight, she was nearly as famous as her husband, and she had been granted more honorary doctorates than he. The colony on their property had become one of the most important creative incubators in the world.

Today the MacDowell Colony encompasses thirty-two studios on 450 acres and hosts 250 artists annually. Among the 6,000 colonists since its inception have been James Baldwin, Amy Beach, Leonard Bernstein, Willa Cather, Michael Chabon, Aaron Copland, Jonathan Franzen, DuBose and Dorothy Heyward (who met at the MacDowell Colony), Alice Sebold, Virgil Thomson, Alice Walker, Thornton Wilder, and numerous other artistic luminaries. According to the colony website, MacDowell Fellows have won "more than sixty-five Pulitzer Prizes, a dozen MacArthur Foundation 'Genius Awards,' and scores of Rome Prizes, Guggenheims, National Book Awards, Academy Awards, GRAMMYs, and Sundance prizes."[12] The list of major works created at the colony includes Wilder's *Our Town* and *The Bridge of San Luis Rey*, the Heywards' *Porgy and Bess*, and Copland's *Billy the Kid*. Edward's dream of synergy among the arts, which he failed to achieve at Columbia University, came to fruition at the artists' colony that bears his name.

MacDowell's compositional achievement has been the subject of ongoing debate since his death. Few composers have earned such high praise or such excoriation, and few composers' posthumous reputations have gone on a similar roller coaster. These extremes reflect both the intensity of feeling he had engendered in his lifetime and the changing musical landscape of the years after his death.

Interest in MacDowell's music was fueled by the growth of MacDowell Clubs across the country. The MacDowell Club of Boston was founded in 1895 by Edward's students, as was the MacDowell Club of New York in 1905. These two

11. Robin Rausch, "American Bayreuth: The 1910 Peterborough Pageant and the Genesis of the MacDowell Colony," paper delivered at the Edward MacDowell Symposium and Festival, Elizabethtown College, 5 December 2010.

12. http://www.macdowellcolony.org/about-FAQ.html, accessed 11 February 2012.

clubs were among the most active in the country because of their direct connection to the composer. They met regularly for decades after his death and presented concerts that often included MacDowell's music. The example of these two clubs proved potent for the rest of the country, where piano teachers and other local music lovers formed clubs for their students and friends in honor of MacDowell. Marian's travels brought her into contact with many of these groups, whose number she estimated at around four hundred in 1945. By 2008 there were still at least fifteen active clubs named for MacDowell.[13] These clubs were led in most cases by piano teachers, for whom the shorter piano works were foundational to teaching. But they also advocated his ideal of the unity of the arts, and many of them were financial contributors to the MacDowell Colony.

Sales of MacDowell's music increased steadily in the years after his death, providing Marian a consistent income for her personal support without drawing on the MacDowell Colony funds. Public interest in MacDowell and his music surged around 1915. In that year, there were multiple articles in the *Etude*, the *Musician*, the *Musical Courier*, *Musical America*, and other journals geared to music teachers. The *Musical Quarterly*, a new journal founded in 1915, established its readership with major articles on MacDowell and his musical influence in each of its first three issues. The British journal *Music Student* devoted its entire August issue to MacDowell, including the first of twelve serialized articles of recollections by Templeton Strong that ran monthly for the next year. Marian had received significant royalties through sales of Edward's music by Schmidt's British subsidiary Elkin & Company, and she was apprehensive that Strong's memoirs would dredge up old animosities, particularly since he promised to set the record straight on inaccuracies in Lawrence Gilman's biography. In the end she was pleased with the articles and their nostalgic memories of her husband by his best friend.[14]

Owing to vagaries in musical culture, though, MacDowell's position in the world declined after World War I. When MacDowell died in 1908, the musical world was already changing. Within a decade, MacDowell's place of honor on the music stands of America's parlor pianos was taken over by Scott Joplin and Irving Berlin; in another ten years, America's parlor pianos ceded their place of honor to console radios. Cultural critics could decry the declining moral and musical standards, but

13. Elizabeth Yackley, "Marian MacDowell and the MacDowell Clubs" (master's thesis, University of Maryland–College Park, 2008), 91, 97.

14. The negotiation behind the publication of these memoirs lasted for more than a year and is recorded in dozens of letters among Marian, Strong, and the editor Percy Scholes. Percy Scholes Fonds boxes 72, 73, 115, and 143, Library and Archives of Canada, Ottawa.

they could not dictate the tastes of American young people. Leonard Liebling asked a series of rhetorical questions in 1916:

> Is ragtime a crime? Does it debase musical tastes? Does it keep the public from buying good music? Is it debauching our children and spoiling them as future concert goers? Would symphony fare better in this country if ragtime were suppressed? Would more songs and piano pieces by MacDowell be bought if there were fewer compositions by Irving Berlin for sale?[15]

As the brassy rhythms of ragtime and jazz supplanted the gentle melodies of parlor music in the home, other forces were at work in the concert hall. There a hard, cool modernism that mocked "sentiment" supplanted the romanticism at the heart of MacDowell's style. Musical styles that had been avant-garde in 1890 were passé by 1910.

In this climate it was easy to forget how innovative MacDowell was during his heyday. For many American composers in the twentieth century, MacDowell served as a foil against which to measure how far they had come. His refusal to participate in nationalistic efforts made him seem in retrospect like someone who had not broken free of European influences. His elevation of salon music to the highest artistic level seemed an unworthy accomplishment in an era when home music making declined. Aaron Copland reflected in 1960 on the passing of generations: "We were rather tough on Edward MacDowell. Whenever I meet some 20-year-old composer nowadays who seems less than admiring, I think 'Well, *we* were pretty tough on Edward MacDowell. I suppose it's *our* turn now!'"[16] Among those whose judgments of MacDowell can now be seen as excessive was Copland's modernist colleague Paul Rosenfeld, who wrote in 1929:

> The feelings entertained about life by him seem to have remained uncertain; and while fumbling for them he seems regularly to have succumbed to "nice" and "respectable" emotions, conventional, accepted by and welcome to, the best people. It is shocking to find how full of vague poesy he is. Where his great romantic brethren, Brahms, Wagner, and Debussy, are direct and sensitive, clearly and tellingly expressive, MacDowell minces and simpers, maidenly and ruffled. He is nothing if not a daughter of the American Revolution.[17]

15. Leonard Liebling, "The Crime of Ragtime," *MC* 72/3 (20 January 1916): 21, quoted in Edward Berlin, *Ragtime: A Musical and Cultural History* (Berkeley: University of California Press, 1980), 40.

16. Aaron Copland, "Making Music in the Star-Spangled Manner," *Music and Musicians* 8 (August 1960): 8–9.

17. Paul Rosenfeld, *An Hour with American Music* (Philadelphia: J. P. Lippincott, 1929), 46; quoted in Newman, *The Sonata Since Beethoven*, 760. This feminization of MacDowell was a recurring

How ironic that a composer known for his strength and virility—not to mention his unwillingness to follow social norms—should have been thus emasculated two decades after his death. Rosenfeld's pen portrait of MacDowell the person is as uninformed as his analysis of the music, whose directness is in stark contrast to the intentional vagueness cultivated by Wagner and Debussy. As Copland implies, this sort of vituperative rhetoric is reserved only for the most powerful of one's elders.

When MacDowell's music is heard for what it *is* rather than what it is *not*, his achievement is clear. For two decades—from the late 1880s through his death in 1908—he captured the American public in a way that no other composer had done before. He proved that an American could earn a worldwide reputation in musical composition, and after MacDowell the question was no longer whether an American could earn an international reputation, but how best to replicate his success. If later composers were bolder or more experimental, they nonetheless aspired to the recognition he had proved was not unattainable by Americans. And he did it on his own terms, with an unmistakable individual stamp that sounded like no other American or European. Copland and his colleagues recognized that MacDowell was not the founder of a school of American music precisely because of his individuality: "A man like MacDowell—there was only one like him—who had a personality of his own that was recognizable in his music, was very rare and did not seem to solve our problems."[18] If twenty-first-century listeners believe his music is indistinguishable from European music, it is because they have lost the power to recognize his uniqueness.

MacDowell created a body of significant concert works that outlived him by generations. His two concertos stand as the most important works in the genre by an American composer other than Gershwin. The four sonatas are rivaled in the American repertoire only by those of Ives, Copland, Griffes, and Barber. These pieces and his two orchestral suites were heard in concert halls and recording studios throughout the twentieth century. But he also left a large repertoire of timeless solo piano works accessible to amateurs. The indefinable charm of his "salon" works transcends the banality of the genre to create miniature masterpieces that remain fresh. The "Witches' Dance," "Shadow Dance," *Sea Pieces*, and *Woodland Sketches* not only sold unprecedented quantities when new, but they continued to appeal

theme among MacDowell's detractors, for instance the Boston organist H. C. MacDougall, who chided editor Percy Scholes for honoring MacDowell in *Music Student* 7/12 (Aug. 1915): "MacD is in truth a sort of Mrs. Grieg and will live as the Northern composer will live as a poet of small pieces" [letter to Percy Scholes, 10 October 1915, Scholes Fonds, Library and Archives of Canada].

18. Copland, "Making Music," 9.

to amateur pianists long after MacDowell was gone. Their combination of emotional directness and musical integrity earned them a lasting place in the repertoire.
In 1958 Angela Diller told an interviewer from the *New Yorker*: "I want to play
a piece of MacDowell's for old times' sake. Something quite sentimental—'To a
Water Lily.'…That's what I mean about music's being indestructible. Monet's 'Water
Lilies' at the Museum of Modern Art went up in smoke, but nothing, by George,
can happen to *this* water lily."[19]

MacDowell's music has continued to be performed and honored, even as the
musical culture changed. Columbia University commemorated him on the thirtieth anniversary of his death in 1938 and again on the one-hundredth anniversary (or so they thought) of his birth in 1961.[20] In 1940, when the United States
Postal Service issued the first series of stamps portraying American composers,
MacDowell was one of the five chosen, along with Stephen Foster, John Philip
Sousa, Victor Herbert, and Ethelbert Nevin. He was elected to the Hall of Fame
for Great Americans in 1960, one of only two musicians (with Stephen Foster) to
be so honored. MacDowell was elected as one of the third class of inductees to the
American Classical Music Hall of Fame in 2000. Significantly, Sousa is the only
other musician from the 1940 group who is in the Music Hall.[21]

In our era, when American music dominates the world, it is easy to forget the
time when Americans could only dream of being taken seriously outside their
own country. MacDowell proved that it could be done, and if this earned him the
jealousy of his contemporaries, that is no less surprising than the patronizing of
the generations that followed him. Edward MacDowell is the first American composer whose breadth of achievement, depth of expression, and unique individuality
qualify him as a master musician. As such he will always stand as a pioneer.

19. "Teachers' Teacher," *New Yorker* 34 (20 September 1958): 34. Diller refers to a fire earlier in the
year that had destroyed two of Monet's *Water Lilies* paintings at the Museum of Modern Art.

20. [Richard S. Angell], *Catalogue of an exhibition illustrating the life and work of Edward MacDowell,
1861–1908* (New York: Columbia University Library, 1938).

21. http://www.americanclassicalmusic.org/web/page.aspx?title=Inductees, accessed 12 February
2012.

Calendar

Year	Age	Life	Contemporary Musicians/ Events
1860		Edward Alexander McDowell born, 18 December, at New York, son of Thomas Fair McDowell, milk dealer, and Fanny (*née* Knapp).	Balakirev, age 22; Berlioz (57); Bizet (22); Borodin (27); Brahms (27); Bristow (34); von Bülow (30); Carreño (6); Chadwick (6); Dvořák (19); Elgar (3); Fauré (15); Foote (7); Stephen Foster (34); Franck (38); Gottschalk (31); Gounod (42); Grieg (17); Victor Herbert (1); Liszt (49); Mahler born, 7 July; William Mason (31); Massenet (18); Mussorgsky (21); Paderewski born, 6/18 Nov.; Paine (21); Puccini (1); Raff (38); Rimsky-Korsakov (16); George F. Root (40); Anton Rubinstein (31); Nikolay Rubinstein (25); Saint-Saëns (25); Clara Schumann (41); Sousa (6); Sullivan (18); Tchaikovsky (20); Verdi (47); Wagner (47); Ambroise Thomas (49); Wolf born, 13 Mar..
1861	I		Charles Martin Loeffler born, 30 Jan.; US Civil War begins with attack on Fort Sumter, 12 Apr.

Year	Age	Life	Contemporary Musicians/Events
1862	2		Delius born, 29 Jan.; Walter Damrosch born, 30 Jan.; Michael ("Chichi") Castellanos born, 11 July; Debussy born, 22 Aug.
1863	3		Horatio Parker born, 15 Sept.
1864	4		Stephen Foster (37) dies, 13 Jan; Eugen d'Albert born, 10 Apr.; Richard Strauss born, 11 June.
1865	5		Civil War ends with surrender at Appomattox Court House, 9 Apr.; Sibelius born, 8 Dec.
1866	6	The McDowell family obtained a piano by this date in defiance of the *Quaker Discipline*.	Busoni born, 1 Apr.; Satie born, 17 May.
1867	7		Amy Cheney [later Beach] born, 5 Sept.
1868	8	Heated debate in the Society of Friends over whether to allow music in members' homes.	Rossini (76) dies, 13 Nov.; Brahms *Deutsches Requiem*; Grieg Concerto in A minor, op. 16; Raff Symphony No. 3, op. 153, "Im Walde."
1869	9		Berlioz (65) dies, 8 Mar.; National Peace Jubilee in Boston, June; Gottschalk (40) dies, 18 Dec.
1870	10	Eddie transfers from public school to the Charlier Institute.	Franco-Prussian War, 19 July 1870–10 May 1871.
1871	11		Leopold Damrosch arrives in New York, 5 Apr.; Auber (89) dies, 12 May; Tausig (29) dies, 17 July; Great Chicago Fire, 8–11 Oct.; first perf. of Verdi *Aïda*, 24 Dec. Boston Apollo Club founded.
1872	12		Arthur Farwell born, 23 Apr.; World's Peace Jubilee in Boston, June; Lowell Mason (80) dies, 11 Aug.; Alexander Zemlinsky born, 4 Oct.; Vaughan Williams born, 12 Oct.; Anton Rubinstein tours the United States.

Year	Age	Life	Contemporary Musicians/ Events
1873	13	Fanny and Eddie tour Europe, June–August.	Six-year depression begins in United States. Sergei Rachmaninov born, 1 Apr.; first perf. of Paine, *St. Peter*, 3 June; Holst born, 27 Sept.; Oscar Sonneck born, 6 Oct.; first concert of Oratorio Society of New York, 3 Dec.
1874	14	Plays Beethoven "Moonlight" Sonata, op. 27, no. 2, in recital, 7 Mar.	Schoenberg born, 13 Sept.; Ives born, 20 Oct. Mussorgsky, *Pictures at an Exhibition*; Saint-Saëns, *Danse macabre*, op. 40; Smetana, *The Moldau*; Wagner, *Götterdämmerung*.
1875	15	Withdraws from Charlier Institute; plays Mendelssohn G-minor Concerto and Grand duet for two pianos "sur Puritani" with Chichi Castellanos in recital, 17 Apr.; Castellanos moves to Paris and enrolls in the Conservatoire.	First perf. of Bizet *Carmen*, 3 Mar.; Ravel born, 7 Mar.; Bizet (37) dies, 3 June; von Bülow tours the United States.
1876	16	In April, Eddie and his mother travel to Paris, where he begins private piano lessons with Marmontel.	First public telephone message by Alexander Graham Bell, 10 Mar.; Ruggles born, 11 Mar.; Centennial Exposition in Philadelphia, 10 May–10 Nov. First perf. of Paine Symphony No. 1, 26 Jan.; first perf. of Wagner complete *Ring* Cycle, Bayreuth, 13–17 Aug.; first perf. of Brahms Symphony No. 1, op. 68, 4 Nov.; MTNA founded, 26 Dec.
1877	17	On 31 Oct., Eddie gains admission to the Conservatoire by audition.	Dohnányi born, 27 July; first perf. of Saint-Saëns *Samson et Dalila* at Weimar, 2 Dec.; patent application for phonograph by Thomas Edison, 24 Dec.
1878	18	Competes unsuccessfully in the *concours*, after which he withdraws in solidarity with his friend Chichi.	First perf. of Gilbert & Sullivan *H. M. S. Pinafore*, 25 May; First perf. of Chadwick String Quartet No. 1 in Leipzig, 29 May; Hoch Conservatory opens in Frankfurt, October.

Year	Age	Life	Contemporary Musicians/ Events
1879	19	Settles in Wiesbaden in January after a month in Stuttgart. Studies privately with Louis Ehlert, then relocates to Frankfurt to enroll in the Hoch Conservatory in May; plays in a conservatory concert on 9 June with Liszt in attendance.	First perf. of Brahms Violin Concerto, 1 Jan.; first perf. of Chadwick String Quartet No. 2 in Leipzig, 29 May; first perf. of Chadwick *Rip Van Winkle* in Leipzig, 20 June; first public demonstration of incandescent lighting by Thomas Edison, Dec.; first perf. of Gilbert & Sullivan *Pirates of Penzance*, New York, 31 Dec. Einstein born, 14 Mar.; John Ireland born, 13 Aug.
1880	20	Debuts with the Wiesbaden Curhaus orchestra, 23 Jan.; plays for Liszt in a conservatory concert on 24 May; completes his studies in July; Heymann resigns from Hoch Conservatory in Sept., but MacDowell is rejected as his successor; accepts Marian Griswold Nevins as a piano student in October.	Chadwick returns to United States. First perf. of Paine Symphony No. 2, 10 Mar. to wild enthusiasm in Boston; Offenbach (61) dies, 4 Oct.
1881	21	Appointed instructor of piano at Darmstadt Conservatory in Mar.; plays Reinecke concerto with Darmstadt orchestra 14 Mar.; plays Beethoven Concerto No. 5 in Frankfurt, 7 Nov.	Nikolay Rubinstein (45) dies, 11/23 Mar.; Bartok born, 25 Mar.; Mussorgsky (42) dies, 16/28 Mar.; President James A. Garfield assassinated, 2 July; Boston Symphony Orchestra founded by Henry Lee Higginson.
1882	22	Resigns Darmstadt position in March; composes First Concerto, op. 15, Mar.–May; travels to Weimar to play for Liszt, 18 June; performs *Erste moderne Suite*, op. 10 at the Allgemeiner deutscher Musikverein in Zürich, 11 July; first and second Modern Suites, opp. 10 and 14, published by Breitkopf & Härtel.	First perf. of Chadwick Symphony No. 1, 23 Feb.; Stravinsky born, 17 June; Raff (60) dies, 24/25 June; Grainger born, 8 July; Kodály born, 16 Dec. Theodore Baker's *Über die Musik der nordamerikanischen Wilden* [On the Music of North American Indians] submitted as a doctoral dissertation at the University of Leipzig.

Year	Age	Life	Contemporary Musicians/ Events
1883	23	Proposes marriage to Marian in Feb.; New York milk strike in March reduces McDowell family income; Marian lives with Edward's parents in New York, July 1883 to July 1884; Hainauer publishes opp. 17 and 18 in Dec.	First perf. of Chadwick *Thalia*, 12 Jan.; Wagner (69) dies, 13 Feb.; Metropolitan Opera House opens, 22 Oct.; Webern born, 3 Dec.; Varèse born, 22 Dec.
1884	24	Marries Marian in New York on 9 July and again in Waterford, CT, on 21 July; attends Shakespeare plays during London honeymoon, which inspires him to write symphonic poems on Shakespearean characters.	Ehlert (58) dies, 4 Jan.; Smetana (60) dies, 12 May; Calixa Lavallée presents American Composers' Concert at MTNA Conference, 3 July, starting a fad for such concerts; Griffes born, 17 Sept.
1885	25	*Hamlet and Ophelia*, op. 22, published by Hainauer; last two movements of First Concerto premiered in New York, 31 Mar.; applies unsuccessfully for a position in Edinburgh in Aug.; moves to Wiesbaden in Sept.	Berg born, 9 Feb.; Leopold Damrosch (52) dies, 15 Feb.; Washington Monument dedicated, 21 Feb.; first perf. of Horatio Parker *König Trojan* in Munich, 15 July;
1886	26	Meets Templeton Strong Jr. in spring; composes *Lancelot and Elaine*, op. 25, in fall; *Hamlet and Ophelia*, op. 22, performed at Wiesbaden Curhaus, 26 Dec.	Saint-Saëns composes *The Carnival of the Animals* but suppresses its performance until after his death; first perf. of Dudley Buck *The Voyage of Columbus*, 4 May; first perf. of Saint-Saëns Symphony No. 3 ("Organ"), 19 May; Liszt (74) dies, 31 July; first perf. of Chadwick Symphony No. 2, 10 Dec.
1887	27	Marian has stillborn child in spring; purchases home on Grubweg in Wiesbaden in Aug., initiating a prolific period of composition; Van der Stucken American festival in New York includes MacDowell's *Hamlet* and Strong's first symphony.	First perfs. of Foote *In the Mountains*, 4 Feb.; Verdi *Otello*, 5 Feb.; Buck *The Light of Asia*, 6 May; Chadwick *Melpomene*, 24 Dec. Frank Van der Stucken stages festival of five American Composers' Concerts in New York, 15–24 Nov. Villa-Lobos born, 5 Mar.

Year	Age	Life	Contemporary Musicians/ Events
1888	28	Carreño premieres *Etude de Concert*, op. 36, on 15 Feb. in Chicago; Carreño plays First Concerto at the MTNA convention in Chicago, 5 July; MacDowell relocates to Boston in Oct., where he resumes active career as a pianist; US debut with Kneisel Quartet, 19 Nov.	First perf. of Chadwick String Quartet No. 3, 23 Jan.
1889	29	A. P. Schmidt publishes opp. 34, 36, and 37, initiating a long and profitable relationship. Plays Second Concerto, op. 23, in New York, 5 Mar.; Boston, 13 Apr.; Paris, 12 July. Spends the summer with Strong in Switzerland.	Exposition Universelle in Paris, May–Nov.; Manuscript Society of New York founded Oct. First perfs. of Strauss *Don Juan*, 11 Nov.; Mahler Symphony No. 1, 20 Nov.; Foote Suite No. 2 in D major, op. 21, 22 Nov.
1890	30	Twelve Etudes, op. 39, and Six Love Songs, op. 40, published. Teresa Carreño performs First Concerto to great acclaim in Berlin, 13 Feb.; MacDowell plays Second Concerto to great acclaim at MTNA convention, 2 July.	First perf. of Strauss *Tod und Verklärung*, 21 June; Franck (67) dies, 8 Nov.
1891	31	*Suite für grosses Orchester*, op. 42, published; MacDowell's attempt to have it removed from an American Composers' Concert in Worcester in Sept. is unsuccessful. Performs three piano recitals in Boston on 6 Nov. 1891, 15 Jan. 1892, and 18 Mar. 1892 that solidify his reputation as a pianist.	Prokofiev born, 13 Apr.; Carnegie Hall dedicated with Tchaikovsky as guest of honor, 5 May; Chicago Symphony Orchestra founded by Theodore Thomas; William Mason, *Touch and Technic*, published 1891–92. Franz Xavier Arens plays nine concerts of American orchestral music in Berlin, Dresden, Hamburg, Sondershausen, Leipzig, Weimar, and Vienna between Mar. 1891 and July 1892.

Year	Age	Life	Contemporary Musicians/ Events
1892	32	MacDowell objects to the Arens tour, despite its enhancement of his European reputation. Marian nearly dies of heat stroke during the summer, after which she spends the winter of 1892/93 undergoing treatment in Philadelphia; Teresa Carreño marries her third husband, Eugen d'Albert, who forbids her playing MacDowell's music.	First perf. of Chadwick cantata *Phoenix expirans*, 5 May; Honegger born, 10 Mar.; Darius Milhaud born, 4 Sept.; Dvořák appointed director of National Conservatory in New York, arrives 26 Sept.; first perf. of Dvořák *Te Deum*, 21 Oct.; Robert Franz (77) dies, 24 Oct.
1893	33	*Sonata tragica*, op. 45, and Eight Songs, op. 47 published by Breitkopf & Härtel. After initially agreeing to play at the Columbian Exposition in May, MacDowell withdraws.	First perfs. of Verdi *Falstaff*, 9 Feb.; Horatio Parker *Hora novissima*, 3 May; Dvořák Symphony No. 9 "From the New World," 16 Dec. World's Columbian Exposition in Chicago, May–Oct.; Gounod (75) dies, 18 Oct.; Tchaikovsky (53) dies, 6 Nov.
1894	34	Twelve Virtuoso Etudes, op. 46, published.	First perf. of Dvořák String Quartet No. 12 in F major, op. 96 "American," 1 Jan.; Piston born, 20 Jan.; Hans von Bülow (64) dies, 12 Feb.; Horatio Parker appointed Battell Professor of Music at Yale; Ives begins studies at Yale, 3 Oct.; first perf. of Chadwick Symphony No. 3, 19 Oct.; Anton Rubinstein (64) dies, 8/20 Nov.; first perf. of Debussy *Prélude à l'après-midi d'un faune*, 22 Dec.
1895	35	*Sonata eroica*, op. 50, published by Breitkopf & Härtel.	Dvořák returns to Bohemia, 16 Apr. but fails to obtain money owed him by the National Conservatory; first perf. of Dvořák *The American Flag*, 4 May; Orff born, 10 July; first perf. of Strauss *Till Eulenspiegel*, 5 Nov.; Hindemith born, 16 Nov.; first perf. of Mahler Symphony No. 2, 13 Dec.

Year	Age	Life	Contemporary Musicians/ Events
1896	36	MacDowell plays First Concerto and premieres Second Suite (Indian), op. 48, in New York, 26 Jan., leading to his appointment as first professor of music at Columbia University in the fall. Purchases 80 acres in Peterborough, NH, in Marian's name. Receives honorary doctorate from Princeton University, 22 Oct. *Woodland Sketches*, op. 51, published by P. L. Jung in Dec., went on to become his biggest seller. A series of compositions published 1896–98 under the pseudonym "Edgar Thorn(e)" benefits Marian's former nurse.	First perf. of Puccini *La Bohème*, 1 Feb.; Ambroise Thomas (84) dies, 12 Feb.; Clara Schumann (76) dies, 20 May; Anton Bruckner (72) dies, 11 Oct.; Howard Hanson born, 28 Oct.; Virgil Thomson born, 25 Nov.; Roger Sessions born, 28 Dec.; first perf. of Chadwick String Quartet No. 4, 21 Dec. Brahms *Vier ernste Gesänge*; first perf of Beach "Gaelic" Symphony, 30 Oct.; first perf. of Saint-Saëns, Piano Concerto No. 5 "Egyptian" with the composer at the piano during his fiftieth jubilee concert, 6 May; Strauss *Also sprach Zarathustra* 27 Nov.
1897	37	Second Suite (Indian), op. 48, published by Breitkopf & Härtel.	Cowell born, 11 Mar.; Brahms (63) dies, 3 Apr.
1898	38	Sea Pieces, op. 55, and Four Songs, op. 56, published by P. L. Jung.	Marmontel (81) dies, 16 Jan.; Roy Harris born, 12 Feb.; first perf. of Strauss *Don Quixote*, 8 Mar.; first perf. of Horatio Parker *The Legend of St. Christopher*, 15 Apr.; Ives graduates from Yale with a D+ average, 29 June; Gershwin born, 26 Sept.; Bristow dies, 13 Dec.
1899	39	Three Songs, op. 58, published by Schmidt. Accepts presidency of Manuscript Society of New York, May.	Poulenc born, 7 Jan.; MTNA presents eight American Composers' Concerts at its annual convention in Cincinnati, 21–23 June (MacDowell refuses to participate); Scott Joplin *Maple Leaf Rag* copyrighted 18 Sept.; Schoenberg completes *Verklärte Nacht*, Dec.

Year	Age	Life	Contemporary Musicians/ Events
1900	40	Resigns presidency of Manuscript Society, 4 Jan. Third Sonata (Norse), op. 57, published by Schmidt.	First perf. of Puccini *Tosca*, 14 Jan.; first perf. of Chadwick *Adonais*, 2 Feb.; Kurt Weill born, 2 Mar.; George Grove (79) dies, 28 May; Antheil born, 8 July; Křenek born, 23 Aug.; Copland born, 14 Nov.; Sullivan (58) dies, 22 Nov.
1901	41	Fourth Sonata (Keltic), op. 59, published by Schmidt. Marian becomes seriously ill in August, requiring surgery.	Verdi (87) dies, 27 Jan.; Ethelbert Nevin (38) dies, 17 Feb.; Ruth Crawford born, 3 July; Louis Armstrong born, 4 Aug.; first perf. of Rachmaninov Second Concerto, 27 Oct.; Rheinberger (62) dies, 25 Nov.
1902	42	Three Songs, op. 60, *Fireside Tales*, op. 61, and *New England Idyls*, op. 62, published by Schmidt. Receives honorary doctorate from the University of Pennsylvania, 18 June. Sabbatical leave 1902–3 results in no new compositions.	First perfs. of Sibelius, Symphony No. 2, 8 Mar.; Ives *The Celestial Country*, 18 Apr.; Debussy, *Pelléas et Mélisande*, 30 Apr. Jadassohn (70) dies, 1 Feb.
1903	43	Concert tour of California in Jan. followed by Midwestern and Eastern cities. Performs Second Concerto in London, 14 May; spends the summer in Switzerland. Friends notice his tired, vacant appearance when he returns to Columbia in the fall.	First perfs. of Bruckner Ninth Symphony, 11 Feb.; d'Albert *Tiefland*, 15 Nov. Claudio Arrau born, 6 Feb.; Hugo Wolf (42) dies, 22 Feb.; Khachaturian born, 6 June; Vladimir Horowitz born, 1 Oct.
1904	44	Resigns his position at Columbia in January; public scandal follows in February as he spars with university president Nicholas Murray Butler in the press over the reasons for his resignation. Resumes private piano teaching in the fall. Elected one of seven founding members of the American Academy of Arts and Letters, 2 Dec.	First perf. of Puccini *Madama Butterfly*, 17 Feb.; first perf. of Strauss *Sinfonia Domestica* in New York, 21 Mar.; first perf. of Chadwick *Euterpe*, 22 Apr.; Dvořák (63) dies, 1 May; first perf. of Chadwick *Cleopatra*, 29 Sept.; first perf. of Mahler Symphony No. 5, 18 Oct.

Year	Age	Life	Contemporary Musicians/ Events
1905	45	Students and friends begin to notice unusual behavior early in the year; MacDowell suffers a nervous breakdown in the summer; signs power of attorney to Marian, 22 July; Hamlin Garland notifies the press of his collapse, 28 Nov.	Theodore Thomas (69) dies, 4 Jan.; first perf. of Schoenberg *Pelleas und Melisande*, 26 Jan.; first perf. of Mahler *Kindertotenlieder*, 29 Jan.; Schoenberg completes String Quartet No. 1 in Sept.; first perf of Debussy *La Mer*, 15 Oct.; first perf. of Strauss *Salome*, 9 Dec.; first perf. of Lehár *The Merry Widow*, 30 Dec.
1906	46	Doctors fail to identify the cause of MacDowell's continuing decline, which is not improved by a summer in Peterborough. The Mendelssohn Glee Club launches a fund-raising campaign that eventually raises $40,000 for the composer's support.	Paine (67) dies, 25 Apr.; Shostakovich born, 12/25 Sept.; Victor Herbert *The Red Mill* opens 24 Sept.
1907	47	Another summer in Peterborough fails to halt his decline; Marian deeds their property to "The Edward MacDowell Foundation" to be used as an artists' colony; they are forced to return to New York on 29 Nov. so that she can be treated for her ailments.	Grieg (64) dies, 4 Sept.

Year	Age	Life	Contemporary Musicians/ Events
1908		Dies (47) in New York, 23 Jan.	First perf. of Chadwick *Symphonic Sketches*, 7 Feb.; August Wilhelmj (62) dies, 22 Jan.; Herbert von Karajan born, 5 Apr.; Rimsky-Korsakov (64) dies, 8/21 June; William Mason (79) dies, 14 July; Sarasate (64) dies, 20 Sept.; Olivier Messiaen born, 10 Dec.; Elliott Carter born, 11 Dec. Antheil age 7; Louis Armstrong 6; Arrau 4; Bartok 26 (completes *Fourteen Bagatelles*, op. 6); Beach 40; Berg 22 (completes Piano Sonata, op. 1); Arthur Bird 51; Buck 69; Busoni 41; Carreño 54; Chadwick 53; Copland 7; Cowell 10; Crawford 6; d'Albert 43; Walter Damrosch 45; Debussy 45; Delius 45; Dohnányi 30; Elgar 50; Farwell 35; Fauré 62; Foote 54; Gershwin 9; Grainger 25; Griffes 23; Hanson 11; Roy Harris 9; Herbert 48; Hindemith 12; Holst 33; Honegger 15; Horowitz 4; Huss 45; Ireland 28; Ives 33; Khachaturian 4; Kodály 25; Křenek 7; Loeffler 46; Mahler 47; Milhaud 15; Orff 12; Paderewski 47; Horatio Parker 44; Piston 14; Poulenc 9; Prokofiev 16; Puccini 49; Rachmaninov 34; Ravel 32; Saint-Saëns 72; Satie 41; Schoenberg 33 (completes String Quartet No. 2); Scriabin 36 (completes *Poem of Ecstasy*); Sessions 11; Shostakovich 1; Sibelius 44; Sonneck 34; Strauss 43; Stravinsky 25; Strong 51; Thomson 11; Varèse 24; Vaughan Williams 25; Villa-Lobos 20; Webern 24; Weill 7; Zemlinsky 35.
1909		Fanny MacDowell dies at Phoenicia, NY, 12 July	Buck dies (70), 6 Oct.

Year	Age	Life	Contemporary Musicians/ Events
1910		Thomas MacDowell dies in New York, 25 Mar.	Frederick Shepherd, *The Pipe of Desire* is first American opera to be produced at the Metropolitan Opera, 18 Mar.; Puccini *La fanciulla del West* produced at the Metropolitan Opera, 10 Dec.

List of Works

Edward and Marian MacDowell were very protective of his reputation by destroying the manuscripts of most of his unfinished and unpublished works. Significant holdings of manuscripts, sketches, and drafts of juvenilia and published works are in EMMC, NYPL, Butler Rare Book and Manuscript Library at Columbia University [CU], and the Lowens Collection.

The ground-breaking study of the published editions of MacDowell's works was O.T. G. Sonneck's *Catalogue of First Editions of Edward MacDowell* (Washington: Government Printing Office, 1917), which is still a useful starting point. Sonneck described the challenges of compiling even a basic works list of MacDowell's compositions in his essay "MacDowell *versus* MacDowell: A Study in First Editions and Revisions," in *Suum Cuique: Essays in Music* (New York: G. Schirmer, 1916), 87–103. The following list treats revised editions as separate works. Publications with the pseudonym Edgar Thorn(e) as well as publications without opus number are listed by genre and in chronological order with the other publications. The early publications had inconsistent bilingual titles; the list below reproduces the titles as printed.

Unpublished Juvenilia

Improvisations (Rêverie), MS op. 1, 1876, EMMC
8 chansons fugitives, MS op. 2, 1876, EMMC
Petits morceaux, MS op. 3, 1876, EMMC, CU
3 petits morceaux, MS op. 4, 1876, EMMC and Columbia University, also as op. 5, NYPL
Suite de 5 morceaux caracteristiques, MS op. 5, 1876, EMMC
    1. Barcarolle; 2. La petite glaneuse; 3. Dans la nuit; 4. Le réveille matin; 5. Cauchemar
Petit rien, MS op. 6, 1876, CU
Trois morceaux caracteristiques, MS op. 7, 1877–78, CU
    1. Prélude; 2. Scherzino; 3. Danse hongroise
Deux Improvisations dediés à Mme. E. Aubert, MS op. 8, 1877, EMMC
Grande valza di bravura, MS op. 8 [*sic*], 1879, EMMC
Deux Mélodies pour piano et violon, MS op. 9, 1879, EMMC

Orchestral

Piano Concerto No. 1, op. 15, 1882 (Two pianos: Leipzig: Breitkopf & Härtel, 1884; full score: Leipzig: Breitkopf & Härtel, 1911)

Hamlet, Ophelia, op. 22, symphonic poem, 1884–85 (Full score, parts, and two-piano score published Breslau: Hainauer; New York: Schirmer, 1885)

Piano Concerto No. 2, op. 23, 1884–89 (Two pianos: Leipzig: Breitkopf & Härtel, 1890; parts: Leipzig: Breitkopf & Härtel, [1902]; full score: Leipzig: Breitkopf & Härtel, 1907)

Lancelot und Elaine, op. 25, symphonic poem after A. Tennyson, 1886 (Full score, parts, and two-piano score published Breslau: Hainauer; New York: Schirmer, 1888)

Lamia, op. 29, symphonic poem after J. Keats, 1887–88 (Full score, parts, and two-piano score published Boston: Schmidt, 1908)

Die Sarazenen, Die schöne Aldâ, op. 30, two fragments after *The Song of Roland,* 1886–90 (Full score, parts, and two-piano score published Leipzig: Breitkopf & Härtel, 1891)

Romanze for cello and orchestra, op. 35, 1887 (Full score, parts, and cello-piano score published Breslau: Hainauer; New York: Schirmer, 1888)

Suite, op. 42, nos. 1, 2, 4, and 5, 1888–91 (Full score, parts, and two-piano score published Boston: Schmidt, 1891); no. 3, 1893 (Boston: Schmidt, 1893)
   1. In einem verwünschten Walde (In a Haunted Forest); 2. Sommer-Idylle (Summer Idyll); 3. Im Oktober (In October); 4. Gesang der Hirtin (The Shepherdess' Song), arr. pf (1906, 1908); 5. Waldgeister (Forest Spirits)

2nd Suite (Indian), op. 48, 1891–95 (Leipzig: Breitkopf & Härtel, 1897)
   1. Legend; 2. Love Song; 3. In War-time; 4. Dirge; 5. Village Festival

Piano solo

Erste moderne Suite, op. 10, 1880–81 (Leipzig: Breitkopf & Härtel, 1883), rev. 1904–5 (Leipzig, 1906)
   I. Praeludium, rev. 1904 (Leipzig, 1904); II. Presto; III. Andantino und Allegretto; IVa. Intermezzo, rev. 1891 (Leipzig, 1891); IVb. Rhapsodie; V. Fuge

Prélude et fugue, op. 13, 1881 (Leipzig: Kahnt, 1883)

Zweite moderne Suite, op. 14, 1882 (Leipzig: Breitkopf & Härtel, 1883)
   I. Praeludium; II. Fugato; III. Rhapsodie; IVa. Scherzino; IVb. Marsch; V. Phantasie-Tanz

Serenade, op. 16, 1882 (Leipzig: Fritzsch, 1883)

Serenata, op. 16, substantially revised 1894 (New York: P. L. Jung, 1895)

Zwei Fantasiestücke, op. 17, 1883 (Breslau: Hainauer; New York: Schirmer, 1884)
   1. Erzählung; 2. Hexentanz

Zwei Stücke, op. 18, 1884 (Breslau: Hainauer; New York: Schirmer, 1884)
   1. Barcarolle; 2. Humoreske

Wald Idyllen, op. 19, 1884 (Leipzig: Kahnt, 1884)
   1. Waldesstille; 2. Spiel der Nymphen; 3. Träumerei; 4. Driadentanz

"Revery," op. 19, no. 3 and "Dance of the Dryads," op. 19, no. 4, substantially revised 1894 (New York: P. L. Jung, 1894)

Vier Stücke, op. 24, 1886 (Breslau: Hainauer, 1887)
   1. Humoreske; 2. Marsch; 3. Wiegenlied; 4. Czardas

Idyllen, op. 28, 1887 (Breslau: Hainauer; and New York: Schirmer, 1887)

1. Ich ging im Walde; 2. Unter des grünen blühender Kraft; 3. Füllest wieder Busch und Thal; 4. Leichte silberwolken Schweben; 5. Bei dem Glanz der Abendröthe; 6. Ein Blumenglöckchen.

Six Idyls after Goethe, op. 28, reissue of above with new titles but no changes to the music (Breslau: Hainauer; New York: Schirmer, 1898)

1. Once through the forest; 2. Under the verdure's vigorous bloom; 3. Bush and vale thou fill'st again; 4. Light and silv'ry cloudlets hover; 5. As at sunset I was straying; 6. A fairbell flower.

Six Idyls after Goethe, op. 28, revised 1901 (Boston: Schmidt, 1901)

1. In the Woods; 2. Siesta; 3. To the Moonlight; 4. Silver Clouds; 5. Flute Idyl; 6. The Bluebell.

Sechs Gedichte nach Heinrich Heine, op. 31, 1887 (Breslau: Hainauer; New York: Schirmer, 1887)

1. Wir sassen am Fischerhause; 2. Fern an schottischer Felsenküste; 3. Mein Kind, wir waren Kinder; 4. Wir führen allein im Dunkeln; 5. König ist der Hirtenknabe; 6. Der Tod, das ist die kühle Nacht.

Six Poems after Heine, op. 31, reissue of above with new titles but no changes to the music (Breslau: Hainauer; New York: Breitkopf & Härtel, 1898)

1. We sat by the fisherman's cottage; 2. Far away on the rock-coast of Scotland; 3. My child, we once were children; 4. We travelled alone in the gloaming; 5. Shepherd boy's a king; 6. Death nothing is but cooling night.

Six Poems after Heine, op. 31, substantially revised 1901 (Boston: Schmidt, 1901)

1. From a Fisherman's Hut; 2. Scotch Poem; 3. From Long Ago; 4. The Postwaggon; 5. The Shepherd Boy; 6. Monologue.

Vier kleine Poesien, op. 32, 1887 (Leipzig: Breitkopf & Härtel, 1888)

1. Der Adler (The Eagle) [after Tennyson]; 2. Das Bächlein (The Brook) [after Bulwer-Lytton]; 3. Mondschein (Moonshine) [after D. G. Rossetti]; 4. Winter [after Shelley]

Etude de concert, op. 36, 1887 (Boston: Schmidt, 1889)

Les orientales [after Victor Hugo], op. 37, 1887–8 (Boston: Schmidt, 1889)

1. Clair de lune; 2. Dans le hamac; 3. Danse andalouse

Marionetten, op. 38, 1888 (Breslau: Hainauer, 1888)

I. Soubrette; II. Liebhaber (Lover); III. Bube (Villain); IV. Liebhaberin (Lady-Love); V. Clown; VI. Hexe (Witch).

Marionettes, op. 38, substantially revised and expanded 1901 (Boston: Schmidt, 1901)

1. Prologue; 2. Soubrette; 3. Lover; 4. Witch; 5. Clown; 6. Villain; 7. Sweetheart; 8. Epilogue.

12 Etüden, op. 39, 1889–90 (Boston: Schmidt, 1890)

1. Jagdlied (Hunting Song); 2. Alla Tarantella; 3. Romanze (Romance); 4. Arabeske (Arabesque); 5. Waldfahrt (In the Forest); 6. Gnomentanz (Dance of the Gnomes); 7. Idylle (Idyll); 8. Schattentanz (Shadow Dance); 9. Intermezzo, 10. Melodie (Melody); 11. Scherzino; 12. Ungarisch (Hungarian)

Sechs kleine Stücke nach Skizzen von J. S. Bach (Boston: Schmidt, 1890)

1. Courante; 2. Menuett; 3. Gigue; 4. Menuett; 5. Menuett; 6. Marsch

Sonata tragica, op. 45, 1891–92 (Leipzig: Breitkopf & Härtel, 1893)

Zwölf Virtuosen-Etüden, op. 46, 1893–94 (Leipzig: Breitkopf & Härtel, 1894)

1. Novelette; 2. Moto perpetuo; 3. Wilde Jagd; 4. Improvisation; 5. Elfentanz; 6. Valse triste; 7. Burleske; 8. Bluette; 9. Träumerei; 10. Märzwind; 11. Impromptu; 12. Polonaise

Air et Rigaudon, op. 49, ?1894; published in *Half Hours with the Best Composers*, ed. Karl
    Klauser (Boston: J. B. Millet, 1894), vol. 4, 837–44
Technical Exercises, Part 1, 1893–94 (Leipzig: Breitkopf & Härtel, 1894)
Technical Exercises, Part 2, 1893–95 (Leipzig: Breitkopf & Härtel, 1895)
Sonata eroica, op. 50, 1894–95 (Leipzig: Breitkopf & Härtel, 1895)
Edgar Thorne, *Amourette*, op. 1, 1896 (New York: P. L. Jung, 1896)
Woodland Sketches, op. 51, 1896 (New York: P. L. Jung, 1896)
    1. To a Wild Rose; 2. Will o' the Wisp; 3. At an Old Trysting-Place; 4. In Autumn;
    5. From an Indian Lodge; 6. To a Water-Lily; 7. From Uncle Remus [after Joel
    Chandler Harris]; 8. A Deserted Farm; 9. By a Meadow Brook; 10. Told at Sunset
Edgar Thorn, *In Lilting Rhythm*, op. 2, 1896 (New York: P. L. Jung, 1897)
Edgar Thorn, *Forgotten Fairy Tales*, op. 4, 1897 (New York: P. L. Jung, 1897)
    1. Sung Outside the Prince's Door; 2. Of a Tailor and a Bear; 3. Beauty in the Rose-
    garden; 4. From Dwarfland
Sea Pieces, op. 55, 1896–98 (New York: P. L. Jung, 1898)
    1. To the Sea; 2. From a Wandering Iceberg; 3. A.D. MDCXX; 4. Starlight; 5. Song; 6.
    From the Depths; 7. Nautilus; 8. In Mid-Ocean
Edgar Thorn, *Six Fancies*, op. 7, 1898 (New York: P. L. Jung, 1898)
    1. A Tin Soldier's Love; 2. To a Humming Bird; 3. Summer Song; 4. Across Fields; 5.
    Bluette; 6. An Elfin Round
3rd Sonata ["Norse"], op. 57, 1898–99 (Boston: Schmidt, 1900)
4th (Keltic) Sonata, op. 59, 1900 (Boston: Schmidt, 1901)
Fireside Tales, op. 61, 1901–02 (Boston: Schmidt, 1902)
    1. An Old Love Story; 2. Of Br'er Rabbit [after Joel Chandler Harris]; 3. From a
    German Forest; 4. Of Salamanders; 5. A Haunted House; 6. By Smouldering Embers
New England Idyls, op. 62, 1901–02 (Boston, Leipzig and New York: Schmidt, 1902)
    1. An Old Garden; 2. Mid-Summer; 3. Mid-Winter; 4. With Sweet Lavender; 5. In
    Deep Woods; 6. Indian Idyl; 7. To an Old White Pine; 8. From Puritan Days; 9. From
    a Log Cabin; 10. The Joy of Autumn

Piano four hands

Drei Poesien, op. 20, 1885 (Breslau: Hainauer; New York: Schirmer, 1886)
    1. Nachts am Meere; 2. Erzählung aus der Ritterzeit; 3. Ballade
Mondbilder nach H.C. Andersen's *Bilderbuch ohne Bilder*, op. 21, 1885 (Breslau: Hainauer; New
    York: Schirmer, 1886)
    1. Das Hindumädchen; 2. Storchgeschichte; 3. In Tyrol; 4. Der Schwan; 5. Bärenbesuch

Solo Songs with piano accompaniment

Drei Lieder, op. 11, 1881 (Leipzig: Kahnt, 1883)
    1. Mein Liebchen; 2. Du liebst mich nicht (Heine); 3. Oben wo die Sterne (Heine)
Zwei Lieder, op. 12, 1880–81 (Leipzig: Kahnt, 1883)
    1. Nachtlied (E. Geibel); 2. Das Rosenband (F. G. Klopstock)
From an Old Garden, op. 26 (Margaret Deland), 1886–87 (New York: Schirmer, 1887)
    1. The Pansy; 2. The Myrtle; 3. The Clover; 4. The Yellow Daisy; 5. The Bluebell; 6. The
    Mignonette
Drei Lieder, op. 33, 1887–8 (Breslau: Hainauer; New York: Schirmer, 1889)

1. Bitte (A Request) (J. C. Glücklich, trans. MacDowell), 2. Geistliches Wiegenlied
   (Cradle Hymn) (Lat. anon.), 3. Idylle (Idyll) (J. W. von Goethe, trans. MacDowell)
Two songs from op. 33, revised 1894 (New York: Breitkopf & Härtel, 1894)
   Cradle Hymn and Idyll
Two Songs, op. 34 (Robert Burns), 1887–88 (Boston: Schmidt, 1889)
   1. Menie; 2. My Jean
Six Love Songs, op. 40 (W. H. Gardner), 1890 (Boston: Schmidt, 1890)
   1. Sweet blue-eyed maid; 2. Sweetheart, tell me; 3. Thy beaming eyes; 4. For sweet love's
   sake; 5. O lovely rose; 6. I ask but this
Eight Songs, op. 47, 1893 (Leipzig: Breitkopf & Härtel, 1893)
   1. The robin sings in the apple-tree (MacDowell); 2. Midsummer Lullaby (after
   Goethe); 3. Folksong (W. D. Howells); 4. Confidence (MacDowell); 5. The west-wind
   croons in the cedar-trees (MacDowell); 6. In the Woods (after Goethe); 7. The Sea
   (Howells); 8. Through the Meadow (Howells)
Two Old Songs, op. 9, 1894 (New York: Breitkopf & Härtel, 1894)
   1. Deserted (Burns); 2. Slumber Song (MacDowell)
Four Songs, op. 56 (MacDowell), 1898 (New York: P. L. Jung, 1898)
   1. Long ago; 2. The swan bent low to the lily; 3. A maid sings light; 4. As the gloaming
   shadows creep
Three Songs, op. 58 (MacDowell), 1899 (Boston: Schmidt, 1899)
   1. Constancy (New England AD 1899); 2. Sunrise; 3. Merry Maiden Spring
Three Songs, op. 60 (MacDowell), 1901 (Boston: Schmidt, 1902)
   1. Tyrant Love; 2. Fair Springtide; 3. To the Golden Rod

Mixed Chorus

Two Northern Songs, op. 43 (MacDowell), 4-part mixed chorus, 1890–91 (Boston: Schmidt,
1891)
   1. The Brook; 2. Slumber Song
Barcarole, op. 44 (F. von Bodenstedt, trans. MacDowell), 8-part mixed chorus and piano 4
hands, 1890 (Boston: Schmidt, 1892)

Male chorus

Drei Lieder für vierstimmigen Männerchor, op. 27, 1887 (Boston: Schmidt, 1890)
   1. Oben wo die Sterne glühen (In the starry sky above us) (Heine, trans. MacDowell),
   2. Schweizerlied (Springtime) [*sic*] (Goethe, trans. MacDowell), 3. Der Fischerknabe
   (The Fisherboy) (F. von Schiller, trans. MacDowell)
Two choruses for men's voices, op. 41, 1890 (Boston: Schmidt, 1890)
   1. Cradle Song (MacDowell, after P. Cornelius); 2. Dance of Gnomes (MacDowell)
Edgar Thorn, *Two choruses for male voices*, op. 3, 1896 and 1897 (New York: P. L. Jung, 1897)
   1. Love and Time (Marion Farley); 2. The Rose and the Gardener (Austin Dobson)
Two Songs from the Thirteenth Century (trans. MacDowell), 1897 (New York: P. L. Jung, 1897)
   1. Winter wraps his grimmest spell (after N. von Reuenthal); 2. As the gloaming shadows creep (after Frauenlob)
Three choruses for male voices, op. 52, 1896–97 (New York: P. L. Jung, 1897)
   1. Hush, hush! (Thomas Moore); 2. From the Sea (MacDowell); 3. The Crusaders
   (MacDowell)
"Die Kreuzfahrer," op. 52, no. 3, translation by the composer (New York: P. L. Jung, 1898)

Two choruses for male voices, op. 53 (Robert Burns), 1897–98 (New York: P. L. Jung, 1898)
    1. Bonnie Ann; 2. The Collier Lassie
Two choruses for male voices, op. 54 (MacDowell), 1897 and 1887 (New York: P. L. Jung, 1898)
    1. A Ballad of Charles the Bold; 2. Midsummer Clouds
Edgar Thorn, *The Witch*, op. 5 (MacDowell), 1897 (New York: P. L. Jung, 1898)
Edgar Thorn, *War Song*, op. 6 (MacDowell), 1898 (New York: P. L. Jung, 1898)
College Songs for Male Voices, 1900–1901 (Boston: Schmidt, 1901)
    1. Columbia's Sons (E. Keppler); 2. We love thee well, Manhattanland (MacDowell);
       3. Columbia! O alma mater (MacDowell); 4. Sturdy and Strong (MacDowell); 5. O
       wise old alma mater (MacDowell); 6. At Parting (MacDowell)

Female Chorus

Two College Songs (MacDowell), rev. of *College Songs for Male Voices*, nos. 3 and 6, ?1901–2
    (Boston: Schmidt, 1907)
    1. Alma mater; 2. At Parting
Summer Wind (Richard Hovey), ?1902 (Boston: Schmidt, 1902)

Editions and arrangements of works by other composers
Orchestra

Raff, Joachim. *Shakespeare Ouverturen*: No. 1 "Romeo und Julie," No. 2 "Macbeth," 1890–91
    (full score, parts, and two-piano score published Boston: Schmidt, 1891)

Piano solo

Alkan-MacDowell. *Perpetual motion* (New York: P. L. Jung, 1896)
Couperin, François. *L'Ausonienne* (Boston and Leipzig: Schmidt, 1900)
Couperin, François. *La Bersan* (New York: P. L. Jung, 1896)
Couperin, François. *Le Bavolet flottant [The waving scarf]* (Boston: Schmidt, 1900)
Cui, César. *Cradle Song*, op. 39, no. 4 (New York: Breitkopf & Härtel, 1895)
Dubois, Theodore. *Sketch* (New York: Breitkopf & Härtel, 1895)
Geisler, Paul. *Episode* (New York: Breitkopf & Härtel, 1895)
Geisler, Paul. *Pastorale* (New York: P. L. Jung, 1896)
Geisler, Paul. *The Princess Ilse* (New York: P. L. Jung, 1896)
Glinka, Michael, transcr. Balakirew. *The Lark* (New York: Breitkopf & Härtel, 1895)
Graun, Carl Heinrich. *Jig* (Boston: Schmidt, 1900)
Grazioli, Giovanni Battista-MacDowell. *Tempo di minuetto* (Boston: Schmidt, 1900)
Huber, Hans. *Intermezzo*, op. 94, no. 4 (New York: Breitkopf & Härtel, 1894)
Lacombe, Paul. *Etude*, op. 33, no. 2 (New York: P. L. Jung, 1896)
Lavignac, Albert. Aria from Haendel's *Susanna* (New York: Breitkopf & Härtel, 1894)
Liszt, Franz. *Eclogue* (New York: Breitkopf & Härtel, 1895)
Liszt, Franz. *Impromptu* (New York: P. L. Jung, 1896)
Loeilly, Jean Baptiste. *Jig* (Boston: Schmidt, 1900)
Loeilly, Jean Baptiste. *Sarabande* (Boston: Schmidt, 1902)
Martucci, Giuseppe. *Improvviso*, op. 17 (New York: Breitkopf & Härtel, 1895)
Mattheson, Johann. *Jig* (Boston: Schmidt, 1900)
Moszkowski, Moritz. *Air de ballet*, op. 36, no. 5 (New York: Breitkopf & Härtel, 1895)
Moszkowski, Moritz. *Etincelles*, op. 36, no. 6 (New York: Breitkopf & Härtel, 1895)

Pierné, Gabriel. *Allegro scherzando*, op. 29 (New York: Breitkopf & Härtel, 1895)

Pierné, Gabriel. *Cradle Song* (New York: Breitkopf & Härtel, 1895)

Pierné, Gabriel. *Improvisata*, op. 22 (New York: P. L. Jung, 1896)

Rameau, Jean Philippe. *The Three Hands (Les trois mains) Courante* (Boston: Schmidt, 1900)

Rameau, Jean Philippe. *Sarabande* (Boston: Schmidt, 1900)

Reinhold, H. *Impromptu in C-sharp minor*, op. 28, no. 3 (New York: Breitkopf & Härtel, 1895)

Rimsky-Korsakov, Nikolai. *Romance*, op. 15, no. 2 (New York: Breitkopf & Härtel, 1895)

Stcherbatchev, Nikolai. *Orientale*, op. 15, no. 2 (New York: Breitkopf & Härtel, 1895)

Ten-Brink, Jules. *Gavotte in E minor* (New York: Breitkopf & Härtel, 1895)

Westerhout, M. van. *Gavotte in A* (New York: Breitkopf & Härtel, 1895)

Westerhout, M. van. *Momento capriccioso* (New York: Breitkopf & Härtel, 1894)

Part-songs

Arnold, Maurice. *Oh! Weep for those* (New York: P. L. Jung, 1898)Beines, C. *Spring Song*, op. 34 (New York: P. L. Jung, 1897)

Borodin, Alexander. *Serenade* (New York: P. L. Jung, 1897)

Filke, M. *The Brook and the Nightingale*, op. 43, no. 2 (New York: P. L. Jung, 1897)

Holstein, Franz von. *Bonnie Katrine*, op. 23, no. 2 (New York: P. L. Jung, 1897)

Ingraham, George. *A Love Song* (New York: P. L. Jung, 1897)

Moniuszko, S. *The Cossack* (New York: P. L. Jung, 1897)

Rimsky-Korsakov, Nikolai. *Folk Song* (New York: P. L. Jung, 1897)

Sokolow, N. *From Siberia*, op. 6, no. 1 (New York: P. L. Jung, 1898)

Sokolow, N. *Spring* (New York: P. L. Jung, 1897)

Wöss, J.V. v. *Under Flowering Branches*, op. 36, no. 2 (New York: P. L. Jung, 1898)

Writings

"Composer *versus* Student," *Boston Musical Herald* 13 (1892): 47–48.

"Music at Columbia," *Columbia University Bulletin*, no.15 (1896): 13–16.

Verses. N.p. [1903]; rev. ed. Boston and New York: Schmidt, 1908.

Critical and Historical Essays: Lectures Delivered at Columbia University, edited by W. J. Baltzell (Boston: Schmidt, 1912; repr. New York: Da Capo, 1969 with introduction by Irving Lowens)

"The Power of Suggestion in Music." *Etude* 33/11 (November 1915): 783–84.

Personalia

Abel, Frederic (1856–1943) A fellow American student at the Hoch Conservatory in Frankfurt. The two were close friends, and MacDowell moved into Abel's apartment when he returned to Detroit after the close of the school year in 1880. As a longtime instructor at the Detroit Conservatory (1881–1900), Abel promoted his friend's music, notably with an all-MacDowell concert in 1888. He founded the Michigan Conservatory of Music in 1900.

Agramonte, Emilio (1844–1918) Cuban-born teacher, composer, pianist, conductor, and singer. He studied in Paris and taught in Cuba (1866–1868) before moving to New York City in 1869, where he continued to teach and conduct choral societies, including the Gounod Society in New Haven, Connecticut. He founded the American Composers' Choral Association in 1890, presenting two seasons of American choral concerts before merging with the Manuscript Society of New York. He became a US citizen in 1886 and returned to Cuba in 1902. MacDowell dedicated *From an Old Garden*, op. 26, to Agramonte.

Apthorp, William Foster (1848–1913) Influential music critic in Boston. A piano and composition student of John Knowles Paine, he graduated from Harvard College in 1869 with a degree in music. In addition to writing books on various musical topics, he wrote music reviews for the *Atlantic Monthly*, *Dwight's Journal of Music*, and the *Boston Evening Transcript*. He also wrote the program notes for the Boston Symphony Orchestra from 1892 to 1901. At first puzzled by MacDowell's music, he was won over by the *Sonata Tragica*, op. 45, in 1893. He retired in 1903 to Switzerland.

Arens, Franz Xavier (1856–1932) Conductor, composer, and voice teacher. Born in Germany, he moved with his family to the Cleveland area at a young age. After music studies with his father, he became the organist and choirmaster of his Cleveland church at the age of fifteen. Later, he studied music in Munich and Dresden (Royal Conservatory). He conducted the Cleveland

Gesangverein and the Cleveland Philharmonic Orchestra in the late 1880s before returning to Germany for vocal study with Julius Hey in Berlin. While there he conducted a series of concerts of American orchestral music throughout Germany in 1891 and 1892, which helped establish MacDowell's reputation. He was head of the vocal department and president of the Metropolitan School of Music of Indianapolis (1892–1896) before moving to New York (1896), where he conducted concerts for the New York Manuscript Society (1898) and founded the People's Symphony Orchestra (1900).

Baker, Theodore (1851–1934) Originally a business student, he was an American music scholar and lexicographer. Baker studied in Germany, receiving his doctorate in Leipzig (1882) with a dissertation on Native American music. His dissertation provided the thematic source material for MacDowell's Second Suite ("Indian") for orchestra and for several piano pieces. He was literary editor and translator for the music publisher Schirmer in America from 1892 to 1926. He is remembered today for his *Biographical Dictionary of Musicians* (1900) and numerous translations of opera libretti.

Buitrago, Juan (1834–1914) Colombian violinist and MacDowell's first piano teacher. After starting Eddie's musical training, he accompanied him to Paris during his studies at the conservatory and lived with the MacDowell parents in New York for many years.

Burgess, John W. (1844–1931) American political scientist and professor at Columbia University from 1876 to 1912. After earning his undergraduate degree at Amherst, he completed his studies at the universities of Göttingen, Leipzig, and Berlin. He worked closely with Nicholas Murray Butler to found the Department of Political Science at Columbia and was influential in bringing MacDowell to Columbia. After MacDowell's resignation in 1904, Burgess convinced Cornelius Rübner to take the position, despite his inability to speak English.

Butler, Nicholas Murray (1862–1947) Twelfth president of Columbia University. When he succeeded Seth Low in 1902, he set about transforming Columbia University into a modern institution, earning the reputation of being materialistic rather than idealistic. Often heavy-handed in personnel decisions, he alienated many on the faculty during his early years. He was president of the Carnegie Endowment for International Peace and a recipient of the Nobel Peace Prize. An enormously important figure in American life, Theodore Roosevelt called him "Nicholas Miraculous" for his achievements.

Carreño, Teresa (1853–1917) Venezuelan concert pianist and singer who studied with Gottschalk, Mathias, and Rubinstein. Also a composer, she wrote primarily for piano and violin. She embodied the Latin temperament in her fiery performances and enjoyed an exceptionally long and successful career. She was a close friend of Fanny MacDowell, and she helped Edward by playing his music often in concert, including more than forty performances of his Second Piano Concerto.

Castellanos, Michael "Chichi" (1862–1940) Friend and fellow piano student of MacDowell in New York and Paris. His expulsion from the Paris Conservatory prompted MacDowell's resignation, and the two of them went to Stuttgart together in Fall 1878, where Castellanos graduated and MacDowell left after a month. Castellanos later served on the faculty of the New York College of Music for over forty years.

Chadwick, George Whitefield (1854–1931) American composer associated with the group known as the Second New England School. He was a founding member of the Music Teachers National Association and assumed the position of director of the New England Conservatory in 1897. He studied in Leipzig and Munich, but like MacDowell he did not complete the prescribed curriculum at any one school. Chadwick was the only Boston composer whom Edward felt he could trust during his residence there from 1888 to 1896.

Charlier, Elie (1826–1896) French teacher who came to New York in 1852. He founded the Charlier Institute in 1873, which became New York's leading preparatory school. In 1887 he sold the school and returned to France. MacDowell enrolled at school about 1870 and withdrew in January 1875. Charlier was also the grandfather of Pete Seeger.

Currier, T. P. (1856–1929) Piano student and friend of Edward MacDowell. After previous studies with B. J. Lang, he switched to MacDowell in 1888. As a critic for one of the Boston papers as well as a student of MacDowell's, he had a unique perspective on his teacher's pianism. He wrote several valuable articles on MacDowell's piano teaching and compositions, and he spent his subsequent career as a piano teacher in Boston.

D'Albert, Eugen (1864–1932) German pianist and composer. He studied with Liszt in Weimar and was present when MacDowell played for Liszt in June 1882. He was married six times, including a three-year marriage to Teresa Carreño from 1892 to 1895, during which time he forbade her playing MacDowell's works.

Damrosch, Walter (1862–1950) American conductor and composer. Born in Breslau, Germany, he was the son of the conductor Leopold Damrosch. After his father's death in 1885, he inherited his conducting responsibilities, including the New York Oratorio Society and Symphony Society, and used these to build a long and successful career. MacDowell had little contact with Damrosch but seems to have disliked him strongly.

Debussy, (Achille-) Claude (1862–1918) One of the most innovative and important composers of his time. He entered the Paris Conservatory in 1872 at the age of ten and was a member of Marmontel's class at the same time as MacDowell. He eventually won the Prix de Rome in 1887 and went on to become the leading representative of impressionism in music, a term that Gilman also applied to the music of MacDowell.

Deland, Margaret (1857–1945) American novelist. Born in Pennsylvania, she was also a writer of poetry and short stories. She moved to Boston in 1880, where she ran a home for unmarried mothers on Beacon Hill. It was during this time that she began her writing. She was known for her novel *John Ward, Preacher* and the poetry collection *The Old Garden*, from which MacDowell drew the texts for *From an Old Garden*, op. 26.

Desvernine, Pablo (1823–1910) Cuban pianist and teacher of Edward MacDowell. He studied in Paris 1840–1847, taking lessons with Kalkbrenner and Thalberg. He was active in Cuban music until moving to New York in 1869. He was responsible for developing MacDowell into an advanced pianist and convincing the family to send him to Paris for further study.

Diller, Angela (1877–1968) Piano student of MacDowell who was the first winner of the Mosenthal Fellowship in 1899. She taught at the New England Conservatory, the University of Southern California, and Mills College, as well as cofounding the Diller-Quaile School of Music in New York. Her piano method was widely used, selling more than 2 million copies.

Dvořák, Antonín (1841–1904) The greatest nineteenth-century Czech composer, known for his use of nationalism. He was already famous when Jeannette Thurber hired him as director of her National Conservatory of Music from 1892 to 1895. While there he wrote his Symphony No. 9, op. 95 ("From the New World") and other American-inspired works. His example and his pronouncements to the press helped to reshape the debate on nationalism in American music.

Ehlert, Louis (1825–1884) Composition teacher and music critic who taught MacDowell in Wiesbaden in the winter of 1879 and served as a mentor until his death five years later.

Erskine, John (1879–1951) Educated at Columbia University (AM, 1901; PhD, 1903) and subsequently served on the English faculty there from 1909 to 1937. He was one of the pioneers of the Great Books movement, a teaching philosophy closely related to MacDowell's methods in his surveys of music history. He was the author of numerous important books, and several of his autobiographical writings contain significant reminiscences of MacDowell and his classes.

Finck, Henry T. (1854–1926) American music critic and advocate of the Romantic composers Liszt, Wagner, Grieg, and MacDowell. He was the music critic of the *Nation* and the *New York Evening Post,* and also a prolific writer on various topics. MacDowell gave Finck the manuscript to his symphonic poem *Lamia*, which was published and performed within a year after the composer's death, despite Marian's reservations.

Foote, Arthur (1853–1937) American teacher, composer, organist, and pianist. He studied with John Knowles Paine at Harvard College, studied organ with B. J. Lang, and was the first American university student to earn an MA in music (Harvard, 1875). He wrote in a conservative Romantic style, specializing in chamber music. He was an especially fine teacher and wrote a theory text

316 · *Appendix C*

with Spalding. MacDowell and Strong did not trust him, as they felt he was jealous of MacDowell's success.

Fritzsch, Ernst Wilhelm (1840–1902) Leipzig music publisher. He published MacDowell's *Prélude et Fugue*, op. 13, and *Serenade*, op. 16, and was the publisher of the *Musikalisches Wochenblatt*.

Garland, Hamlin (1860–1940) Author who wrote on American topics and impressions. He especially focused on native Amerindian life in his writings. He first heard MacDowell perform when he was a penniless student in Boston, and the two became close friends in later years.

Gericke, Wilhelm (1845–1925) Austrian conductor. He led the Boston Symphony Orchestra (1884–1889 and 1898–1908), during which time he featured many of MacDowell's works, including the 1889 Boston premiere of the Second Piano Concerto.

Gilbert, Henry F. (1868–1928) American composer. A composition pupil of MacDowell after his arrival in Boston, he later became interested in Negro melodies and folk songs. His recollections provide important perspectives on MacDowell's early years in Boston.

Gilman, Lawrence (1878–1939) Music critic and MacDowell's first biographer. After early studies in art, he learned music on his own, becoming enamored of MacDowell's works in his early twenties. He published two books and numerous articles that did much for his hero's reputation. His enthusiasm led him to make intemperate statements about MacDowell's American contemporaries, which Marian believed contributed to professional jealousy by other composers. He later became a respected musical authority for *Harper's Weekly* and the *New York Herald Tribune*.

Gleason, Frederick Grant (1848–1903) American composer, teacher, and performer. The first president of the Chicago Manuscript Society, he was also music critic for the *Chicago Tribune*. He wrote music in many styles, including the use of leitmotifs. Theodore Thomas conducted much of his music.

Glücklich, J. C. MacDowell's realtor in Wiesbaden and the librettist of "Bitte," op. 33, no. 1.

Godowsky, Leopold (1870–1938) Lithuanian American pianist and composer. He was also a friend and colleague of W. S. B. Mathews in Chicago. Godowsky's phenomenal technique was reflected in a series of fifty-three *Studies on the Chopin Études* (1894–1914), free fantasies on the melodies and pianistic patterns of Chopin. When Godowsky dedicated his *Concert Study*, op. 11, no. 3, to MacDowell in 1899, the latter objected strenuously.

Grieg, Edvard (1843–1907) Norwegian composer, conductor, and pianist. A student at the Leipzig Conservatory, he studied piano with Moscheles and harmony and counterpoint with Richter, Hauptmann, and Reinecke. Known as a nationalist composer, he is famous for his incidental music to Ibsen's play *Peer Gynt*. MacDowell developed a friendship with Grieg by correspondence and dedicated his last two sonatas to him.

Hainauer, Julius (1827–1897) Music publisher in Breslau, Germany. He published many of MacDowell's early piano works with no royalties to the composer, as well as the orchestral works *Hamlet and Ophelia*, op. 22, *Lancelot and Elaine*, op. 25, and *Romanze* for cello and orchestra, op. 35, for which the composer paid substantial subventions. After MacDowell became famous and his works began selling in large quantities, he and Hainauer had an acrimonious dispute over US copyrights to the works published in Germany.

Hale, Philip (1854–1934) American music critic and program annotator. He studied in Europe with Haupt, Rheinberger, Bargiel, and Guilmant. He began his career as music critic for the *Boston Post*, moving to the *Boston Journal* the following year. He also wrote for the *Musical Courier*, and the *Boston Herald*. From 1901 to 1933 he wrote the program notes for the Boston Symphony Orchestra, developing the previously lightweight genre into one more scholarly and literary. He and his wife, Irene, bought a summer home near the MacDowells in New Hampshire.

Henderson, W. J. (1855–1937) Music critic for the *New York Times*. His enthusiastic reviews of MacDowell's performances and compositions did much to seal the composer's New York reputation.

Herbert, Victor (1859–1924) American cellist and composer. He studied at the Stuttgart Conservatory with Max Seifritz. He was also a conductor as well as a member of the faculty of the National Conservatory of Music. Most famous for operettas such as *Naughty Marietta*, he also composed concert works, including his cantata *The Captive*, premiered on the same Worcester Music Festival concert that premiered MacDowell's *Suite für grosses Orchester*, op. 42.

Heymann, Carl (1854–1922) An outstanding German piano virtuoso who taught at the Hoch Conservatory during the three semesters of MacDowell's attendance. Plagued by mental illness, he resigned his position in 1880 to settle in Bingen am Rhein and spent the last third of his life in a mental hospital.

Hinrichs, Gustav (1850–1942) Born in Mecklenburg, Germany, and trained as an orchestral musician. Hinrichs moved to San Francisco in 1870, where he taught, conducted, and composed for fifteen years. In 1885 he was named assistant to Theodore Thomas in the short-lived American Opera Company. He worked closely with MacDowell as conductor at Columbia University from 1899 to 1906. He was also assistant conductor at the Metropolitan Opera from 1903 to 1908 before relocating to San Francisco. He shared MacDowell's interest in new music, conducting the American premieres of *Cavalleria Rusticana*, *I Pagliacci*, and *Manon Lescaut* in San Francisco.

Humiston, William Henry (1869–1923) Organist, composer, and conductor. After early studies with W. S. B. Mathews in Chicago, he studied under MacDowell at Columbia University from 1896 to 1899. During a relatively brief career, he worked as an organist at various churches, as a conductor (including the post of assistant conductor of the New York Philharmonic from 1916), annotator of the New York Philharmonic programs from 1912, and composer in his own right. His large collection of early editions of MacDowell works is now in the Lowens Collection.

Huneker, James G. (1857–1921) American critic and writer. Author of "The Raconteur" columns for the *Musical Courier*, he was also critic for the *Philadelphia Press*, the *New York Times*, and the *New York World*. He edited piano pieces and songs by Chopin, Brahms, and Strauss, and published numerous books. His *New York Herald* essay on his visit with MacDowell in 1906 did much to shape public opinion on the composer's condition.

Huss, Henry Holden (1862–1953) New York composer, pianist, and teacher. He corresponded briefly with MacDowell during his Paris years and later studied at the Royal Music School in Munich with Rheinberger and Giehrl. He married the soprano Hildegard Hoffmann, with whom he gave recitals. He considered himself MacDowell's rival for the Columbia position, but there is no evidence that he was in serious contention.

Johnson, Robert Underwood (1853–1937) American writer and diplomat. He was on the staff of *Century Magazine* from 1873 to 1913, serving as associate editor and eventually editor. He was instrumental in creating Yosemite National Park and was also involved in forming the Sierra Club. He worked closely with MacDowell as secretary of the American Academy of Arts and Letters and later served as US ambassador to Italy after World War I.

Joseffy, Rafael (1852–1915) Hungarian pianist who studied with E. F. Wenzel, Tausig, and Liszt. He made his American debut in 1879 and later toured with Theodore Thomas and his orchestra. He was one of the first pianists in America to play Brahms on a regular basis. As a piano instructor at the National Conservatory from 1888 to 1906, he was in regular contact with Fanny MacDowell.

Kahnt, C. F. (1823–1897) German music publisher who featured works by contemporary composers such as Liszt, Busoni, Nielsen, and Mahler as well as lesser-known composers of the sixteenth and seventeenth centuries. He published MacDowell's songs, opp. 11 and 12, as well as his *Wald Idyllen*, op. 19, for piano.

Krehbiel, Henry E. (1854–1923) American music critic and scholar. He was the longtime musical editor of the *New York Tribune,* where his opinions exerted a strong influence on contemporary taste. He was the author of various books on musical topics, including one of the first books on African American music. He translated German language libretti and biographies, including Thayer's Beethoven biography.

Lachmund, Carl Valentine (1853–1928) American pianist who studied music in Germany. He became a close friend of Liszt while studying with him in Weimar. He eventually moved to Minneapolis to teach piano and tour as a concert pianist. Later, he moved to New York to establish the Lachmund Conservatory of Music. He met MacDowell during his 1882 visit to Weimar and corresponded with him in years after.

Lang, Benjamin Johnson (1837–1909) One of Boston's most powerful musicians and the man credited with convincing MacDowell to return to his homeland in 1888. Lang had studied in Berlin in the 1850s and went on to become an influential musician in Boston through his conducting and keyboard playing. He founded and directed the Apollo Club, a male chorus, and the Cecilia Society, a mixed chorus. A very busy teacher, he was able to amass a significant fortune over the course of his long career, which enabled his talented daughter Margaret Ruthven Lang (1867–1972) to devote her life to composition.

Langs, John Pierce (1882–1967) Piano student of MacDowell. Langs studied in Berlin from 1897 to 1898 before enrolling at Columbia University, where he studied composition and piano. After a year spent teaching at the University of Colorado at Boulder, Langs returned to New York to study piano privately during the winter of 1904–1905. Langs's detailed personal diary gives first-hand evidence of MacDowell's decline in the months before his breakdown.

Liszt, Franz (1811–1886) Hungarian composer, pianist, and leader of the group known as the "New German School." He was the greatest piano virtuoso of his time, causing students by the hundreds to flock to Weimar for lessons. A forward-looking composer, he is credited with the harmonic experimentation and use of thematic transformation that helped to drive musical ideas into the twentieth century. It was his advocacy that allowed MacDowell to perform at the 1882 festival of the Allgemeiner Deutscher Musikverein in Zürich, but there is no evidence to support the oft-repeated story that he convinced Breitkopf & Härtel to publish MacDowell's two piano suites.

Low, Seth (1850–1916) University president and politician. After making his fortune in the silk trade, Low served as mayor of Brooklyn from 1881 to 1885. As president of Columbia University from 1890 to 1901, he established a pension system and sabbatical leaves for faculty, oversaw the transformation from college to university, and shepherded the move from Midtown Manhattan to its current location in Morningside Heights. He donated $1 million to build the Low Memorial Library in the center of the new campus in honor of his late father. After running unsuccessfully for mayor of New York in 1897, he won the post in 1901, resigning as president of Columbia in order to devote full time to his new position. During a two-year term as mayor he reformed the police department and civil service system, lowered taxes, and improved educational opportunities, but he failed to win reelection. He hired MacDowell as first professor of music at Columbia University in 1896 and raised funds for his support after his collapse in 1905.

Marmontel, Antoine François (1816–1898) French pianist and teacher. He taught a large part of his career at the Paris Conservatory, where he had studied piano with Zimmermann and had won the "premier prix." His pupils included Albéniz, Debussy, MacDowell, and Pierné.

Mason, William (1829–1908) An important American piano teacher, performer, and composer. After studying with Liszt and others in the 1850s, Mason became established as a teacher in New York. His *Touch and Technic*, op. 44 (1889) is one of the most influential pedagogical texts of the nineteenth century. Mason admired the works of MacDowell and played them often, helping to popularize the piano sonatas and Virtuoso Etudes.

Mathews, W. S. B. (1837–1912) Music critic and piano teacher in Chicago. He was MacDowell's most vocal detractor, launching a series of diatribes in the pages of his journal *Music*. He particularly took issue with MacDowell's pianism, claiming that he did not play his own works as indicated in the scores.

McKim, Charles Follen (1847–1909) American architect. His firm designed the Boston Public Library, the Morningside Heights campus of Columbia University, Pennsylvania Station, the New York Herald building, and other icons of prewar architecture. He was instrumental in founding the American Academy in Rome, working closely with MacDowell.

McWhood, Leonard B. (1870–1939) Student and colleague of MacDowell at Columbia University. Already a student when MacDowell arrived in 1896, McWhood began teaching theory classes the following year. MacDowell requested a promotion for him in 1902 but was denied. After MacDowell's resignation, he was promoted to adjunct instructor, a position he held until 1910. The rumor circulated in the months after MacDowell's resignation that McWhood had done the bulk of the department's teaching in previous years, which MacDowell vigorously denied. McWhood incurred MacDowell's ire by refusing to issue a public statement refuting the rumor.

Moebius, Kurt New York representative of the Breitkopf & Härtel firm during the 1890s. Under his own imprint of P. L. Jung, Moebius published MacDowell's opp. 51–56 along with Thorn's opp. 1–7. These included some of the composer's most remunerative publications, but he was forced to sell his catalog to Schmidt when he got into financial trouble in 1899.

Nikisch, Arthur (1855–1922) Austro-Hungarian conductor who studied violin and composition at the Vienna Conservatory. He later became the principal conductor for the Leipzig Opera as well as the Boston Symphony Orchestra, the Budapest Opera, the Leipzig Gewandhaus Orchestra, and the Berlin Philharmonic Orchestra, earning a reputation as the most influential conductor of his day. His tenure in Boston from 1889 to 1893 was rocky, as the conservative audiences bridled at his interpretational liberties. He often featured MacDowell's works on his concerts, including twice during the 1892/93 season.

Paderewski, Ignace (1860–1941) Polish pianist and composer. He studied music in Warsaw, Berlin, and Vienna before embarking on an international career as a concert pianist. He was also a composer of piano music and the opera *Manru*. He became a matinee idol as much for his high level of pianistic virtuosity as for his striking appearance and stage mannerisms.

Parker, Henry Taylor (1867–1934) Boston music critic. He signed his reviews "H.T.P.," which was variously interpreted as "Hard to Please" or "Hell to

Pay." Although he did not read music, his perceptive comments and incisive writing earned him a loyal following. As critic for the *Boston Evening Transcript* from 1905, he opined that MacDowell's orchestral works were weak, passing a negative judgment on the premiere of *Lamia* in 1908.

Parker, Horatio (1863–1919) American church musician and important composer who studied composition with Chadwick in Boston. An accomplished organist, he studied at the Royal Music School in Munich with Josef Rheinberger. He became organist and choirmaster at Trinity Church in Boston in 1893. He was appointed Battell Professor of Music at Yale University in 1894, where he exerted an important influence on music in higher education. Like MacDowell, his works were highly regarded in England in the early twentieth century.

Paur, Emil (1855–1932) Austrian violinist, conductor, and composer. He succeeded Nikisch as the conductor of the Boston Symphony Orchestra, replaced Seidl at the New York Philharmonic Society, and was Dvořák's successor as director of the National Conservatory of Music.

Pierné, Gabriel (1863–1937) French composer and conductor. He studied at the Paris Conservatory, winning premiers prix for organ, harmony, and counterpoint. He was appointed principal conductor at the Concerts Colonne, where he conducted many premieres of works by important composers of his day.

Raff, Joachim (1822–1882) Swiss composer, teacher, and critic. He worked closely with Liszt in Weimar in the early 1850s before relocating to Wiesbaden in 1856 to teach piano, singing, and harmony. He became the director of the Hoch Conservatory in Frankfurt in 1878, where he taught Edward MacDowell. Among the most famous composers in Europe at his death in 1882, his reputation declined rapidly in the succeeding decades. His life and works are chronicled extensively at www.raff.org.

Raff, Doris (1826–1912) Wife of Joachim Raff. She was the daughter of Eduard Genast, Weimar Court Theatre Director. Raff fell in love with her in 1850 while working with Liszt in Weimar. She left to become an actress with the Royal Theatre in Wiesbaden in 1853, and they were married there in 1859. After Raff's death in 1882, she struggled to publish his remaining works. Edward MacDowell helped her negotiate with A. P. Schmidt for the publication of the *Four Shakespeare Overtures*, only two of which appeared in print.

Riedel, Carl (1827–1888) German composer and choral conductor. He studied music at the Leipzig Conservatory with Hauptmann and joined the faculty upon graduation. He became a supporter of the "New German School" through his presidency of the Allgemeiner Deutscher Musikverein.

Rübner [Rybner], Cornelius (1853–1929) Danish pianist and teacher. After MacDowell's resignation from Columbia University in 1904, Burgess hired Rübner on the recommendation of some American women who had heard him play at a German resort. Even though he did not speak English and had no musical reputation, he succeeded in ingratiating himself with students and administrators as MacDowell had not.

Riemenschneider, Georg (1848–1913) German conductor, critic, and composer. He often performed the orchestral works of MacDowell with his orchestra in Breslau, and he wrote laudatory reviews of MacDowell's works for German periodicals.

Saint-Saëns, Camille (1835–1921) French composer, organist, and pianist with close ties to Liszt and the "New German School." A member of the 1878 piano jury at the Paris Conservatory, he resigned in protest over biased judging. MacDowell dedicated his *Zweite moderne Suite*, op. 14, to Saint-Saëns.

Sauret, Emile (1852–1920) French violinist and composer. The first husband of Teresa Carreño, he had access to their daughter, Emilita, who lived with the Bischoff family in Wiesbaden and was prohibited from contact with her mother.

Schirmer, Gustav (1829–1893) One of America's most important music publishers. The firm published only one of MacDowell's works, *From an Old Garden*, op. 26 (1887). The composer was so angry over the appearance of the cover, for which he had given detailed instructions, that they never collaborated again. In 1906, after MacDowell's breakdown, the firm paid Marian MacDowell back royalties, which her husband had refused to accept in his fit of pique.

Schmidt, Arthur P. (1846–1921) German-born American publisher who specialized in works by New England composers Chadwick, Beach, Bird, Paine, Parker, Foote, and MacDowell in gratitude for his success in America. He believed strongly in MacDowell's talent, promoting his works and supporting his widow Marian despite the composer's often-ungrateful behavior.

Seidl, Anton (1850–1898) Austro-Hungarian by birth, he became a naturalized American citizen. He championed the operatic works of Wagner, bringing the operas performed at the Met up to a very high standard. His protégés included Victor Herbert and Arthur Farwell, and he famously stated that he preferred the works of MacDowell to those of Brahms.

Sinclair, Upton (1878–1968) Studied at Columbia University briefly after studying at City College in New York. Financial exigencies forced him to leave before earning a degree, but he achieved fame with his 1906 novel *The Jungle*, the eleven novels of the Lanny Budd series, and numerous other works of fiction. He published recollections of his student days with MacDowell.

Sonneck, Oscar George Theodore (1873–1928) American musicologist, librarian, and editor. He studied in Heidelberg, Munich, and Sondershausen in Germany. He was head of the music division of the Library of Congress from 1902 to 1917 and edited the *Musical Quarterly*. An ardent champion of American music, he published a seminal work on early American secular music, laid the foundation of the exemplary collection of American scores at the Library of Congress, and published the foundational study on MacDowell's published editions. The Sonneck Society for American Music was named in his honor at its founding in 1975.

Strong, George Templeton, Jr. (1856–1948) American composer and painter and Edward MacDowell's best friend. The two met in 1886 when Strong moved to Wiesbaden. Strong's works include two symphonies, numerous choral works, and compositions for piano. Despite MacDowell's urging, Strong lacked initiative to promote his own works. He taught at the New England Conservatory from 1891 to 1892 but returned to Switzerland when his marriage fell apart. MacDowell again convinced him to move to America in the summer of 1896, but when Strong learned of his friend's impending move to New York, they had a falling out, and he abandoned music to become a watercolorist in Switzerland. After three years of estrangement, they reestablished contact in 1899.

Thomas, Ambroise (1811–1896) French composer, teacher, and pedagogical writer. He studied at the Paris Conservatory with Zimmerman, Doulen, and Le Sueur, winning the Prix de Rome in 1832. He was primarily an opera composer, famous for his *Mignon* and *Hamlet.* As director of the Conservatory during MacDowell's student years, he instituted reforms to remove underperforming students.

Thomas, Theodore (1835–1905) American conductor. Born in Germany, his formal music training came to a halt after moving to America. He toured the country with his orchestra, introducing orchestral music to small towns on the "Thomas Highway." He was famous for his Cincinnati May Festival concerts and later directed the New York Philharmonic before becoming the first conductor of the Chicago Symphony Orchestra. He played a vital role in American musical life, premiering many great masterpieces of European music to the American public. He served as music director for the Philadelphia Centennial Exhibition in 1876 and the World's Columbian Exposition in Chicago in 1893.

Thurber, Jeannette Meyer (1850–1946) American music patron. She studied at the Paris Conservatory, which served as the model for her National Conservatory of Music in New York City. Students were accepted according to talent and not barred because of race or religion. MacDowell refused her offer of a position on the faculty in 1888, but his mother Fanny became Thurber's secretary in 1889. Dvořák served as director of the conservatory from 1892 to 1895.

Tretbar, Charles F. (ca. 1829–1909) Joined the firm of Steinway and Sons in 1864, where he served for forty years. During this time he was instrumental in building the Steinway roster of concert artists, arranging US tours for numerous European luminaries. MacDowell used his services as agent for a number of years in the 1890s.

Van der Stucken, Frank (1858–1929) American conductor and composer born in Fredericksburg, Texas. He studied music in Holland and went on to an important career in New York and Cincinnati. He organized and conducted concerts of American music in New York and for the 1889 Paris Exposition. The founder of the Cincinnati Symphony (1895), he was also the dean of the

Cincinnati College of Music (later merged with the Conservatory of Music as the Cincinnati College-Conservatory of Music in 1955). He was the music director for the Cincinnati May Festival from 1906 to 1912 and from 1923 to 1927.

Whiting, Arthur (1861–1936) American composer, pianist, and teacher who studied with Chadwick at the New England Conservatory and later with Rheinberger at the Munich Conservatory. He lived in Boston from 1885 to 1895 and in New York thereafter. His music—mostly for piano and chamber ensembles—was conservative in style. Despite a personal antipathy to Whiting, MacDowell proposed him as a member of the National Institute of Arts and Letters.

Wilson, George H. (1854–1908) Critic for the *Boston Traveller* when MacDowell returned from Europe in 1888. Shortly afterward, he purchased the *Boston Musical Herald* and used this journal as a platform from which to attack F. X. Arens for his American Composers' Concerts in Germany in 1892. MacDowell refused to endorse Wilson's smear campaign, despite his own reservations about the Arens tour. As music secretary of the World's Columbian Exposition in 1893, Wilson incurred MacDowell's wrath by prematurely announcing that the composer would set the Columbian Ode to music for the dedication ceremony. MacDowell subsequently incurred Wilson's wrath by agreeing to perform at the Exposition but pulling out at the last minute. Wilson later settled in Pittsburgh as manager of the Carnegie Music Hall and the Pittsburgh Symphony. He and MacDowell reconciled their differences and arranged for performances of his orchestral works in Pittsburgh.

Woodberry, George E. (1855–1930) Professor of comparative literature at Columbia University from 1891 to 1904. A brilliant author and lecturer, his unconventional teaching made him a favorite of students and a target of the administration. After humiliating confrontations with Columbia's president Nicholas Murray Butler, Woodberry took a sabbatical in 1903/04, submitting his resignation letter to the university on 14 January 1904, four days before MacDowell's resignation.

Zerrahn, Carl (1826–1909) German-born American conductor and flutist. He conducted the Harvard Musical Association Orchestra and the Worcester Festival orchestra. He was also a respected choral conductor and taught singing, harmony, and composition at the New England Conservatory.

Bibliography

Aborn, Merton Robert. "The Influence on American Musical Culture of Dvořák's Sojourn in America." PhD diss., Indiana University, 1965.

Adams, Mrs. Crosby. *What the Piano Writings of Edward MacDowell Mean to the Piano Student.* Chicago: Clayton F. Summy, 1913.

Albuquerque, Anne E. "Teresa Carreño: Pianist, Teacher, and Composer." DMA thesis, Cincinnati College-Conservatory of Music, 1988.

Aldrich, Richard. *Concert Life in New York: 1902–1923.* New York: G. P. Putnam's Sons, 1941.

"America's First Composer Honored." *San Francisco Chronicle*, 7 January 1903, 9.

"America's Leading Composer is Here." *San Francisco Chronicle*, 3 January 1903, 14.

"America Mourns the Loss of Its Greatest Composer." *Musical America* 7/12 (1 February 1908): 5–6.

"An American Music House in Europe." *Boston Musical Herald* 11/7 (July 1890): 152–53.

Anderson, Hilary. "Building *A House of Dreams Untold.*" *Historical New Hampshire* 51/1 and 2 (Spring/Summer 1996): 47–56.

Anderson-Gilman, Wilma. "Mrs. Edward A. MacDowell Appears at Convention of Minnesota Music Teachers' Association." *MC* 70/26 (30 June 1915): 35.

[Angell, Richard S.] *Catalogue of an exhibition illustrating the life and work of Edward MacDowell, 1861–1908: professor of music in Columbia University 1896–1904: together with the addresses delivered at the opening ceremony, April 27, 1938.* New York: Columbia University Library, 1938.

Angell, Richard S. *Supplement to Sonneck's MacDowell Catalogue, Containing Notes on Columbia Copies of MacDowell First Editions.* New York: n.p., 1942.

"Another Correction by Professor MacDowell." *New York Evening Post*, 23 April 1904, 4.

Armstrong, William. "Edward MacDowell on the Relations of Music and Poetry." *Etude* 20/7 (July 1902): 247–48.

Baker, Theodore. *Über die Musik der Nordamerikanischen Wilden.* Leipzig: Breitkopf & Härtel, 1882.

Baker, Theodore. *On the Music of the North American Indians.* Translated by Ann Buckley. New York: Da Capo Press, 1977.

Barnes, Edwin N. C. *Near Immortals? Stephen Foster, Edward MacDowell, Victor Herbert.* Washington: Music Education Publications, 1940.

Barzun, Jacques, ed. *A History of the Faculty of Philosophy: Columbia University.* New York: Columbia University Press, 1957.

Bauer, Emilie Frances. "Teresa Carreño Tells of MacDowell's Youth." *New York Evening Mail*, 31 March 1908, 7.

Beckerman, Michael. "Henry Krehbiel, Antonin Dvořák, and the Symphony 'From the New World.'" *Notes* 59 (December 1992): 447–73.

Bertrand, Jean. "Drame et musique." *La République française*, 5 August 1878, 2.

Blasing, Francesca. "The Legacy of Edward MacDowell." *American Music Teacher* 46/4 (1997): 28.

Block, Adrienne Fried. "Boston Talks Back to Dvořák." *I.S.A.M Newsletter* 18/2 (May 1989): 10.

Block, Adrienne Fried. "Amy Beach's Music on Native American Themes." *American Music* 8/2 (Summer 1990): 141–66.

Bobo, Richard. "Edward MacDowell as Pianist." *American Music Teacher* 46/4 (February/March 1997): 25–28, 75.

Bobo, Richard. "Edward MacDowell's Wonderful Etudes." *Clavier* 33/4 (April 1994): 22–29.

Bobo, Richard. "MacDowell's Twelve Virtuoso Etudes: A Closer Look." *American Music Teacher* 42/2 (October/November 1992): 32–35.

Bomberger, E. Douglas. "Edward MacDowell, Arthur P. Schmidt, and the Shakespeare Overtures of Joachim Raff: A Case Study in Nineteenth-Century Music Publishing." *Notes* 54/1 (September 1997): 11–26.

Bomberger, E. Douglas. "The German Musical Training of American Students, 1850–1900." PhD diss., University of Maryland, 1991.

Bomberger, E. Douglas. "Kelley vs. Lebert: An American Confronts a German Piano Method." *American Music Teacher* 43/4 (February/March 1994): 14–17, 81.

Bomberger, E. Douglas. *"A Tidal Wave of Encouragement": American Composers' Concerts in the Gilded Age.* Westport, CT: Praeger, 2002.

"Boston's Discovery of 'Lamia.'" *Literary Digest* 37/19 (7 November 1908): 670.

Brancaleone, Francis. "Edward MacDowell and Indian Motives." *American Music* 7/4 (Winter 1989): 359–81.

Brancaleone, Francis. "The Short Piano Works of Edward MacDowell." PhD diss., City University of New York, 1982.

"Breitkopf & Härtel: The Leipzig House Represented in New York." *MC* 23/2 (8 July 1891): 44.

Brower, Edith. "New Figures in Literature and Art: E. A. MacDowell." *Atlantic Monthly* 77/461 (March 1896): 394–402.

Brower, Harriette. *Piano Mastery: Talks with Master Pianists and Teachers.* New York: Frederick A. Stokes, [1915].

Brower, Harriette. *Piano Mastery, Second Series: Talks with Master Pianists and Teachers.* New York: Frederick A. Stokes, 1917.

Brower, Harriette. *Story-Lives of Master Musicians.* New York: Frederick A. Stokes, 1922.

Brower, Harriette. *The World's Great Men of Music.* New York: Frederick A. Stokes, 1922.

Brown, Abbie Farwell. *The Boyhood of Edward MacDowell.* New York: Frederick A. Stokes, 1924.

Brown, Rollo Walter. *Lonely Americans.* New York: Coward-McCann, 1929.

Browner, Tara. "'Breathing the Indian Spirit': Thoughts on Musical Borrowing and the 'Indianist' Movement in American Music." *American Music* 15/3 (Autumn 1997): 265–84.

Browner, Tara C. "Transposing Cultures: The Appropriation of Native North American Musics, 1890–1990." PhD diss., University of Michigan, 1995.

Bruton, Carole Diane. "A Pedagogical and Performing Analysis of Edward MacDowell's *Zwölf Virtuosen-Etuden*, Op. 46." DMA diss., Southwestern Baptist Theological Seminary, 1996.

Burgess, John W. *Reminiscences of an American Scholar: The Beginnings of Columbia University.* New York: Columbia University Press, 1934.

Burgess, Ruth Payne. "Teresa Carreño as a Teacher." *Etude* 48/11 (November 1930): 779–80, 826.

Burnaman, S. P. "The Solo Piano Music of Edward MacDowell and Mrs. H. H. A Beach: A Historical Analysis." PhD diss., University of Texas, 1997.

Butler, Nicholas Murray. *Across the Busy Years: Recollections and Reflections.* 2 vols. New York: C. Scribner's Sons, 1939–40.

Cadman, Charles Wakefield. "The 'Idealization' of Indian Music." *MQ* 1/3 (July 1915): 387–96.

Cahn, Peter. *Das Hoch'sche Konservatorium in Frankfurt am Main: 1879–1978.* Frankfurt am Main: Kramer, 1979.

Calcaño, José Antonio. *La Ciudad y su música: Crónica Musical de Caracas*. Caracas: Conservatorio Teresa Carreño, 1958.

Carney, M. W. P. "Bromism–A Clinical Chameleon." *Nursing Times* (5 July 1973): 859–60.

Carreño, Teresa. "My Interpretation of MacDowell's Barcarolle." *Delineator* 75 (January 1910): 47.

"Carreño and MacDowell." *Musical America* 7/8 (4 January 1908): 12.

"The Case of Prof. MacDowell." *New York Evening Post*, 10 February 1904, 9.

"Chair of Music for Columbia. E. A. MacDowell Named as the First Professor—Gifts to the University." *NYT*, 5 May 1896, 5.

C[heatham], K[atharine] S[miley]. "A Wider Field for New York's Most Exclusive Singing Organization." *Musical America* 15 (27 April 1912): 3.

Cho, Hyunjung. "The Four Piano Sonatas of Edward MacDowell." DMA diss., Boston University, 2001.

Cipolla, Wilma Reid. "Marketing the American Song in Edwardian London." *American Music* 8/1 (Spring 1990): 84–94.

Clapham, John. "Dvořák's Musical Directorship in New York." *Music and Letters* 48/1 (January 1967): 40–51.

Clapham, John. "The Evolution of Dvořák's Symphony 'From the New World.'" MQ 44/2 (April 1958): 167–83.

Clute, Fayette J. *The ABC of Photography by an Amateur*, rev. ed. Chicago: Burke and James, 1909.

Cohen, Henry. "Concours du conservatoire." *L'Art Musical* 16/31 (2 August 1877): 243.

"College Men Boors, says Professor." *New York World*, 4 February 1904.

"Columbia and the Department of Music: Statement by President Butler." *NYT*, 8 February 1904, 8.

"The Columbia Snarl: Versions of the MacDowell Affair that Clash." *Boston Evening Transcript*, 12 February 1904.

"Columbia's Coming Celebration." *Bookman* 3/3 (May 1896): 224–27.

Comettant, Oscar. "Revue musicale," *Le Siècle*, 30 July 1877, 2.

Cooke, James Francis. *Edward MacDowell: A Short Biography*. Philadelphia: Theodore Presser, [1928].

Copland, Aaron. "Making Music in the Star-Spangled Manner." *Music and Musicians* 8 (August 1960): 8–9.

Corey, N[ewton] J. "Mr. Mathews on MacDowell." *MC* 42/10 (6 March 1901): 9–10.

Crawford, Richard Arthur. "Edward MacDowell: Musical Nationalism and an American Tone Poet." *Journal of the American Musicological Society* 49/3 (Autumn 1996): 528–60.

Crawford, Richard, R. Allen Lott, and Carol J. Oja, eds. *A Celebration of American Music: Words and Music in Honor of H. Wiley Hitchcock*. Ann Arbor: University of Michigan Press, 1990.

"Criticizes Butler and Quits Columbia." *NYT*, 4 February 1904, 16.

"Crystal Palace Concerts." *Musical Times* 41/687 (1 May 1900): 320.

Currier, T[homas] P[arker]. "Edward MacDowell as I Knew Him." *MQ* 1/1 (January 1915): 16–51.

Currier, T[homas] P[arker]. "MacDowell's Compositions." *Musician* 17/5 (May 1912): 305 and 351.

Currier, T[homas] P[arker]. "MacDowell's Etudes." *Musician* 15/12 (December 1910): 806–7.

Currier, T[homas] P[arker]. "MacDowell's Technic as Related to his Piano Music." *Musician* 13/3 (March 1908): 113.

D. L. L. "Edward MacDowell as an Instructor: Edith Thompson Tells of Incidents in her Study with Late Composer." *Musical America* 7/24 (25 April 1908): 19.

Deaville, James. "Allgemeiner Deutscher Musikverein." *New Grove Dictionary of Music and Musicians*, vol. 1, 403–4, 2nd ed. London: Macmillan, 2001.

Dempsey, Delia A. "Bromides." In *Poisoning & Drug Overdose*, Kent R. Olson, ed., 5th ed. New York: Lange Medical Books/McGraw-Hill, 2007. P. 140.

Derby, Ellen S., and Ann D. Grummon. "Why Peterborough? The Appeal of a Small Town." *Historical New Hampshire* 51/1 and 2 (Spring/Summer 1996): 41–46.

[Dickinson, Edward]. "Edward MacDowell." *Oberlin Review* 30 (12 February 1903): 297–98.

Dillon, John J. *Seven Decades of Milk: A History of New York's Dairy Industry.* New York: Orange Judd, 1941.

Dilsner, L. "Edward MacDowell—The Man, His Times." *American Music Teacher* 19/4 (April 1970): 31–32.

Dinsmoor, William Bell. "The Department of Fine Arts and Archaeology." In *A History of the Faculty of Philosophy: Columbia University.* Ed. Jacques Barzun. New York: Columbia University Press, 1957. Pp. 252–69.

Downes, Olin. "Early Views of MacDowell." *NYT*, 12 June 1927, sect. 7, 6.

Dumm, Robert W. "The Piano Music of Edward MacDowell." *Clavier* 35/5 (May/June 1996): 24–27.

Dvořák, Antonín, assisted by Edwin Emerson Jr. "Music in America." *Harper's New Monthly Magazine* 90/537 (February 1895): 429–34.

Eagle, Nancy Louise. "The Pianoforte Sonatas of Edward A. MacDowell, a Style-Critical Study." Master's thesis, University of North Carolina–Chapel Hill, 1952.

"E. A. MacDowell a Wreck: His Days of Work Over." *New York Tribune*, 28 November 1905, 1.

"E. A. MacDowell's Funeral." *Brooklyn Daily Eagle*, 25 January 1908, 2.

"Edgar Thorn: An Appreciation." *Musical World* 3/4 (April 1903): 63–64.

Editorial. *Columbia Literary Monthly* 4/8 (May 1896): 342.

Editorial. *MC* 40/6 (7 February 1900): 26.

Editorial. "Society of American Musicians." *MC* 40/7 (14 February 1900): 26.

"Edward A. MacDowell." *Brooklyn Daily Eagle*, 24 January 1908, 3.

"Edward A. MacDowell Dead." *MC* 56/5 (29 January 1908): 23–24.

"Edward Alexander MacDowell: Something about Columbia University's New Professor of Music." *Sun*, 10 May 1896.

"Edward MacDowell: A Biographical Sketch," *Musical Times* 44/734 (1 April 1904): 222.

"Edward MacDowell, Composer." *Queen* (13 September 1923): 302.

"The Edward MacDowell Fund." *MC* 54/5 (30 January 1907): 48–49.

"Edward Mac Dowell Greatly Improved: Eminent Composer Rallies in an Astonishing Manner and May Recover." *Musical America* 3/22 (14 April 1906): 1.

"Edward MacDowell: The Spirit of American Individuality in Music." *Musician* 20/6 (June 1915): 167–68.

Elkin, Robert. "Great American Composer." *Radio Times*, 25 March 1938, 12.

Elson, Louis C. *The History of American Music.* Revised by Arthur Elson. New York: Macmillan, 1925.

Erskine, John. "MacDowell at Columbia: Some Recollections." *MQ* 28/4 (October 1942): 395–405.

Erskine, John. *The Memory of Certain Persons.* Philadelphia, New York: Lippincott, 1947.

Erskine, John. *My Life in Music.* New York: Morrow, 1950; repr. Westport, CT: Greenwood, 1973.

"Etude Master Study Page: MacDowell." *Etude* 33/11 (November 1915): 793–94.

Falconer-Salkeld, Bridget. *The MacDowell Colony: A Musical History of America's Premier Artists' Community.* Lanham, MD: Scarecrow, 2005.

"Fate of Robert Schumann and Edward MacDowell." *Metronome* 21/9 (September 1906): 15.

Festschrift für das fünfundzwanzigjährige Jubiläum des Konservatoriums für Musik in Stuttgart, den 30. Mai bis 2. Juni 1882. Stuttgart: J. B. Metzler, [1882].

Finck, Henry T. "An American Composer: Edward A. MacDowell." *Century Magazine* 53/3 (January 1897): 449–54.

Finck, Henry T. "Creative Americans: Edward MacDowell, Musician and Composer." *Outlook* 84/17 (22 December 1906): 983–89.

Finck, Henry T. "Edward MacDowell as a Man and Artist." *Musician* 13/3 (March 1908): 111–12.

Finck, Henry T. "Musical Genius and Insanity." *Etude* 33/5 (May 1915): 339–40; repr. as "MacDowell's Last Days." *Music Student* 7/12 (August 1915): 257.

Finck, Henry T. "Musical News and Gossip." *Evening Post Magazine*, 23 August 1919.

Finck, Henry T. *My Adventures in the Golden Age of Music*. New York: Funk & Wagnalls, 1926.

Finck, Henry T. "Representative American Composers." Translated by Gustav Saenger. *Metronome* 21/9 (September 1906): 9; 21/10 (October 1906): 9; 21/11 (November 1906): 9.

Finck, Henry T. *Songs and Song Writers*. New York: Charles Scribner's Sons, 1900.

Finck, Mrs. Henry T. "We Visit MacDowell and Listen Secretly to what He Called his 'Rotten Melodies.'" *Musical America* 49 (25 February 1929): 13.

"Fine Arts and MacDowell." *MC* 48/7 (17 February 1904): 23.

"First Award of the Mosenthal Fellowship in Music." *Columbia Spectator* 42/21 (2 May 1899): 2.

Fountain, Richard Daniel. "Edward MacDowell and the Formation of an American Musical Culture." DMA diss., University of Nebraska–Lincoln, 2008.

Frankfurt um 1900: "Schöne bunte Welt." Köln: Emons, [1998].

Frey, Martin. "Edward MacDowell." *Musikalisches Wochenblatt* 40/47 (24 February 1910): 669–71.

Gardner, Kara Anne. "Edward MacDowell, Antimodernism, and 'Playing Indian' in the Indian Suite." *MQ* 87/3 (Fall 2004): 370–422.

Garland, Hamlin. *Companions on the Trail: A Literary Chronicle.* New York: Macmillan, 1931.

Garland, Hamlin. *Crumbling Idols.* Chicago: Stone and Kimball, 1894.

Garland, Hamlin. *Roadside Meetings.* New York: Macmillan, 1930.

Gates, W. Francis. "Robert Franz and Edward MacDowell—A Parallel." *Musical Review* 9/6 (October 1906): 28–29.

Gerner, R. H. "Bromism from over-the-counter medications." *The American Journal of Psychiatry* 135/11 (November 1978): 1428.

Gilbert, Henry F. "Personal Recollections of Edward MacDowell." *New Music Review* 2 (November 1912): 495.

Gilbert, Henry F. "The American Composer." *MQ* 1/2 (April 1915): 169–80.

Gilman, Lawrence. "An American Tone-Poet." *Harper's Weekly* 46 (17 May 1902): 623.

Gilman, Lawrence. "The Art of Fiona Macleod." *North American Review* 183/4 (October 1906): 674–79.

Gilman, Lawrence. "Edward MacDowell: An Appreciation." *Musical Record* 463 (1 August 1900): 339–40.

Gilman, Lawrence. *Edward MacDowell: A Study.* New York: John Lane, 1908.

Gilman, Lawrence. "The MacDowell Club: A New Force in the Art Life of New York." *Critic* 48/6 (June 1906): 516–22.

Gilman, Lawrence. "MacDowell's 'Keltic Sonata.'" *Musical World* 1/5 (June 1901): 60–61.

Gilman, Lawrence. "Mr. MacDowell's Recent Work." *Musical World* 3/10 (October 1903): 163–64.

Gilman, Lawrence. "The Music of Edward MacDowell." *North American Review* 178/6 (June 1904): [927]–32.

Goetschius, Percy. *The Material Used in Musical Composition: A System of Harmony Designed and Adopted for Use in English Harmony Classes of the Conservatory of Music, at Stuttgart.* Stuttgart: Zumsteeg, 1882.

Goler, Robert I. "A Collective Vision of Artistry: The MacDowell Colony and the Organizational Design of Creativity." *Journal of Arts Management, Law, and Society* 35/3 (Fall 2005): 217–27.

Golomb, Beatrice Alexandra. "Bromism." In *A Review of the Scientific Literature as it Pertains to Gulf War Illnesses*, chap. 10. Rand, 1999. http://www.gulflink.osd.mil/library/randrep/pb_paper/mr1018.2.chap10.html, accessed 28 January 2012.

Gottschalk, [Clara] Aimée. "A Memory of MacDowell." *Bulletin of the Stojowski Students' Association* (May 1940): 3–4.

Grant, Mark N. *Maestros of the Pen: A History of Classical Music Criticism in America.* Boston: Northeastern University Press, 1998.

Greene, Gary A. *Henry Holden Huss: an American Composer's Life.* Metuchen, NJ: Scarecrow, 1995.

[Hale, Philip.] "London Estimates of MacDowell: MacDowell's English Critics." *Boston Sunday Herald,* 7 June 1903, 39.

Hale, Philip. "Music in Boston." *MC* 27/26 (27 December 1893): 20.

Halverson, William H. "Grieg and MacDowell: A Tale of Two Edwards." *Sonneck Society Bulletin* 23/1 (Spring 1997): 5–6.

Hanson, Howard. "MacDowell: American Romantic Supreme." *Music Journal* 19/8 (Nov/Dec 1961): 30, 76–77.

Hartmann, Arthur. *"Claude Debussy as I Knew Him" and Other Writings of Arthur Hartmann.* Edited by Samuel Hsu, Sidney Grolnic, and Mark Peters. Rochester: University of Rochester Press, 2003.

Henderson, W. J. "American Composers." *Mentor* 6/3 (1 February 1918): 1–12.

[Henderson, William J.] "Mr. E. A. MacDowell's Recitals: An American Composer and Pianist Who Ranks Among the Best." *NYT,* 1 March 1895, 2.

Hier, Ethel Glenn. *The Boyhood and Youth of Edward MacDowell: Seven Scenes with Prologue and Epilogue.* Peterborough, NH: Nubanusit Press, 1926.

Hill, Edward Burlingame. "MacDowell's Marionettes." *Musician* 15/10 (October 1910): 653, 703.

Hill, Edward Burlingame. "Musical Boston in the Gay Nineties." Five-part article in *Etude* (January–May 1949).

Hill, E[dward] B[urlingame]. "Program Music (Conclusion)." *Music* 20/7 (November 1901): 391–95.

Hinson, Maurice. "Edward MacDowell: America's Great Tone Poet." *Clavier* 20/4 (April 1981): 22–23.

"Hope for American Music." *MC* 37/11 (12 September 1898): 5.

Horn, Julia Bachus. "Edward MacDowell: Personal Recollections." *Louisville Courier-Journal,* 11 December 1932.

Horowitz, Joseph. *Classical Music in America: A History.* New York: Norton, 2007.

Horowitz, Joseph. "Reclaiming the Past: Musical Boston Reconsidered." *American Music* 19/1 (Spring 2001): 18–38.

Howard, John Tasker. *Our American Music: Three Hundred Years Of It.* New York: Thomas Y. Crowell, 1946.

Howard, John Tasker. "The American Composer: The Victim of His Friends." *MQ* 8/3 (July 1922): 313–18.

Howland, Stephen Norman. "Edward MacDowell's 'Woodland Sketches' arranged for guitar: Performance Edition, Biography, and Literature Review." DMA diss., Arizona State University, 1998.

Hughes, Rupert, *Contemporary American Composers.* Boston: L. C. Page, 1900.

Hughes, Rupert. *Famous American Composers.* Boston: Page, 1900; rev. ed. 1914.

Hughes, Rupert. "Music in America: Edward Alexander MacDowell." *Godey's Magazine* 131 (July 1895): [80]–87.

Hughes, Rupert. "Music in America: The Manuscript Society and Its President." *Godey's Magazine* 133 (July 1896): 80–86.

Hume, Paul, and Ruth Hume. "The Great Chicago Piano War." *American Heritage* 21/6 (October 1970): 16–21.

Humiston, William H[enry]. *MacDowell*. New York: Breitkopf & Härtel, 1921.

Humiston, William H[enry]. "Personal Recollections of Edward MacDowell." *Musician* 13/3 (March 1908): 160–61.

Humiston, William H[enry]. "The Work of Edward MacDowell." *Papers and Proceedings of the Music Teachers' National Association at its Thirtieth Annual Meeting*. Hartford, CT: Published by the Association, 1909.

Huneker, James. "An American Composer: The Passing of Edward MacDowell." *New York Herald*, 24 June 1906, magazine sec., 2; repr. in James G. Huneker. *Unicorns*. New York: Charles Scribner's Sons, 1924. 6–17.

[Huneker, James]. "Personals: E. A. MacDowell." *MC* 18/15 (10 April 1889): 284.

Irgang, W. "E. A. MacDowell, Op. 10 und Op. 14, Erste und zweite moderne Suite für Pianoforte," *Neue Zeitschrift für Musik* 79/31 (27 July 1883): 350.

Jonson, G. C. Ashton. "Some Aspects of the Work of Edward MacDowell. *Music Student* 3/7 (April 1911): 115–17.

Jonson, G. C. Ashton. "The Poetry of Edward MacDowell." *Music Student* 7/12 (August 1915): 255–56.

Kaiserman, David. "Edward MacDowell—The Keltic and Eroica Piano Sonatas." *Music Journal* 24 (February 1966): 51, 76ff.

Kearns, William Kay. *Horatio Parker, 1863–1919: His Life, Music, and Ideas*. Metuchen, NJ: Scarecrow, 1990.

Kefferstan, Christine Bane. "The Piano Concertos of Edward MacDowell." DMA thesis, University of Cincinnati, 1984.

Kenny, Ellen. "Some Letters to Emil Paur." *Notes* 8/4 (September 1951): 631–49.

Kinscella, Hazel Gertrude. "A Half Century of Piano Playing as Viewed through Teresa Carreño's Eyes." *Musical America* 25/9 (30 December 1916): 5.

Klauser, Karl. ed. *Half Hours with the Best Composers*. 6 vols. Boston: J. B. Millet, 1894.

Koch, Juan Martin. "Franz Liszt und das Klavierkonzert in der zweiten Hälfte des 19. Jahrhunderts." In *Liszt und die Neudeutsche Schule*, edited by Detlef Altenburg, 143–69. Weimarer Liszt-Studien, vol. 3. Germany: Laaber, 2006.

[Krehbiel, Henry E.] "More Gifts to Columbia. Meeting of the University Trustees. Edward Alexander MacDowell Appointed Professor of Music—A Telegram from President Cleveland." *New York Tribune*, 5 May 1896, 5.

Krehbiel, Henry E. "Music in Columbia College: What the New Department Ought To Be," *New York Tribune*, 10 May 1896; repr. in *Music* 10/1 (May 1896): 205–9.

Lachmund, Carl V. "E. A. MacDowell and other Americans in Europe." *American Art Journal* 46/3 (6 November 1886): 37.

Lachmund, Carl V. *Living with Liszt: from the Diary of Carl Lachmund, An American pupil of Liszt, 1882–1884*. Edited, annotated, and introduction by Alan Walker, Franz Liszt Studies Series No. 4. Stuyvesant, NY: Pendragon Press, 1994.

Lahee, Henry C. *Annals of Music in America*. Boston, 1922; repr. New York: AMS Press, 1969.

"The Late Professor MacDowell and Columbia University." *Bookman* 27/1 (March 1908): 16–18.

Law, Frederick S. "E. A. MacDowell." *Musician* 9/7 (July 1904): 257–58.

Law, Joe K. "Toward the Condition of (Absolute) Music: Edward A. MacDowell and the Arthurian Twilight." In *The Arthurian Revival: Essays on Form, Tradition, and Transformation*. Ed. Debra N. Mancoff. New Yor: Garland, 1992. Pp. 191–204.

Lawrence, Vera Brodsky, ed. *Strong on Music: The New York Music Scene in the Days of George Templeton Strong, 1836–1862*. 3 vols. Chicago: University of Chicago Press, 1988–1999.

Le, Bonnie M. "American Landscapes: The Pastoral Topoi of Edward MacDowell's New England Idylls." Master's thesis, University of Louisiana–Lafayette, 2007.

Lebert, Sigmund, and Ludwig Stark. *Große theoretisch-praktische Clavierschule für den systematischen Unterricht nach allen Richtungen des Clavierspiels vom ersten Anfang bis zur höchsten Ausbildung*, 4 vols. Stuttgart: Cotta, 1858.

LeClair, Lynn Bridget. "A Historical and Comparative Study of the Influences of Edvard Grieg and Robert Schumann on the Piano Suites of Edward MacDowell." Master's thesis, University of Cincinnati, 1994.

Ledbetter, Steven. "Edward MacDowell, American Romantic." *Historical New Hampshire* 51/1 and 2 (Spring/Summer 1996): 23–34.

Lee, Min-ju. "A Study of Edward MacDowell's 'Twelve Etudes, op. 39.'" Master's thesis, National University of Taiwan, 2007.

Leggett-Abel, May. *The Story of Frederic L. Abel: The Musician, The Soldier*. N.p., 1945.

Lehman, Donna Hollister. "The Choral Music of Edward MacDowell." Master's thesis, University of South Carolina, 1991.

Leichtentritt, Hugo. "Music in Boston in the 'Nineties." *More Books* 21/10 (December 1946): 367–80; 22/1 (January 1947): 11–19.

Leonard, Neil. "Edward MacDowell and the Realists." *American Quarterly* 18/2 (Summer 1966): 175–82.

"Les musicians des Etats-Unis et leurs rapports avec la France." *Le Courrier Musical de France* 55 (1976): 92.

"A Letter from E. A. M'Dowell." *MC* 25/6 (10 August 1892): 6.

Levy, Alan Howard. *Edward MacDowell: An American Master*. Lanham, MD: Scarecrow Press, 1998.

Levy, Alan Howard. *Musical Nationalism: American Composers' Search for Identity*. Contributions in American Studies, No. 66. Westport, CT: Greenwood, 1983.

Liebling, Leonard. "The Crime of Ragtime." *MC* 72/3 (20 January 1916): 21. Quoted in Edward Berlin, *Ragtime: A Musical and Cultural History*. Berkeley: University of California Press, 1980, 40.

Lien, Beatrix. "An Analytical Study of Selected Piano Works by Edward MacDowell." Master's thesis, University of Rochester, 1940.

Loring, William C., Jr. *An American Romantic-Realist Abroad: Templeton Strong and his Music*. Composers of North America, No. 4. Lanham, MD: Scarecrow, 1996.

Lowens, Irving. "Edward MacDowell's Critical and Historical Essays (1912)." *Journal of Research in Music Education* 19/1 (Spring 1971): 17–34.

Lowens, Irving. "Edward MacDowell." *Hi Fi/Stereo Review* 19 (December 1967): 61–72.

Lowens, Irving. "Music: The Peterboro Principle." *Washington Sunday Star*, 11 July 1971, D–14.

Lowens, Margery Morgan. "The New York Years of Edward MacDowell." PhD diss., University of Michigan, 1971.

[Low, Seth.] "Columbia University: President Low's Report to the Trustees Today." *New York Evening Post*, 5 October 1896, 5.

Lucke-Kaminiarz, Irina. "Der Allgemeine Deutsche Musikverein und seine Tonkünstlerfeste 1859–1886." In *Liszt und die Neudeutsche Schule*, edited by Detlef Altenburg, 221–35. Weimarer Liszt-Studien, vol. 3. Germany: Laaber, 2006.

Lucke-Kaminiarz, Irina. "Die Tonkünstlerversammlungen des ADMV—ein internationales Forum zeitgenössischer Musik?" In *Liszt und Europa*, edited by Detlef Altenburg and Harriet Oelers, 63–75. Weimarer Liszt-Studien, vol. 5. Germany: Laaber, 2008.

Lythgoe, Clive. "Wake up to MacDowell!" *Music Journal* 32/6 (July 1974): 12.

M. v. F. "Louis Ehlert." *Rheinischer Kurier*, erste Ausgabe. 6 January 1884, 1–2.

McCusker, Honor. "Fifty years of Music in Boston." *More Books* 12/10 (December 1937): 451–62.

The MacDowell Colony: A History of its Architecture and Development. Peterborough, NH, 1981.

MacDowell, Edward. "The Power of Suggestion in Music." *Etude* 33/11 (November 1915): 783–84.

MacDowell, Edward. *Critical and Historical Essay*. Edited by W. J. Baltzell. Boston: Schmidt, 1912; repr. New York: Da Capo, 1969 with introduction by Irving Lowens.

MacDowell, Edward. "Composer versus Student." *Boston Music Herald* 13/3 (January 1892): 47–48.

MacDowell, Edward. "Music at Columbia." *Columbia University Bulletin*, No. 15 (December 1896): 13–16.

MacDowell, Edward. *Benedick: A Sketch for the Scherzo from the Second Concerto for Pianoforte*. New York: Edward MacDowell Association, Inc., 1947.

MacDowell, Edward. "What Prof. MacDowell Says." *NYT*, 14 February 1904, 22.

"The MacDowell Fund." *Musical America* 6/11 (27 July 1907): 15.

"MacDowell Fund $19,912.50." *Musical America* 5/15 (23 February 1907): 3.

"MacDowell Haven for Art Students." *Boston Sunday Herald*. 1 November 1908, 1.

MacDowell, Marian. "Edward MacDowell as a Teacher of Pianoforte." *Etude* 32/11 (November 1914): 779–80.

MacDowell, Marian. "MacDowell's 'Peterborough Idea.'" *MQ* 18/1 (January 1932): 33–38.

MacDowell, Marian. *Random Notes on Edward MacDowell and His Music*. Boston: Schmidt, 1950.

MacDowell issue. *Music Student* 7/12 (August 1915).

MacDowell issue. *Musician* 13/3 (March 1908).

"MacDowell on 'American' Concerts." *Musical America* 2/20 (20 May 1899): 5.

"MacDowell to Resign. Head of Department at Columbia." *New York Evening Post*, 3 February 1904, 1.

"MacDowell Works Hidden Under Assumed Name." *Musical America* 12/24 (22 October 1910): 14.

"MacDowell's Distinguished Career." *Etude* 33/11 (November 1915): 787–88.

"MacDowell's Justification." *MC* 48/20 (18 May 1904): 22.

"MacDowell's Music Charms." *San Francisco Chronicle*, 11 January 1906, 16.

Maddox, Craig Wood. "The Songs of Edward A. MacDowell: A Critical Analysis." DM diss., Florida State University, 1989.

Malham, Vincent. "The Eighteen Part Songs for Male Chorus of Edward MacDowell: A Study and Performing Edition." DM diss., Laval University, 1977.

Mann, Brian. "The Carreño Collection at Vassar College." *Notes* 47/4 (June 1991): 1064–83.

Mansfield, Helen C. "The Rounds in Gotham." *Bellman* 1 (22 September 1906): 224–25.

Martin, John Gares. "A Study of the Educational Theory of Edward A. MacDowell and Its Implications for Curricular Change in the Elementary School." D Ed thesis, Ball State University, 1966.

Mason, Daniel Gregory. "Memories of William Mason and His Friends." *Etude* 54/9 (September 1936): 543–44.

Mason, William. *Memories of a Musical Life*. New York, 1901; repr. New York: AMS Press, 1970.

Mathews, John Lathrop. "Mr. E. A. MacDowell." *Music* 10/1 (May 1896): 31–36.

[Mathews, W. S. B.] "Editorial Bric-A-Brac." *Music* 9/4 (February 1896): 429–32 [Sonata trag-ica]; 10/2 (June 1896): 186–89; 17/5 (March 1900): [509]–7; 17/6 (April 1900): 638–39; 19/4 (February 1901): 410–13.

Mathews, W. S. B. "The XIXth Century and National Schools of Music." *Music* 19/4 (February 1901): [335]–54.

Mathews, W. S. B. "Things Here and There: Music at Columbia." *Music* 11/1 (November 1896): 90–92.

Mathews, W. S. B. "Things Here and There: Music in Chicago." *Music* 9/5 (March 1896): 565–66.

Matthey, Jean-Louis. *Inventaire du Fonds Musical: George Templeton-Strong*. Lausanne, Switzerland: Bibliothèque Cantonale et Universitaire, 1973.

McDermott, Inez. "A House of Dreams Untold: The Story of the MacDowell Colony." *Historical New Hampshire* 51/1 and 2 (Spring/Summer 1996): 5–21.

McWhood, Leonard B. "Edward MacDowell at Columbia University." In *Papers and Proceedings of the Music Teachers' National Association*, 18th series (1924): 71–77.

McWhood, Leonard B. "The Department of Music." *Columbia University Quarterly* 6 (September 1904): 436–38.

Mears, Mary. "The Work and Home of Edward MacDowell, Musician." *Craftsman* 16/4 (July 1909): 416–27.

Memorial Book of the Sesquicentennial Celebration of the Founding of the College of New Jersey and of the Ceremonies inaugurating Princeton University. New York: Charles Scribner's Sons, 1898.

"The Memorial to Anna Baetz, Nurse of Edward MacDowell." *Trained Nurse and Hospital Review* 76/6 (June 1926): [631]–34.

"Miguel Castellanos" [obituary], *NYT*, 26 July 1940, 17.

Milinowski, Marta. *Teresa Carreño "by the grace of God."* New Haven: Yale University Press, 1940; repr. New York: Da Capo, 1977.

Moore, Charles. *The Life and Times of Charles Follen McKim*. Boston: Houghton Mifflin, 1929.

Moore, Douglas. "The Department of Music." In *A History of the Faculty of Philosophy: Columbia University*. Ed. Jacques Barzun. New York: Columbia University Press, 1957. Pp. 270–88.

Morgan, John E. and Edgar N. Weaver. "Chronic Bromism Simulating Neurological Diseases." *Virginia Medical Monthly* 96 (May 1969): 262–64.

"Mr. M'Dowell Appointed the Chair of Music in Columbia College—Next Year's Budget." *New York Evening Post*, 5 May 1896, 9.

"Mr. MacDowell's Preferences." *Boston Journal*, 6 March 1893, 6.

"Mr. MacDowell's Recital." *Washington Evening Star*, 7 March 1903, 16.

"Mrs. Hearst Presents Professor MacDowell." *Berkeley Daily Gazette*, 19 January 1903, 5.

"M.T.N.A.: The Fourteenth Annual Meeting in Detroit," *MC* 21/2 (9 July 1890): 52.

"M.T.N.A.: The President, Secretary, Executive and Program Committees in Council in Detroit." *MC* 20/1 (1 January 1890): 25.

Munro, David. "The Background of American Music." *Musical Times* 94/1330 (December 1953): 580–81.

"Music and Musicians: Edward MacDowell." *Los Angeles Times*, 31 December 1902, 6.

"Music at Columbia." *MC* 32/16 (15 April 1896): 29.

"Music at Columbia." *NYT*, 5 February 1904, 8.

"Music in Colleges." *NYT*, 14 February 1904, 6.

"Music: Notes of the Season." *Critic* 29 (5 February 1898): 97.

"A New MacDowell Club." *New York Evening Post*, 25 November 1905, 5.

Newman, William S. "The Four Sonatas by MacDowell." In *The Sonata Since Beethoven*, 758–68. Chapel Hill: The University of North Carolina Press, 1969.

"No Row, Says MacDowell." *New York Globe and Commercial Advertiser*, 4 February 1904, 3.

Noh, Ohran. "Edvard Grieg's Influence on American Music: The Case of the Piano Concertos in A-Minor from the Pen of Edvard Grieg and Edward MacDowell," Paper presented at The International Edvard Grieg Society Conference in Bergen, Norway, 30 May 2007.

The Old Discipline: Nineteenth-Century Friends' Disciplines in America. Glenside, PA: Quaker Heritage Press, 1999.

Olle, Mary C. "Three Pioneers in American Composition, Edward MacDowell, John Knowles Paine, Horatio Parker." Master's thesis, University of Wisconsin, 1951.

"Open Letters: American Musical Authorities against the Treloar Bill." *Century Magazine* 52/3 (July 1896): 474–76.

Ottenberg, June C. *Gustav Hinrichs (1850–1942): American Conductor and Composer*. Warren, MI: Harmonie Park Press, 2003.

H. F. P. "America Gradually Coming Into a True Appreciation of its Greatest Composer." *Musical America* 25/12 (20 January 1917): 3–4.

Page, Elizabeth Fry. *Edward MacDowell: His Work and Ideals*. New York: Dodge, 1910.

Partington, Blanche. "Modesty Marks the Appearance of MacDowell." *San Francisco Call*, 9 January 1903, 6.

Pesce, Dolores. "MacDowell's Eroica Sonata and its Lisztian Legacy." *Music Review* 49/3 (August 1988): 169–89.

Pesce, Dolores. "New Light on the Programmatic Aesthetic of MacDowell's Symphonic Poems." *American Music* 4/4 (Winter 1986): 369–89.

Pesce, Dolores. "The Other Sea in MacDowell's Sea Pieces." *American Music* 10/4 (Winter 1992): 411–40.

"Philip Woolf on MacDowell." *Music* 16/1 (May 1899): 100–102.

Pierre, Constant. *Le Conservatoire national de musique et de declamation: documents historiques et administratifs*. Paris: Imprimerie Nationale, 1900.

Pisani, Michael V. "Exotic Sounds in the Native Land: Portrayals of North American Indians in Western Music." PhD diss., Eastman School of Music, 1996.

Pisani, Michael V. "From Hiawatha to Wa-Wan: Musical Boston and the Uses of Native American Lore." *American Music* 19/1 (Spring 2001): 39–50.

Pisani, Michael V. *Imagining Native America in Music*. New Haven: Yale University Press, 2005.

Pisani, Michael V. "Issues of Chronology Surrounding the Composition of MacDowell's 'Indian Suite' (1891–1896)," appendix D in "Exotic Sounds," 573–75.

Pita, Laura. "Presencia de la Obra de Edward MacDowell en el Repertorio de Teresa Carreño." Master's thesis, Universidad Central de Venezuela, 1999.

"Plans for Columbia's New Dormitories…Changes in Departments." *NYT*, 8 March 1904, 9.

Porte, John Fielder. *Edward MacDowell: A Great American Tone Poet, His Life and Music*. London: K. Paul, Trench, Trubner, 1922.

"Prof. Edward A. MacDowell." *Peterborough Transcript*, 30 January 1908, [1].

"Prof. MacDowell Dies at Forty-Six: Foremost of American Composers had Suffered a Long Illness." *NYT*, 24 January 1908, 7.

"Prof. MacDowell's Funeral. Simple Services at St. George's Church in Memory of the Composer." *NYT*, 26 January 1908, 9.

"Prof. Woodberry Regretted." *New York Evening Post*, 3 February 1904, 7.

Purcell, William L. "Lawrence Gilman, America's Greatest Music Critic." *American Record Guide* 44/8 (June 1981): 2–7, 57.

Putnam, Natalie Alden. *Edward MacDowell, Reminiscences and Romance*. Los Angeles: United Printing Co., 1919.

Putnam, Natalie Alden. *MacDowellish Miniatures*. Los Angeles: Times-Mirror Publishing and Binding House, 1942.

"Queries and Answers." *Photographic Times* 22/581 (4 November 1892): 568.

Ranck, Edward Carty. "The MacDowell Colony at Peterborough." *MQ* 6/1 (January 1920): 24–28.

Rausch, Robin. "The House that Marian Built: The MacDowell Colony of Peterborough, New Hampshire." In *American Women: A Gateway to Library of Congress Resources for the Study of Women's History and Culture in the United States*, http://memory.loc.gov/ammem/awhhtml/aw08e/aw08e.html#ack, accessed 11 February 2012.

Reisfeld, Bert. "Edward MacDowell (†23.1.1908)." *Musica* 12/1 (January 1958): 46–47.

Rempel, Siegfried and Wolfgang. *Health Hazards for Photographers*. New York: Lyons & Burford, 1992.

Riemann, Hugo. *Musik-Lexicon*, dritte Auflage [third edition]. Leipzig: Max Hesse, 1887.

Riemann, Hugo. *Musik-Lexicon*, vierte vollständig umgearbeitete Auflage [4th fully rev. ed.]. Leipzig: Max Hesse, 1894.

Robinson, Allan. "The MacDowell Fund." *MC* 56/13 (25 March 1908): 11.

Robinson, Edward. "MacDowell's Protesting Demon." *American Mercury* 23/92 (August 1931): 500–504.

Robinson, Edward Arlington. "The Peterborough Idea." *Historical New Hampshire* 51/1 and 2 (Spring/Summer 1996): 35–40.

Rosenfeld, Paul. "The Advent of American Music." *Kenyon Review* 1/1 (Winter 1939): 46–56.

Rosenfeld, Paul. *An Hour with American Music*. Philadelphia: J. P. Lippincott, 1929.

Rosenthal, Michael. *Nicholas Miraculous: The Amazing Career of the Redoubtable Dr. Nicholas Murray Butler*. New York: Farrar, Straus and Giroux, 2006.

Rosenthal, Norman E. *Winter Blues: Everything You Need to Know to Beat Seasonal Affective Disorder*. Rev. ed. New York: Guilford, 2006.

Rubin, Emanuel. "Jeannette Meyers Thurber and the National Conservatory of Music." *American Music* 8/3 (Fall 1990): 294–325.

Rubin, Emanuel. "Jeannette Meyer Thurber (1850–1946): Music for a Democracy." In *Cultivating Music in America: Women Patrons and Activists since 1860*, edited by Ralph P. Locke and Cyrilla Barr, 134–63. Berkeley: University of California Press, 1997.

Runge, Nancy W. "'Moon Pictures'—Music of Edward MacDowell." *Piano Quarterly* 25/97 (1977): 26.

Saerchinger, César. "Musical Landmarks in New York." *MQ* 6/2 (April 1920): 227–56.

Salter, Sumner. "Early Encouragements to American Composers." *MQ* 18/1 (January 1932): 76–105.

Salter, Sumner. "The Music Teachers' National Association in its Early Relation to American Composers." *Proceedings of the Music Teachers' National Association*. Oberlin, OH: Published by the Association, 1933.

Schabas, Ezra. *Theodore Thomas: America's Conductor and Builder of Orchestras, 1835–1905*. Urbana: University of Illinois Press, 1989.

Schafer, William J., Johannes Riedel. "Indian Intermezzi ('Play It One More Time, Chief!')." *Journal of American Folklore* 86/342 (October–December 1973): 382–87.

Schempf, Ruthanne. "The New England Character Piece: A Comparative Study of Four Representative Composers—Arthur William Foote, Edward Alexander MacDowell, Ethelbert Nevin, and Mrs. Henry Harris Aubrey (Amy Marcy Cheney) Beach." DMA diss., Manhattan School of Music, 1995.

Schlup, Leonard. "Democrats, Populists and Gilded Age Politics." *Manuscripts* 50/1 (Winter 1998): 27–40.

Scholes, Percy A. "An Interview with Mrs. MacDowell." *Music Student* 7/12 (August 1915): 235–37.

Scholes, Percy A. "MacDowell's Piano Works: An Annotated List for Players and Hearers." *Music Student* 7/12 (August 1915): 243–47.

"Schurman on MacDowell: Disagrees with Professor's Views on Art in Colleges—New Coach for Cornell Football Team." *NYT*, 12 February 1904, 3.

Schwab, Arnold T. "Edward MacDowell's Birthdate: A Correction." *MQ* 61/2 (April 1975): 233–39.

Schwab, Arnold T. "Edward MacDowell's Mysterious Malady." *MQ* 89/1 (Spring 2006): 136–151.

Schwab, Arnold T. *James Gibson Huneker: Critic of the Seven Arts.* Stanford, CA: Stanford University Press, 1963.

Schwimmer, Franciska. *Great Musicians As Children.* Garden City, NY: Doubleday Doran & Co., 1929.

Seidl, Anton. "The Development of Music in America." *Forum* 13 (May 1892): 386–93.

Shah, Uttamlal Thomas. "The Solo Songs of Edward MacDowell: An Examination of Style and Literary Influence." DA diss., Ball State University, 1987.

Sinclair, Upton. "MacDowell." *American Mercury* 7/25 (January 1926): 50–54; repr. *ISAM Newsletter* 19/1 (November 1989): 9, 14–15.

Sinclair, Upton. "Memories of Edward MacDowell." *Sackbut* 6 (December 1925): 127–32.

Smith, Evelyn Maxine. *"The Piano Compositions of Edward A. MacDowell."* Master's thesis, Oberlin College, 1942.

Smith, Gail. *The Life and Music of Edward MacDowell.* Pacific, MO: Creative Keyboard Publications, 1996.

Smith, Lily Althaus. "MacDowell Anecdotes." *Musician* 19/8 (August 1914): 515.

Smith, Wilson G. "American Compositions in the Class and Concert Room." *Etude* 6/8 (August 1888): 129.

Sonneck, Oscar George Theodore. "The American Composer and the American Music Publisher." *MQ* 9/1 (January 1923): 122–44.

Sonneck, Oscar George Theodore. *Catalogue of First Editions of Edward MacDowell.* Washington: Government Printing Office, 1917.

Sonneck, Oscar George Theodore. "Edward MacDowell." *Zeitschrift der Internationalen Musikgesellschaft* 9/1 (1907–1908): 1–13.

Sonneck, Oscar G. "MacDowell versus MacDowell: A Study in First Editions and Revisions." In *Suum Cuique: Essays in Music*, 87–103. New York: G. Schirmer, 1916.

Sorce, Richard. "An Investigation into the Compositional Techniques of Edward MacDowell." PhD diss., New York University, 1991.

Spalding, Albert. "Boy with Violin: Beginning a Musical Autobiography." *Harper's Magazine* 184/1102 (March 1942): 358.

Starr, M. Allen. "Bromide Poisoning Mistaken for Paresis." *Monthly Cyclopaedia of Practical Medicine* 9/5 (May 1906): 193–95.

Stephenson, Mary Lee. "The Life and Works of Edward MacDowell." Master's thesis, Catholic University of America, 1952.

Stevens, Ashton. "A Chat with Composer MacDowell." *San Francisco Examiner*, 11 January 1903, 45.

Strong, Templeton. "Edward MacDowell as I Knew Him." *Music Student* 7/12 (August 1915): 233–57; 8/1 (September 1915): 5–7; 8/2 (October 1915): 29–30; 8/3 (November 1915): 51–52; 8/4 (December 1915): 81–82; 8/5 (January 1916): 127–28; 8/6 (February 1916): 151–53; 8/7 (March 1916): 189–90; 8/8 (April 1916): 223–24; 8/9 (May 1916): 276; 8/10 (June 1916): 298 and 300; 8/11 (July 1916): cccxxiii and cccxxiv.

Summerville, Suzanne. "The Songs of Edward MacDowell." *NATS Bulletin* 35/4 (1979): 36–40.

Tawa, Nicholas E. *Arthur Foote: A Musician in the Frame of Time and Place*. Lanham, MD: Scarecrow Press, 1997.

Tawa, Nicholas E. *From Psalm to Symphony: A History of Music in New England*. Boston: Northeastern University Press, 2001.

"Teachers' Teacher." *New Yorker* 34, 20 September 1958, 34.

Thompson, Vance. "A Double Triumph, M'Dowell's Success as a Soloist and Composer." *New York Commercial Advertiser*, 24 January 1896, 8.

Thorpe, Harry Colin. "Interpretive Studies in American Song." *MQ* 15/1 (January 1929): 88–116.

Thurber, Jeannette M. "Dvořák as I Knew Him." *Etude* 37/11 (November 1919): 693–94.

"A 'Transit of Idealism' at Columbia University." *Literary Digest* 28/8 (20 February 1904): 253–54.

Upton, William Treat. "Our Musical Expatriates." *MQ* 14/1 (January 1928): 143–54.

Walker, Francis A. *The Statistics of the Population of the United States*. Washington: Government Printing Office, 1872.

Watson, Jo Shipley. "At Edward MacDowell's Lectures, Columbia University." *Musician* 12/9 (September 1907): 426–27.

"Welcome the MacDowell Club." *MC* 51/22 (29 November 1905): 20.

"What inspired the Scherzo of MacDowell's 'Eroica'? A Dispute Ended." *Music Student* 8/6 (February 1916): 153.

Wheeler, Opal, and Deucher, Sybil. *Edward MacDowell and his Cabin in the Pines*. New York: E. P. Dutton, 1940.

Whybrow, Peter C. and John A. Ewing. "Self-Perpetuation of Bromide Poisoning." *British Medical Journal* (8 October 1966): 886–87.

"Wife of Edward MacDowell, Famous Composer, Lived Here; Now in New Hampshire." *New London Day* (CT), 11 July 1968, 16.

Wilkinson, Alec. *The Protest Singer: An Intimate Portrait of Pete Seeger*. New York: Knopf, 2009.

Williams, Alexander. "Music: The Pops." Review of Indian Suite and Concerto No. 2. *Boston Herald*, 25 May 1936.

Wilson, Gary Paul. "A Conductor's Analysis of Edward MacDowell's Original Choral Music for Mixed Voices and Women's Voices, and Arrangements for Men's Voices." DMA diss., University of Nebraska–Lincoln, 2004.

Wisehart, M. K. "'I've Done the Best I Could, and That's Victory.'" *American Magazine* 100 (November 1925): 18–21, 222, 224, 226, and 228.

Wiseman, Carter, ed. *A Place for the Arts: The MacDowell Colony, 1907–2007*. Peterborough, NH: The MacDowell Colony, 2006.

Yackley, Elizabeth. "Marian MacDowell and the MacDowell Clubs." Master's thesis, University of Maryland at College Park, 2008.

Yang, Hon-Lun. "German Influence and American Symphonic Music: Lisztian Legacy and the Symphonic Poems of John K. Paine and Edward MacDowell." In *Liszt und Europa*, edited by Detlef Altenburg and Harriet Oelers, 283–93. Weimarer Liszt-Studien, vol. 5. Germany: Laaber, 2008 .

Index

Abel, Frederic L., 50–51, 54, 108, 312
Abschrift, 83, 101
Academy Award, 288
ADMV. *See* Allgemeiner Deutscher
    Musikverein
African American music, 192–93, 196, 316, 318
Agramonte, Emilio, 98, 113–15, 312
Allgemeiner Deutscher Musikverein [ADMV],
    59–60, 62–64, 67–70, 72, 78, 83, 87–88,
    239, 319, 321
American Academy in Rome, 268, 287, 320
American Academy of Arts and Letters, x, 23n22,
    268, 301, 318
American Classical Music Hall of Fame, 292
American Composers' Choral Association,
    184, 312
American Composers' Concerts, ix, 99–100,
    118, 143, 180–81, 183–85, 189–91,
    189n15, 237, 240, 297, 313, 324
Americanism in music, ix, 117–18, 180–83,
    189–93, 196, 229
American Symphony Orchestra, 282
Amringe, John Howard Van, 242
André, 84
antimodernism, 230
apartments, 41, 54, 74, 102, 108–9, 127, 216,
    227–28, 245, 269
Apollo Club, 130, 148, 171, 176, 225, 294, 319
Apthorp, William F., 175, 177, 312
Arens, Franz Xavier, 188–92, 298–99,
    312–13, 324
Arion Society, 100
Arthurian legends, 165
Aubert, Madame, 26, 28

Bach, Johann Sebastian, 29, 51, 73–74, 160–61,
    165, 231
Baden-Baden, 55, 110
Bad Homburg, 97
Baermann, Carl, 150
Baetz, Anna, 273–74, 277, 279–82, Pl. 11
Baker, Theodore, 313
Balakirev, Mili, 59, 63, 293
Baldwin, James, 288
Baltzell, W. J., 285
Barber, Samuel, 291

Bargiel, 317
Barton, George Edward, 199
baseball, 119, 145, 148
Bassermann, Fritz, 47, 51, 54, 56
Bayreuth Festival, 120, 295
Beach, Amy, 133, 192, 288, 294, 300, 303, 322
Beethoven, Ludwig van, 21, 51, 66, 73–74, 89,
    108, 138, 231, 280, 296, 318
    WORKS
      "Emperor" Concerto, op. 73, 51, 60
      "Moonlight" Sonata, op. 27, no. 2, 21,
        254, 295
Beethoven Club, 148
Bellaigue, Camille, 32, 34–36
Benoit, Pierre, 100, 185
Berlin, 40, 43, 46, 55, 68, 72, 78, 82, 98, 110, 154,
    189, 243, 268, 298, 313, 319–20
Berlin, Irving, 289–90
Bernstein, Leonard, 100, 288
Bird, Arthur, 111, 144, 182, 303, 322
Bischoff, James, 45, 52, 103, 322
Bischoff, Mrs. James, 72, 98, 103–4
Bismarck, Otto von, 116n37
Bizet, Georges, 29, 293, 295
Blumenberg, Marc, 140
Borodin, 59, 293, 311
borrowing, thematic, 117, 160–61, 194, 200, 237,
    247, 313
Boston, ix, x, 12, 18, 118–21, 125–32, 134–35,
    139–40, 142–43, 145, 147–57, 161, 164–65,
    167–77, 180, 182, 185–90, 192–94, 197–99,
    204, 213, 216, 225–29, 234–35, 241, 245,
    258, 268, 270, 277, 288, 294, 296, 298, 312,
    314–17, 319, 321, 324
Boston Art Club, 134, 137
Boston Museum of Fine Arts, 127
Boston Public Library, 127, 245, 320
Boston Symphony Orchestra, 127, 129–30,
    141–42, 147, 151–52, 171, 173–74, 177,
    285, 312, 316–17, 320–21
Bote & Bock, 84
Brahms, Johannes, 13, 48, 59, 74, 159, 200,
    231–32, 237, 290, 293–96, 300,
    318, 322
Brancaleone, Francis, xi, 247, 250
Braud, Paul Aimé, 32, 34–35, 37–38

Breitkopf & Härtel, 61, 73–74, 73n4, 75–76, 82–84, 87, 97, 99–102, 115–16, 132, 161, 164–65, 168, 188, 204, 216, 222, 228, 235–36, 245, 257, 271n9, 285, 296, 299–300, 319–20
Brendel, Franz, 59
Breslau, 85–86, 100, 171, 314, 317, 322
bromides, 136, 152, 275–76, 281
bromism, 275–76, 281–82
Bromo-seltzer, 275
Brooklyn, NY, 253, 319
Brooks, Phillips, 173
Brown, Abbie Farwell, 29, 59n9
Browner, Tara, 194
Browning, Robert and Elizabeth, 178
Bruneau, Alfred, 182
Buck, Dudley, 144, 182, 297, 303
Budapest, 63, 76, 320
Budget, 274–75
Buffalo, NY, 253
Buitrago, Juan, 15–18, 23, 26, 28, 30, 44, 44n13, 313
Bülow, Hans von, 46, 63, 89, 154, 299
Burgess, John, 96, 217n13, 259, 265–66, 313, 321
Burgmüller, 158
Busoni, Ferruccio, 173, 294, 303, 318
Butler, Nicholas Murray, 243–44, 251, 258–65, 270, 301, 313, 324
Buzby, Mordecai, 6
Byron, Lord, 59, 96

Cahn, Peter, 53
California, 253, 301
Carnegie, Andrew, 215
Carnegie Foundation for the Advancement of Teaching, 279
Carnegie Music Hall, 215, 221, 324
Carreño, Teresa, 17–18, 22–23, 45, 73, 82, 86, 93, 98–99, 102–3, 111, 114, 119, 125, 129, 133, 140–41, 154–55, 181, 190, 237, 293, 298–99, 303, 313–14, 322, Pl. 3
Castellanos, Michael "Chichi," 22–23, 28–29, 32–39, 39n36, 43, 108, 294–95, 314
Cather, Willa, 288
Catholic Church, 12, 38
Cecilia Society, 148, 176, 319
Central Park, 14–15, 268
Century Club, 228
Chabon, Michael, 288
Chabrier, 100
Chadwick, George Whitefield, 119, 133, 144, 151–55, 176–77, 181–82, 188, 192, 293, 295–301, 303, 314, 321–22, 324
  WORKS
    Symphony No. 1, 296
    Symphony No. 2, 297
Champlin, J. D., 112–13

Charlier, Elie, 19, 23n22, 314
Charlier Institute, 19–23, 26, 53, 314
Cherubini, Luigi, 27
Chevillard, 37
Chicago, 98, 104, 119, 141, 181, 185, 227, 229, 231, 240–41, 253–54, 256, 294, 298–99, 316–17, 320, 323
Chicago Fair. *See* World's Columbian Exposition
Chickering Hall, New York, 115, 131
Chickering & Sons, 127, 129, 131, 167
Chopin, Frédéric, 12, 18, 31, 51, 58, 60, 67, 158, 237, 316, 318
Christmas, 85, 87, 103–4, 110, 113, 127, 253, 269
Cincinnati, 143, 181, 238, 300, 323–24
Civil War, 5, 9, 34, 213, 293–94
Clemens, Samuel L. [Mark Twain], 268
Cleveland, 99, 188, 312–13
Cleveland, Grover, 216
Cody, Buffalo Bill, 144
Cohen, Henry, 32
Collis, Sister Kathleen (Marian's nurse), 79–81, 81n24, 206, 300
Cologne, 20, 40, 43, 171
Columbia University, 106, 196–97, 204, 207, 211–23, 225–28, 230, 234, 236, 240, 243–45, 251–52, 256–68, 270, 273, 275, 277, 284, 288, 292, 299–301, 313, 315, 317–22, 324
  fine arts, combined department of, 214–15, 242–45, 251–52, 258–59, 261–63, 288
  Forty-ninth Street campus, 215, 243
  Morningside Heights campus, 215, 221, 243, 319–20
  music curriculum, 217, 221, 242, 250–51, 257–59
  music library, 216, 222, 242
  role of music in, 211–13, 225–26, 243–44, 250–51, 260–62, 264–65
  Teachers College, 243, 258–59, 263
  Trustees, 106, 196, 211–12, 220, 225–26, 242, 251, 260–65, 267
Comettant, Oscar, 33
Composers' Club (Boston), 151
Conservatoire national de musique. *See* Paris Conservatory.
conservatories, German, 40–41
Copland, Aaron, 288, 290–91, 303
copyright, 84–85, 99, 114–15, 134, 176n5, 187–88, 235, 317
Corbaz, Antonin-Emile-Louis, 34
Corey, N. J., 240–41
Cornelius, Peter, 59, 63
Cornell University, 263
Cornwall, NY, 4, 6, 9
cosmopolitan style in music. *See* international (cosmopolitan) style in music
Cossmann, Bernhard, 48

Crawford, Richard, 193n25, 194
Crocker, Mary, 257
Cuba, 15, 17, 22, 26, 28–29, 33, 113, 312, 315
Cuchullin, 231
Cui, César, 59, 310
Curhaus Wiesbaden, 52, 55, 89, 103, 108, 110, 296–97
Currier, T[homas] P[arker], 129, 137, 156–57, 161, 164, 168–69, 175, 202, 216–17, 234, 241, 270, 314

D'Albert, Eugen, 18, 67, 78, 237, 294, 299, 301, 303, 314
Damrosch, Leopold, 49, 100, 294, 297, 314
Damrosch, Walter, 215, 274, 294, 303, 314
Danforth, Dr. Loomis L., 271–72, 277, 279, 281
Darmstadt Conservatory, 58, 61, 64, 69, 74, 102, 213, 245, 296
Darmstadt Saalbau, 58
Dayas, William H., 111
Deas, Lindsay, 102
Debussy, Claude, 29, 32, 34–35, 37, 144, 165, 202, 290–91, 294, 299, 301–3, 314, 319
Deirdre, 231
Deland, Margaret, 113, 172–73, 315
Desvernine, Pablo, 17–18, 21–23, 98, 315
Detroit, 50, 99, 181, 183–84, 240, 312
Detroit Conservatory of Music, 50, 181, 312
Dickinson, Edward, 254
Dierich, Carl, 88, 98
Diller, Angela, 219, 225–26, 292, 315
Diller-Quaile school, 226, 315
D'Indy, Vincent, 29, 185
Ditson, Oliver, 132–33, 147
Dohnanyi, Ernö, 164
Donizetti, Gaetano, 279
Doré, Gustave, 109, 165
Draeseke, Felix, 59
Dresden, 40, 50, 189, 298, 312
Dresel, Otto, 151
Dubois, Théodore, 29, 310
Duvernoy, Alphonse, 182
Dvořák, Antonín, 85, 100, 173, 191–93, 195, 293, 299, 301, 315, 321, 323
    MacDowell's jealousy of Dvorak, 173, 191–93
    WORK, Symphony "From the New World," 193, 299, 315

Easter, 79
eclecticism in music, 48–49
Edinburgh, Scotland, 20, 102
Ehlert, Louis, 46, 52, 60–61, 64, 72–74, 77, 81n24, 84, 89, 110, 296–97, 315
Elkin & Company, 289
Émancé, France, 38–39
England, 10, 19, 24, 93–94, 102–3, 108, 254–55
Erbach-Fürstenau, Count of, 58–59

Erskine, John, 94, 217–20, 242, 315
Exposition Universelle of 1878, 24, 39
Exposition Universelle of 1889, 142–44, 146, 182, 204, 298, 323

Faelten, Carl, 129
Fair, Alfred, 14
Fair, Thomas, 3
Farwell, Arthur, 194, 234, 294, 303, 322
Federated Music Clubs, 238
Ferdinand the Bull, 16
Fiedler, Max, 285
Finck, Henry, 36, 41, 57, 111, 212, 271, 277, 279, 285, 315
Fiona Macleod. *see* Sharp, William
Fleisch, Max, 58
Fletcher, Alice, 194
Foote, Arthur, 119, 129, 133, 144, 150–51, 173, 177, 181–82, 293, 297–98, 303, 315–16, 322
    WORKS
        In the Mountains, op. 14, 144
        String Suite No. 2, op. 21, 151, 298
Foster, Stephen, 200, 292–94
Fournier, 32, 36
Fox, George, 4–5
Franco-Prussian War, 19, 294
Frankfurt, 41, 46–53, 57–59, 68, 74, 78, 84, 91, 94, 96–97, 102, 110, 127, 178, 225, 245, 295–96, 312, 321, Pl. 5
Frankfurt Philharmonic Society, 60
Franko, Sam, 282
Franz, Robert, 279, 299
Franzen, Jonathan, 288
Frauenlob, 207
Frène, 37
Friends, Religious Society of, 3–13
    birthright members, 3–4, 6
    childrearing, 8–9
    clergy, attitude toward, 4, 6, 92
    disownment, 5–6, 8, 92
    dress, 5
    equality, 4, 9
    Fifteenth-Street Quaker Meeting, 4, 282
    Hicksite branch, 4, 5n2, 11
    Inward Light, 4, 11–12
    marriage to non-member, 57
    Monthly Meeting, 5–6
    music, 9–13, 148
    and music, 4
    pacifism, 4, 9
    silent meeting, 3–4, 12, 72, 148
    speech, 5
Fritzsch, Ernst Wilhelm, 76, 316

Gabrilowitsch, Ossip, 254
Garland, Hamlin, 194, 220, 228–29, 258, 272, 302, 316

Gates, Francis, 279
Geibel, Emanuel, 59, 308
Geneva, Lake, 20, 136
Gericke, Wilhelm, 129–31, 142, 147, 151, 316
German orthography, 71
Gershwin, George, 291, 300, 330
Giehrl, 318
Gilbert, Henry F., 113, 128–29, 194, 316
Gilman, Lawrence, 42, 49, 52, 64–65, 76n10, 97,
    102, 165, 241, 289, 314, 316
Glazunov, Alexander, 185
Gleason, Frederick Grant, 181, 185, 227, 316
Glücklich, J. C., 316
Glücklich, J. Ch., 133
Godowsky, Leopold, 237, 240, 316
Goethe, Johann Wolfgang von, 47, 59, 96, 133,
    246, 307, 309
Goetschius, Percy, 42
Goldmark, Karl, 51, 130
Gottschalk, Aimée, 226
Gottschalk, Louis Moreau, 27, 293–94, 313
Gounod Society, 312
Grammy Award, 288
Grant, Ulysses S., 34
Great Books movement, 315
Grieg, Edvard, 100, 138, 229–30, 232–33, 273,
    291n17, 293–94, 302, 315–16
Griffes, Charles T., 291, 297, 303
Guggenheim Foundation, 288
Guiard, 32
Guilmant, 317

Hainauer, Julius, 84–88, 97–98, 110–11, 116,
    132–33, 171, 235, 245, 285, 297, 317
Hale, Philip, 241, 284–85, 317
Hall of Fame for Great Americans, 292
Hambourg, Mark, 254
Hamburg, 189, 298
Hanson, Howard, 187, 300, 303
Harris, Joel Chandler, 200
Harvard Musical Association, 130, 324
Harvard University, 100, 127, 212, 312, 315
Haupt, 317
Havemeyer, Henry Osborne, 244
Hay, John, 268
health care, universal, 115n37
Heidingsfeld, Ludwig, 185
Heine, Heinrich, 59, 110, 118, 246, 307–8
Heller, Stephen, 36, 158
Henderson, W. J., 117, 139, 317
Henschel, George, 130, 147
Herbert, Victor, 188, 292–93, 302–3, 317, 322
Herz, Henri, 22, 36
Hey, Julius, 313
Heymann, Carl, 45–49, 52, 56–57, 68, 110, 156,
    296, 317
Heyward, Dorothy, 288

Heyward, DuBose, 288
Higginson, Henry Lee, 130, 142, 147, 151, 296
Hillcrest, 198–99, 207, 277, 280, 287
Hinrichs, Gustav, 221–22, 317
Hoch, Dr. Joseph, 47
Hoch Conservatory, 46–54, 56, 67, 102, 110, 127,
    213, 245, 296, 312, 317, 321
Hoffmann, Hildegard, 318
Holy Grail, 255n28
homeopathic remedies, 256, 271–72
Homer, Winslow, 224
Horowitz, Joseph, 213
Howe, Granville L., 141
Howells, William Dean, 268
Huber, Hans, 77, 98
Hughes, Rupert, 232
Humiston, William Henry, 219, 250, 255n28, 282,
    284, 317–18
Huneker, James G., 112–13, 113n28, 139–40, 190,
    277–79, 318
Huss, Henry Holden, 30–31, 104, 108, 144,
    181–82, 303, 318

impressionism, 314
Indianapolis, 190–91, 253, 313
international style in music, ix, 118, 144, 181,
    189–92, 195
Ireland, 3, 19–20, 231
Irgang, W., 83
Irving, Henry, 93–94, 96–97
Italy, 16, 80, 108, 115, 230, 318
Ives, Charles, 291, 295, 299–301, 303

Jadassohn, Salomon, 63, 134, 301
Jaëll, Marie, 78
jazz, 290
Jimenes, José, 28, 32–33
Johnson, Robert Underwood, 228, 318
Joplin, Scott, 289, 300
Joseffy, Rafael, 51, 318
Jost & Sander, 136
Jules, F. H., 140
Jung, P. L., 165, 204, 228, 235–36, 300, 320

Kahnt, Christian Friedrich, 87–88, 318
Kalkbrenner, 315
Keats, 59, 285, 306
Kelley, Edgar Stillman, 41–42, 181
Klauser, Karl, 165
Klopstock, F. G., 59, 308
Knapp, Benjamin, 9
Knapp, Darius, 5, 9
Knapp, Frances Mary. *see* McDowell, Frances
Kneisel, Franz, 129–30
Kneisel Quartet, 129, 137, 156–57, 171, 177, 298
Krehbiel, Henry E., 117, 139, 190, 212, 214,
    287, 318

Lachmund, Carl Valentine, 18, 66n24, 104, 108, 110–12, 117, 181, 192
Lachmund, Carrie, 104
LaFarge, John, 268
Lang, Benjamin Johnson, 118–20, 125–27, 129–33, 140, 144, 148–50, 154–55, 171, 174, 176, 192, 225, 314–15, 319
Lang, Margaret Ruthven, 126, 177, 183, 319
Lang, Mrs., 126, 133, 174
Langs, John Pierce, 268–70, 274–75, 319
Latin Americans, 15–18, 22–23, 26, 28–29, 37–39, 43, 312–13, 315
Lavallée, Calixa, 99, 297
Lears, T. Jackson, 230
Lebert, Sigmund, 41–42
Leipzig, 40, 43, 59, 73, 73n4, 76, 78, 87, 100, 107, 119, 133–34, 159, 185, 189, 194, 228, 257, 295–96, 298, 313, 316, 320
Leipzig Conservatory, 40, 43, 46, 134, 316, 321
Library of Congress, x, 94, 111, 138, 169, 217, 246, 322
Liebling, Leonard, 290
Liszt, Franz, 13, 22, 27, 45, 47–48, 50–52, 58–59, 62–63, 66–67, 69, 72, 76, 78, 83, 88, 97–98, 100, 102, 104, 107, 110, 117, 119, 121, 130, 138, 149, 151, 175, 268, 280, 285, 293, 296–97, 310, 314–15, 318–19, 321
    influence on MacDowell, 66–67, 76–77, 97, 110, 117, 119, 138, 151, 158–59, 161–63, 175, 285
    WORKS, Hungarian Rhapsodies, 51, 159
London, 20, 82, 93–94, 96, 102, 105, 108, 137, 255, 297, 301
Loring, David, 171, 176
Louisville, KY, 237
Low, Seth, 197, 211, 213–16, 217n13, 221, 224–26, 228, 242–43, 252, 265, 273, 279, 313, 319
Lowens, Margery Morgan, xi, 113
Lowens Collection, 318
Loyer, 35, 37
Luckie, Miss H. O., 54, 57, 94, 98
Lüstner, Louis, 52, 110

Maas, Louis, 129
MacArthur Foundation, 288
MacDowell, Edward Alexander
    accident with cab, 273
    administrative duties at Columbia University, 221–23, 244, 251, 259
    affection for Marian, 74–75, 80–81, 91–92, 105, 120, 178, 280
    aloofness, 151–52, 175, 238
    anxiety, 80–81, 88–89, 91–92, 173–74, 177–78, 274
    aphasia, 270, 278
    appearance, 38, 57, 93, 220, 226, 255, 270, 272, 278, 301, Pl. 1–Pl. 2, Pl. 4, Pl. 6, Pl. 8–10
    appetite, 108–9, 126, 133, 135
    as artist, 17, 20–21, 23n22, 26, 32n21, 94, 135, 214
    birthdate, ix, 7, 111–13, 292
    as boy, 24–26, 280, Pl. 1–Pl. 2
    burial, 282–83
    cabin, 145, 199, 277, Pl. 12
    cause of death, 281–82
    Celtic heritage. *See* Irish heritage
    commissions, attitudes toward, 148, 165
    compositional process, 199–200
    composition teaching, 128, 212–14, 217, 221, 242, 257, 268–69
    concert tours, 55, 167–68, 227, 245, 253–55, 258, 301
    as conductor, 206, 225
    conflict between composition and performance, 13, 71–72, 134, 167
    counterpoint, 54, 65–66, 77, 128
    daily routine, 107–9, 119, 234
    death, 281–82
    dedications, 30, 68, 74, 76–77, 87, 97–98, 103, 110–11, 113, 133, 140, 165, 230, 234, 236–37, 285, 312, 316
    depression, 50–51, 64, 170, 174, 178, 245–46, 256, 259
    detractors, 240–41, 290–92
    doctorates, honorary, 216–17, 252, 300–301
    drinking, 107, 119, 133
    earnings, 127, 150, 170–71, 227
    education, 8, 19, 22–53, 211, 294–96
    European education, 24–53
    European influences, 229
    exercise, 119, 171
    feminization of, 290–91, 290n17
    fever, 254, 276
    finances, 55–56, 61–62, 81, 83–84, 94–96, 101–2, 157, 170, 197–98, 207, 228, 246, 253, 258, 268, 270
    French influences, 85
    friendships, 107–8
    funeral, 282, 286
    generosity to strangers, 233–34
    German habits and appearance, 57, 128, Pl. 4, Pl. 6
    German influences, 229
    hiking, 145, 256
    house purchases, 116, 198–99, 233, 287
    humor, 50, 107, 113, 120, 125, 128–29, 134–35, 152, 219–21, 226–27, 255–56, 258
    idealism, 227, 263–64
    illnesses, 254–55, 270–81, 287, Pl. 9–10
    independence, 46, 48, 53, 62, 148, 154, 197
    individualism, ix, 39, 291
    insomnia, 174, 267, 272–75, 277–78
    introversion. *See* shyness
    Irish heritage, 3, 85, 230–31

MacDowell, Edward Alexander (*Cont.*)
  irritability, 84, 114–15, 187–88, 233, 256–57,
    274, 277
  Jews, attitudes toward, 57
  journalists, attitudes toward, 140–41
  language difficulties, 28, 44–45, 57, 71,
    101, 256
  lectures, 195–96, 217–20, 250, 256, 284–85
  letterbooks, 71
  literary influences, 59
  locomotor ataxia, 278
  loving cup, 267
  marriage proposal, 79–80, 297
  memory problems, 274
  name, spelling of, 3, 28, 236
  nationalism, views on, 117–18, 192, 195–
    96, 232
  nature, 39
  nervous breakdown, 270–73, 302, 319, 322
  ocean crossings, 24–25, 91, 120–21, 125,
    143, 204
  organ playing, 38
  outsider, ix, 13, 107, 175
  overwork, 50–51, 216, 234, 258, 267, 270,
    272–74, 277–78
  pension, 279
  personality, ix–x
  piano playing, 54–55, 58, 68–69, 71–72, 119,
    129–30, 156–58, 161, 171, 225, 227, 253
  piano teaching, 54–56, 58–61, 127–28, 149–50,
    156–57, 164, 226, 233, 245, 268–69
  piano textures, 66, 87, 157–59, 162–68,
    200–203, 205, 231–32
  as poet, 7, 64, 69, 139, 175, 189, 205–6, 230–32,
    248–49, 283–84, 290n17
  posthumous reputation, 283
  power of attorney, 271, 302
  programmatic music, 159–65, 186, 247–50
  publishers, conflicts with, 76, 83–87, 100–101,
    114, 132, 152–53, 204, 228, 235–37, 245,
    256–57
  Quaker heritage, 3–13, 15, 57, 72, 92, 118, 148.
    See also Friends, Religious Society of
  reading, love of, 8, 16, 23, 59, 109, 194–95, 200,
    214, 230, 280
  reputation, ix, 98–99, 110–11, 115, 118, 129,
    156–57, 184, 227, 232–33, 255, 268, 283,
    288–92, 313, 317
  resentment of Lang, 148–50
  resignation from Columbia, 259–65, 273
  return to U.S., 91, 118, 120–21, 125–26
  revisions, 12–13, 76, 246–47, 267, 284, 305
  rumination, 173, 258–59, 267, 270
  sabbatical year, 250
  sabbatical year, 246, 252–57, 301
  salary, 61–62, 81, 102, 191–92, 197, 246
  sarcasm, 219, 226, 234

  self-doubt, 258
  shyness, 13, 18–19, 21, 66n24, 68, 104, 106,
    152, 154, 178, 194–95, 226, 229, 259
  smoking, 119, 133, 256
  stage fright, 157, 173–74
  stubbornness, 114–15, 239–40, 259
  summer vacations, 19–21, 38, 145, 169,
    197–200, 204, 255–56, 297, 301, Pl. 8
  talkativeness, 269–70
  as teacher at Columbia, 217–20, 258
  weight gain, 38, 57, 119, 135n34
  weight loss, 280
  work ethic, 13, 27, 36, 46, 58, 64–65, 72, 109,
    127, 148, 156, 177, 199, 204, 216, 222–23,
    227, 233–34, 272, 278
  WORKS, 305–11
    Air et Rigaudon, op. 49, 164
    arrangements of works by others, 164–65,
      310–11
    Chansons Fugitives, op. 2, 30
    College songs, 220–21, 310
    Columbia fanfares, 220
    "Dance of Gnomes," op. 41, 176
    Deux Mélodies pour Piano et Violon, op. 9, 30
    Die Sarazenen and *Die schöne Alda,* op. 30,
      116, 188
    Drei Poesien, op. 20, 98
    Etude de Concert, op. 36, 116, 133
    12 Etudes, op. 39, 158–59, 202, 291–92, 298
    Fireside Tales, op. 61, 245–47
    First Modern Suite, op. 10, 53, 62, 67, 67n26,
      83, 98, 101–2, 130, 267
    First Piano Concerto, op. 15, 64–67, 82–83,
      87, 96, 98, 100–101, 154, 162, 229n16,
      291–92, 296–97, 300
    Four Songs, op. 56, 205–6, 228
    Fourth "Keltic" Sonata, op. 59, 230–32, 254,
      291–92, 301, 308
    From an Old Garden, op. 26, 98, 113, 132,
      312, 315
    Hamlet, Ophelia, op. 22, 93, 96–97, 110
    Lamia, op. 29, 116, 285, 315, 321
    Lancelot und Elaine, op. 25, 97–98, 104, 109
    Les Orientales, op. 37, 116, 133, 153n12
    Lieder, op. 11, 88, 98, 318
    Lieder, op. 12, 98, 103, 318
    3 Lieder, op. 27, 116
    3 Lieder, op. 33, 116, 133
    Marionetten, op. 38, 116, 246–47
    2 Mélodies pour piano et violon, MS op.
      9, 30
    Mondbilder, op. 21, 96, 98
    New England Idyls, op. 62, 245–50
    Prelude and Fugue, op. 13, 76–77, 98, 316
    projected works, 93, 96, 137, 188, 254–55,
      255n28
    Romanze, op. 35, 116

Sea Pieces, op. 55, 204–5, 228, 248
Sechs Gedichte nach Heinrich Heine (Six Poems after Heine) op. 31, 116, 246
Second "Indian" Suite, op. 48, 193–96, 248, 282, 291–92, 300, 313
Second Piano Concerto, op. 23, 93, 98, 104, 116, 121, 130, 137–38, 141–42, 144, 153, 182–84, 291–92, 298, 301, 313, 316
Serenade, op. 16, 76–77, 98, 316
Six Fancies for the Piano, op. 7, 205
Six Idyls after Goethe, op. 28, 116, 246
Sonata Eroica, op. 50, 161, 165–67, 236
Sonata Tragica, op. 45, 161–63, 165, 171, 312
2 Songs, op. 34, 116, 133
3 Songs, op. 60, 245–46, 301
4 Songs, op. 56, 206–7, 228, 300
8 Songs, op. 47, 299
4 Stücke, op. 24, 111
Suite für grosses Orchester, op. 42, 171, 185–89, 291–92, 298, 317
Technical Studies, 164
Third "Norse" Sonata, op. 57, 230–32, 291–92, 301, 308
Three Songs, op. 58, 206, 300
Trois petits morceaux [three short pieces], op. 5, 30, 30n17
Vier kleine Poesien, op. 32, 116, 249
Wald Idyllen, op. 19, 83, 87, 98, 318
War Song, op. 6, 205, 225
Woodland Sketches, op. 51, 199, 201–4, 228, 248–49
Zwei Fantasiestücke, op. 17, 85–86, 98
Zwei Stücke, op. 18, 83, 86, 98
Zweite moderne suite, op. 14, 59, 67n26, 83, 98, 101
Zwölf Virtuosen-Etüden [Twelve Virtuoso Etudes], op. 46, 163
MacDowell, Marian Nevins, x, 62, 68, 79–81, 87–88, 91, 98, 102, 120, 148, 157, 188, 198–99, 217, 234, 253, 256, 258, 265n61, 269–70, 274, 277–79, 284–88, 315–16, 322
affection for Edward, 62, 75, 81, 115, 120, 174, 270, 280
appearance, 57, 93, Pl. 8, Pl. 10–12
biographical half-truths, 96, 281
as copyist, 109
doctorates, honorary, 288
Fanny MacDowell's assessment of, 57–58
grief for Edward, 281–82, 286
Hillcrest, purchase of, 198–99, 233, 287, 300
honeymoon in England, 93–94, 297
illnesses, 57–58, 79–80, 92, 105, 108–9, 115–16, 169–79, 245–46, 252, 280–81, 286, 299, 301
inheritance, 80, 95–96, 102, 105, 116

MacDowell compositions, comments on, 161–62, 165, 168, 187, 202–3, 206, 247–49, 285, 1673
miscarriage, 115, 297
as pianist, 60, 126, 288
protection of Edward, x, 228, 233, 258–59, 305
relationship with EAM's parents, 81, 94–96, 105, 118, 196, 228, 282–83, 286, 297
relationship with Templeton Strong, 106, 108, 120, 197, 241, 273, 277
studies with Edward, 56, 60, 296
"Toddles," Edward's nickname for, 93
MacDowell Clubs, 286–89
MacDowell Colony, 288–89, Pl. 12
MacDowell Fund, 279, 301
MacDowell Memorial Association, 287–88, 301
Machado, Hilario, 94
Macleod, Fiona. *See* Sharp, William
MacMonnies, Frederick William, 245
Magdeburg, 59
Mahler, Gustav, 168, 204, 247, 293, 298–99, 301–3, 318
Maine, 169, 198
male chorus, 58, 68, 171, 221, 224, 247, 319
Mansfield, Howard and Helen, 244–45
Manuscript Music Society (Philadelphia), 185
Manuscript Society of Chicago, 185, 316
Manuscript Society of New York, 184–85, 227, 238–39, 245, 298, 300–301, 312–13
Margulies, Adele, 100
Marmontel, 39n36
Marmontel, Antoine-François, 23, 27, 29–37, 42–43, 77, 94, 98, 137, 145, 156, 295, 300, 314, 319
Martin, Hugh, 219
Martinet, Jean Eugène André, 35, 37–38
Mason, William, 47–48, 63, 163, 165, 237, 293–94, 298, 303, 319–20
Massenet, Jules, 232–33, 293
Mathews, W. S. B., 141, 231, 240–41, 316–17, 320
Mathias, Georges, 31–33, 36–37, 313
Matthew, George, 219
McDowell, Alexander (grandfather), 3
McDowell, Alexander (great-grandfather), 3
McDowell, Charles, 6, 9, 271
McDowell, Edward Alexander
Carreño, friendship with, 103–4
personality, 17
social connections, 103–4
McDowell, Elizabeth Ann, 6
McDowell, Frances (Fanny) Mary Knapp, 5, 16–17, 22–23, 30, 39, 41, 44, 44n13, 45, 57, 92, 111, 118, 120, 141, 193, 228, 246, 252, 286, 293, 295, 303
Carreño, friendship with, 17–18, 140, 237, 313

McDowell, Frances (Fanny) Mary Knapp (*Cont.*)
  Columbia University, contact with, 196, 265
  Edward MacDowell, relationship with, 22,
    24–27, 35, 38, 55–57, 92, 95–96, 105, 107,
    228, é5
  Marian MacDowell relationship with, 56–58,
    81, 95–96, 170, 196, 228, 282–83, 286
  National Conservatory, work at, 136–37, 142,
    183, 318, 323
  personality, 7, 9, 13, 81
  Quakers, relationship to, 6–10
  social connections, 8–9, 15, 17, 19, 27, 126, 137,
    196, 228
McDowell, Frank (son of Thomas), 6
McDowell, Frank (son of Walter), 252
McDowell, Joseph, 6
McDowell, Sarah Thompson, 3, 6, 14, 112
McDowell, Thomas Fair, 3–6, 22, 38, 62, 92,
    95–96, 105, 293, 304
  business, 78–79, 94
  Marian, relationship to, 94–95
  personality, 7–8, 13, 142–43
McDowell, Walter, 6–9, 14–16, 25–26, 35, 38, 44,
    55, 57, 78, 88, 92, 252
McKim, Charles Follen, 268, 270, 320
McMurran, Ann, 3
McWhood, Leonard B., 221–22, 251, 257, 259,
    264–65, 267, 270, 320
Mears, Helen Farnsworth, 287
Mears, Mary, 287
medieval, 58–59, 194, 200
Mees, Arthur, 225
Meissner, Dr., 78, 82
Mendelssohn, Felix, 22, 35, 40, 46, 51, 73, 85,
    182–83, 204, 269, 295
Mendelssohn Glee Club, 206, 224–27, 234, 271,
    279, 279n32, 282, 286–87, 302
Merington, Marguerite, 173
Meyerbeer, Giacomo, 117
Michelstadt, 58–59, 213
Michigan Conservatory of Music, 312
Milk strike of 1883, 79, 94, 297
Moebius, Kurt, 167–68, 228, 236, 320
Monet, Claude, 292
Morgan, J. P., 286
morphine, 275
Mosenthal, Joseph, 224–25
Mosenthal Fellowship, 225, 315
Moszkowski, Moritz, 78, 85
motivic development, 65–66, 161–63, 187
Mount Monadnock, 282
Mozart, W. A., 21–22, 73, 222
Müller-Reuter, Theodor, 50
Munich, 31, 40, 119, 134n28, 297, 312, 314, 318,
    321–22, 324
Munroe, A. C., 187–88
music in higher education, 211–23, 242–66

Music Teachers' National Association [MTNA],
    99, 181, 183–84, 188, 238, 265n61, 295,
    297–98, 300
Mussorgsky, Modest, 59, 293, 295–96

National Book Award, 288
National Conservatory of Music, 118, 120,
    136, 142, 153, 183, 191, 299, 315, 317–18,
    321, 323
National Institute of Arts and Letters, 268, 324
nationalism, 117–18, 193, 195–96, 229, 232, 315
Native Americans, 192–93, 200, 203, 248,
    313, 316
nature, 186, 200–203, 205, 247
Nervine, Dr. Miles', 275
Nevin, Ethelbert, 292, 301
Nevins, Anna, 93, 105, 108–10, 120, 169–70, 281
Nevins, Cornelia [Nina], 93, 105, 108–10, 116,
    118, 270, 281
Nevins, David, 56, 60, 62, 74–75, 79, 95
Nevins, Harry, 282
Nevins, Marian Griswold. *See* MacDowell,
    Marian
New England, 127, 186, 197, 200, 234,
    245–50, 322
New England Conservatory of Music, 129,
    314–15, 323–24
New German School, 48, 59, 73, 83, 88, 102, 107,
    138, 319, 321–22
Newman, William S., 161n6, 232, 232n20, 290n17
New Orleans, 216
New York Church Music Society, 107
New York College of Music, 314
New York Homeopathic College, 271
New York Oratorio Society, 215, 314
New York Philharmonic Society, 54, 131, 142,
    224, 317, 321, 323
New York Symphony Society, 215, 314
Nielsen, 318
Nietzsche, Friedrich, 279
Nikisch, Arthur, 142, 147, 151, 171, 173–75,
    320–21
Nobel Peace Prize, 243, 313
Norton, Charles Eliot, 212
nostalgia, 200, 248, 289

Oberlin, OH, 253–54
O'Kelly, Henri-Joseph, 32, 37

Paderewski, Ignace, 8, 131, 173–75, 196n32,
    233–34, 240n16, 254, 264–65, 293, 303, 320
Paine, John Knowles, 100, 129, 133, 144, 182, 192,
    212, 293, 295, 302, 312, 315, 322
  WORKS
    Symphony No. 1, 295
    Symphony No. 2 "Spring," 133, 296
Paladilhe, Émile, 36

paresis, 281–82
Paris, performances in, 141, 143–44, 153, 182–83
Paris Conservatory, 12, 17, 23–39, 42, 112, 183,
  213, 314, 319, 321–23
  concours, 27–28, 31–36, 38–39, 69, 295
  expulsions from, 38–39, 39n36
Paris Expositions. *See* Exposition universelle
Parker, Henry Taylor, 285, 320–21
Parker, Horatio, 177, 294, 297, 299–300, 303,
  321–22
Paumgartner, Hans, 189
Paur, Emil, 321
Pesce, Dolores, 204
Peterborough, NH, 145, 169, 197–207, 214, 234,
  252–55, 267, 270–71, 277, 280, 282, 284,
  286–88, 300–302, Pl. 12
Peterborough Pageants, 287–88
Pettee, S. L., 98
Phelps, Elizabeth, 30
Philadelphia, 6, 10, 169–70, 177–78, 185, 252, 280,
  295, 299, 323
Philharmonic Society of London, 255
photography, 135–36, 145, 152, 172, 214,
  255–56, 276
Pierné, Gabriel, 29, 35–37, 319, 321
Pittsburgh, PA, 253, 324
Porte, John F., 160
Princeton University, 216, 300
Prix de Rome, 314, 323
Prochazka, J. O., 102
Pulitzer Prize, 243, 288

Quakers. *See* Friends, Society of
Quesada family, 25, 28

Rabaud, 32
Raff, Doris, 68, 94, 98, 134, 161, 321
Raff, Helene, 68, 134
Raff, Joachim, 47–53, 56, 61–63, 66–69, 72,
  76n10, 81, 89, 110, 117, 134, 161, 163, 269,
  293–94, 296, 310, 321
ragtime, 289–90
Rahter, 84
Ranney, Helen, 178
Reinecke, Carl, 35, 50, 58, 100, 296, 316
Reisenauer, Alfred, 78
René, 35
Revolutionary War, 4, 9
Rheinberger, Josef, 31, 301, 317–18, 321, 324
Riedel, Carl, 59–60, 62–63, 88, 321
Riemann, Hugo, 112, 118
Riemenschneider, Georg, 98n21, 171, 322
Ries & Erler, 84
Rimsky-Korsakov, 59, 185, 293, 303
Rome, 268, 280, 287
Roosevelt, Theodore, 243, 313
Root, George F., 9, 293

Rosenfeld, Paul, 290–91
Rosenthal, Michael, 243
Rosenthal, Moriz, 149
Royal Academy of Music, 102
royalties, 86, 88, 99–101, 115, 132, 152, 159, 185,
  204, 206, 228, 235–36, 245–46, 256–57,
  268, 273, 285, 289, 317, 322
Rubinstein, Anton, 42, 60, 131, 134, 293–94, 299,
  313
Rubinstein, Joseph, 48
Rubinstein, Nicholas (Nikolay), 24, 39, 269, 293,
  296
Rübner, Cornelius, 264–65, 270, 313, 321
Ruggles Street Baptist Church, 48, 165

Saint-Gaudens, Augustus, 263, 268
Saint-Saëns, Camille, 36–37, 50, 58–59, 63, 69, 74,
  98, 269, 293, 295, 297, 303, 322
San Francisco, 171, 176, 253, 317
Sarasate, 51, 303
Saratoga, NY, 98
Sauret, Émile, 18, 45, 48, 55, 72–73, 94, 322
Sauret, Emilita, 45, 103, 322
Savard, Augustin, 27, 29
Schiller, 59, 309
Schirmer, G. (Gustav), 113–14, 132–33, 236–37,
  313, 322
Schmidt, Arthur P., 87, 116, 132–34, 147, 153,
  159–60, 165, 176, 185, 188, 221, 228,
  235–36, 241, 245–46, 250, 256, 273, 277,
  284–85, 289, 298, 300–301, 321–22
Schnorr von Carolsfeld, Malvina, 48
Schoenefeld, Henry, 192
Schott's Söhne, 60, 73, 84
Schumann, Clara, 48, 51, 56, 293, 300
Schumann, Robert, 46, 64, 83, 128, 138, 204, 231,
  279, 279n29
  WORKS
    Quintet, op. 44, 51
    Sonata No. 2, op. 22, 31, 33
    Symphony in B minor, 128
Schurman, Jacob Gould, 263
Schwarz, Max, 48
Scotch snap, 162, 202–3, 206
Scotland, 3, 19–20, 102
Seasonal Affective Disorder [SAD]. *See* seasonal
  depression
seasonal depression, 64–65, 135, 135n34, 154, 169,
  178–79, 239, 245, 259–60
Sebold, Alice, 288
Seeger, Pete, 314
Seidl, Anton, 232, 321–22
Seifritz, Max, 317
Sessi, Eugenia, 54–55
Sgambati, Giovanni, 117
Shakespeare, William, 93–94, 229, 297, 310, 321
Sharp, William, 230

Shelley, Percy Bysshe, 59, 307
Sinclair, Upton, 217–20, 253, 322
sleeping medicine, 275–76, 281–82
Smetana, Bedrich, 279, 295, 297
Smith, Wilson G., 180
social mobility, 107
Society of American Musicians and Composers.
    See Manuscript Society of New York
Sondershausen, 40, 98, 189, 298, 322
Sonneck, Oscar, 165n14, 176n5, 246, 247n11, 266,
    295, 303, 305, 322
Sousa, John Philip, 292–93
Spalding, Albert, 16–17
St. Botolph Club, 130, 175
St. George's Church, 282
Starr, M. Allen, 272, 281
Stedman, Edmund Clarence, 268
Steindorff, Paul, 253
Steinway and Sons, 131, 167, 323
Stockhausen, Julius, 48
Stratton, Isabella, 6
Strauss, Richard, 200, 247, 285, 294, 298–303, 318
Strong, George Templeton, Jr., 7, 21, 98, 100,
    106–22, 152–53, 182, 197–98, 214, 241,
    245, 255–56, 258, 273, 277, 289, 297–98,
    303, 316, 323, Pl. 6
    correspondence with MacDowell, x, 120–22,
        125–31, 133–40, 143, 145, 147–52, 157,
        160, 169, 181, 192–93, 234–35, 255–56, 258
    lack of initiative, 136, 143, 234, 323
    loyalty to MacDowell, 108, 120–22, 138, 143,
        234–35
    MacDowell compositions, comments on, 77,
        138–39, 157
    marital problems, 172, 323
    personality, 106, 108, 113, 234
    photographic hobby, 136, 145, 152, 256
    WORKS, Symphony No. 1, 117, 181, 297
Strong, George Templeton, Sr., 106–7
Strong, Lizzie, 172, 214
Strong, Veronica, 107, 120, 172
Stuttgart, 39–43, 103, 296, 314, 317
Stuttgart Conservatory, 40–43, 53, 317
subventions, 82–84, 87, 110, 132, 236, 285, 317
Sundance Prize, 288
Switzerland, 19–20, 29, 38, 63, 68–70, 80, 108,
    113, 120, 143, 145, 172, 198, 234, 255–58,
    298, 301, 312, 323, Pl. 8
syphilis, 278n26, 279, 281

Tagliapietra, Arturo, 18
Tagliapietra, Giovanni, 18
Tausig, Carl, 63, 294, 318
Tchaikovsky, Pyotr, 39, 60, 63, 100, 138, 293,
    298–99
Tennyson, Alfred Lord, 59, 109, 306–7
Terry, Ellen, 93, 96–97

Thalberg, Sigismond, 22, 315`
Thanksgiving, 57, 109
Thomas, Ambroise, 27–28, 33, 35–36, 293, 300,
    323
Thomas, Theodore, 131, 137–39, 142, 145, 181,
    184, 298, 302, 316–18, 323
Thomson, Virgil, 288, 300
Thorn, Edgar [pseudonym for MacDowell], 206,
    225, 228, 300, 305, 320
Thurber, Jeannette Meyer, 26, 30, 118, 126, 136,
    153, 183, 191, 315, 323
Torchet, Julien, 144
Toronto, 253
Trago, José Maria, 32–33
Tretbar, Charles F., 167, 323
Trinity Church (Boston), 177, 321
Trinity Church Wall Street (New York), 106
Trocadéro, Palais du, Pl. 7

United States Postal Service, 292
University of Pennsylvania, 252, 301

Van der Stucken, Frank, 99–100, 111, 117–18,
    142–44, 153, 181–83, 297, 323–24
Vassar College, 251
Venezuela, 17, 103n36, 111, 313
Verdi, Giuseppe, 117, 293–94, 297, 299, 301
Vevey, Switzerland, 136, 143, 198
Vienna, 43, 189, 298, 320
Villars-sur-Ollon, Switzerland, 255

Wagner, Richard, 13, 21, 31, 48, 59, 63, 67, 73–74,
    83, 97, 100, 107, 117, 120, 138, 142, 151,
    153, 175, 186, 189–90, 193, 202, 205, 222,
    231, 247, 285, 290–91, 293, 295, 297, 315,
    322
Walker, Alice, 288
Wallenstein, Martin, 58, 62
Ware, William R., 244–45, 264
Warsaw, 43, 320
Washington, DC, 153, 183, 189, 191, 253, 268, 297
Waterford, CT, 56, 81, 91–92, 297
Weber, Carl Maria von, 36, 205
Weddings, 5–6
weddings, 91–93, 297
Weimar, 40, 47–48, 63, 67, 76, 78, 87–88, 104, 121,
    163, 189, 296, 298, 314, 318–19, 321
Weingartner, Felix, 185
Wells College, 253
Wenzel, E. F., 318
Westminster Hotel, 257, 271, 277
Whiting, Arthur, 129, 150, 152, 181, 324
Wieniawski, Henryk, 63
Wiesbaden, 43–47, 52, 58, 64, 72, 89, 98, 102–5,
    107–8, 110, 115–19, 121–29, 133, 135, 138,
    148, 151, 154, 184, 245, 249, 285, 296–97,
    315–16, 321–22, Pl. 6

Wilder, Thornton, 288
Wilder, Victor, 145, 182
Wilhelmj, August, 45, 89, 303
Wilson, George H., 190, 324
winter blues. *See* seasonal depression
Wolf, Hugo, 247, 279, 293, 301
Wolff, Auguste, 36
Wolff, Hermann, 154
Woodberry, George, 220, 261, 264, 324
Worcester, MA, 99, 187–89, 298, 317, 324

World's Columbian Exposition, 245, 299, 323–24
World War I, 3, 161, 289, 318
World War II, 73n4
Würzburg Conservatory, 40, 94

Yale University, 299–300, 321

Zerrahn, Carl, 187–88, 324
Zimmerman, Pierre, 27, 319, 323
Zürich, 63, 68–73, 296